THE WHOLEFOOD CATALOG

A Complete Guide to Natural Foods

JUN

Also by Nava Atlas

VEGETARIANA
A Rich Harvest of Wit, Lore and Recipes

AMERICAN HARVEST
Regional Recipes for the Vegetarian Kitchen

THE WHOLEFOOD CATALOG

A Complete Guide to Natural Foods

Written and Illustrated by

NAVA ATLAS

Fawcett Columbine • New York

A Fawcett Columbine Book
Published by Ballantine Books
Copyright © 1988 by Nava Atlas

Library of Congress Catalog Card Number: 87-62013

ISBN: 0-449-90197-1

Cover and text design by Nava Atlas
Manufactured in the United States of America

First Edition: April 1988
10 9 8 7 6 5 4 3 2 1

For my brothers,
Dan and Ron

ACKNOWLEDGMENTS

I'd like to thank the following publishers and authors for granting permission to adapt recipes from their books:

Ballantine Books, Inc., NY:
   From *American Harvest* by Nava Atlas, © 1987: Recipes for Hopping John and Frijoles Refritos, adapted by permission.

William Morrow, Inc., NY:
   From *Classic Indian Vegetarian and Grain Cookery* by Julie Sahni © 1985: Recipe for Mung Dal, adapted by permission.

Naturegraph Publishers, Inc., Happy Camp, CA:
   From *Sea Vegetables: Harvesting Guide and Cookbook* by Evelyn McConnaughey © 1985: Recipe for Tempeh Split Pea Soup, adapted by permission.

Quinoa Corporation, Boulder, CO:
   From company literature by Rebecca Theurer Wood: Recipe for Mother Grain Crackers, adapted by permission.

Rodale Press Books, Inc., Emmaus, PA:
   From *Tofu, Tempeh and Other Soy Delights* by Claire Cusumano, © 1984: Recipe for Italian-Style Green Soybeans, adapted by permission.

In addition, I am grateful to the following companies and organizations for sending me literature and answering questions that were so essential to this book: The Amaranth Research division at the Rodale Food Center; Arrowhead Mills; Eden Foods; Erewhon (US Mills); Fearn Natural Foods; The Food Learning Center; Grainaissance; Great Eastern Sun; Hain Pure Food Company; Health Valley Foods; Maine Coast Sea Vegetables; Natural Food Associates; The Quinoa Corporation; The Soyfoods Center; and Walnut Acres. I also thank Dr. Robert Buchsbaum of The Massachusetts Audubon Society and Dr. Rod Fujita of the Harbor Branch Oceanographic Institute for answering my questions on the safety of sea vegetables.

As always, I am indebted to my agent Diana Price, especially in her determination to find a good home for this project. Finally, and most importantly, I wish to acknowledge my editor, Virginia Faber, whose support of this long-term project gave me the incentive to consolidate the massive amounts of materials at a steady pace and with the ongoing enthusiasm required; thanks also to the staff at Ballantine Books, who help make the production of a book a very pleasant and gratifying experience.

CONTENTS

INTRODUCTION

Natural-food stores have always held a special fascination for me. I'm drawn to the bins of earth-colored grains and flours, the colorful dried beans, the exotic condiments and fragrant spices, and the array of wholesome products wrapped in colorful, "new age" packaging. Here is a treasure trove of foods that helps underscore my long-held belief that healthy, natural eating need never be routine or boring.

After completing my second vegetarian cookbook, *American Harvest*, which kept me with more familiar, traditional ingredients for some time, I was very anxious to delve back into the more exotic realms of food. I began shopping more frequently at natural-food stores for the items that I wished to reinstate as staples in my pantry. Being an inveterate experimenter, I also explored unusual bulk items and exotic, imported products. It seemed to me that wonderful new products like amaranth, quinoa, mochi cakes, and amazaki were appearing all the time, but that easily accessible information on all these natural foods was lagging behind. Bulk foods are sold with no packaging information at all, and even many of the packaged items come with only rudimentary cooking instructions. Many natural foods receive only cursory attention in cookbooks and other print. Due to their growing popularity, however, I felt it was time for a comprehensive food-by-food guide, and the idea for *The Wholefood Catalog* was born.

To begin, I imagined what sort of questions interested consumers might have as they scanned the aisles of a natural food store or food co-op: What sort of grain is triticale? I love bulgur, but should I try cracked wheat instead? Look at all those types of brown rice—long grain, short grain, glutinous, basmati—what's the difference among them? What is this *seitan*, looking so meatlike in its plastic tub? I've heard that sea vegetables are good for you, but how would I use them? Should I pay all that money for that special grain sweetener?

The popularity of ethnic cuisines and the acceptance of the benefits of a high-fiber, low-fat diet, have contributed to a growing interest in natural foods by the general public and the rapid expansion of the health-food industry. The resurgence of interest in hearty, whole-grain breads, the mania for pastas, and an increased appreciation of exotic seasonings and condiments indicates that at least a portion of our population is reacting against overly processed, highly refined, and additive-laden foods. An increasing number of supermarkets contain natural-food sections, featuring nuts and dried fruits in bulk, packages of stone-ground flours and cornmeals, whole-grain noodles, and more. Twenty years ago, yogurt, an ancient food, was a relative newcomer to North America; today, it would seem odd *not* to find it in any supermarket. Ten years ago, tofu was an oddity, and now it, too, is a familiar sight in the supermarket. Many are predicting that tempeh, another soy food, will make similar inroads in the years to come.

With *The Wholefood Catalog* I hope to take the mystery out of shopping for and using hundreds of natural foods. Under the entry for each item, you will find purchasing hints, storage tips, and general nutritional information. Also included are recipes as well as additional cooking and serving suggestions that allow cooks to use their creativity. So whether you are simply interested in finding out more about the basics like whole-wheat flour, brown rice, soybeans, and peanuts, or if you wish to experiment with more unusual foods like cloud-ear mushrooms, hijiki, chick-pea flour, and umeboshi plums, you will have all the information you need to make use of and enjoy these purchases.

Note: This guide does not cover numerous specific brands of healthfood snacks or prepackaged mixes for baked goods, cereals, pilafs, and the like. These are fixtures in natural-food stores, and many are good and quite convenient. However, the ingredients that go into these products are certainly covered here, and once you're familiar with these, it will be easier to decide whether you'd like to try them. Also not covered here is the boundless array of vitamins, mineral supplements, and general tonics found in the world of health foods. These, too, are a volume unto themselves.

THE WHOLEFOOD CATALOG

A Complete Guide to Natural Foods

Chapter 1

GRAINS

Grains are the seed-bearing fruits of plants known as cereal grasses. The seeds can be either sown for subsequent crops or harvested for use as food. The cultivation of grain crops put an end to the wandering of ancient tribes for the purpose of foraging for food and represents the beginning of formal agriculture. Agriculture, in turn, led to commerce, and thus grain cultivation is widely considered to be a cornerstone of civilization.

Over half of the world's cultivated land is used to produce grain crops, and for most of the world's people grains are the proverbial staff of life. This has been less true in the United States and other Western nations, where much of the grain grown is exported or used as feed for animals. However, the use of a wide range of both common and exotic whole grains is on the increase, in part because of the popularization of international and vegetarian cookery and also due to the growing recognition that complex carbohydrates are an essential part of a healthy diet. Whole grains are life-sustaining, satisfying, and versatile.

NUTRITIONAL BENEFITS OF GRAINS

Whole grains consist of a usually inedible outer layer, called the *hull*, which houses the germ, the bran, and the endosperm. The *germ* is the embryo of the seed, the part that gives life to a new plant. It is the germ that sprouts when the seed is sown. Rich in protein, unsaturated fats, and carbohydrates, the germ is also a fine source of the B-complex vitamins, vitamin E, and minerals such as iron. The *bran* comprises the several layers of protective coating that surround the germ and endosperm. It provides the greatest concentration of fiber in the whole grain. Fiber is vital for the proper functioning of the digestive system. Bran also provides B vitamins and minerals such as phosphorus and potassium. The heart of the seed, the *endosperm*, is the part from which the plant is nourished before it sprouts leaves. It consists basically of starch and protein and contains a small percentage of the vitamins and nutrients of the grain.

When grains are refined for commercial use, the germ and bran are removed, leaving primarily the simple starch and protein present in the endosperm. This processing increases their shelf life, but it strips away many of the valuable nutrients. Processed grains are sometimes "enriched," that is, a handful of the lost nutrients are added back, but many of the original nutrients are not restored, and there is no way to put back the fiber that is lost.

Whole grains are a superb source of complex carbohydrates, nutrients comprising starches and fiber. Starches are an excellent fuel source for the body, and fiber, the parts of the plant that pass through the body undigested, provides the bulk crucial to the regulation of the digestive system. Whole grains and their derivatives, as well as legumes, nuts, and seeds have become widely accepted antidotes to the overly refined Western diet. For further discussion on the importance of fiber, see the glossary entry *Fiber*, page 185.

Although they are good sources of protein, whole grains provide protein that is incomplete. In order for protein to be readily used by the body, it must be complete, that is, contain all eight of the essential amino acids in specific proportions. Grains are deficient in certain of these amino acids, but if they are eaten in conjunction with legumes, dairy products, or soy foods, what occurs is *protein complementarity*, which means that the amino acids present in one food group combine with the amino acids in the other, and a readily usable, complete protein is formed. The eating of grains and legumes together in the same meal is the most common example of protein complementarity.

A 1977 Senate committee on nutrition recommended that the diet consist of 58 percent carbohydrates, preferably complex carbohydrates. Many nutritionists feel that this percentage should be even higher. A diet rich in whole grains and whole-grain-flour products is now accepted as an ideal to strive for.

STORAGE AND BULK BUYING

Grains keep well for some time, but all the same, it is desirable that your source have a good turnover so that you can be assured of freshness. Look for grains that are uniform, plump rather than shriveled, and with a good, even color. Organically grown grains (grown without pesticides, in soil free of chemical fertilizers) are an option available in natural-food stores and food co-ops.

Store grains in tightly lidded jars in a cool, dry place. Moisture is highly detrimental to grains, causing them to grow stale and moldy. Most grains will keep well for several months, but the sooner they are used, the better.

Whether bought in bulk or packaged, whole grains will occasionally contain mealworm eggs. These dormant eggs are laid while the grain is still in the field. Most of the eggs are loosened and removed when the grain is cleaned for distribution, but inevitably a few slip through. The practically invisible eggs hatch during hot, humid summer months when they are snug in your cozy grain jars. (Refrigeration and moisture control are the most effective ways of preventing the occasional stray egg from hatching.) From time to time, little gray moths will escape when you open the jars. Though these moths are perfectly harmless, it is nevertheless annoying to have them flying all over the kitchen.

Suffice it to say that suppliers and retailers do not wish to sell buggy grains, but the eggs are so tiny that all it takes is one or two to create a problem. If you find that a given batch of grain turns into a breeding ground, throw it out, let your retailer know, and avoid buying that particular grain from that source for a while.

Brown rice seems particularly susceptible to this problem, while oats seem particularly resistant. Rinsing grains well in a fine sieve before cooking them is an extra measure you can take to flush away stray eggs. However, the eggs are very difficult to see, so be assured that if one or two end up in your food, they are perfectly harmless and do not carry disease.

TOASTING GRAINS

Almost any grain benefits from being toasted before it is cooked, to bring out its nutty flavor. Use a dry skillet or add 1 tablespoon oil per cup of grain for a slightly richer effect. Simply toast the grain in a heavy skillet over moderate heat, stirring frequently, for 4 to 7 minutes, or until the grain is aromatic. Then proceed to cook as your recipe directs.

COOKING GRAINS

Unless a grain is cooked by simply soaking it, as is the case with couscous or bulgur, most grains may be cooked in the following manner. Refer to the chart below for proportion of water to grain.

1. Rinse the grain thoroughly in a colander or fine sieve.

2. Bring the amount of water needed to a boil in a heavy saucepan or cooking pot.

3. Stir in the grain. Return the water to a boil, then lower the heat and simmer over low heat, covered, until the water is absorbed. Stirring during the cooking time is not recommended, since doing so can make the grain mushy.

COOKING TIMES AND YIELDS FOR GRAINS

Use the method indicated above in "Cooking Grains," unless otherwise specified. For more detailed information, see under each individual entry. Amounts given are based on 1 cup dry grain used. Don't forget to rinse the grain!

Grain (1 cup dry measure)	Water Needed (cups)	Approximate Cooking Time (minutes)	Approximate Yield (cups)	Comments
Amaranth	2½–3	20–25	2½	Use less water for drier effect
Barley				
Pot or Scotch	3–3½	50–55	3	
Pearl	2½–3	40–45	3	
Grits	4	20–25	3	
Buckwheat Groats	2	15–25	2½	Toast grain first as described under entry
Hominy Grits	4	25–30	3	
Millet	2½	35–40	3½	Flavor is improved by toasting
Oats				
Whole	3–4	45–60	3	Soak overnight to reduce cooking time
Steel-cut	4	40–45	3	Flavor is improved by toasting
Rolled	1½	10	2½	Remove from heat after stirring in, then let stand
Quinoa	2	15	4	Nice toasted first or cooked in stock

Grain *(1 cup dry measure)*	Water Needed *(cups)*	Approximate Cooking Time *(minutes)*	Approximate Yield *(cups)*	Comments
Rice				
Long- or medium-grain	2½	35–40	3	
Short-grain	2	35–40	3	
Basmati	2½	35–40	3	
Flakes	1¼	5–8	2–2¼	
Rye				
Whole	3½–4	50–60	2½–3	Soak overnight to reduce cooking time
Cracked	3	40–45	3	Toasting improves flavor
Flakes	2	15–20	2½	
Triticale				
Whole	3–3½	45–60	2½	Soak overnight to reduce cooking time
Flakes	2	15–20	2½	
Wheat				
Whole	3½–4	50–55	2½	Soak overnight to reduce cooking time
Bulgur	2	15–20	2½	See entry for two cooking methods

Grain (1 cup dry measure)	Water Needed (cups)	Approximate Cooking Time (minutes)	Approximate Yield (cups)	Comments
Couscous	2	15	3	Grain is soaked rather than cooked (see entry)
Cracked	3	35–40	2½–3	Toasting improves flavor
Flakes	2	15–20	2½	
Wild rice	2½	35–40	3	

AMARANTH

Amazing amaranth, once a revered crop of the ancient Aztecs, is now coming back into use via the natural-food market. Native to Mexico, Guatemala, Peru, and Bolivia, grain amaranth (as it is often called, to distinguish it from vegetable amaranth, a closely related plant) is a tiny, round seed, about half the size of a millet seed. So impressive is the nutritional profile of amaranth that it has been cited as one of the world's most promising foods by the National Academy of Sciences and has been the subject of several significant conferences highlighting so-called foods of the future. The United States and several Third World countries have set up research institutes to explore its potential.

Grain amaranth, despite its fine qualities, is not yet a staple offering in natural-food stores; it is still grown as a specialty crop in the Americas rather than on a mass scale. This is a situation that many hope will change, since it is a hardy crop, resistant to drought and cold. Where amaranth is found, amaranth flour is usually also available. In many ways it is a more versatile product than the whole grain (see page 92). Popped amaranth, made by heating the seeds until they explode (akin to, but much tinier than popcorn), is a specialty item available mainly through mail-order sources. It can be added to cold cereals and makes a nice topping for green salads and casseroles. Some large natural-food companies have also recently begun to manufacture tasty, crisp cold cereals made from amaranth. Explore mail-order sources for amaranth products if local stores don't carry them. Walnut Acres and Nu-World Amaranth are two such sources (see appendix B).

Amaranth and its companion grain, quinoa (page 17), are to other grains what the soybean is to its fellow legumes. Higher in fat and oil than other grains (which is not to say these are high-fat foods), these "supergrains" contain the highest percentage as well as the highest quality protein of all the grains. Amaranth contains 16 percent protein and is unusually high in lysine and methionine, amino acids that are often in short supply in grains. The high quality of protein makes amaranth a good complement to legumes, nuts, and seeds. In addition, it is among the grains highest in fiber and is quite rich in calcium and iron. Amaranth even contains vitamin C, a vitamin not usually found in significant amounts in grains.

The flavor of cooked amaranth is quite strong. It has been described as nutty and sweet, but it is more complex than that. Even its aroma is distinct and is not to everyone's liking. Amaranth cooks to a rather sticky and glutinous texture, which limits its versatility. It can't easily be substituted for other grains in recipes and is a bit too overpowering to be used as a simple bed of grains for vegetable or bean dishes. Amaranth's unusual texture calls for a different approach.

Basic Cooked Amaranth: Use a ratio of 2½ to 3 parts water to 1 part grain, depending on the texture you want. The smaller amount of water yields a chewier result. Using more water will yield a consistency like a mushy cooked cereal. Bring the water to a boil and stir in the grain. Return to a boil, then lower the heat and simmer, covered, until the water is absorbed, about 20 to 25 minutes.

- As a hot cereal, cook as instructed above. Add a little milk if desired and embellish as you would any other hot cereal, with dried or fresh fruit, honey or rice syrup, nuts, and so on.

- Cooked with fruit juice in place of water, with the optional addition of fresh fruit, amaranth yields an unusual, jamlike spread when cooled. Use it on crackers, muffins, or griddle cakes. High in a starch called amylopectin, amaranth gels as it cools.

- Try this casserole idea: Spread cooked amaranth, seasoned to taste with salt and pepper, into an oiled, shallow casserole dish. Arrange over it a layer of broiled eggplant slices, then a layer of sliced tomatoes, then some rings of sautéed onion. Top with grated mild cheese. Bake at 350°F until the cheese is bubbly, about 20 to 25 minutes.

- The flavor of amaranth is compatible with that of various squashes. Use cooked amaranth laced with raisins, nuts, cinnamon, and grated ginger to stuff prebaked winter squash. Or simply slice a large onion and a medium yellow summer squash and sauté in olive oil until lightly browned; then stir in a cup or so of cooked amaranth. Serve as a nutritious side dish, garnished with chopped fresh parsley.

- Cook amaranth in the evening, then spread it about 1½ inches thick in a lightly oiled pie pan, and refrigerate overnight. In the morning cut the "pie" into wedges. Fry on a non-stick skillet with a bit of soy margarine until the wedges are golden brown on both sides; serve with maple or rice syrup for breakfast.

- Toast a small amount of the raw grain in a dry skillet and use as a topping for green salads, casseroles, or noodles.

- Add a small amount of cooked amaranth to muffin and quick-bread batters for a moist, chewy texture. About ½ cup per average recipe is right.

AMARANTH SPOONBREAD

Yield: 4 to 6 servings

2½ cups water
⅔ cup amaranth
⅓ cup cornmeal
1 teaspoon salt
2 tablespoons soy margarine, cut into bits
1 medium onion, finely chopped
1 small green or red bell pepper, finely chopped
½ cup low-fat or soy milk
2 eggs, separated, at room temperature
1 cup firmly packed grated sharp Cheddar cheese
Freshly ground pepper to taste

Bring the water to a boil in a heavy saucepan. Pour in the amaranth, then lower the heat and slowly pour in the cornmeal, stirring constantly to prevent lumps. Add the salt, then simmer, covered, until the water is absorbed, about 20 to 25 minutes. When done, stir in half the margarine.

Preheat the oven to 375°F.

Heat the remaining tablespoon of margarine in a small skillet. Add the onion and sauté over moderate heat until it is translucent. Add the chopped green or red pepper and continue to sauté until the onion is golden. Stir into the amaranth and cornmeal mixture, followed by the milk, egg yolks, and cheese.

In a small bowl, beat the egg whites until they form stiff peaks. Gently fold into the amaranth mixture along with a few grindings of pepper. Pour into a deep, lightly oiled 1½-quart casserole dish or soufflé pan. Bake for 30 to 35 minutes, or until puffed and golden brown.

━━━━━ BARLEY ━━━━━

Barley is believed to be the most ancient of cultivated grains—records of its use date back to Egypt of 5000 B.C. It was a staple bread grain of the ancient Greeks and Romans and likewise predominated as a bread grain in Europe before rye and wheat replaced it. Historically, barley has been an important food grain among Asiatic peoples and in the Middle East, and its ability to withstand heat, cold, and drought has made it a staple crop in climates as diverse as Scandinavia's and Africa's. In the United States, approximately 30 percent of the barley crop goes toward making hops for brewing beer, 10 percent is used for human consumption, and the rest goes for animal feed. With its mild flavor, pleasantly chewy texture, and good nutritional profile, barley certainly deserves more use; it can be just as versatile as rice and combines well with bold seasonings.

Two kinds of barley are available in natural food stores: *pearl barley* and *pot barley*, sometimes called *Scotch barley*. Unhulled barley is occasionally available, but it is not recommended except for the purposes of sprouting, since it takes a very long time to cook—and to chew. The most familiar form of barley is the pearled variety. Pearling is accomplished by grinding off the tenacious hulls of the grain with the use of abrasive disks called carborundum wheels. Pearl barley goes through five or six pearlings, removing all of the hull, plus most of the bran and germ. To make pot or Scotch barley, the grain goes through three pearlings to remove most of the hull and some of the bran. It is therefore more nutritious than pearl barley.

Don't assume that just because you buy it in a natural-food store, the grain you have must be the less refined pot barley; make sure it is labeled as such if that is what you want. Pot barley has a deeper tan color than pale pearl barley.

The protein content of pearl barley is 8 percent, whereas that of pot barley is 9½ percent. Pot barley is rich in the B vitamins, particularly niacin and thiamine, and provides good quantities of minerals, particularly potassium, as well as iron, phosphorus, and calcium. Pearl barley loses half of the vitamin and mineral content through the removal of the bran and germ. Much of the good fiber content is lost, too.

Basic Cooked Barley: Use 2½ to 3 parts water to 1 part grain for pearl barley, and 3 to 3½ parts water for pot or Scotch barley, depending on how firm and chewy you like the texture. Bring the water to a boil, then stir in the barley and return to a boil. Lower the heat and simmer, covered, until the water has been absorbed, about 40 minutes for pearl barley and 50 to 55 minutes for pot barley.

- Barley is a favorite soup grain. In addition to the classic mushroom-barley combination, tomato-barley soups are excellent as are bean-barley soups (try adzuki, white, or pinto beans).

- In the summer, a cold potato-barley soup is truly refreshing. For 4 to 6 servings, combine 3 medium potatoes, cooked and diced; 1⅓ cups cooked barley; and 1 cup grated cucumber in a serving bowl. Pour in 1 cup low-fat milk and 2 cups buttermilk, or enough to give the soup a medium-thick consistency. Add ⅓ cup finely chopped fresh herbs (a combination of parsley, dill, and chives tastes great) and season to taste with salt and pepper. Serve at once or chill until needed.

- Barley may be used as a substitute for rice in almost any type of recipe—in casseroles, as a bed of grains for vegetable and bean dishes, and as a stuffing for green bell peppers, tomatoes, or other vegetables.

- In hearty stews and casseroles, barley is always compatible with mushrooms, browned onions, and any legume.

- Barley has a nice affinity with the flavors of green beans, chick-peas, and fresh green peas. Combine any or all of them with cooked barley in more or less equal amounts and embellish with chopped tomatoes and fresh herbs. Served warm and seasoned with nat-

9

ural soy sauce, this combination makes a simple main dish, or served cold with an Italian dressing, it makes a satisfying grain salad.

- A small quantity of cooked barley added to breads and muffins lends a pleasant, chewy texture.

- Barley is excellent in marinated salads, such as the following:

SPRING BARLEY SALAD

Yield: 6 servings

1 cup pearl or pot barley
2 1/2 cups water
1 1/2 cups steamed asparagus, cut into
  1-inch pieces
1 cup shelled fresh peas, steamed
1/2 cup chopped cucumber
1/2 cup finely shredded cabbage
1 medium stalk celery, finely diced
1/4 cup sliced black olives
2 tablespoons finely minced fresh dill
1 teaspoon chopped fresh mint leaves
  (optional)
3 tablespoons olive oil
2 tablespoons safflower oil
3 tablespoons cider vinegar
Salt and freshly ground pepper to taste

Cook barley as directed above in "Basic Cooked Barley." Allow to cool to room temperature.

Combine the barley with all of the remaining ingredients in a mixing bowl. Toss together thoroughly. Refrigerate for at least one hour before serving to allow the flavors to blend.

BARLEY GRITS

Barley grits are most often available in bulk in natural-food stores. To make barley grits, pot barley is cracked into five or six pieces. Barley grits are excellent when added raw to soups, where they cook in about half the time of whole barley. Cooked barley grits may be used as a hot cereal, served with milk, honey, dried or fresh fruits, and nuts. Try them as a substitute for whole barley or rice in casseroles, or as a substitute for rice in rice pudding recipes. You may not want to use them where a fluffy grain texture is called for, since they cook to a stickier texture than the whole grain.

Basic Cooked Barley Grits: Use 4 parts water to 1 part grain. Bring the water to a boil, stir in the grits, return to a boil, then lower the heat and simmer, covered, until the water is absorbed, about 20 minutes.

———— BUCKWHEAT GROATS ———— (KASHA)

An oddity among grains, buckwheat is not a cereal grain in the botanical sense, but a beautiful pink-flowered plant related to rhubarb. First cultivated in ancient China, buckwheat was later taken to Eastern Europe by traveling tribes. Its flowers attract bees, which produce a dark, strong-flavored honey (see Buckwheat Honey, page 160). The soft, pyramidal seeds, when hulled and cracked, are known as buckwheat groats. Further milling produces buckwheat flour (page 93).

The use of this ancient food in the Near and Far East as well as Eastern Europe is still extensive. However, apart from buckwheat pancakes, which were all the rage in the nineteenth century (and continue to be popular in the South today), the use of buckwheat is minimal in North America. Toasty, brown buckwheat groats may either be passionately disliked for their strong, distinct flavor and aroma or greatly savored for the same reasons.

Buckwheat groats have long been available either in grain or kosher food sections of supermarkets, where they come in a box labeled kasha. In bulk sections of natural-food stores, buckwheat groats are available in various grinds—fine, medium, and coarse, which, predictably, will vary their cooking times. They are often sold lightly toasted, which brings out their distinct aroma.

Buckwheat groats contain 11 percent protein and are a rich source of minerals, particularly iron, as well as phosphorus and potassium. They are one of the best grain sources of calcium. Buckwheat groats contain nearly the entire range of B vitamins and are particularly strong in thiamine and niacine.

Basic Cooked Buckwheat Groats: Use 2 parts water to 1 part grain. Bring the water or stock to a boil in a heavy saucepan. In the meantime, heat 1 tablespoon oil for every cup of groats in a heavy skillet. Add the groats and stir quickly to coat them with the oil. Toast over moderate heat, stirring frequently, until they become a shade darker and very aromatic, about 4 to 5 minutes. Pour the boiling liquid over them and cover. Simmer over low heat until the water is absorbed, about 15 to 25 minutes, depending on the grind. The traditional Jewish method calls for mixing the groats with a well-beaten egg before toasting them, then proceeding as above. Once the groats are cooked, they may be used in any number of ways.

- For a simple side dish, dress up cooked groats with lots of browned onions and a bit of chopped parsley or dill.

- Cooked groats are highly compatible not only with onions but also with mushrooms, celery, cabbage, and almonds. For a simple pilaf-style dish, sauté any or all of these and combine with cooked groats; season with salt, pepper, and fresh or dried herbs.

- Use groats as a stronger-flavored substitute for brown rice; try them in stuffed cabbage or in soups.

- Use groats as a substitute for, or mixed with, bulgur. They are similar in texture and appearance.

- In India and Eastern Europe, cooked buckwheat groats are simply eaten as a hot cereal. Add milk and a sweetener, dried fruits, or nuts of your choice.

- Jewish or Eastern European cookbooks often contain a number of traditional recipes using kasha. The best known are kasha varnishkas, which is groats combined with egg noodles, and kasha knishes, which are groats wrapped in a savory potato dough.

BUCKWHEAT GROATS WITH VERMICELLI

Yield: 6 servings

1 cup buckwheat groats
2 cups vegetable stock (homemade, or made with one vegetable bouillon cube)
1 cup vermicelli, broken into 2-inch lengths
2 tablespoons soy margarine
1 medium red bell pepper, cut into 1 1/2-inch-long matchsticks
1 medium turnip, cut into 1 1/2-inch-long matchsticks
1 cup firmly packed finely shredded cabbage
1 medium stalk celery, finely diced
3 bunches scallions, chopped

1/4 cup finely chopped fresh parsley
Juice of 1/2 lemon
2 teaspoons poppy seeds
Salt and freshly ground pepper to taste

Cook the groats in the stock as directed in "Basic Cooked Buckwheat Groats," above. Cook the vermicelli until just *al dente*, then immediately rinse with cool water.

Heat the margarine in a large, heavy skillet or wok. Add the red pepper, turnip, cabbage, and celery and stir-fry over moderate heat until they are just tender-crisp. Stir in the cooked groats and vermicelli along with the remaining ingredients and cook over low heat, stirring frequently, for 10 to 12 minutes. If the mixture seems dry, add just a bit of water. Serve at once.

————— CORN PRODUCTS —————

CORN NUTS

Used primarily as a snack food, corn nuts are whole hulled, roasted corn kernels. They are most often sold in the nuts section of natural-food stores. Nutritional information on them is not available, since they have not been specifically analyzed by the USDA. Corn nuts can be tasty, but are often overly salted. Because they are real jawbreakers, they may not be the best snack for children. Perhaps the best way to use them is as an ingredient in fruit-and-nut trail mixes.

HOMINY GRITS

Grits are prepared from corn that has been soaked in lime (calcium hydroxide) to remove the hull. The whole, hulled kernels are known as *whole hominy*; when the hominy is dried and cracked, it is known as *grits*. Grits were a much more esteemed dish, from north to south and across class boundaries, in the nineteenth century. They're still a mainstay in the cooking of the Deep South, and have been adopted for use by some "new American chefs." At their very best, grits can have the flavor of creamed, sweet corn. (But don't expect this level of taste from commercial grits, especially "instant grits," which are so highly processed that they are almost totally devoid of flavor.)

Grits are readily available in the supermarket, courtesy of Quaker Oats. These commercially prepared grits have been degerminated (that is, stripped of the nutritious germ in order to increase shelf life) and enriched. There is very little nutritional difference between varieties that are long cooking (25 minutes or so) and quick cooking (about 5 minutes), so you might as well opt for convenience. Avoid flavorless "instant" grits. If you like grits, it is worth seeking out whole, undegerminated grits. Though these are difficult to find in natural-food stores, some natural-food mills offer them (see appendix B).

A serving of enriched grits is high in fiber and low in calories and fat, but it is not exactly a powerhouse of nutrition, containing only modest amounts of protein, vitamin A, calcium, iron, and B vitamins. Though specific nutritional analysis is not available on undegerminated grits, it's safe to assume that they have all that the supermarket variety have and then some.

Basic Cooked Grits: For long-cooking grits, use 4 parts water to 1 part grits. Bring to a boil in a heavy-bottomed saucepan or double boiler (nonstick cookware is recommended), then slowly sprinkle in the grits, stirring to avoid lumping. Lower the heat immediately; cook over very low heat until thick and creamy, about 25 to 30 minutes. For hot cereal, use 3 to 4 tablespoons of uncooked grits per serving.

- Grits are traditionally eaten simply buttered and salted alongside eggs for breakfast.

- Stir a small amount of grated Cheddar cheese into cooked grits to make cheese grits, a favorite in the Deep South.

- Spread cooked grits on a dinner plate to a thickness of 1/2 inch. Chill overnight or until firm, then cut into squares or wedges and fry in a small amount of soy margarine on

each side until golden brown. Fried grits are delicious with maple syrup or fruit butter.

- Add a small amount of cooked grits to batters for muffins, griddle cakes, or quick breads, for extra moisture and flavor.

- Serve grits as a side dish for supper in place of mashed potatoes or rice.

GRITS WITH FRESH CORN AND TOMATOES

Yield: 4 to 6 servings

This is a quick and interesting late-summer supper dish, with the flavors of the Southwest.

3/4 cup grits
3 cups water
2 tablespoons soy margarine
1 medium onion, chopped
1 small green bell pepper, diced
1 pound ripe tomatoes, preferably plum tomatoes, chopped
2 green chilies, chopped (optional)
2 cups cooked fresh corn kernels (about 2 medium ears)
1/2 teaspoon each dried oregano and cumin
Salt and freshly ground pepper to taste
1 cup firmly packed grated Cheddar cheese

Cook the grits in the water as directed in "Basic Cooked Grits," above. In the meantime, heat the margarine in a large skillet until it foams. Add the onion and sauté until it is translucent. Add the green pepper and continue to sauté until the onion is golden. Add the tomatoes and green chilies and sauté until the tomatoes have softened, about 5 to 7 minutes. Stir in the corn kernels and seasonings. When the grits are done, stir them into the skillet. Sprinkle in the Cheddar cheese and cook until it melts. Serve at once.

POPCORN

Believed to have been first cultivated by the ancient Incas, popcorn is a variety of corn grown especially as a snack food. The kernels contain a high percentage of hard endosperm (the starchy heart of the kernel) and thus pop easily when exposed to high heat. When they reach a certain temperature, the moisture inside them creates pressure, causing the endosperm to burst through the hull.

As a snack, plain, unsalted popcorn is not especially nutritious, but it is low in calories and fat and very high in fiber. A cup of plain popcorn contains 23 calories. Large amounts of butter and salt, obviously, take away from the advantages of this snack. But all in all, popcorn is certainly preferable to oil-laden chips and the like. Natural-food stores sometimes offer organically grown popcorn.

One-third cup unpopped kernels makes about 8 cups popcorn. Hot-air poppers, widely available and inexpensive, provide an easy, convenient way to make popcorn with no fat at all. Each brand is different, so follow the manufacturer's instructions. To make popcorn without a popper, use a large, deep, heavy-bottomed saucepan (a 4-quart pot is comfortable for popping 1/3 cup kernels). Pour in enough oil to coat the bottom of the pot and place over moderately high heat. Sprinkle in the kernels and cover. Once the kernels begin to pop, shake the pot occasionally to make sure the unpopped kernels remain on the bottom. Do this until the popping stops. Transfer to a serving bowl. Salt in moderation! Here are some simple ideas for embellishing popcorn. These recipes assume the use of one-third cup unpopped kernels (8 cups popped):

- CHILI-SPICED POPCORN: Melt 2 tablespoons soy margarine. Add 1 teaspoon chili powder, 1/2 teaspoon paprika, 1/4 teaspoon each dry mustard and garlic powder, and salt to taste. Drizzle over the popcorn and toss well.

- POPCORN PARMESAN: Melt 2 tablespoons soy margarine and drizzle it over the popcorn. Stir in 1/4 cup grated Parmesan cheese and toss well.

- PEANUT "CARMEL" CORN: Combine the popcorn with 1 1/2 cups peanuts. In a small saucepan, heat 2 tablespoons soy margarine with 1/3 cup honey until melted. Drizzle into the popcorn and toss to coat the pieces. Spread on two baking sheets and bake at 275°F for 15 minutes. Let cool and break apart.

- ALMOND-MAPLE POPCORN: In a small saucepan, melt 2 tablespoons soy margarine. Remove from the heat and stir in 1/3 cup maple syrup and 1 teaspoon vanilla extract. Drizzle into the popcorn, then toss in 1 cup coarsely chopped or slivered almonds. Spread on two baking sheets and bake at 275°F for 15 minutes. Let cool and break apart.

- CINNAMON-RAISIN POPCORN: Melt 2 tablespoons soy margarine. Stir in 1/4 cup honey and 1 1/2 teaspoons cinnamon. Toss into the popcorn with 1 1/2 cups raisins. Spread on two baking sheets and bake at 275°F for 10 minutes. Let cool and break apart.

MILLET

Millet's place in the history of grains is about as venerable as can be. This tiny, round yellow seed was a staple food in ancient India and Egypt and was widely used in China before rice became its staple grain. It has always been an important grain in Africa, since it thrives even in poor, dry soil, and has long been a popular grain in India. Millet's most legendary claim is as a favored food of the Hunzas, the denizens of the foothills of the Himalayas, renowned for their longevity. Today, millet is grown in North America as well, but only a small percentage of the crop is used for human consumption, with most going for use as birdseed and cattle feed. Bland in flavor and rather mushy in texture, millet is no cause for culinary excitement, but it is nonetheless versatile and nourishing. It is available in natural-food stores as well as Indian food shops.

At about 10 percent protein, millet compares favorably with other grains, especially since its protein is of high quality. It is a particularly rich source of iron and contains good amounts of potassium, calcium, and other minerals, and a good range of the B-complex vitamins. Millet is a highly digestible food.

Basic Cooked Millet: Use 2 1/2 to 3 parts water to 1 part grain (use the greater proportion of water if a porridgelike consistency is desired). Bring the water to a boil, stir in the millet, return to a boil, then lower the heat and simmer, covered, for 35 to 40 minutes, or until the water is absorbed and the grains have burst. Millet's flavor is much improved by toasting it lightly before cooking. Use 1 tablespoon oil for every cup of grain. Heat the oil in a heavy skillet. Add the millet and stir to coat the grains with the oil. Toast over moderate heat, stirring frequently, until the millet is aromatic and lightly browned, about 5 minutes. Proceed to cook as directed above.

- MILLET PORRIDGE: Cook as directed above. When the water is absorbed, add 3/4 cup milk per every cup of uncooked millet that was used and cook over low heat until it, too, is absorbed. Serve with sweetener, nuts, and dried fruits.

- For a tasty cheese soufflé, to serve 4, combine 2 cups cooked millet with 1 packed cup sharp Cheddar cheese in a mixing bowl. Stir in 3 beaten egg yolks, 1/3 cup milk or soy-milk, 1 teaspoon curry powder, and salt and pepper to taste. Beat 3 egg whites until stiff and fold them into the millet mixture. Pour into a deep, lightly oiled 1 1/2-quart casserole dish. Bake at 325°F for 30 to 40 minutes, or until puffed and golden.

- To make a savory, Indian-inspired stew to serve 4 to 6, sauté a large, chopped onion and 3 cloves garlic, minced, in a Dutch oven or large, heavy saucepan until they are golden. Add 2 cups cooked millet, 1 1/2 to 2 cups cooked mung beans (see page 47) and one 14-ounce can imported tomatoes, chopped. Flavor with grated fresh ginger, chopped fresh cilantro, mustard seeds, and whole cloves. Simmer over low heat for 30 minutes. Add salt to taste and serve.

- Combine cooked millet with freshly cooked sweet corn, scraped off the cob, and season simply with soy margarine, salt, and pepper. Stir in a little milk or soy milk if the mixture seems dry. Serve as a side dish.

- Use millet in casseroles, layered with steamed vegetables and cheese.

- Serve millet as a bed of grain for stir-fried Chinese vegetables or seafood in place of rice.

- Substitute millet for rice in your favorite rice pudding recipe.

- The texture of millet makes it a perfect stuffing for vegetables. It works well in bell peppers, eggplant, and winter squashes. The following recipe makes for a bright winter entrée:

MILLET-STUFFED BUTTERNUT SQUASH

Yield: 4 servings

2 medium butternut squashes
2/3 cup millet
1 2/3 cups water
2 tablespoons soy margarine
1 large onion, chopped
1/3 cup finely chopped cashew nuts or almonds

1/2 cup mixed dried fruit (a combination of apricots and raisins is nice)
1/2 cup orange juice
1 teaspoon honey
1 teaspoon salt, or to taste
1/2 teaspoon each: curry powder, cumin, cinnamon
Dash of nutmeg

Preheat the oven to 400°F.

With a sharp knife, cut the squashes in half lengthwise. Scrape out the seeds and fibers. Cover the squash halves with aluminum foil, then place in shallow baking dishes filled to 1/2 inch with water. Bake until tender, but do not overbake, about 45 to 55 minutes.

While the squashes are baking, cook the millet as instructed above in "Basic Cooked Millet." When the squash is done, set it aside until it is cool enough to handle. Reduce the oven to 350°F.

In a large skillet, heat the margarine until it foams. Add the onion and sauté over moderate heat until it is lightly browned. In the meantime, scoop the pulp out of the squash halves, leaving a 1/2-inch shell all around. Chop the pulp finely and add it to the onion. Sauté for 2 minutes, stirring, then add the millet and all the remaining ingredients. Stir together well and remove from the heat.

Stuff the squash shells with the millet mixture. Bake for 15 minutes. Serve at once.

OATS

The history of the cultivation of oats is not as ancient as that of most other grains. It's known that they grew wild in the Near East and North Africa around 2500 B.C., but the first written record of their cultivation dates back only to the beginning of the Christian era. Nevertheless, oats have become one of the most familiar and widely used cereal crops in the Western world. They are valued for their hardiness in cold climates, such as Scandinavia, and they have long been a favored grain in the cool, damp British Isles, especially in Scotland, where they are included in many traditional dishes. Half of the world's oat crop is grown in North America, where oats have been widely used since colonial times. Their mild, pleasantly nutty flavor and the variety of ways in which they can be processed make them a good, all-around grain whose uses go far beyond that of the familiar breakfast cereal.

At 14 percent protein, oats have the highest protein content of all common grains, second only to the newly revived "supergrains," amaranth and quinoa, and the man-made hybrid triticale. Oats contain seven B vitamins, vitamin E, and are mineral-rich, with a significant amount of iron, as well as a good supply of calcium and phosphorus. Oat bran provides a good amount of fiber and has recently been credited with the ability to reduce cholesterol in the blood. Oats contain a higher proportion of fat than most other grains (although they cannot be considered a high-fat food by any stretch of the imagination). Some claim that this accounts for their value as a warming food in cold weather, because fat helps the body store heat and energy. Since oats are never refined (that is, their bran and germ are left intact), they retain their nutritional qualities through many phases of arduous processing.

Oats have the additional benefit of containing an antioxidant substance that acts as a natural preservative to extend their shelf life. Still, for optimal freshness, store oats in all their forms in a cool, dry place as you would other grains. Oats can be purchased in a number of forms, as follows:

WHOLE OAT GROATS

Whole oat groats are the basis of all other oat products. To prepare the grain for consumption, the outer husks are removed, and then the kernel is cleaned and toasted. The toasting makes two layers of tough hull easier to remove and also deactivates an enzyme (lipase) that can produce an odd, soapy taste. The kernel is then scoured to remove the tough hull material. The edible, beneficial bran remains, as does the germ of the kernel. Whole oat groats are softer than wheat or rye berries, so lend themselves well to rolling, slicing, and milling. They may also be used in their whole form and in this way resemble pot barley in texture and taste.

Basic Cooked Whole Oat Groats: There is a considerable range in the recommended cooking time for oat groats, from 45 minutes to 2 hours! After 45 minutes the grain is still quite firm and chewy; after 2 hours, the grain will burst and become mushy. Use your discretion and cook the grain to suit particular recipes—a firmer texture is nice for pilafs and grain salads, for instance, whereas a softer texture is better for soups or as cooked cereal. Use 3 parts water to 1 part grain. Bring the water to a boil, stir in the grain, return to a boil, then lower the heat and simmer until the water is absorbed, about 45 minutes. Taste the grain, and if you'd like a softer texture, add another 1/2 cup of water for every cup of raw grain that was used, then simmer until it is absorbed. Repeat until the grain is cooked to your liking. To reduce cooking time somewhat, whole oat groats may be presoaked overnight in water.

- Soaked overnight, oat groats may be added to bread dough without further cooking. For a standard bread recipe for 2 loaves, use 1/4 cup groats soaked in 1/2 cup water.

- Substitute whole oat groats for barley in long-cooking soups.

- Cooked groats make a chewy addition to grain pilafs, especially when used in conjunction with a fluffy grain such as couscous, long-grain rice, or quinoa.

- Oat groats are good for sprouting (see appendix A). Oat sprouts are useful in salads, grain dishes, and homemade breads.

- The pleasantly chewy texture of whole oats makes them an interesting basis for hearty winter salads such as this one:

WHOLE OATS SALAD WITH BUTTERMILK MARINADE

Yield: 6 servings

3/4 cup whole oat groats
2 1/4 cups water
1 cup cooked chick-peas
2 cups finely chopped broccoli florets, steamed tender-crisp
1 medium carrot, coarsely chopped
1 medium stalk celery, finely diced
1/3 cup chopped black olives
2 to 3 bunches scallions, chopped
2 tablespoons sunflower seeds, toasted

Marinade:

1/3 cup buttermilk
3 tablespoons olive oil
3 tablespoons wine vinegar
1/2 teaspoon salt
1 teaspoon dry mustard
1/2 teaspoon dried oregano
1/2 teaspoon dried basil

**¹/₂ teaspoon cumin
Freshly ground pepper to taste**

Cook the oats as directed in "Basic Cooked Whole Oat Groats," above. A fairly firm texture is desirable here, so don't let them get mushy. When done, rinse them in cool water and combine them in a mixing bowl with the remaining salad ingredients. Combine the marinade ingredients in a small bowl and mix well. Pour over the salad and toss together. Refrigerate, covered, for about an hour before serving, stirring once or twice.

STEEL-CUT OATS

Sometimes called *Scottish* or *Irish oatmeal*, steel-cut oats are made by slicing the whole groat into small pieces with sharp blades. To give them a toasty flavor, they are sometimes lightly roasted before being marketed. Because steel-cut oats cook to a thick, very sticky consistency, they're more useful as a cooked cereal (albeit a rather long-cooking one) than as a grain for general cookery. Hearty, gritty, and nutty in flavor, they have far more texture when cooked than rolled oats or oatmeal.

Basic Cooked Steel-Cut Oats: Use 4 parts water to 1 part grain. Bring the water to a boil, stir in the grain, return to a boil, then reduce the heat to low and simmer, covered, until the water is absorbed, about 45 to 50 minutes.

- Use as a hot cereal with honey, milk, nuts, and dried fruit.

- Add small amounts to baked goods, such as griddle cakes and muffins, for hearty texture.

- Add cooked steel-cut oats to vegetable or bean soups to lend thickness and substance. Or you can add them raw to long-cooking soups in place of barley or other grains.

ROLLED OATS

Rolled oats (sometimes referred to as *old-fashioned oats* or simply *oatmeal*) are whole oats that have been steamed then run through rollers to flatten them. These are what you get most often when buying in bulk. To make oats know as *quick-cooking*, the whole oats are steamed, then sliced into three or four pieces before being flattened in rollers. *Instant oats* have been partially cooked and dried. Rolled,

quick, and instant oats contain most of the original nutrients in whole oats; however, be aware that instant oats are often packaged with salt and sugar.

Basic Cooked Rolled Oats: For old-fashioned rolled oats, use 1 ¹/₂ parts water to 1 part grain. Bring the water to a boil, then stir in the oats. Cover and remove from the heat. Let stand until done to your liking, about 10 minutes. For packaged quick-cooking oats, follow package directions. Allow ¹/₃ cup dry oats per serving as a hot cooked cereal.

Serve cooked oats as a hot cereal with raisins or other dried fruits (for a change of pace, use dried fruits such as prunes or black figs that have been soaked in water overnight to plump them) and the optional sweetener of your choice. Or add an unusual twist with chopped apricots, cashews, and cinnamon.

Uncooked rolled oats are very versatile and, in addition to their well-known role in oatmeal cookies, may be used to add a pleasant texture and mild, nutty flavor to many recipes. Old-fashioned and quick-cooking oats may be used interchangeably. Here are some ideas:

- Substitute ¹/₂ cup rolled oats for the equivalent amount of flour in your favorite recipe for banana bread.

- For delicious pancakes, replace up to half the wheat flour in a standard recipe with rolled oats.

- Use rolled oats instead of bread crumbs in casseroles or as a topping.

- For an easy savory pancake: Combine 1 cup rolled oats with an equivalent amount of grated zucchini, 2 beaten eggs, 1/4 cup milk, 1 teaspoon each of mixed dried herbs and cumin, and salt and pepper to taste. Ladle quarter-cupfuls onto a hot, oiled skillet and fry on both sides until golden brown. Drain on paper towels and serve at once. This makes about a dozen pancakes.

- For a delicious granola, skillet-roast some rolled oats along with sesame seeds, wheat germ, and crushed almonds until the mixture smells toasty and fragrant. Add dried fruit and a touch of carob powder, then let cool and store in jars. The result is a naturally sweet and nutty cereal, considerably lighter than the heavy, baked oil-and-honey versions of the 1960s!

- To make a delightful topping for pies and fruit crisps, stir together 1 cup rolled oats with 1/4 cup whole wheat pastry flour, 1/4 cup finely chopped or ground walnuts, 2 tablespoons melted soy margarine, 1 tablespoon light brown sugar, and a pinch of cinnamon.

ROLLED-OAT PIECRUST

Yield: One 9-inch crust

This cookie-type piecrust is less buttery, but just as satisfying as conventional pastry crust. The crust may be filled and baked further, but it is especially good with chilled, pudding-style fillings.

1 cup rolled oats
1/4 cup whole wheat pastry flour or oat flour
4 tablespoons soy margarine
3 tablespoons honey
3 tablespoons water, or as needed

Preheat the oven to 350°F.

In a mixing bowl, combine the oats with the flour. Work in the margarine with the tines of a fork until the mixture resembles a coarse meal. Work in the honey and enough water to hold the mixture together. Very patiently, press the mixture into the bottom and up the sides of a 9-inch pie pan. Bake for 10 to 12 minutes, or until golden. Allow to cool before filling.

OAT BRAN

Oat bran is the edible outer covering of the whole oat groat and is most often sold in bulk in natural-food stores. It has recently been recognized as one of the richest sources of a soluble form of fiber that helps to reduce cholesterol levels in the blood. Nutritionist Jane Brody, in her *Good Food Book*, cites studies that showed significant lowering of cholesterol levels in men who consumed oat bran on a daily basis in the form of muffins or cereal. Oat bran may be used in the same ways as wheat bran (see page 29 for ideas).

——— QUINOA ———

Quinoa (pronounced KEEN-wa) is a historic companion to grain amaranth (see page 7), one of two esteemed ancient staple crops that gradually fell into disuse after the sixteenth-century Spanish conquests of the Andean and Central American cultures. The nutritional profiles of quinoa and amaranth are remarkably alike.

Traditionally grown in the South American Andes, quinoa has recently begun to be cultivated in the Rocky Mountains of Colorado. The seeds, which grow in clusters at the end of the plant's stalk, are generally harvested by hand. Quinoa thrives in the thin air, low rainfall, and extreme temperatures of high altitudes. It grows well even in very poor soil. All these factors explain why quinoa has long been a valued crop in the mountainous regions of South America, where few other crops can survive.

Like amaranth, quinoa is slowly making a comeback via the natural-food market. It is marketed in this country by the Quinoa Corporation who were the first to promote its use outside South America. It is also available as a versatile flour (page 99). Somewhat smaller than millet seeds, quinoa seeds are irregularly roundish and of a sandy color. Because it grows in mountain regions and is harvested by hand, quinoa is relatively expensive as compared with other grains (but less expensive than wild rice, so it need not be considered a gourmet item). You get a lot of nutritional value for your money, and the fact that cooked quinoa expands to four times its dry volume means that a little goes a long way. If your natural-food store does not carry quinoa, either ask them if they will do so or order it directly from the Quinoa Corporation, who will also send recipes, as well as nutritional and agricultural information (see appendix B).

Nutritionally, quinoa is similar to grain amaranth. At 16 percent protein, it surpasses other grains not only in quantity but also in quality of protein, with substantial amounts of all the essential amino acids. It is also rich in minerals, particularly calcium, phosphorus, and iron. Quinoa also provides a wide range of the B-complex vitamins as well as vitamin E.

Where quinoa and amaranth part company is in their culinary differences. Whereas amaranth has an assertive flavor and cooks to a heavy, somewhat sticky consistency, quinoa is mild and distinctly nutty, and its texture is very light and fluffy. An additional advantage is its quick cooking time (about 15 minutes). Quinoa is delicious simply seasoned with soy margarine, scallions, and black pepper. In fact, it's so good on its own that it hardly needs embellishments. However, here are some further suggestions for using this versatile "grain of the future."

Basic Cooked Quinoa: The basic recipe for quinoa calls for 2 cups water (for variety, you might like to occasionally use a light vegetable stock) to 1 cup grain. Rinse the quinoa in a very fine sieve. Bring the water to a boil, stir in the grain, return to a boil, then lower the heat and simmer, covered, until the water is absorbed, about 15 minutes. Like other grains, the nutty flavor and aroma of quinoa is enhanced by toasting it lightly in a dry or lightly oiled skillet for about 5 minutes before cooking.

- Substitute quinoa in any recipe calling for bulgur. For instance, quinoa makes a light and very tasty tabouli.

- Use as a bed of grains for bean dishes, curries, stir-fried vegetables, or seafood—in fact, anywhere you'd use rice.

- Use as a base for pilafs, laced with nuts, dried fruits, and exotic spices, such as saffron, fenugreek, and whole roasted cumin or mustard seeds.

- Seasoned quinoa makes an excellent stuffing for vegetables. Heat olive oil or soy margarine in a skillet and sauté chopped onions and minced garlic until golden. Add quinoa, chopped fresh herbs, a pinch of ground cumin, and salt and pepper. Use to stuff prebaked zucchini, winter squashes, green bell peppers, or eggplant.

- To make tasty griddle cakes, combine 2 cups cooked quinoa with 1/2 cup flour of any kind, 2 beaten eggs, and 2/3 cup milk or soy milk. Stir until blended and drop by quarter-cupfuls onto a hot, lightly oiled griddle. Cook on both sides until golden (this will yield about 16 griddle cakes). Serve hot with maple syrup, fruit butter, or applesauce.

- Quinoa makes a more nutritious substitute for refined durum couscous. Prepare a Moroccan-style couscous using a stew of chickpeas, carrots, onions, zucchini, tomatoes, and raisins and serve by surrounding it with a ring of quinoa.

- Quinoa is great in casseroles, too. Here's a simple idea: Make layers in an oiled 1 1/2-quart casserole dish as follows: 1 1/2 cups quinoa (seasoned with salt and pepper), 1 1/2 cups steamed chopped broccoli, 2 beaten eggs, and 3/4 cup grated Cheddar cheese. Repeat the layers. Bake at 350°F until the top is very golden and crisp, about 30 to 40 minutes.

- Use quinoa in place of rice in your favorite rice pudding recipe.

- A delicious topping for plain cooked quinoa is a combination of stir-fried onions, bok choy, and soybean or mung bean sprouts, seasoned with dark sesame oil and natural soy sauce.

QUINOA AND SUMMER SQUASH SAUTÉ

Yield: 4 to 6 servings

1 tablespoon safflower oil
1 cup quinoa
2 cups water or vegetable stock
2 tablespoons olive oil
1 medium onion, chopped
2 cloves garlic, minced
2 medium zucchinis (about 1 1/2 pounds)
or 1 zucchini and 1 medium pattypan
squash, sliced into bite-size pieces
1 medium yellow summer squash, sliced
into bite-size pieces
6 large or 10 medium mushrooms, sliced
1 or 2 green chilies, seeded and minced
2 to 3 tablespoons chopped cilantro or
fresh parsley
1 teaspoon oregano
1/2 teaspoon ground cumin
Salt and freshly ground pepper to taste

Heat the safflower oil in a large, heavy skillet. Toast the quinoa until it is lighty browned and aromatic, about 5 minutes. In the meantime, bring the water or stock to a boil in a heavy saucepan. Stir in the quinoa and cook as directed in "Basic Cooked Quinoa," above.

Heat the olive oil in the same heavy skillet. Add the onion and garlic and sauté over moderate heat until it is translucent. Add the squashes, mushrooms and chilies, and stir-fry until the squashes are touched with golden spots. Stir in the cooked quinoa along with the seasonings. Cook over very low heat, stirring frequently, for 8 to 10 minutes. Serve at once.

RICE

Rice is the staple grain of half the world's population. Written records of its cultivation date back to 2800 B.C. in China, though it is believed to have originated in India prior to this. Rice arrived in Europe only in the fifteenth century, and in North America in the seventeenth century, when it was presented to the colony of South Carolina as a gift of seed from a ship from Madagascar. Rice is intrinsic to numerous cuisines all over the globe; however, white rice is used overwhelmingly in favor of brown. For those accustomed to eating white rice, brown rice takes some getting used to—with its nutty taste and chewy texture it doesn't fade into the background of dishes as does white rice. The most compelling reason to switch is that nutritionally brown rice is far superior.

When purchased in bulk, brown rice is very economical. It stores well for several months, provided that storage conditions are consistently cool and dry. Most natural-food stores also offer organically grown brown rice, at a slightly higher price. The only drawback to buying brown rice in bulk is the occasional presence of mealworm eggs and the subsequent moths that hatch from them. If brown rice is left unrefrigerated during warm, humid months, it can become quite a hatching ground, sending annoying, yet perfectly harmless tiny gray moths flying out of your grain jar when opened. The way to minimize the problem is to rinse your rice very well in a fine sieve before cooking it and to refrigerate it during the summer. Be assured that distributors as well as retailers do their best to avoid selling buggy grains.

Brown rice is high in fiber, low in fat, and very easy to digest. It provides a good range of the B vitamins, particularly thiamine, niacin, and folacin, and minerals, notably phosphorus,

calcium, and potassium. At 7½ percent protein, brown rice is not as high in protein as some other common grains, such as millet, oats, and barley. When brown rice is refined, the bran, polish, and germ are removed, leaving only the starchy white endosperm. White rice contains roughly only one-third of the vitamins and fiber, one-half of the minerals, none of the vitamin E, and 80 percent of the protein. To enrich white rice, iron and three B vitamins are added back, but the overall nutritional value of whole brown rice is not nearly approximated.

In Asia, there is an insistence on using only white rice, since at some point polished rice became a status symbol. Nutritionists consider this an ironic tragedy, particularly in light of the fact that rice is the primary food in many underdeveloped nations. For some time, this situation resulted in the proliferation of beriberi, a disease caused by thiamine deficiency. The white rice consumed by Asians is now enriched.

THE VARIETIES OF BROWN RICE

Brown rice is available in a variety of forms, but the differences among the types are culinary rather than nutritional. When deciding which to buy, keep in mind how you plan to use the rice.

Long-grain brown rice cooks to a firm, fluffy texture and the grains remain separate when cooked. This texture and the mild, lightly nutty flavor make long-grain brown rice a good all-purpose rice. It's especially good in pilafs, rice salads, and as a bed for vegetables, seafood, and bean dishes.

Medium-grain brown rice cooks to a fluffy texture like long-grain, but is slightly more tender and has more of a nutty, sweet flavor. Medium grain rice is also good as an all-purpose rice and works especially well in baked goods, griddle cakes, and as a stuffing for vegetables.

Short-grain brown rice, whose kernels are almost round, cooks to a denser, chewier texture and is sweeter than both long-grain and medium-grain brown rice. If it is cooked to more than a just-done consistency, it becomes sticky. It's a great choice for using in rice puddings and, like medium-grain rice, may also be used in baked goods and griddle cakes.

Glutinous brown rice is a variant of short-grain rice. Its name refers to its texture and not literally to gluten, which it does not contain. Glutinous rice is a fairly common offering in natural-food stores as well as Oriental groceries (though in the latter, it is much more likely to be refined). Alternately called *sweet rice* or *sticky rice*, glutinous rice is a much-used staple in Japan and other Southeast Asian countries. It is used in the making of sushi, rice balls, sweet puddings, and mochi cakes (see page 22).

Basic Cooked Rice: The amount of water recommended for cooking long- and medium-grain brown rice varies widely, from as little as 1½ parts water to as much as 3 parts water per 1 part rice. I recommend using a ratio of 2½ parts water to 1 part rice. Use 2 parts water to 1 part rice for short-grain and glutinous rice. Remember to rinse the rice well before cooking. Bring the water to a boil, stir in the rice, return to a boil, lower the heat, then simmer, covered, for 35 to 40 minutes, until the water is absorbed.

Few grains are as versatile as rice. In North America, rice is a staple of the Southwest, where it is often served alongside tortilla specialties. Rice has also long been an important staple on Southern tables, from the Carolinas to Louisiana, where it is teamed with legumes (such as in the famous New Orleans red beans and rice) and used in everything from soups to desserts. In Southeast Asia, China, India, and Japan, hardly a meal is served that doesn't include rice. Rice pilafs, fragrant with spices, herbs, and nuts, are well known in the cuisines of the Near and Middle East, and in the Mediterranean rice goes into classic dishes such as the stuffed grape leaves of Greece, the risottos of Italy, and the paellas of Spain. White rice is traditionally used in these classic recipes, but there is no reason that wholefood enthusiasts can't substitute brown rice in homemade versions. If you find the more assertive flavor and texture a little odd at first, try mixing brown rice half and half with white rice (cooked separately, of course). The heartier character of brown rice is not difficult to grow accustomed to—and to relish.

Here are a few additional suggestions for using brown rice:

- Add well-cooked, leftover brown rice to muffin or quick-bread batters for a wonderful flavor and chewy texture—about ½ cup per average recipe.

- For a hearty breakfast treat, make brown rice griddle cakes. Combine 1 cup whole wheat, barley, or oat flour in a mixing bowl with ½ teaspoon each salt and baking soda. Stir in 2 beaten eggs, 1 cup buttermilk, and 1 cup well-cooked brown rice (medium-grain is preferable). Mix thoroughly, then drop the batter onto a hot, lightly oiled griddle or skillet to form 3-to-4-inch cakes. Cook on both sides until golden brown and serve hot with maple syrup, preserves, or fruit butter. This makes 14 to 16 cakes.

- For excellent cold rice salads, combine cooked long-grain brown rice with steamed or raw vegetables, fresh herbs, and chopped nuts of your choice. Dress with a good nut oil or olive oil and vinegar.

- As a soup grain, brown rice has a special affinity with tomato-based soups and is also good in split pea and lentil soups. Add ½ to ⅔ cup raw brown rice at the time you begin cooking the peas or lentils for the soup.

- Cook brown rice together with soy flakes in a ratio of 3 parts rice to 1 part soy flakes to boost the protein quality.

CAULIFLOWER RICE PILAF

Yield: 6 or more servings

2 tablespoons safflower oil
3 to 4 cloves garlic, minced
1 small head cauliflower, cut into small florets
1-inch piece fresh ginger, grated
3 cups cooked long-grain brown rice (about 1 cup raw)
⅓ cup raisins or currants
1 teaspoon good curry powder
½ teaspoon coriander
¼ teaspoon each cinnamon and ground cloves
3 bunches scallions, chopped
1 tablespoon soy margarine
½ cup yogurt
2 tablespoons sesame seeds

Heat the oil in a very large, wide skillet. Add the garlic and sauté over moderate heat for 1 minute. Add the cauliflower and ginger and sauté until the cauliflower is lightly browned. Add all the remaining ingredients except the last three. Stir together and cook, covered, over very low heat, for 15 minutes. Stir in the margarine, yogurt, and sesame seeds. Remove from the heat and serve at once.

BROWN BASMATI RICE

A long-grain rice that originated in northern India, Basmati's special appeal lies in its exceptionally nutty flavor and enticing fragrance. The Basmati rice used in traditional Indian cookery is usually refined, but a whole, unpolished version is available in natural-food stores. Brown Basmati is grown in California under conditions approximating those of the plant's native Punjab region. California Basmati is sometimes labeled, appropriately, *calmati*.

Brown Basmati is generally available in bulk and is a bit more expensive than ordinary brown rice, but not so much as to make it prohibitive. It is especially appropriate to use in Indian recipes, enhanced with aromatic spices. Basmati may be substituted in any recipe calling for long- or medium-grain brown rice. Cook it exactly as you would those types of rice (see "Basic Cooked Rice," page 20).

BASMATI AND WILD RICE PILAF WITH CASHEWS

Yield: 6 servings

The simplicity of this recipe will highlight the aroma and flavor of Basmati rice without overshadowing it, making for a nice introduction to its special character.

1 cup brown Basmati rice
1/2 cup wild rice
1 quart water
3 tablespoons soy margarine
3 bunches scallions, minced
3 tablespoons minced fresh parsley
Juice of 1/2 lemon
Salt and freshly ground pepper to taste
1/2 cup cashew pieces, toasted

Rinse the Basmati and wild rice and combine them in a heavy saucepan with the water. Bring to a boil, then simmer, covered, until the water is absorbed, about 35 to 40 minutes.

In a large skillet, heat the margarine until it melts. Add the cooked rice along with all the remaining ingredients except the cashews. Sauté over low heat for 10 minutes, stirring frequently. If the mixture seems dry, add a small amount of water. Stir in the cashews and serve at once.

RICE FLAKES

Rice flakes (sometimes labeled *flaked brown rice*) are made from partially cooked rice that is sliced, flattened with rollers, and dehydrated, making them a quick-cooking, convenient cereal food. They cook to a soft, mushy, but not overly gummy or glutinous consistency. Their flavor is somewhat bland.

Basic Cooked Rice Flakes: Use 1 1/4 cups water to 1 cup flakes. Bring the water to a boil in a heavy saucepan, sprinkle in the flakes, lower the heat, and simmer, covered, for 5 to 8 minutes, or until the water is completely absorbed. Alternately, simply remove from the heat after sprinkling in the flakes and let stand, covered, until the water is absorbed, about 10 to 12 minutes. Keep in mind that cooked rice flakes expand only about 25 percent from their dry volume. Allow 1/2 to 3/4 cup dry flakes per serving as a hot cereal. Embellish with dried fruit, nuts, and sweeteners such as honey, rice syrup, or barely malt.

- Add 1/2 cup or so cooked rice flakes to the batter for muffins and quick breads to provide a pleasant flavor and moist texture. Or add 1/4 to 1/3 cup uncooked flakes to those batters, as well as to pancake batters, for a chewier texture.

- Substitute cooked rice flakes in recipes that call for cooked cornmeal or mashed potatoes.

- Substitute cooked rice flakes for cooked rice in rice pudding recipes.

CHEDDAR-RICE WEDGES

Yield: 4 to 6 servings

This simple recipe becomes something rather elegant when baked; it's almost like spoon-bread and goes nicely with bean soups.

1 1/4 cups water
1 cup rice flakes
1 egg, beaten
1/2 cup low-fat milk or soy milk
1/3 cup whole wheat flour
1/2 teaspoon salt
1/2 teaspoon baking powder
2 tablespoons soy margarine, melted
3/4 cup firmly packed grated Cheddar
  cheese

Preheat the oven to 400°F.

Bring the water to a boil in a heavy saucepan. Sprinkle in the rice flakes, lower the heat, and simmer for 5 to 8 minutes, or until the water is absorbed. In a mixing bowl, combine the cooked rice flakes with the remaining ingredients and mix thoroughly. Pour the mixture into an oiled 9-inch pie pan. Bake for 20 to 25 minutes, or until the top is nicely browned. Allow to cool somewhat, then cut into four or six wedges to serve.

RICE BRAN AND RICE POLISH

When brown rice is refined to make white rice, the bran and polish are removed. Some of this nutritious material is rescued in order to be marketed as two slightly different products. Rice bran and rice polish are the outer layers covering the starchy endosperm of the rice kernel. Rice bran is very rich in fiber, most of which passes through the body undigested, adding bulk to the diet and aiding in the regulation of the digestive process. Rice polish is a thin layer of skin under the bran and is fully digestible. Both are rich in B vitamins, particularly thiamine, niacin, and folic acid, and house about half of the mineral content of brown rice. Though not as flavorful as wheat germ, these products can be used in much the same ways—sprinkled over cereals and casseroles, used instead of bread crumbs, and used to replace a small portion of the flour in baked goods, such as muffins, breads, and griddle cakes.

MOCHI (Sweet Rice Cakes)

A traditional Japanese specialty, mochi cakes are made from sweet, glutinous brown rice that has been steamed, then mashed. The mashed rice is pressed into trays, then dried, becoming very hard and dense. Finally, the hardened mass is cut into small sections for storage or packaging. Mochi is a low-fat, high-carbohydrate food with all the nutritional characteristics of brown rice. It is available plain or in flavors such as sesame-garlic or raisin-cinnamon.

Look for cellophane-wrapped mochi cakes, which are about 6 inches square and 1/2 inch thick, in the refrigerator section of natural-food stores. Mochi is perishable and must be kept refrigerated until used. It may also be stored in the freezer for several months. Once the package is opened, any leftovers should be wrapped in an additional plastic bag and refrigerated or frozen.

The most popular way to prepare mochi cakes is to bake them at a high temperature to create their characteristic puffiness. The outside becomes crisp while the inside becomes rather sticky and pleasantly chewy. The puffing of the cakes also causes an air pocket to form on the inside. With a sharp knife, cut the cakes into four or six pieces, or break them along the serrations that are often provided. Place on a baking sheet and bake in a 450°F oven for 10 minutes, or until they are puffed and golden brown. Mochi cakes may be done very successfully in a toaster oven. Serve the mochi cakes hot, either plain or filled. The hollow pocket inside a mochi cake is small, but may be filled in many different ways. A major North American producer of mochi, Grainaissance, provides a list of suggestions on how mochi may be filled. Here are just a few:

• Peanut butter and honey

• Butter or margarine and honey

• Soy sauce, honey, and ginger

• Grated cheese

• Avocado, tomato, and sprouts

• Beans, cheese, tomato, and onions

• Scrambled eggs

In addition to baking, Grainaissance provides these alternative ideas for preparing mochi:

• Cut the cakes along the marked serrations. Brush them with oil and pan-fry in a heavy skillet for 6 minutes on each side. Top with sliced cheese, mashed potatoes, honey, jam, or fruit butter.

- Cook in a lightly oiled waffle iron for 10 minutes and serve for breakfast with honey or syrup.
- Cut into small cubes and cook in a soup broth to make chewy dumplings.

Grainaissance sends free pamphlets with recipes and suggestions to consumers who write them (see appendix C).

RYE

The first records of the cultivation of rye date from just before the Christian era. Its ability to withstand cold, wet climates soon made it a staple bread grain in Scandinavia, Russia, and Germany. Wheat eventually supplanted rye, but rye is still a well-loved bread grain in those countries. North Americans have learned to relish the chewy texture and pleasant, faintly sour flavor of rye bread, too. Besides bread flour, whole-grain rye yields several versatile products, including rye flakes and cracked rye. Despite all it has going for it, however, worldwide rye cultivation is declining.

The retail and mail-order natural-food markets are good sources for whole rye and its derivatives. Rye products should be stored in a cool, dry place, where they will keep well for several months.

Whole-grain rye is 12 percent protein, is rich in the B-vitamin complex, and provides generous amounts of iron, calcium, phosphorus, and potassium. Overall, it contains higher concentrations of these nutrients than does whole wheat.

RYE BERRIES

Whole rye berries are widely available in natural-food stores. Shaped somewhat like a grain of rice, with a deep furrow in the middle, rye berries may be used in much the same way as wheat berries (see page 26 for suggestions). Note also that the uncooked berry is excellent sprouted and can be added to bread doughs or tossed into green salads (see appendix A).

Basic Cooked Rye Berries: Use 3 1/2 parts water to 1 part grain. Bring the water to a boil, stir in the grain, return to a boil, then lower the heat and simmer, covered, until the water is absorbed, about 45 to 55 minutes. If the grain is still too firm for you, add another 1/2 cup water for every cup of raw grain that was used, and simmer until it is absorbed. The berries may be presoaked in water overnight to reduce the cooking time somewhat.

CRACKED RYE

Just as the name implies, this is whole, uncooked rye that has been cracked into small pieces. Cracked rye may be used as a tasty substitute for cracked wheat. See the entry for cracked wheat (page 28) for ideas.

Basic Cooked Cracked Rye: Use 3 parts water to 1 part grain. Bring the water to a boil, stir in the grain, return to a boil, then lower the heat and simmer, covered, for 40 to 50 minutes, or until the water is absorbed.

RYE FLAKES (Rolled rye)

Rye flakes are made from whole rye berries that have been steamed, then flattened with steel rollers. Faster cooking than both the whole berry and cracked rye, rye flakes may be eaten as a substantial hot cereal, added to baked goods, or incorporated into stews and soups. If you enjoy the taste of rye, you'll find rye flakes a very pleasant way to enjoy its unique flavor. Their cooked texture is just chewy enough to offer a bit of resistance to the tooth. Use them in the same ways as suggested for wheat flakes. See the entry for wheat flakes (page 29) for ideas.

Basic Cooked Rye Flakes: Use 2 parts water to 1 part grain. Bring the water to a boil, stir in the rye flakes, return to a boil, then lower the heat and simmer, covered, for about 15 to 20 minutes, or until the water is absorbed. For use as a hot cereal, allow 1/3 to 1/2 cup flakes per serving.

SPICY EGGPLANT WITH RYE FLAKES

Yield: 4 to 6 servings, or more as an appetizer

This recipe may be used as a main or side dish, or cooled and spread on crackers or pita bread as an appetizer. It also makes an excellent stuffing for tomatoes.

2 tablespoons safflower oil
1 medium onion, chopped
2 to 3 cloves garlic, minced

1 large eggplant, peeled and finely diced
2 fresh green chilies, seeded and minced
1 cup rye flakes
2 cups water
1 teaspoon good curry powder
1/2 teaspoon each: ground coriander,
    cumin, dry mustard
2/3 cup yogurt
Salt and freshly ground pepper to taste
2 tablespoons finely minced fresh
    parsley or cilantro

In a large skillet, heat the oil and sauté the onion until it is translucent. Add the garlic and continue to sauté until the onion is golden. Add all the ingredients except for the last three. Stir together and simmer over low heat, covered, until the eggplant and rye flakes are tender and the water is absorbed, about 30 minutes. Remove from heat and stir in the yogurt. Season to taste with salt and pepper. Stir in the parsley or cilantro. Serve warm or at room temperature.

SORGHUM

Sorghum, an important grain in much of Asia (including India and China) and Africa, is resistant to drought and will grow where rice or wheat won't. Worldwide, sorghum is the third largest cereal crop; thousands of acres a year are used to grow it in the United States (although here it is used almost exclusively as feed for cattle). Nevertheless, few Americans have even heard of it, much less tasted it.

The small, round seeds are somewhat larger than those of millet and grow in clusters at the end of a strong stalk. This stalk is the source of an excellent sweetener called *sorghum molasses* (page 162).

In North America, sorghum is not marketed to consumers for use as food, though why it is not is unclear. Those who want some can buy it in rural agricultural feed stores, but caution must be taken that the grain has not been treated with harmful pesticides. The two varieties of sorghum, milo and kefir, are reputed to be as flavorful as they are healthful. Sorghum has not undergone nutritional analysis by the USDA, but it is known that it contains very high quality protein that is deficient only in the amino acid lysine.

This entry is included for the purpose of definition only. Perhaps in the future sorghum will be recognized as a viable grain for marketing and will become available to consumers.

TRITICALE

After decades of research which began over a hundred years ago, triticale (pronounced tri-ti-CAY-lee) was developed in the 1960s by crossbreeding two types of wheat with rye, resulting in a hybrid that is nutritionally superior to its parts. It was originally developed to create a grain with the generous yield of wheat and the cold-hardiness of rye. However, the crop yields have been disappointing, and triticale has proved susceptible to the fungus disease ergot. Because of these agricultural difficulties, its potential for becoming a "superfood of the future" has diminished, and its use has not become as widespread as was hoped.

Triticale is available through mail-order sources and in natural-food stores. It comes in the form of flour (see page 102), whole berries, and flakes, either prepackaged or in bulk. If you have trouble finding triticale products in your local natural-food store, you might write to Arrowhead Mills, one of the major distributors of this grain, for outlets near you. They will also send recipes to those requesting them (see appendix C). Store triticale products in a cool, dry place, where they will keep well for several months.

At 16 percent protein, triticale is higher in protein than wheat or rye and contains larger percentages of the essential amino acids than its parent grains. It even has a good supply of lysine, the amino acid usually deficient in grains. Though triticale has not been fully analyzed by the USDA, it is believed that its B-vitamin, vitamin-E, and mineral content is similar to that of rye. In terms of flavor, triticale falls between wheat and rye, with more of wheat's nuttiness and just a hint of rye's pleasantly sour taste.

TRITICALE BERRIES

Similar to rye berries, with a long, slender shape, whole triticale berries can be used in the same way as rye or wheat berries. See the entry for wheat berries (page 26) for ideas for use.

Basic Cooked Triticale Berries: Use 3 1/2 parts water to 1 part grain. Bring the water to a boil, stir in the grain, return to a boil, then lower the heat and simmer, covered, about 50 to 55 minutes. If the grain is still too chewy for you, add another 1/2 cup water for every cup of raw grain that was used and simmer until it is absorbed. The berries may be presoaked in water overnight to reduce the cooking time some-what.

TRITICALE FLAKES (Rolled Triticale)

These are triticale berries that have been toasted and thinly rolled. They resemble wheat flakes in flavor and texture, but have the extra chewiness of rye. See the entries for rye flakes (page 23) and wheat flakes (page 29) for suggestions for use.

Basic Cooked Triticale Flakes: Use 2 parts water to 1 part grain. Bring the water to a boil, stir in the grain, return to a boil, then lower the heat and simmer, covered, for about 15 to 20 minutes, or until the water is absorbed. For use as a hot cereal, allow 1/3 to 1/2 cup dry flakes per serving.

─── WHEAT ───

Wheat, currently the world's most widely cultivated grain crop, has been grown for human consumption for thousands of years. Records of its cultivation have been found in the writings of ancient cultures of Egypt and China, among others. Wheat is a fairly hardy crop, growing in a variety of climates, though it is dependent on adequate rainfall. The United States is the world's leading producer of wheat; some 60 percent of the crop is exported.

There are several common varieties of wheat, including hard red winter wheat, hard red spring wheat, soft red winter wheat, and durum wheat. The differences among them are more apparent in their flour form (see page 103). After wheat is harvested, it is threshed in order to remove the hard hull, or *chaff*, and what remains is the whole kernel, called the *wheat berry*. The wheat berry is made up of three parts. *The germ* is a tiny area inside the base of the grain. It makes up about 2 to 3 percent of the wheat berry and contains 8 percent of the protein and the entire amount of vitamin E. *The bran* is the six or so outer layers covering the grain and contains most of the fiber. The bran makes up about 15 percent of the whole kernel and contains 20 percent of the protein. *The endosperm* comprises the greatest part of the kernel at 83 percent. It is mainly starch and protein, containing 72 percent of the protein in the grain.

Whole wheat contains substantial amounts of twenty-two major vitamins and minerals, no-tably eleven B vitamins, including B_6, folacin, niacin, thiamine, and riboflavin; vitamin E; and the minerals calcium, iron, magnesium, zinc, phosphorus, and potassium. In fact, according to nutrition expert Jane Brody, only four of the forty-four known essential nutrients are missing from wheat (those are vitamins A, B_{12}, and C and the trace mineral iodine). Whole wheat contains a wide range of the essential amino acids and is a fine source of good-quality protein. The exact amount of protein varies among the different types of wheat, but averages at about 12 percent.

When wheat is refined, that is, stripped of the bran and germ, as much as 80 percent of the vitamins and minerals are removed. The fiber content is diminished by about 93 percent, but the protein level remains high, since much of it is concentrated in the starchy endosperm. When wheat is enriched, only iron and three B vitamins are added back.

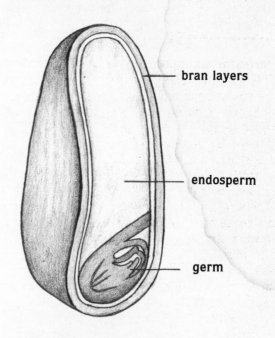

bran layers

endosperm

germ

WHEAT BERRIES

Wheat berries are perhaps the most impractical way to enjoy whole wheat in grain form, since they take so long to cook and their intense chewiness may be a bit overwhelming for some. Nevertheless, their slightly sweet, nutty taste and chewy texture add interest to many dishes, and those who don't mind the long cooking time will find them useful.

Basic Cooked Wheat Berries: Use 3 1/2 parts water to 1 part grain. Bring the water to a boil, stir in the grain, return to a boil, then lower the heat, and simmer, covered, for 50 to 55 minutes. If they're still too chewy at this point, add another ½ cup water for every cup of grain that was used and simmer until it is absorbed. To cut down on cooking time, you may presoak the berries overnight in water.

- Sauté cooked wheat berries in a bit of soy margarine to bring out their nutty flavor and use them as a garnish for puréed soups. They're particularly nice with cream of broccoli soup.

- Toss a handful of cooked wheat berries into green salads; marinate them first in a vinaigrette if time allows.

- For a filling, high-protein main dish, combine cooked wheat berries with black beans, in more or less equal proportions. Add lots of sautéed chopped onion and garlic, season with natural soy sauce, and garnish with chopped fresh parsley.

- Add small amounts of cooked wheat berries to less intense grains, such as rice, to make chewy pilafs.

- For a simple main or side dish, cook ½ pound mild-flavored noodles, such as Japanese udon or somen or ordinary spaghetti. Combine with a cup or so of cooked wheat berries and a cupful of steamed snow peas or bean sprouts. Season simply with scallions and natural soy sauce.

- Add a handful of wheat berries to bread doughs for texture and nutty flavor.

- Sprout raw wheat berries and add to bread doughs, green salads, or pasta salads (see appendix A).

BULGUR

The origins of this versatile wheat product can be traced back to the ancient Near and Middle East, when bulgur was cited as a favorite delicacy of the conquering armies of Genghis Khan. Bulgur is produced by parboiling the whole wheat berry, which is then dried and cracked. Sometimes bulgur is partially refined by removing some of the layers of bran. It's not difficult to spot the difference: When the bran layers are intact, the bulgur is a deep, toasty brown. Unrefined bulgur retains much of the original nutritional value of the whole berry. When

cooked, it has a chewy texture and slightly nutty flavor similar to that of brown rice.

The most economical way to buy bulgur is in bulk. It is also occasionally sold in preweighed 1- or 2-pound packages. Stored in a cool, dry place, bulgur will keep well for several months. Bulgur has made its way into packaged mixes for tabouli and pilaf, which are available in natural-food stores as well as gourmet food sections of many supermarkets.

Basic Cooked Bulgur: Bulgur may be cooked in two ways. The more common is simply to place the grain in a heatproof, deep casserole dish and pour boiling water over it in a ratio of 2 to 1. Cover the dish and let stand about 30 minutes, or until the water is absorbed. Fluff with a fork. The other way is to boil 2 parts water to 1 part grain in a heavy saucepan. Stir in the bulgur, lower the heat and simmer, covered, until the water is absorbed, about 15 to 20 minutes. To heighten the nutty flavor of bulgur, toast it first in a heavy skillet, either dry or with 1 tablespoon oil for every cup of grain used. Stir over moderate heat until it turns a slightly deeper shade of brown and is aromatic.

Explore Middle or Near Eastern cookbooks for classic bulgur recipes. The following list suggests only a few of the ways in which this healthful, convenient, and versatile food may be used:

- Use bulgur as a bed of grains in place of rice for vegetable stir-fries and stews or for bean dishes such as chili.

- Bulgur pilafs of all kinds are possible, using any of the following: lots of sautéed onion, chopped dried fruit and nuts, aromatic spices, fresh herbs, chick-peas, fresh peas, mushrooms.

- Bulgur works very well in casseroles, as in this simple recipe that serves 4: Spread 2 cups cooked bulgur, seasoned with salt, pepper, and a pinch of mixed dried herbs, into an oiled, shallow 1½-quart baking dish. Top with the sautéed rings of one large onion, sautéed diced eggplant pieces (from 1 large eggplant), sliced tomatoes, and 1 to ½ cups grated cheese. Bake for 20 minutes at 350°F, or until the cheese is bubbly.

- Use bulgur to stuff vegetables such as winter squashes.

- Cook bulgur further in a small amount of

milk or soy milk to make a hot breakfast cereal. For every serving (about 3/4 cup cooked bulgur), cook further in 1/3 cup milk or soy milk until nearly absorbed. Embellish with honey or other sweetener, dried fruits, chopped nuts, and a sprinkling of cinnamon.

- Add leftover cooked bulgur in small amounts to bread doughs and muffin batters for great texture.

BULGUR SALAD WITH FRUITS AND NUTS

Yield: 6 to 8 servings

Perhaps the most famous of bulgur recipes is tabouli, a delicious salad of Middle Eastern origin that combines the grain with tomatoes, fresh parsley, mint, scallions, olive oil, and lemon juice. Most Middle Eastern cookbooks and many vegetarian cookbooks contain this recipe. Here is another tasty bulgur salad, not of any particular origin save for my own inspiration, and one that may be enjoyed in any season.

1 cup bulgur
2 cups water
2/3 cup coarsely chopped walnuts
1/2 cup raisins or currants
1 large stalk celery, finely diced
1/4 cup sunflower seeds, toasted
2 tablespoons minced chives
1 medium apple
Juice of 1/2 lemon
1/4 cup (scant) safflower oil
1 tablespoon honey, or to taste
1/2 teaspoon cumin
1/4 teaspoon cinnamon
Dash of nutmeg

Cook the bulgur in either of the two ways suggested in "Basic Cooked Bulgur," above. Cool to room temperature.

In a serving bowl, combine the bulgur with the walnuts, raisins or currants, celery, sunflower seeds, and chives. Core (but don't peel) and finely dice the apple and toss with half the lemon juice, then add it, along with the remaining lemon juice and the rest of the ingredients, to the bulgur mixture. Toss until thoroughly combined. Serve at once or chill until needed.

COUSCOUS

Couscous is the name of the spicy, complex Moroccan dish of stewed meats and vegetables served over steamed grain. The cracked grain used in this famous North African recipe is usually millet. In North America, what is sold as couscous is made from the starchy endosperm of hard spring durum wheat. To make North American couscous, the wheat kernel is refined (that is, the bran and germ are removed), leaving the endosperm, which is then steamed, dried, and cracked. Semolina, the flour used to make pasta, is also made from the endosperm of durum wheat, explaining why couscous and refined pastas taste remarkably alike. The appeal of couscous lies in its light texture, its mild, familiar flavor, and its ease and speed of preparation.

Commonly sold in bulk, couscous stored in a tightly lidded jar in a cool, dry place will keep very well almost indefinitely. Because it is a refined product, the risk of rancidity is minimal.

Couscous has not been analyzed for precise nutritional statistics by the USDA, but its benefits are comparable to those of refined pastas. By definition, these are not whole foods, but they are nonetheless low in fat, fairly high in protein and, if made with enriched durum wheat flour, contain good amounts of iron and the B vitamins thiamine, niacin, and riboflavin.

Basic Cooked Couscous: Use 2 parts water to 1 part couscous. Place the amount of grain needed in a heatproof bowl or deep casserole dish. Bring the amount of water needed to a boil, then pour it over the couscous. Cover and allow to sit for 15 minutes, then fluff with a fork. It is now ready to use in a variety of interesting ways.

- Use couscous as a bed of grains in place of rice for stir-fried vegetables, curried vegetables, and the like. Because it's so light, couscous offers a nice contrast to heavy bean dishes.

- For a delicious, simplified vegetarian version of the Moroccan dish make a stew of some characteristic ingredients—tomatoes, chickpeas, zucchini, carrots, and onions, spiced with ginger and turmeric. Spread cooked couscous on a large round serving platter and make a well in the center; pour in the vegetable stew. Garnish the vegetables with raisins and chopped almonds and serve.

- Use leftover cooked couscous to make light and tasty griddle cakes. For every cup of cooked couscous, add 1 beaten egg, 1/4 cup milk, and 2 tablespoons wheat germ. Drop in heaping tablespoonfuls on a lightly oiled griddle. Serve hot with applesauce, fruit butter, jam, or syrup. The proportions given here make about a dozen cakes.

- For a delicious hot cereal, combine couscous in a saucepan with 1/2 cup milk for every cup of cooked grain. Simmer over low heat until absorbed. Sprinkle with wheat germ and serve with honey, raisins, and nuts.

- Make couscous a base for light summer salads. Toss diced tomatoes, cucumbers, radishes, and green or red bell peppers with cooked couscous and dress in a mild vinaigrette. Season with fresh herbs and scallions. Place each serving atop a bed of lettuce. Or try the following roasted vegetable salad, which is just a bit more involved, but special enough to serve to company:

COUSCOUS SALAD WITH ROASTED VEGETABLES

Yield: 6 servings

1 medium eggplant
1 large green or red bell pepper
2 medium firm, ripe tomatoes
1 cup couscous
2 cups boiling water
1/4 cup chopped fresh parsley
2 tablespoons minced fresh dill
2 bunches scallions, chopped
1 medium stalk celery, minced
1/4 cup olive oil
Juice of 1/2 lemon
1 teaspoon turmeric
1/2 teaspoon cumin
Salt and freshly ground pepper to taste

Preheat the oven to 375°F.

Place the eggplant on a baking sheet lined with aluminum foil. Bake for 35 to 45 minutes, or until it has "collapsed." In the meantime, roast the pepper and tomatoes under a broiler, turning so that the skin on all sides becomes quite blistered. Place these in a paper bag to cool.

Place the couscous in an ovenproof bowl. Pour the boiling water over it and cover. After 15 minutes, fluff with a fork.

When all the vegetables have cooled to room temperature, slip their skins off and chop into bite-size pieces.

Combine the couscous, vegetables, and all the remaining ingredients in a serving bowl and toss thoroughly to mix. This salad is best served at room temperature.

CRACKED WHEAT

Cracked wheat is similar to bulgur, in that it is whole wheat that has been cracked into large pieces. Unlike bulgur, however, cracked wheat is not presteamed, so it takes longer to cook. It cooks to a stickier texture, with the pieces tending to gum together rather than remain separate. This makes cracked wheat less desirable for use as a base for pilafs, grain salads, or as a bed of grain under vegetable or bean dishes. Cracked wheat is available boxed or in bulk in natural-food stores and will keep well for several months stored in a cool, dry place.

Basic Cooked Cracked Wheat: Use 3 parts water to 1 part grain. Bring the water to a boil, stir in the grain, return to a boil, then lower the heat and simmer, covered, for 35 to 40 minutes, or until the water is absorbed. Cracked wheat may be toasted on a hot, lightly oiled skillet before cooking to bring out the nutty flavor. Allow 1/4 cup raw cracked wheat per serving for use as a hot cereal.

There is little advantage in using cracked wheat over bulgur unless you will simply be eating it as a hot cereal. The texture of bulgur makes it more of a general-purpose grain. Cracked wheat may, however, be used as a soup grain instead of barley or as an element in savory baked nut loaves or casseroles, where its cohesive qualities prove useful.

WHEAT BRAN

Bran is the multilayered outer coating of the wheat berry. It is available in either a fine or a coarse grind. Which you choose is a matter of preference, but fine bran is easier to incorporate into all forms of baked goods. Coarse bran is sometimes labeled *bran flakes*. This refers to the flaky texture of the product and is not to be confused with prepared breakfast cereals that incorporate bran into crisp flakes. Kretschmer, the company that markets wheat germ, has also brought finely milled toasted bran in jars to supermarket shelves.

Bran is valued above all for its high fiber content. A 1-ounce serving (about 1/4 cup) contains 12 grams of fiber, nearly half the amount needed daily for a diet to be considered high in fiber. The bran contains half of the minerals present in the wheat berry, including significant amounts of magnesium and phosphorus. It is a good source of B vitamins, particularly B_6 and niacin, and also provides riboflavin, thiamine, and pantothenic acid.

Since bran and wheat germ may be used in similar ways, it's tempting to compare the two. Wheat germ is high in fiber, too, though not quite so much as bran. It has a pleasantly nutty flavor and aroma, whereas in those respects bran is rather flat. It's fair to say that in purely aesthetic terms, wheat germ has the greater appeal to the palate, though nutritionally both products are valuable additions to the diet.

Sprinkle a tablespoon or two of bran per serving over cold cereals and improve refined hot cereals such as farina by stirring in a similar amount of bran per serving. Bran muffins are a well-known way of taking advantage of bran in baking, but think of using it also in cookies, breads, and pancakes. Replace 2 to 3 tablespoons flour with bran (or more, if you'd like) for each cup of flour used. For more ideas, refer to the list under the entry for wheat germ (page 30). Fine bran may be substituted in any of those.

RAISIN-BRAN-HONEY COOKIES

Yield: 3 dozen cookies

1/2 cup (1 stick) soy margarine
3/4 cup honey
1 egg, beaten
1 teaspoon vanilla extract
1 1/2 cups fine bran
1 cup whole wheat pastry flour
1 teaspoon baking powder
1/2 teaspoon salt
1 teaspoon cinnamon
1 cup raisins
1/2 cup finely chopped walnuts or pecans

Preheat the oven to 375°F.

In a mixing bowl, cream together the margarine and the honey. Beat in the egg and the vanilla.

In another bowl, combine the bran, flour, baking powder, salt, and cinnamon. Work the wet ingredients together with the dry to form a stiff batter. Work in the raisins and nuts. Drop by heaping teaspoonfuls onto a cookie sheet. Bake for 10 to 12 minutes. Cool on a rack.

WHEAT FLAKES (Rolled Wheat)

These are wheat berries that have been steamed until soft, then flattened with steel rollers. They resemble rolled oats, but are darker and a bit firmer. Wheat flakes are excellent as a cooked cereal—very hearty and chewy. They may also be used in other ways as well.

Basic Cooked Wheat Flakes: Use 2 parts water to 1 part flakes. Bring to a boil, stir in the flakes, return to a boil, then lower the heat and simmer, covered, for 15 to 20 minutes, or until the water has been absorbed.

- Add about 1/3 cup dry wheat flakes for every serving of cereal to be cooked. Stir together and cook according to directions for the main grain. Serve with a little milk, dried or fresh fruit, honey, and some chopped nuts.

- Add some uncooked wheat flakes to long-simmering recipes such as chili, curried vegetables, bean stews, or even soups, to add texture.

- Substitute wheat flakes for rolled oats in baked goods. It's a good idea to soften the flakes first by pouring an equal volume of boiling water over them in a heatproof bowl. Cover and let stand 10 minutes, then proceed (manufacturers recommend adding them directly to batters, but this results in a product that is hard and dry).

- To make hearty griddle cakes, combine 2 cups cooked wheat flakes in a mixing bowl with 2 well-beaten eggs, 1/2 cup milk, and 2 tablespoons ground nuts. Stir until well blended, then drop by quarter-cupfuls onto a hot griddle. Cook on both sides until golden. Serve hot with syrup, fruit butter, or applesauce. This makes about a dozen cakes.

- Add a small amount of cooked wheat flakes to baked goods for great texture and moistness. Below is a recipe for muffins that are terrific with thick winter soups:

BUTTERMILK WHEAT FLAKE MUFFINS

Yield: 1 dozen

1/2 cup wheat flakes
1 cup water
2 tablespoons soy margarine
2 eggs, beaten
1 cup buttermilk
2 tablespoons honey
1 1/2 cups whole wheat flour
1/4 cup oat or barley flour
1 teaspoon baking powder
1/2 teaspoon baking soda
1/2 teaspoon salt
Sesame seeds for topping

Cook the wheat flakes as directed in "Basic Cooked Wheat Flakes," above. Remove from the heat. Stir in the margarine until it melts, then add the eggs, buttermilk, and honey.
Preheat the oven to 375°F.
In a mixing bowl, combine the remaining ingredients except for the sesame seeds. Pour in the wheat flakes mixture and stir vigorously until thoroughly combined. Spoon into 12 oiled muffin cups and sprinkle the tops with sesame seeds. Bake for 20 to 25 minutes, or until the tops are golden brown and a toothpick inserted into the center of a muffin tests clean.

WHEAT GERM

The germ of the wheat berry is also referred to as its embryo, because it sprouts when planted, germinating a new plant. Wheat germ, which is marketed in the form of tiny flakes, is widely available in jars in supermarket cereal sections, as well as in bulk in natural-food stores. While buying in bulk is more economical, you need to be concerned about freshness, since the wheat germ contains fats that quickly go rancid at room temperature. Wheat germ should be refrigerated at all times for maximum freshness. Raw wheat germ is good in homemade granola, where further toasting takes place. It is also fine to use in breads. Toasting wheat germ brings out its naturally nutty, slightly sweet flavor.

Wheat germ is a concentrated source of vitamin E (which also acts as a natural preservative). It contains generous amounts of nearly the entire B-vitamin complex as well as many minerals, with particularly good amounts of iron, zinc, and magnesium. Wheat germ is high in fiber, though slightly less so than bran. The fat in wheat germ consists of several essential fatty acids, including linoleic acid, a component of fat associated with cardiovascular health.

The flavor of wheat germ is both easy to like and easy to incorporate into many different types of dishes. For example:

- Top toasted wheat germ with milk and fruit for a tasty cold cereal. Or sprinkle some on any hot or cold cereal for a nutritional boost.

- Mix equal parts wheat germ with stone-ground cornmeal for a very tasty breading for fried foods.

- Use wheat germ as a topping on casseroles or pies, where it is an excellent substitute for bread crumbs.

- Substitute up to 25 percent of the flour with wheat germ in your favorite pancake recipe.

- Substitute up to 25 percent of the flour with wheat germ in recipes for muffins, quick breads, cookies, and even cakes. It adds a rich, nutty flavor.

- Add a tablespoon of wheat germ to high-protein milk or soy milk shakes.

- Substitute wheat germ for 2 to 3 tablespoons of the flour in homemade piecrusts.

- Sprinkle wheat germ over yogurt.

Kretschmer, the national manufacturer of the wheat germ sold in supermarkets, will send you a colorful recipe booklet featuring many enticing ways of incorporating wheat germ into cooking and baking. The order blank is on the back of the label. It's inexpensive and well worth having.

WHEAT GERM–ZUCCHINI PIE

Yield: 6 sevings

3/4 cup wheat germ, toasted
1/4 cup ground sunflower seeds, toasted
1/2 cup grated Parmesan cheese
2 1/2 tablespoons soy margarine
1 medium onion, halved and sliced
2 medium zucchinis, about 1 pound, sliced
1 teaspoon dried oregano
1 teaspoon dried dill

Salt and freshly ground black pepper to taste

1 cup firmly packed grated mild white cheese, such as Monterey Jack or Muenster

2 large tomatoes, thinly sliced

Preheat the oven to 350°F.

In a mixing bowl, combine the wheat germ, the ground sunflower seeds, and the Parmesan cheese. Melt 1 tablespoon of the margarine, then toss well with the wheat germ mixture. Heat the remaining margarine in a large skillet. Add the onion and sauté until it is golden. Add the zucchini, cover, and sauté until the zucchini is tender-crisp, stirring occasionally. Sprinkle with the oregano and dill and season to taste with salt and pepper.

In an oiled, 1 1/2-quart casserole, layer as follows: a fine layer of the crumbs mixture followed by half of the zucchini mixture, half of the cheese, half of the tomato slices, and half of the crumbs. Repeat. Bake for 30 to 35 minutes. Let cool for 10 minutes, then cut into squares to serve.

WHEAT GLUTEN (Seitan)

Seitan is one of the latest of ancient foods to make its way into Western use via the natural foods market. Seitan is the Japanese name for cooked wheat gluten. It is a commonly used food in Japan, China, Korea, and Russia. Gluten is the protein that gives wheat flour the ability to rise. Its unique characteristic is that it becomes stretchy and elastic when dough is kneaded. Any wheat flour milled from hard wheats, which contain a higher percentage of gluten than soft wheats, may be used to make seitan. It can be made from whole wheat flour, refined flour, or a combination of the two.

To make seitan, flour is combined with water to make a dough of about the same density as a bread dough. This dough is left to rest for 45 minutes or so, to allow the gluten to develop. It then undergoes many rinsings under running water, a process that is done either mechanically or by hand. Most of the starch (and much of the bran, if unrefined flour is used) is rinsed away, leaving a firm, stringy mass of gluten. The gluten is then sliced and cooked. The traditional Oriental method of cooking gluten is often used by North American manufacturers of seitan as well. It calls for cooking the seitan in a broth flavored with soy sauce and the sea

vegetable kombu. The cooked seitan is then packaged in tubs similar to those used for tofu and distributed to natural-food stores and co-ops, where it is kept in the refrigerator section.

The texture of seitan is remarkably meatlike. Its medium-brown color and porous surface give it an appearance that is uncannily like that of beef. These analogous qualities can be very desirable to those seeking meat substitutes, but may be off-putting to those who have an aesthetic aversion to meat! As for the taste, good seitan retains a hint of the flavor of wheat, but it should not taste of raw dough. It can be quite tasty when creatively prepared.

There is another form of wheat gluten called *fu gluten cakes*, which are occasionally available in natural-food stores, but those are not as easy to find as seitan. Fu is gluten that is toasted and steamed, then dried. To use, the cakes are simply soaked in warm water for 5 to 10 minutes and then prepared in much the same way as seitan.

Despite the fact that much of the bran has been rinsed away, seitan is still fairly nutritious. It contains nearly complete, high-quality protein (with more protein per serving than tofu) and provides a modest amount of B vitamins and iron. A 4-ounce serving supplies 15 grams of protein, but only 70 calories and 1 gram of fat.

One producer of this product, Upcountry Seitan, will send recipe pamphlets to consumers who write in (see appendix C).

Because of its rather full-bodied flavor and texture, seitan is not quite as versatile as tofu, but it nevertheless lends itself to a myriad of preparations. What's more, it is ready to use, making it very convenient. Before cooking, drain the seitan and reserve the flavorful liquid it comes in to use in sauces or soup stocks. You might wish to press some of the liquid out of the seitan to give it a firmer texture, but this is entirely optional.

- To make seitan cutlets, slice seitan into pieces approximately 1 1/2 by 2 inches by 1/2 inch thick. Dip into egg, then into seasoned bread crumbs and fry on both sides until the breading is golden and crisp. Serve with a mushroom gravy, made with sautéed mushrooms, flour or arrowroot, and the reserved liquid from the seitan, or with Sweet and Savory Grilling Sauce (page 161).

- Marinate 1/2-inch cubes of seitan in Rice Vinegar Marinade (page 181) or in your favorite vinaigrette dressing for an hour or two. Add to grain salads, hot bean dishes, or cold sesame noodles or sauté in a little oil and serve as an hors d'oeuvre with an herbed yogurt dip.

- Slice seitan thinly and use it as is or sauté lightly. Sandwich between rye or pumpernickel bread and embellish with mustard, lettuce, tomatoes, and pickles.

- To make a *seitan "Reuben,"* slice the seitan thinly and layer on hearty dark rye bread with well-drained cole slaw and Swiss cheese. Place under a broiler briefly to melt the cheese. Top with another slice of bread, spread with mustard if desired, or eat open-faced. Serve with potato salad and dill pickles.

- Incorporate thinly sliced bits of seitan into eggplant parmesan or lasagna.

- Simply add diced seitan to stir-fried vegetables as you would tofu.

- Use diced seitan as a substitute for beef in hearty stews, shish kebabs, and Mexican dishes.

- Barbecued or broiled seitan is excellent. Cut into 1/2-inch-thick slices, then baste with your favorite barbecue sauce or Sweet and Savory Grilling Sauce (page 161). Broil or barbecue for 5 to 7 minutes on each side.

SWEET-AND-SOUR SEITAN "PEPPERSTEAK"

Yield: 4 to 6 servings

This stir-fry is rather elaborate to prepare, but it is offbeat and very satisfying.

2 tablespoons peanut oil
1 teaspoon sesame oil
1 medium onion, halved and sliced
2 cloves garlic, minced
2 medium green bell peppers (or 1 green pepper and 1 sweet red pepper), cut into 1-inch-square pieces
1/2 pound mushrooms, sliced
1 cup snow peas, trimmed
2 plum tomatoes, diced
One 16-ounce can unsweetened pineapple chunks, with juice
1 teaspoon freshly grated ginger
2 to 3 tablespoons rice vinegar, to taste

2 tablespoons natural soy sauce, or to taste
1/2 pound seitan, diced (save the liquid for another use)
1 1/2 tablespoons cornstarch or arrowroot
Hot cooked rice
Sesame seeds for topping

Heat the oils in a wok. Add the onion and garlic and stir-fry over moderately high heat until the onion is just beginning to turn golden. Add the peppers, mushrooms, and snow peas and stir-fry for 3 to 4 minutes. Add the tomatoes, pineapple with liquid, ginger, vinegar, and soy sauce. Stir together and simmer over moderate heat until the snow peas are just tender-crisp. Stir in the seitan. Remove about 1/4 cup of the liquid in the wok and transfer to a cup. Dissolve the cornstarch or arrowroot in it, and stir back into the wok. Simmer for another 5 minutes. Serve at once over hot cooked rice, garnishing each serving with sesame seeds.

—————— WILD RICE ——————

Wild rice is actually the seed of a tall aquatic grass that is not a form of rice, nor even a grain at all. It is included in this section, however, because it is cooked and used as one. Native to parts of North America, most of our domestic crop is harvested by Native Americans in and around Minnesota and other Great Lakes states, where it thrives in freshwater lakes or rivers. The fact that wild rice is literally a wild grass has made attempts at large-scale commercial cultivation difficult. Its relative scarcity makes it very expensive. Because its flavor is quite pronounced, however, it can be successfully mixed with regular rice. Even in small quantities it lends elegance to any meal. The most economical way to buy wild rice is in bulk.

Since wild rice is never polished or refined, it is rich in nutrients. At 14 percent protein, it is higher in protein than many grains. The protein is of a high quality, with good percentages of lysine and methionine, amino acids that are usually deficient in grains. Wild rice is rich in the minerals iron and phosphorus and also provides magnesium, calcium, and zinc. It has higher concentrations of the B vitamins thiamine, niacin, and riboflavin than most common grains and is high in fiber while very low in fat.

Wild rice is often mixed with another grain, usually rice. Conveniently enough, the cooking times of brown and wild rice are similar, so they can be cooked together. A fifty-fifty mix of brown and wild rice is a good balance, but you can combine them in whatever proportion you like. If you enjoy the bold flavor and are feeling extravagant, there is no reason that wild rice can't be used on its own.

Basic Cooked Wild Rice: Use 2 1/2 parts water to 1 part grain. Bring to a boil, stir in the grain, return to a boil, then lower the heat and simmer, covered, for about 40 minutes, until the water is absorbed.

- Wild-rice pilafs lend themselves to many types of embellishment. Apples and nuts are common additions, with pecans a favorite. For variety, try using slivered almonds or chopped hazelnuts. Dried fruits (apricots, currants, chopped prunes) or fresh herbs are also nice additions.

- Wild-rice pilafs incorporating bright-colored steamed vegetables such as broccoli or carrots are tasty and visually appealing. Season with a good nut oil (such as walnut or hazelnut oil) or extra-virgin olive oil and chopped fresh herbs. The same ingredients make a delightful cold salad, with the addition of a mild vinegar.

- Try adding a small amount of cooked wild rice to pureed soups. It's especially delicious in pumpkin and butternut squash soups.

- Cooked wild rice combined with more or less equal parts cooked quinoa (page 17) is so tasty that all you need to add is a little soy margarine and salt and pepper. Use as a side dish.

WILD-RICE PILAF WITH SPINACH AND ALMONDS

Yield: 6 to 8 servings as a side dish

2/3 cup wild rice
2/3 cup long-grain brown rice
3 1/2 cups water
3 tablespoons soy margarine
1 medium onion, finely chopped
1 small stalk celery, finely chopped
1 clove garlic, minced
2 cups sliced mushrooms
3/4 pound spinach, washed, steamed, and finely chopped, or one 10-ounce package frozen spinach, thawed
Juice of 1 lemon
2 tablespoons finely chopped fresh parsley
1/4 teaspoon each thyme and cumin
Salt and freshly ground pepper to taste
1/2 cup slivered almonds

Rinse the wild and brown rice and combine them with the water in a heavy saucepan. Bring to a boil and simmer, covered, until the water is absorbed, about 35 to 40 minutes. Remove from the heat.

Heat 2 tablespoons of the margarine in a large, heavy skillet until it foams. Add the onion and sauté over moderately low heat until it is translucent. Add the celery and garlic and continue to sauté until the onion is lightly browned. Add the mushrooms and sauté until they have softened, about 4 minutes. Stir in the cooked wild and brown rice mixture along with the spinach, lemon juice, parsley, thyme, and cumin. Cook, stirring, for 5 minutes. Add the remaining tablespoon of margarine and the slivered almonds and cook for another 10 minutes over very low heat, stirring frequently. Season to taste with salt and pepper and serve at once.

Chapter 2

BEANS AND PEAS

Beans and peas are the fruits of leguminous plants, encased in pods that grow on long, running stems. They come in an array of colors, sizes and shapes, from tiny, round red lentils to large, flat, pale lima beans. Legumes have been cultivated for thousands of years, serving as an important source of protein and sustenance. However, most of the beans and peas that are commonplace today were unknown to the New World until after the Christian era.

From the very beginning of their appearance in Western societies, legumes have been stuck with an image problem. The fact that they are extremely economical has given them a long-standing reputation as a "poor man's food." And they were widely believed to be fattening, which couldn't be further from the truth—an average serving of beans contains only a moderate amount of calories and a negligible amount of fat, yet beans are very filling and satisfying.

Happily, the increased popularity of ethnic and regional cuisines, as well as the acknowledgment of the importance of fiber in the diet, have helped to convince the general public of legumes' value. To name but a few classic bean dishes, think of spicy Indian dals, made of lentils or peas, Mexican frijoles refritos, the satisfying refried beans, made from pinto beans, which accompany tortillas and enchiladas; falafel and hummus from the Middle East, both made with chick-peas; and American classics such as New Orleans red beans and rice, southern Hopping John, with black-eyed peas and rice, and the traditional New England baked beans, using navy beans. The list could go on and on, encompassing delicious classics from every corner of the globe. And this is all in addition to the versatile soybean, which has been acknowledged supreme among all the legumes (and is discussed, along with its many derivatives, in the next chapter).

NUTRITIONAL BENEFITS OF BEANS AND PEAS

Legumes provide a great deal of nutritional mileage relative to their cost. A cup of cooked legumes (which is slightly more than an average serving) contains between 200 and 250 calories, with fat content ranging from a mere trace to just over 2 grams. (Oil-rich soybeans, by contrast, contain more fat than other legumes, but are still far from being a high-fat food.) What's more, the fat in beans and peas is polyunsaturated, and is thought to have a cholesterol-lowering effect.

Beans and peas are excellent sources of complex carbohydrates, that is, starches, complex sugars, and most important, dietary fiber. An average serving of beans or peas contains from 6 to 8 grams of fiber, closely rivaling the fiber content of cereal bran and making them one of the richest sources available. (The importance of fiber in the diet is discussed in the glossary, page 185.) This high-fiber content along with the fact that they are digested slowly, contributes to the feeling of fullness most people experience after eating bean dishes. Since hunger doesn't return rapidly, beans are excellent choices for inclusion in weight-loss or weight-maintenance diets.

Dry beans and peas (including soybeans and their derivatives) are a superb source of protein, with amounts ranging from 14 to 20 grams per cooked cup. The quality of the protein is very good, containing a wide range of the essential amino acids. With the exception of soybeans, the protein in legumes is not complete, that is, some of the amino acids are not present in the correct proportions to make the protein immediately usable by the body. This is easily remedied by eating legumes along with grains, nuts, seeds, or dairy products, whose amino acid structure balances theirs in order to create complete protein. For example, while legumes are high in lysine and low in methionine, grains are just the opposite. Many classic dishes are perfect examples of complementarity—Cuban black beans and rice, tacos (pinto beans and cheese on corn tortillas), and hummus (pureed chick-peas and sesame tahini, usually served with a wheat pita), to name just a few.

Beans and peas contain vitamin A and are a good source of the B-complex vitamins, particularly B_6, folacin, thiamine, and niacin. (These vitamins are water soluble, and some are inevitably lost to the cooking water as is a small amount of the protein. So save the flavorful, nutritious cooking water to use as a soup stock or as a base for sauces.) Minerals, too, are in excellent supply. Iron is a standout, and generous amounts of calcium, phosphorus, and potassium are provided.

BULK BUYING AND STORAGE

In addition to natural-food stores or food co-ops, explore Indian and Spanish groceries to find interesting varieties of dry beans. Supermarkets, too, usually provide a good selection. Natural-food stores also offer organically grown varieties. Buy dry legumes where you feel there is a good turnover. Unlike other foods, they don't spoil under long storage, and since they are so low in fat, they aren't as susceptible to rancidity as are nuts or certain grains. But once they start to get old, more than a year or so, they take longer to cook and will cook to a grainy texture, which can be unpleasant. When buying legumes, look for uniform size (ensuring even cooking time), rich color, and a plump, smooth look. Wrinkled, faded-looking beans signal that they've seen better days.

Try storing beans in Mason jars on visible shelves in your kitchen. Not only will they look attractive, but you'll be reminded to use them more often than if they were tucked away in your pantry. Dry beans and peas keep for up to a year, but like any food, the sooner they are used, the better.

CANNED BEANS VERSUS DRY BEANS

Although canned beans are not generally thought to be a nutritionally inferior product, cooking dry beans is more economical and you can control the amount of salt. If you do buy canned beans, look for those that have no additional additives aside from salt. Rinse the canned beans well in a colander to remove the salty sauce. Dry beans are not a convenience product, so if your schedule does not allow you the time to cook them from scratch, it makes sense to opt for good-quality canned beans. In the summer, it is nice to have a few cans on hand, particularly of the long-cooking varieties, such as chick-peas and kidney beans.

If you're interested in organically grown cooked beans, Eden Foods offers them in large jars, seasoned with natural soy sauce. Ask your natural foods retailer about them.

DIGESTIVE PROBLEMS CAUSED BY BEANS AND POSSIBLE SOLUTIONS

Some people avoid beans because of the digestive problems they can cause, specifically, intestinal gas. This problem is caused by oligosaccharides, complex sugars that arrive intact in the large intestine and are not easily broken down by its enzymes. The reaction to these sugars varies from individual to individual. Many are not troubled by them in the least, whereas others are decidedly uncomfortable after eating beans. Several studies have shown that if legumes are consumed regularly rather than only on occasion, digestive problems are minimized considerably. This is believed to be due to the gradual adjustment of the intestine's enzymes to the sugars.

If you are troubled by these digestive problems but would like to add more beans into your diet, try starting with green and yellow split peas, black-eyed peas, and lentils. These are among the most easily digestible legumes. Gradually add small servings of chick-peas, adzuki beans, and navy beans. Bear in mind that the most difficult beans to digest are kidney beans, soybeans, and fava beans.

Following are two techniques that sometimes help minimize the gas-producing property of beans:

- *Discard the original soaking water:* Ideally, the water used for soaking the beans should be the water that they are cooked in, since many nutrients leach into it during soaking. However, discarding the soaking water and cooking beans in fresh water helps eliminate some of the oligosaccharides. Since many people who actually like beans very much will avoid them for their gas-producing property, it seems more reasonable to discard the soaking water than to avoid beans altogether.

- *The vinegar method:* Fred Rohe, author of *The Complete Book of Natural Foods* (Shambala Publications, 1983), swears by the vinegar method of reducing the gas-causing properties of beans. For each cup of dry beans used, remove 1/4 cup cooking water from the pot about 30 minutes before the beans are done and replace it with 1/4 cup apple cider vinegar.

PREPARING DRY BEANS FOR SOAKING

When a recipe calls for "sorting" or "picking over" dry beans or peas, this simply means that they should be examined carefully for stones and grit and that withered-looking beans should be discarded. This is easily done in a colander. Once the beans are sorted, give them a good rinsing under briskly running water. They are now ready to presoak.

PRESOAKING AND COOKING BEANS

While cooking beans is admittedly a time-consuming process, it really requires little effort. Presoaking beans, either overnight or by the quick-soak method, greatly reduces the cooking time, contributes to a better texture, and helps to reduce the gas-causing indigestible sugars. Certain legumes require no presoaking at all. These are mung beans, yellow and green split peas, and lentils.

As they cook, beans need very little attention, so the trick is to organize yourself to begin well ahead of time, not just when you need them, because then you will find yourself anxiously hovering over the pot. Here are two methods:

- *THE LONG-SOAK METHOD:* Rinse and sort the beans and place them in a large cooking pot with water in a ratio of 3 to 4 parts water to 1 part beans. Cover and refrigerate (this prevents possible fermentation and spoilage, especially during warm months) until the next day. When ready to cook the beans, add more water if necessary, for the beans will have absorbed most of the presoaking water. Although no exact amount of water is needed for cooking, make sure there is plenty of room for the beans to simmer in the pot. A good rule of thumb is that the water be about double the volume of the beans. Bring to a boil, then lower the heat and bring to a gentle simmer. Cover the pot, but leave it ajar to prevent foaming. Cook the beans until tender, then drain (save the flavorful stock for soups and sauces) and either use the beans at once or cool and refrigerate them for later use.

   If you are concerned about reducing the gas-causing properties of beans, discard the original soaking water and cover with fresh water.

- *THE QUICK-SOAK METHOD*: Rinse and sort the beans. Place them in a cooking pot with water in a ratio of 3 to 4 parts water to 1 part beans. Bring the water to a rolling boil, then remove from the heat and allow to stand, covered, for an hour or so. Then, cook as described above.

MORE COOKING TIPS

- *Additions to the cooking water—what's good, what's not*: Beans are just fine cooked in plain water. Avoid adding salt until the very end, since salt hardens the skins and lengthens the cooking time. Acids, such as tomatoes, tend to do the same. Seasonings such as chopped onion and garlic, or a bay leaf or two, however, may be added to the cooking water at any time; they enhance the flavor and aroma wonderfully. Baking soda, often prescribed to shorten the cooking time or to reduce the gas-causing sugars, destroys nutrients. The sea vegetable kombu has properties that help soften the beans and make them more digestible; add a 4-inch strip to the water when you begin to cook the beans. Peas, lentils and mung beans can be cooked with other ingredients, such as grains or long-cooking vegetables, especially in the case of soups.

- *Cook extra*: Once you are making the effort, you might as well cook more than you need and freeze the rest. Except for lentils, cooked beans freeze well.

- *Cook beans slowly and thoroughly*: Cooking beans at a gentle simmer prevents their skins from bursting and helps them to develop a better flavor and texture. This is one case where overcooking is preferable to undercooking, because well-cooked beans are easier to digest. A good way to test for doneness is to press one between your thumb and forefinger. If it yields to pressure very easily, it's done.

- *Explore pressure-cooking*: Pressure-cooking beans greatly minimizes cooking time. It is best to follow the specific manufacturer's directions as to relative water and pressure needs. Using a pressure cooker can sometimes be problematic because of the tendency of some types of beans to foam (particularly soybeans, lima beans, and black beans) and thus clog the vents of the cooker.

COOKING TIMES AND YIELDS FOR BEANS AND PEAS

Several factors determine the exact cooking time of dry beans, including the temperature at which the beans are simmered, how long the beans were soaked, and the size and age of the beans. Altitude is also a factor; they take longer at higher altitudes. Likewise, the cooking time is extended in hard water (water with a high mineral content). Consult the chart below for average cooking times.

Depending on the variety, the average yield is 2 1/4 to 2 1/2 cups cooked beans for every cup of dry beans used. One notable exception is large dry lima beans, which expand only about 50 percent when cooked.

——————AT-A-GLANCE COOKING CHART FOR BEANS AND PEAS——————

	Presoak	Approximate Cooking Time
Adzuki beans	Yes	45 minutes to 1 hour
Black beans	Yes	1 to 1 1/2 hours
Black-eyed peas	No	1 to 1 1/4 hours
Chick-peas (garbanzos)	Yes	2 1/2 to 3 hours
Cowpeas	Yes	1 to 1 1/2 hours
Fava beans	Yes	1 to 2 hours
Great Northern beans	Yes	1 1/2 to 2 hours
Kidney or red beans	Yes	1 1/2 to 2 hours
Lentils, red or brown	No	30 to 45 minutes
Lima beans, large	Yes	1 to 1 1/2 hours
Lima beans, baby	Yes	45 minutes to 1 1/4 hours
Mung beans	No	45 minutes to 1 hour
Navy or pea beans	Yes	1 to 1 1/2 hours
Peas, split	No	45 minutes to 1 hour
Pinto beans	Yes	1 1/2 to 2 hours

ADZUKI BEANS

Relatively new to the Western food market, adzuki (alternatively spelled *aduki*) beans are very popular in Japan and are said to be among the most digestible of beans. Small, round, and of a pretty, dark red color, adzuki beans are among the fastest cooking of dry beans.

Though adzuki beans have not been analyzed by the USDA, they are known to be rich in high-quality protein and to contain good amounts of phosphorus, iron, potassium, and the B-complex vitamins.

The taste of adzukis is similar to that of kidney and small red beans, though they are somewhat more flavorful. They look appealing mixed with cooked grains or other cooked beans that have been cooked separately. Try combining them with medium-grain rice, millet, or quinoa. Perhaps due more to their Oriental origins than to their particular flavor, they take well to flavorings not usually associated with beans, such as natural soy sauce, ginger, and miso. Adzuki beans are welcome as a substitute in any dish where red or pinto beans are called for—even Mexican chilies. They're also very good tossed into green salads, in marinated bean salads, and in soups and stews. In Japan, adzukis are even used in desserts; if you're adventurous, you might look for such recipes in Japanese cookbooks.

ADZUKI BEANS WITH SQUASH AND BULGUR

Yield: 4 to 6 servings

1 cup bulgur
2 cups boiling water
2 tablespoons safflower oil
1 large onion, quartered and sliced
2 cloves garlic, minced
2 heaping cups cooked diced butternut
   squash
2 to 3 tablespoons miso, to taste,
   dissolved in 1/2 cup warm water
2 tablespoons dry red wine
2 tablespoons honey
1 to 2 teaspoons freshly grated ginger,
   to taste
2 cups cooked adzuki beans (about
   3/4 cup dry)
3 bunches scallions, minced
Freshly ground pepper to taste

Place the bulgur in a heatproof bowl. Cover with the boiling water. Cover and let sit for 30 minutes.

Heat the oil in a large skillet. Add the onion and sauté over moderate heat until it is translucent. Add the garlic and continue to sauté until the onion is lightly browned. Add the squash, miso, wine, honey, and ginger and simmer over reduced heat for 2 minutes. Stir in the cooked adzuki beans and simmer over low heat for 10 minutes. When the bulgur is done, stir it in along with the scallions and simmer over low heat for another 5 to 10 minutes. Serve at once.

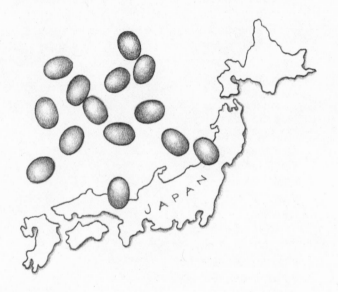

BLACK BEANS

Dark and tasty, black beans are often referred to as *turtle beans*. Especially popular in Cuban, South American, and Mexican cuisines, they also appear in Mediterranean and Oriental repertoires.

Black beans are 22 percent protein and contain average amounts of all the nutrients common to beans, including calcium, phosphorus, iron, potassium, and the B-vitamin complex.

The flavor of black beans lends itself to many complementary enhancements and is strong enough to hold up under the boldest of seasonings. Compatible herbs include thyme, savory, parsley, and oregano; onions, garlic, and shallots, added in quantities to one's heart's content, are always welcome; and lemon juice or cider vinegar and olive oil all are wonderful enhancements.

Black beans are perhaps best known as the basis for the filling, hearty soups they make and for the Cuban-inspired dish known simply as black beans and rice. Black beans make a pleasant change of pace from pinto beans in Mexican or Southwestern specialties such as tostados or tacos. Black beans are also wonderful as a base for salads (see the recipe below); or they may be tossed into green salads either as is or lightly marinated.

- *MARINATED BLACK BEANS*: Combine 2 to 2 1/2 cups cooked black beans in a bowl with 1/4 cup good olive oil and the juice of 1 lemon or 3 tablespoons (more or less to taste). Stir well and refrigerate, covered, for several hours. Toss some of these marinated beans into green salads, hot cooked grains, or try serving them atop cottage cheese, garnished with some chopped ripe tomato.

- *SIMPLE SEASONED BLACK BEANS*: Sauté onions and garlic, as much as you'd like, in a small amount of good, fragrant olive oil in a heavy skillet. Add black beans along with some of their cooking liquid. Mash some of the beans with the back of a wooden spoon, enough to thicken the liquid. Add salt, pepper, a dash of cumin, and lemon juice or cider vinegar to taste. Add some parsley or other herbs if desired. Simmer over very low heat for 10 to 15 minutes. This is an excellent side dish. To make it a protein-balanced main dish, spoon some over hot cooked grains or serve atop a crisp tortilla with shredded lettuce, chopped tomato, and shredded cheese.

BLACK BEAN SALAD WITH FETA CHEESE

Yield: 4 to 6 servings

3 cups cooked black beans (about 1 1/4 cups dry)
1/4 cup olive oil
Juice of 1 lemon
1/4 cup chopped fresh parsley
1 teaspoon dried oregano
1 small green bell pepper, cut into julienne strips
2 bunches scallions, minced
1/4 pound feta cheese, crumbled
2 medium tomatoes, diced
Freshly ground pepper to taste

In a serving bowl, combine the black beans with all but the last three ingredients. Mix thoroughly and allow to marinate for 1 to 2 hours. Just before serving, add the feta cheese, tomatoes, and pepper. Toss well and serve at once.

BLACK-EYED PEAS

Black-eyed peas came to the shores of colonial Virginia as part of the slave trade in the eighteenth century. They are occasionally referred to as cowpeas or field peas, though these are actually different, but related varieties. The use of black-eyed peas is prominent in Africa and in the American South, and they are also popular in India and China. Botanically, they are more closely related to beans than to peas. Like peas, though, they need not be presoaked and cook fairly quickly compared with other dry beans. It's especially advisable in the case of black-eyed peas to know that your source has a good turnover, because old ones cook to an unpleasant, dry, and grainy texture.

Black-eyed peas are 23 percent protein. They contain moderate amounts of calcium, phosphorus, and iron, but are quite high in potassium. Of the B vitamins they provide, the standouts are thiamine, folacin, and B_6. Black-eyed peas also contain a small amount of vitamin C.

Black-eyed peas are very nice added to salads of strong greens (try them in a spinach salad) or tomato salads with lots of fresh herbs, such as dill or basil. Try marinating the black-eyed peas first in a light vinaigrette for a nice touch. They also combine nicely with brown rice or bulgur as the basis for a protein-balanced main dish. The flavor of black-eyed peas is enhanced by tomatoes, garlic and onion, and cider vinegar. They are highly compatible with steamed greens such as Swiss chard, collards, or kale, seasoned simply with butter or margarine and lots of garlic and black pepper. The somewhat "green" flavor of black-eyed peas is not particularly suitable for cheesy dishes.

HOPPING JOHN (BLACK-EYED PEAS WITH RICE)

Yield: 4 to 6 servings

This is a famous dish from the American South that, in its original form, always includes a piece of salt pork. In this Creole-influenced adaptation, the tomatoes and herbs more than make up for the absence of meat.

2 tablespoons safflower oil
1 cup chopped onion
2 cloves garlic, minced
2 cups ripe, juicy tomatoes, chopped
1/4 cup water or cooking liquid from the black-eyed peas
1 tablespoon minced fresh basil or 1 teaspoon dried basil
1 teaspoon dried thyme
2 cups cooked black-eyed peas (about 3/4 cup dry)
3 cups cooked brown rice
Salt and freshly ground black pepper

Heat the oil in a large skillet. Add the onion and sauté over low heat until it is translucent. Add the garlic and continue to sauté until the onion is golden. Stir in the tomatoes along with the water or cooking liquid and herbs and cook until the tomatoes have softened, about 5 minutes. Add the peas and rice and season to taste with salt and lots of freshly ground pepper. Stir together well and simmer over very low heat for 15 minutes. Add a bit more water or cooking liquid if the mixture needs more moisture. Serve at once.

CHICK-PEAS
(GARBANZOS, CECI)

Well-loved in Middle Eastern, Mediterranean, North African, and Indian cuisines, chick-peas are also commonly known by their Spanish name, *garbanzo beans*, and less frequently by their Italian name, *ceci*. Those who profess not to care for beans will often make an exception for delicious chick-peas. Their chief disadvantage is their long cooking time (up to 3 hours), second only to soybeans. However, their versatility and unique flavor makes the extra time involved worthwhile. Barring that, this is definitely a case where buying them canned is preferable to not using them at all. Buy a brand without additives and rinse away the salty liquid.

Chick-peas are 20.5 percent protein. At 4.8 percent fat, they are higher in fat than all other legumes except soybeans, but are far from being a high-fat food. Chick-peas are rich in the minerals calcium, phosphorus, iron, potassium, and zinc and contain average amounts of the B-vitamin complex relative to other legumes.

You are likely to find many ideas for utilizing chick-peas in Middle Eastern cookbooks, including falafel, deep-fried balls of spiced chick-peas, and also *hummus*, a spread made of a puree of chick-peas, tahini (sesame paste), lemon juice, and spices. In Indian cuisine, chick-peas are commonly simmered in aromatic cumin-and-coriander sauces or combined with fresh herbs. Check Indian cookbooks for more ideas.

- Toss a handful of chick-peas into fresh green salads, pasta salads, or grain salads. Added to the classic Middle Eastern grain salad tabouli, they not only taste great, but also create complete protein when combined with the bulgur.

- Here's another refreshing salad idea that serves 4 to 6: Combine 2 cups cooked chick-peas with 1 cup steamed green beans (cut into 1-inch lengths), 1 cup chopped cucumbers, and fresh basil to taste. Dress in olive oil, lemon juice, and yogurt, and grind in lots of black pepper.

- For a simple main or side dish, chick-peas are good combined with fluffy grains such as long-grain rice, couscous, bulgur, or quinoa.

- Well-cooked, pureed chick-peas make a flavorful thickener for certain soup stocks. When making soups of strong-flavored vegetables such as cabbage or broccoli, add to the soup 1 to 2 cups pureed chick-peas, enough to achieve a slightly thick consistency, when the vegetables are nearly tender.

- Whole cooked chick-peas are very good in tomato-based soups and vegetable soups.

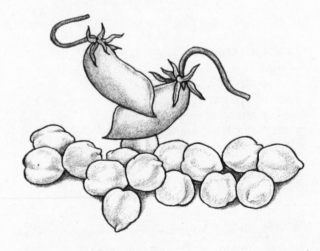

- Sauté a large onion and 3 or 4 cloves garlic in good olive oil. Add about a pound of chopped fresh or imported canned tomatoes, 3 cups cooked chick-peas, cumin to taste, and lots of freshly ground black pepper. Add a bit of chopped fresh cilantro or parsley. Simmer until saucy and aromatic and serve over hot cooked rice. This makes 4 to 6 servings.

CHICK-PEA SANDWICH SPREAD

Yield: About 2 cups

This easy preparation is equally good as an hors d'oeuvre spread on whole-grain crackers as it is on a hearty bread, such as dark rye, for lunch.

2 cups well-cooked chick-peas (about 3/4 cup dry)
1/4 cup minced green bell pepper
2 tablespoons minced fresh parsley
1 tablespoon minced scallion or chives
Juice of 1/2 lemon
2 tablespoons sesame paste (tahini)
1/2 teaspoon dried dill
1/2 teaspoon cumin
Salt and freshly ground pepper to taste

Mash the chick-peas well and combine with the remaining ingredients in a mixing bowl. Mix thoroughly and pat into an attractive serving container. Serve at once or cover and refrigerate until needed.

COWPEAS

Black-eyed peas are often referred to as cowpeas, but in the southern United States, the legume referred to as a cowpea is a slightly different, but related variety. The cowpea also has an "eye," but is smaller, brown, and perhaps even a bit tastier. The cowpea's cooking time is similar to that of the black-eyed pea (see chart, page 39); it is nutritionally similar, and its comparable flavor makes its uses the same as those recommended for black-eyed peas (see page 41).

FAVA BEANS

Cultivated in Europe for many centuries, fava beans were the only beans known there before the discovery of the New World. Alternatively called broad, Windsor, or horse beans, fava beans are now grown in the United States but are still used most extensively in the Mediterranean region of Europe as well as in South America. A large bean, resembling the lima bean in appearance and taste, dried fava beans have not caught on to any great extent with the American public.

Dry fava beans are high in protein at 28 percent. They are rich in the minerals calcium, phosphorus, and iron and provide good amounts of the B vitamins, particularly niacin.

Fresh fava beans have a strong flavor, but as with limas, cooked dry fava beans tend to be rather bland and benefit from strong seasoning and tomato-based sauces. Fresh herbs or lots of onion and garlic also heighten their flavor. Use fava beans in soups (such as minestrone) and stews, or puree them for use as a soup base, pâté, or sandwich spread.

FAVA BEANS AND GREEN BEANS PARMESAN

Yield: 6 servings

3 tablespoons olive oil
1 small onion, minced
3 cloves garlic, minced
1 pound ripe, juicy tomatoes, chopped
2 cups cooked fava beans (about 3/4 cup dry)
1 pound green beans, trimmed and cut in half
1/4 cup fresh basil
1 teaspoon paprika
1 tablespoon lemon juice
Salt and freshly ground pepper
Freshly grated Parmesan cheese

Heat the oil in a large, heavy skillet. Add the onion and garlic and sauté over moderate heat for 2 minutes. Add the tomatoes and sauté for 3 to 4 minutes. Add the remaining ingredients and simmer, covered, over very low heat for 15 minutes. Serve at once on its own or over hot cooked rice, passing around some fresh Parmesan cheese to top each serving.

GREAT NORTHERN BEANS

These are the familiar large white beans (and are in fact, often referred to in recipes as *large white beans*, as well as by their Italian name, *cannellini*).Their mild flavor and creamy texture make them very versatile.

Great Northern beans are about 22 percent protein. They are very high in potassium and contain average amounts of calcium, phosphorus, iron, zinc, and the B-vitamin complex compared with other legumes.

The flavor of Great Northern beans is compatible with that of tomatoes, garlic, molasses, honey, mild vinegars, and mustard. This bean makes an excellent kitchen staple, since it can be used in many general ways.

- Great Northern beans are classic soup beans. They are used in Italian pasta and bean soups as well as in minestrone. These soups, accompanied by crusty bread and a green salad, are meals in themselves. Try them in potato soups or potato-cheese soups as well.

- Combine them with whole-grain pasta, a cream or cheese sauce, and mushrooms for a hearty main dish.

- Toss some into green salads or pasta salads, either plain or premarinated.

- Use Great Northern beans in stews or baked bean recipes. Their flavor, as mentioned above, is especially compatible with tomato-based sauces, especially those with a sweet and sour flavor or with barbecue flavorings.

- Because they have a smooth, creamy texture when cooked, Great Northern beans puree beautifully. This puree may be added in small amounts to baked goods and is excellent for thickening soup, especially milk-based soups such as chowders. It may also be used to make an easy and eleqant pâté, as in the following recipe:

GREAT NORTHERN PÂTÉ

Yield: 2 cups

Serve this as an appetizer with whole-grain crackers, rye bread, or crisp cut vegetables.

1 tablespoon safflower oil
1 medium onion, chopped
1 clove garlic, minced
1 medium stalk celery, chopped
2 tablespoons miso, or to taste
Juice of ¹/₂ lemon
1 sprig parsley
1 ¹/₂ cups well-cooked Great Northern beans (about ²/₃ cup dry)
2 tablespoons tahini, sesame butter, or sunflower butter
2 tablespoons water
Freshly ground black pepper to taste
Paprika for garnish

Heat the oil in a small skillet. Add the onion, garlic, and celery and sauté over moderate heat until all are tender and golden. Transfer to the container of a food processor or blender along with all the remaining ingredients except the paprika. Process until creamy and smooth. Pour into a shallow serving container and sprinkle with paprika. This may be made ahead of time and refrigerated, but bring to room temperature before serving.

——KIDNEY OR RED BEANS——

Deep red kidney beans and a slightly smaller, related variety, commonly referred to as *small red beans*, are among the most popular in the United States. These beans are very high in fiber, which works to their advantage nutritionally but also makes them mealier in texture and harder to digest than most other beans. Be sure to cook them well.

Kidney and red beans are 22.5 percent protein. Rich in phosphorus and iron, they contain only average amounts of calcium and potassium in comparison with other beans. They contain good amounts of the B-complex vitamins, especially thiamine, and their vitamin A content is higher than that of most other legumes.

The flavor of kidney and red beans is mild, but not bland, and they lend themselves well to strong seasoning. Their success in spicy dishes is proven by the popularity of red bean chili. Kidney or red beans star in New Orleans classic red beans and rice and are commonly used in marinated bean salads. Use them in well-seasoned vegetable soups such as minestrone, in winter stews, or combine them with beaten eggs and spices to make fried "burgers" to eat in sandwiches.

SUMMER PASTA SALAD WITH RED BEANS

Yield: 6 or more servings

1/2 pound corkscrew- or seashell-shaped pasta
2 cups cooked kidney or small red beans (about 3/4 cup dry)
1 cup diced zucchini
1 small green bell pepper, finely chopped
1 pound ripe, juicy tomatoes
1/3 cup green olives
1/4 cup chopped fresh basil
1/4 cup grated Parmesan cheese
3 tablespoons olive oil
2 to 3 tablespoons wine vinegar
1/2 cup plain yogurt
1/2 teaspoon chili powder, or to taste
Salt and freshly ground pepper to taste

Cook the pasta *al dente* and rinse with cool water. Drain the pasta well and transfer it to a serving bowl. Add the remaining ingredients and mix thoroughly. Serve at room temperature or chill.

————— LENTILS —————

Long considered a "poor man's food," lentils are actually a rich source of protein and nutrients and are easily digested. Best known as a main component of thick, filling soups, lentils are an important staple in Indian cuisine. Small and rather flat, lentils cook quickly and are highly flavored and aromatic. Two types of lentils are commonly available: the more familiar brown lentils, sometimes referred to as green lentils, which are generally found in supermarkets as well as natural-food stores, and the tiny red lentils, which are occasionally found in natural-food stores and are staples in Indian specialty shops.

Lentils are nearly 25 percent protein and are rich in minerals, particularly zinc, iron, phosphorus, and potassium. They contain an average amount of the B-vitamin complex relative to other legumes and a small amount of vitamin A.

Neither brown nor red lentils require pre-soaking. Brown lentils take 40 to 45 minutes to cook, and the red take about 30 minutes. Their flavor and texture, once cooked, are very similar, the difference being that the red lentils are just slightly milder and cook to a pale, golden-brown color, whereas the brown retain their rather muddy hue. There are some instances where you want to cook lentils down to a mushy texture, while for other recipes you want them to retain their shape. Watch them closely during the final stages of cooking, since they go from just done to mushy very quickly. Here are some serving ideas:

- Lentils have a special affinity with curry spices and fresh ginger. Make a curried stew combining firm-cooked lentils with cooked potatoes, chopped fresh spinach, diced tomatoes, and finely-chopped cauliflower. Cook slowly with the spices until the flavors blend and the cauliflower is tender.

- Mash a cupful of cooked lentils and combine them with 1/4 cup each finely ground walnuts and bread crumbs. Mix in 2 beaten eggs and season to taste with cumin, garlic powder, natural soy sauce, and freshly ground black pepper. Shape into palm-size croquettes and fry on each side in safflower oil until golden brown. This makes 10 to 12 croquettes.

- Marinate lentils and use them as a base for marinated salads. One delicious idea: Combine them with crumbled feta cheese, green peppers, scallions, tomatoes, olive oil, and lemon juice.

- Dal is a thick, saucelike dish that is used as a side dish with Indian meals. The lentils are cooked to a mushy texture and are laced with chilies, onions, garlic, ginger, and other flavorings. Any Indian cookbook will have at least one version of it.

- Combine lentils, cooked until done but still firm, with an approximately equal volume of fine egg noodles. Flavor with lots of fried onion, garlic, and celery and season simply with natural soy sauce.

LENTIL, POTATO, AND CAULIFLOWER SOUP

Yield: 8 servings

2 tablespoons soy margarine
1 large onion, chopped
1 cup dry brown or red lentils, rinsed
3 to 4 cloves garlic, minced
1 large stalk celery, finely chopped
2 bay leaves
7 cups water
One 14-ounce can imported plum
   tomatoes, with liquid, chopped
2 medium potatoes, scrubbed and diced
2 cups finely chopped cauliflower pieces
2 teaspoons good curry powder, or to
   taste
1/2 teaspoon each ground coriander and
   dry mustard
1 cup chopped spinach leaves
2 tablespoons minced cilantro (optional)
Juice of 1/2 lemon
Salt and freshly ground black pepper to
   taste

Melt the margarine in a large soup pot or Dutch oven. Sauté the onion over moderate heat until golden. Add the lentils, garlic, celery, bay leaves, and water. Bring to a boil, then reduce the heat, cover, and simmer for 10 minutes. Add the tomatoes and potatoes and simmer until the potato is about half done, about 10 to 15 minutes. Add the cauliflower and spices and simmer until the lentils and vegetables are tender, about 30 to 35 minutes. Add the spinach and cilantro and simmer over low heat for another 10 minutes. Stir in the lemon juice and season to taste with salt and pepper. Let the soup stand, if possible, for an hour of more before serving, to allow the flavors to blend. Heat through as needed.

LIMA BEANS

Lima beans, sometimes called *butter beans* or *fordhooks*, come in large and small, or "baby," sizes. The larger bean has a slightly stronger flavor and takes a bit more time to cook. Fresh, or green, lima beans in the pod are rarely available, but are commonly available frozen and generally thought to be more flavorful than the dry beans, which are rather bland. Believed to have originated in South America, fresh lima beans are especially well loved in the southern states of North America. Most of those grown for domestic use, however, come from California.

Dry lima beans are 20 percent protein. They are quite high in potassium and also provide calcium, phosphorus, and iron. Limas provide a range of the B vitamins and are particularly rich in vitamin B_6. They are one of the few legumes that provide an appreciable amount of vitamin C.

You might think of fresh or frozen green lima beans primarily as a vegetable, to be combined with other fresh vegetables, such as with corn in succotash or with tomatoes and fresh herbs as a simple side dish. Cooked dry limas can also be used as are other dry beans—in hearty soups or stews, or pureed and spiced to be used as a pâté or sandwich spread. However, there is nothing rigid about these guidelines. Green lima beans and dry lima beans may usually be used interchangeably in recipes, except for pureeing—green limas are a little too crunchy for that. The bland flavor of cooked dry limas takes well to strong seasonings. Highly flavored soups, tomato-based stews, and recipes utilizing lots of fresh herbs are good venues for them. Dry lima beans expand much less than other beans when cooked (only about 50 percent, or 1 1/2 cups cooked for every cup dry).

LIMA BEAN AND CORN RELISH

Yield: 6 to 8 servings

2 cups cooked dry baby lima beans
   (about 1 1/3 cups dry) or frozen green
   baby lima beans, thawed
2 cups cooked corn kernels, preferably
   fresh, scraped from 2 medium ears
1 medium red or green bell pepper,
   minced
2 tablespoons fresh chopped dill
2 tablespoons fresh chopped parsley
2 tablespoons minced onion
1/4 cup cider vinegar
3 tablespoons safflower oil
1 teaspoon dry mustard
1 teaspoon turmeric
1/2 teaspoon salt

Combine the first six ingredients in a mixing bowl and mix together thoroughly. Combine the remaining ingredients in a small mixing bowl and stir well. Pour over the lima and vegetable mixture and toss together. Refrigerate for several hours, stirring occasionally. Serve as a small, relish-type side dish.

MUNG BEANS

Very popular in Asian and Indian cuisines, these are the small legumes from which come the familiar bean sprouts commonly used in Oriental stir-fries. Mung beans can be sprouted at home very successfully, so they are a good choice for the beginning sprouter (see appendix A). Considering their relatively quick cooking time (they do not require presoaking) and pleasant flavor (akin to, but milder than, dry green peas), it is surprising that their use has not become more widespread. Look for these small, round beans in natural-food stores and Indian and Oriental specialty shops. Mung beans are most commonly found in an olive-green color, but more exotic varieties come in golden or black.

Mung beans have not been analyzed by the USDA, but they are known to be quite nutritious, with high-quality protein and good amounts of potassium, calcium, phosphorus, iron, zinc, and the B-vitamin range. They are among the most highly digestible of legumes.

- Use mung beans as a substitute for dry green peas or lentils in soups and other recipes.

- Toss a small amount of cooked mung beans into Oriental-style stir-fried vegetable or noodle dishes for a protein boost.

- Mung beans have a special affinity with the following: curry spices, ginger, garlic, tomatoes, green chilies, and spinach. Use any or all of the following to make thick soups or stews for topping grains.

- Try a recipe for mung dal, an Indian classic that is a cross between a soup and a sauce. Here's a simple version:

MUNG DAL

Yield: 4 to 6 servings

This classic recipe is adapt from Julie Sanhi's *Classic Indian Vegetarian and Grain Cooking;* © *1985.*

1 cup mung beans, rinsed and sorted
3 1/2 cups water
2 tablespoons safflower or peanut oil
1 teaspoon cumin seeds
1 teaspoon freshly grated ginger

1 or 2 green chilies, mild or hot, seeded and minced
Juice of 1/2 lemon
3 to 4 tablespoons minced cilantro
Salt to taste

Cook the mung beans in the water until they are soft, about 1 hour.

Heat the oil in a small skillet. Add the remaining ingredients and cook over moderate heat, stirring, until fragrant, about 5 to 7 minutes. Add to the mung beans and cook for 10 minutes. Serve hot as a side dish with vegetable curries or grain dishes.

NAVY BEANS

Navy beans, also known as *small white beans*, *pea beans*, or *Yankee beans*, are the beans traditionally used in New England baked-bean recipes and in Yankee bean soup. Quite similar to Great Northern beans in overall flavor and texture, navy beans cook a bit faster and may be used for exactly the same purposes as their larger counterparts. Their nutritional profile, too, is comparable. See the entry for Great Northern beans (page 43) for specifics and serving suggestions.

SAUERKRAUT BAKED BEANS

Yield: 4 to 6 servings

2 tablespoons safflower oil
1 large onion, chopped
3 cups cooked navy beans (about 1 1/4 to 1 1/3 cups dry)
One 16-ounce can sauerkraut, well drained
1/4 cup firmly packed brown sugar
2 to 3 tablespoons molasses, to taste
1 cup thick tomato sauce

1 teaspoon dry mustard
1 teaspoon paprika
¹/₂ teaspoon salt
1 cup grated sharp Cheddar cheese
¹/₄ cup toasted wheat germ

Preheat the oven to 350°F.

Heat the oil in a small skillet. Add the onion and sauté over moderate heat until it is lightly browned. In a mixing bowl, combine the cooked beans with the onion and all the remaining ingredients except for the cheese and the wheat germ. Pour into an oiled 1¹/₂-quart casserole and bake, covered, for 25 minutes. Sprinkle with the cheese and wheat germ, then bake, uncovered, for another 20 to 25 minutes. Allow to stand for 5 minutes, then serve.

————— PEAS —————

Yellow and green dry split peas are excellent sources of protein, and both are commonly available. Though yellow peas have a milder flavor, they may be used interchangeably in recipes.

Dry peas are 24 percent protein. They provide average amounts of minerals compared to other legumes, including calcium, phosphorus, and iron, and are rich in the B vitamins thiamine, riboflavin, and niacin. They also contain a small amount of vitamin A. Split peas are highly digestible.

Both yellow and green peas have a special affinity with potatoes and tomatoes; pea soups are very good with the addition of brown rice, which can be cooked right along with the peas. Good flavor enhancers are onions and garlic, green chilies, lemon juice, curry spices, and fresh or dried dill.

Since dried split peas invariably cook to a mushy texture, they are most suited for making soups of the stick-to-the-ribs variety. (For an unusual version of pea soup, see page 129, under the entry for the sea vegetable alaria.) In India, peas, like mung beans and lentils, are commonly used to make dal, a spiced saucelike side dish, and are also used in making croquettes.

SPICED SPLIT PEA CROQUETTES

Yield: 20 to 22 croquettes

Though quite tasty, these Indian-inspired croquettes have the rather mealy texture inherent

in peas, and so are enhanced by topping them with plain yogurt or with a dressing, such as tofu tartar sauce (see page 66).

1 cup dry yellow or green split peas
3 cups water
1 small onion, grated
1 clove garlic, crushed
2 eggs, beaten
2 tablespoons lemon juice
2 tablespoons cornmeal
1 to 2 teaspoons good curry powder, to taste
1 teaspoon salt
¹/₂ teaspoon ground coriander
¹/₄ teaspoon ground cardamon
Pinch each of ground nutmeg and cinnamon
Oil for frying

Rinse and sort the peas. Combine them in a large, heavy saucepan with the water. Bring to a boil, then lower the heat and simmer, covered (leave the cover slightly ajar), for 1 hour, or until the peas are mushy and the water is absorbed. Transfer to a large mixing bowl and combine with all the remaining ingredients. Stir to mix thoroughly.

Heat just enough oil to coat the bottom of a wide skillet. When hot, drop the pea mixture by heaping tablespoonsful onto the skillet and fry on both sides until touched with golden brown. Drain on paper towels. Serve warm with yogurt or sauce.

————— PINK AND PINTO BEANS —————

Pink beans and pinto beans are related varieties of beans that are slightly smaller and lighter in color than the kidney or red variety. When cooked, pink and pinto beans have a very similar flavor and texture and may be used interchangeably.

Dry pink and pinto beans are about 23 percent protein. They provide good amounts of the minerals calcium, iron, phosphorus, and potassium. They also provide a good range of the B vitamins and are particularly high in vitamin B₆.

Pintos are the traditional beans of the southwestern United States and of Mexico. When dry, the pinto has a spotted surface, which disappears and turns a dull pink when cooked. Both pink beans and pintos cook to a pleasant texture, making them an excellent substitute for the tougher, mealier kidney or red beans. See the entry for kidney or red beans (page 44) for further suggestions for use. They lend themselves well to casseroles, soups, and stews, especially spicy chilies. Their flavor is highly compatible with green chilies (hot varieties such as jalapeño or serrano, or milder types; such as poblano or Anaheim, are all appropriate), cilantro, onions, garlic, green bell peppers, and tomatoes.

- Pink and pinto beans are excellent in salads, whether as the main component or tossed in with greens. They are also pleasing in combination with pasta, rice, or avocado in composed salads and take to creamy as well as oil-and-vinegar dressings.

- Lightly mash well-cooked pinto beans in a skillet over low heat and add enough water to form a consistency resembling a very thick sauce. Season to taste with salt, chili powder, garlic powder, and cumin. Spread atop a crisp tortilla and sprinkle with finely diced tomato and grated Monterey Jack cheese. Bake in a hot oven just until the cheese melts.

- Combine pink or pinto beans with fresh corn kernels for a simple main dish, enhanced with any of the flavorings suggested in the introductory paragraph.

- Look for recipes using pinto beans in Mexican and American regional cookbooks. Pink beans may be used as a substitute.

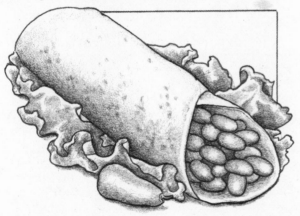

FRIJOLES REFRITOS
(Refried Pinto Beans)

Yield: 6 to 8 servings

There are few preparations more common to the cuisine of the Southwest than refried pinto beans. They show up at nearly every meal. Traditionally, they are made with lard, but today many home and restaurant cooks are lightening the dish by using oil. This simple preparation may be served on the side of eggs or wrapped in corn or flour tortillas and embellished with a spicy salsa, then baked with some additional melted cheese if desired.

1 2/3 cups dry pinto beans
1 large onion, chopped
3 tablespoons safflower oil
1 teaspoon salt
1 cup grated Monterey Jack cheese

Soak the beans overnight. Drain and rinse them and place them in a large soup pot or Dutch oven with plenty of fresh water. Add the onion and 1 tablespoon of the oil, bring to a boil, then cover and simmer until the beans are tender, about 2 hours. The bean should yield easily when pressed between your thumb and forefinger. Drain and store the beans until they're needed.

When you are ready to "refry" the beans, heat the remaining oil in a very large skillet. Add the cooked pinto beans and fry over moderate heat, stirring frequently, for 10 minutes. Mash the beans coarsely with a mashing implement. Add the salt and cook, covered, adding small amounts of water until the beans have the consistency of a very thick sauce. Sprinkle in the cheese and cook, covered, for another 10 minutes.

Chapter 3

SOY FOODS

The source of all manner of wondrous products, the humble soybean is the king of all legumes and is the most inexpensive source of high-quality protein available. The Western world is only beginning to scratch the surface of the vast trove of soy-foods knowledge that has been part of Asian cultures for eons. The cultivation of soybeans is believed to have existed in China by the second century B.C. Their use spread to Japan and other parts of the Orient by the eighth century A.D. as a result of the travels of Buddhist monks.

In agricultural terms, nothing beats soybeans for yielding usable protein. An acre of land on which soybeans are grown produces twenty times as much protein as an acre used to graze beef cattle. Compared with cereal crops, an acre of soybeans will yield about one-third more protein than the average grain crop. Frances Moore Lappé's landmark book *Diet for a Small Planet* did much to underscore just how much less wasteful and more efficient it is for people to eat soy and grain protein directly rather than feed these protein sources to animals and get our protein indirectly from them as meat. For example, only 5 to 7 percent of the vegetable protein fed to a steer or cow is returned in meat for human consumption. In other animals, the percentage of protein returned is higher, but not by much.

Ironically, it is the United States that is the world's leading producer of soybeans. With an output of two-thirds of the world's total soybeans, it is our leading cash crop. According to soy-foods expert William Shurtleff, 95 percent of all nonexported soy protein ends up as feed for livestock, with only 1.5 percent of the domestic crop being used directly as food here in the United States. However, statistics prove that the use of soy foods is increasing dramatically in the West. Shurtleff and other experts predict that low-cost, high-quality soy protein will become increasingly important in the near future as a way of meeting human protein needs on a worldwide scale.

As a culinary item in and of themselves, soybeans are disappointing; most people don't find them particularly tasty, and they take an inordinately long time to cook. Soybeans are perhaps most valued for the foods they spawn: Tofu and miso are important parts of the everyday diet in China and Japan and other parts of Asia; tempeh is a staple food in Indonesia (natural soy sauce, otherwise known as shoyu or tamari, is another important soy derivative; see page 180). All of these soy-derived foods offer complete protein, containing all eight of the essential amino acids in proportions that make it readily usable by the body. They are the only vegetable sources that do so.

From soybeans and their derivatives, a myriad of preparations can be made, and the imaginative cook will delight in their versatility. If yogurt was the "new" natural food of the seventies, then tofu is, arguably, the new food of the eighties. Perhaps in the nineties, tempeh will come into its own. This chapter will serve as a basic, brief introduction to those who'd like to get to know more about soy products. For more in-depth information and recipes, some very good books are available (see appendix C).

──── DRY WHOLE SOYBEANS ────

Whole soybeans are not, despite their nutritional superiority, a legume that most people look forward to using. Their flavor is rather bland, and their long cooking time (3 hours or more) and tendency to foam while cooking require the attention of a most patient cook; however, if you do have the patience, soybeans can be quite a worthwhile kitchen staple.

Soybeans are the only legume with complete protein—that is, the full range of the eight essential amino acids. These amino acids are in the correct proportion to be readily used by the body and need not be complemented by other foods. Containing about 35 percent more protein on average than other legumes, soybeans are rich in polyunsaturated oils, which help lower the blood cholesterol level. A $3^1/_2$-ounce serving contains 11 grams of protein and only 130 calories. High in fiber, soybeans are also rich in the minerals iron, calcium, phosphorus, and potassium, as well as vitamins B_1 and B_2. The oil in soybeans contains vitamin E. It is the abundance of oil that makes them far higher in fat than other legumes. A $3^1/_2$-ounce serving contains about 6 grams of fat. However, this does not by any means make soybeans a high-fat food.

Sold in bulk in natural-food stores, dry soybeans may be kept for up to a year if stored in a cool, dry place. Look for smooth beans with an even, creamy-white color and no surface imperfections, such as holes and cracks.

Basic Cooked Soybeans: Rinse and sort the beans, discarding any stones or withered ones. Place the beans in a cooking pot with 3 to 4 times their volume of water. Cover and soak the beans overnight in the refrigerator (soybeans immersed in water are particularly susceptible to fermentation and spoilage). When ready to cook the beans, drain them and cover with fresh water to about double their bulk. Draining off the original soaking water of soybeans is often recommended, because this helps to eliminate some of the indigestible sugars, thus making them more digestible.

Bring the water to a boil, then lower the heat and simmer the soybeans slowly for at least 3 hours, with the lid of the pot slightly ajar to prevent the water from foaming over. Make sure there is always plenty of water covering the beans; add more during cooking if necessary. Soybeans should be cooked thoroughly to make them more digestible. Avoid cooking soybeans in a pressure cooker, since the foam tends to clog the vents. Like other beans, 1 cup of dry soybeans will yield about $2^1/_4$ cups cooked beans. Cooked soybeans will keep in the refrigerator for a week, but they taste best if used in 4 to 5 days. Or they may be frozen and will keep for several months.

• Mash cooked soybeans coarsely and use as a substitute for ground meat in chili, stews, and Mexican dishes such as tacos and burritos.

• *Soyburgers*: For every cup of cooked soybeans, use 1 beaten egg, 1 tablespoon minced or grated onion, and 1 tablespoon natural soy sauce (more or less to taste). Combine in a mixing bowl with spices—try chili spices or curry spices—and mix thoroughly. Shape into patties and fry in a small amount of oil on both sides until golden. Serve on a whole wheat bun with lettuce and tomato.

• For a mock chicken salad, mash soybeans coarsely, add minced celery, chives, or scallion, and dress in mayonnaise (or tofu mayonnaise, see page 66) and mustard.

• Substitute soybeans in whole or in part in recipes calling for white beans; see for example, Sauerkraut Baked Beans (page 47) or any of the recipe ideas listed under "Great Northern Beans" (page 44).

• Combine 1 cup soybeans in equal parts with $1/_3$ cup sunflower or sesame butter in a food processor or blender. Add the juice of $1/_2$ lemon, or more if you wish, and $1/_2$ teaspoon each of cumin, ground coriander, and garlic powder. Process until smoothly pureed and use as a high-protein sandwich spread.

• Simmer cooked soybeans in highly seasoned tomato-based sauces, such as an Italian marinara sauce. Try serving over whole wheat pasta.

• Marinate soybeans in a vinaigrette dressing overnight, then use as a condiment or an ingredient in green salads.

• Puree soybeans thoroughly and add small amounts to soups and baked goods for texture and a protein boost.

• Stir-fry soybeans in a combination of oil and soy sauce until well browned. Toss them into rice or noodle dishes, such as the following:

JAPANESE NOODLES WITH FRIED SOYBEANS

Yield: 6 servings

2 1/2 tablespoons safflower oil
1 1/2 tablespoons natural soy sauce
1 1/2 to 2 cups cooked soybeans
1 teaspoon sesame oil
2 tablespoons sherry or dry white wine
1 large onion, halved and sliced
1 cup cabbage, finely shredded
1 cup snow peas, trimmed and halved
　　crosswise
1 cup mung bean sprouts
1/2 pound Japanese noodles, cooked (use
　　udon, somen, or jinenjo)

In a large skillet or wok, heat 1 1/2 table-spoons of the safflower oil and the soy sauce. Add the soybeans and fry over moderately high heat until they are well browned and crisp. Remove from the skillet or wok and set aside.

Add the remaining safflower oil, plus the sesame oil and the sherry or wine to the skillet or wok. Add the onion and cabbage and stir-fry until the onion is golden. Add the snow peas and bean sprouts and stir-fry until all the vegetables are tender-crisp. Stir in the soybeans and cooked noodles and season with additional soy sauce if desired. Serve at once.

FRESH GREEN SOYBEANS

Commonly used and well loved as a vegetable in their summer-to-early fall season in Japan, fresh green soybeans have not yet caught on in the West. Fresh green soybeans come in fuzzy green pods usually containing two bright green soybeans. Their flavor is a cross between fresh green peas and fresh lima beans.

Fresh green soybeans are not readily available, but you might search for them in farm markets (especially in regions where soybeans are grown), or try buying them canned through mail-order sources. Walnut Acres carries them sporadically (see appendix A).

Fresh green soybeans are more easily digested than the dry variety. They are high in protein at 12 percent, as high in vitamin C as oranges, and are rich in thiamine as well as vitamin A. Some of these nutrients are lost in the drying process.

To prepare them, cover the pods with boiling water. Let stand for 5 minutes, then drain. When cool enough to handle, break the pods crosswise and squeeze out the beans. One pound of soybeans in the pod will yield approximately 1 1/2 cups shelled green soybeans. To cook, bring 1 cup water to a boil in a saucepan. Add the shelled soybeans and simmer, covered, for 15 to 20 minutes, or until tender but firm. Cooked green soybeans may be frozen for up to a year. Canned green soybeans are ready to use and need not be cooked as above.

Green soybeans may be used in any way that fresh green peas or fresh or frozen lima beans are used. They're very nice as a vegetable side dish simply seasoned with butter or margarine and salt and pepper. They are also good in soups or mixed with hot rice, and they have an affinity with tomatoes and tomato-based sauces.

ITALIAN-STYLE GREEN SOYBEANS

Yield: 4 to 6 servings

This excellent recipe is from *Tofu, Tempeh and Other Soy Delights*, by Claire Cusumano, which has several interesting recipes for green soybeans. See also *The Book of Tofu*, by William Shurtleff and Akiko Aoyagi, for more ideas.

2 large cloves garlic, minced
2 cups sliced mushrooms
2 tablespoons olive oil for shallow frying
2 cups fresh green soybeans
1 teaspoon dried basil

½ teaspoon dried oregano
Pinch of dried tarragon
2 tablespoons wine vinegar
One 28-ounce can imported plum
tomatoes, with liquid, crushed
½ cup grated Romano cheese
Cooked spaghetti or other pasta

Sauté the garlic and mushrooms in the oil for 2 minutes. Add the soybeans, basil, oregano, tarragon, vinegar, and tomatoes. Cover and simmer for 10 minutes. Remove the lid and simmer for 10 minutes more. Stir in half the cheese. Spoon the mixture over the pasta in a large bowl and sprinkle with the remaining cheese. Serve at once.

MISO

A ubiquitous staple in Japanese and Chinese cookery, miso, or fermented soybean paste, is a powerhouse of concentrated flavor and nutrition. Three types of miso are commonly available in the Western natural-food market: soybean miso, rice miso, and barley miso (rice and barley misos actually combine soybeans with the grain). Within each category of miso exists a range of earthy hues and subtle flavor variations, all more or less in the realm of a pungent saltiness. The texture resembles that of peanut butter. Miso is best known as the base for simple, broth-type soups, although it is equally useful as a basis for sauces, dressings, and dips.

Miso is commonly sold in either plastic packages or tubs. Once the tubs are opened, it is best to reseal them tightly and refrigerate. Once the plastic packages are opened, they should be additionally protected by placing them in another container, such as a tightly lidded glass jar or plastic container. Refrigerated miso keeps very well for several months. After some time, a white mold may develop around the edges. Although this may be scraped off and the rest of the miso used, it is your signal that the freshness is waning.

Miso has been produced in the Orient for several centuries, and the methods used today are little different from the ancient ones. The important first step in making miso is to prepare the mold culture, called *koji*, which will ferment the soybeans or the soy and grain combination, depending on what type of miso is being made. For soybean-only miso, cooked soybeans rest for 2 to 3 days in a special room, called the *koji-room*, during which a mold called *Aspergillus hatcho* develops on them. For soybean and rice miso or soybean and barley miso, cooked grain is similarly put in a koji-room, and a mold called *Aspergillus orizae* grows on either grain.

To make soybean miso, or, as it is commonly called, *hatcho miso*, the soy koji is combined with cooked soybeans, salt, and water. To make *rice or barley miso*, the grain koji is combined with cooked soybeans, cooked rice or barley, salt, and water. These ingredients are then stored in large cedar kegs. The mold cultures release beneficial enzymes that stimulate the fermentation process. These enzymes assist in breaking down the starches in the soybeans and grains into simple sugars and cause the protein to be broken down into separate amino acids. Miso is aged for periods of 1 to 3 years, depending on the type that is being made. The length of time, the temperature at which the fermentation process takes place, and the proportions of the ingredients used all contribute to the final result and are responsible for the differences between the various types of miso. Miso packaged for exportation is required to be pasteurized as an extra safety measure.

"Quick" misos are not uncommon and, predictably, are a modern innovation. Through temperature control, the fermentation process can be speeded up to completion within a few weeks. Often, flavorings, additives, and preservatives are added to quick misos, and they don't taste as fine and complex as traditionally aged misos. There is no real advantage to buying quick miso. If in doubt as to what you are getting, read the ingredients—natural, aged miso contains only soybeans (and grain, in the case of rice or barley miso), salt, and water.

The protein content in miso ranges from about 13 percent in rice miso and about 18 percent in barley miso to about 20 percent in soybean miso. One tablespoon of miso provides an average of 2.5 grams of protein and contains only 27 calories. All misos are excellent sources of iron, calcium, phosphorus, and the B vitamin range, including vitamin B_{12}, which is rarely found in vegetable sources. Fermentation makes miso very easily digestible, and the live lactic-acid bacteria and enzymes that it contains aid in general digestion.

Miso serves as a substitute for both salt and soy sauce in that you would be unlikely to use them in tandem in any given dish; even the sweetest rice misos are salty (miso contains an average of 12 percent salt, which acts as a preservative, preventing harmful bacterial growth). The concentrated flavor of miso goes a long way; rarely will you see more than 2 or 3 tablespoons called for in a recipe that serves 4 to 6. Miso is easier to use if it is diluted in a small amount of warm water and stirred until smooth. When cooking with miso, do not boil it, because this destroys the beneficial enzymes.

The essential differences between soybean, barley, and rice misos are outlined below and are followed by some basic ways in which to use miso in general.

SOYBEAN (HATCHO) MISO

Hatcho miso is named for the Chinese city of the same name, where it originated. The darkest, firmest, most intensely flavored of misos, hatcho resembles a thick chocolate fudge. Its fermentation process is a long one, optimally between 2 and 3 years. Because its flavor is exceptionally strong, soybean miso is often mixed with other misos.

Made with soybeans, soybean koji, salt, and water, hatcho miso has the highest protein content among misos at about 20 percent, as well as the highest fat content at about 10 percent. It is richest in calcium, phosphorus, and iron and is comparable to other misos in its content of the B-complex vitamins.

The robust flavor of hatcho makes it a favorite winter miso, most appropriate for use with cold-weather foods such as root vegetables and in hearty dishes such as stews. If you enjoy the strong flavor of this miso, however, you need not adhere to this rule religiously.

BARLEY (MUGI) MISO

Barley, or mugi, miso is made by mixing barley, soybeans, barley koji, salt, and water. The fermentation period is shorter than for soybean miso, the optimal time being between 18 months and 2 years. Barley miso has become the most widely accepted by Westerners and is also very popular in Japan. Its not-too-sweet, not-too-overpowering flavor makes it appropriate for both summer and winter use. It is an ideal base for almost all miso soups, sauces, and spreads. In Japan, mugi miso is considered a "country-style" food; it is available in smooth and chunky textures.

RICE MISO

Rice miso is made from a combination of rice,

soybeans, rice koji, salt, and water. This type of miso has the shortest fermentation period, since the starches in rice are rapidly converted to sugars. Rice miso tends to have a somewhat sweet flavor, which mellows the salty taste. It is considered most appropriate for summer cooking since it is the lightest in flavor.

Several varieties of rice miso are marketed through natural-food outlets, with colors ranging from brown to red to creamy white.

The most common of these is *kome miso* (also known as *sendai*, or *red miso*), made from white rice. This miso is quite popular in Japan, where it has been made, using a time-honored formula, since the seventeenth century. A recent innovation is *genmai miso*, made from brown rice instead of white. Unpolished rice was once considered too resistant to fermentation, but a method was developed that resulted in genmai miso, which has proven to be very pleasing to the Western palate. *Shiro miso* is a variety of the very mild, white sweet misos, which age relatively quickly. Shiro miso uses sweet rice and less salt. Another variation on this is a product made in North America that is labeled a "mellow white miso." These white misos are the lightest in flavor and so are ideal for using in nontraditional ways, such as blending with buttermilk and herbs for salad dressing, where they will add zest but never overpower.

• *Miso Soups*: A staple of Japanese cuisine and of macrobiotic diets, miso soup is often a simple affair, made of a combination of few ingredients. Here is one very basic recipe: First, make a dashi (a basic stock), by combining in a large saucepan a quart of water with a 7-inch strip of kombu (a sea vegetable; see page 132) and a handful of shiitake mushrooms (page 177). Bring to a boil, then cover and remove from the heat. Let stand for 30 minutes. Strain the stock (reserve the kombu and mushrooms for other uses), return it to the saucepan, and bring to a simmer. Add 1/2 cup each of finely diced or grated carrot and daikon radish. Cook until they are just tender-crisp. Dissolve a tablespoon of miso in enough warm water to make it pourable and stir in. If you'd like a more intense flavor, add one additional tablespoon of dissolved miso at a time until the desired taste is obtained. Remove from the heat at once. Garnish each serving with thinly sliced scallions. Any of the different types of miso may be used, or a combination of any two. This makes 4 to 6 servings.

MISO SOUP WITH CABBAGE AND BABY CORN

Yield: 4 to 6 servings

Miso soup may also be more elaborate than the simple recipe given above. This simple, quick preparation is a nice introduction for those who have never tasted miso soup before.

1 tablespoon peanut oil
2 cups thinly sliced savoy or white cabbage
5 cups water
1/2 cup loosely packed dried shiitake mushrooms, stems and caps
One 15-ounch can baby corn, with liquid
2 bunches scallions, minced
1/4 pound tofu, finely diced
1/4 teaspoon freshly ground ginger
2 to 3 tablespoons miso, or to taste

In a soup kettle or Dutch oven, heat the peanut oil. Add the cabbage and stir-fry over high heat for 1 minute. Add the water and mushrooms and bring to a boil, then lower the heat and simmer for 10 minutes. Scoop out the mushrooms with a slotted spoon; trim and discard the tough stems, then slice the caps and return them to the soup. Add the remaining ingredients, except for the miso, and simmer over very low heat for 10 minutes. Dilute the miso in just enough warm water to make it smooth and pourable. Stir into the soup, then remove from the heat and serve immediately.

• *Miso Sauces:* To make miso sauces, use 2 to 4 tablespoons of the miso of your choice, to taste, diluted in about 3/4 cup water or unsalted stock, and embellish with other flavorings. Heat just until warm; do not boil. Try adding wine, sautéed garlic or onions, fresh herbs, or even a sharp cheese, in combinations to your liking. Miso sauces are excellent over tofu, tempeh, seitan, grains, noodles, or root vegetables, such as turnips, daikon radish, and even potatoes. Here's an easy one to try:

MISO-GINGER SAUCE

Yield: About 1 1/2 cups

1 tablespoon sesame oil
1 large onion, quartered and thinly sliced
1 clove garlic, minced
1 to 2 teaspoons freshly grated ginger, to taste
3 tablespoons miso, or to taste
2/3 cup water or unsalted vegetable stock
1 tablespoon sesame seeds
Dash of cayenne pepper (optional)

Heat the oil in a heavy saucepan. Add the onion and sauté over low heat until it is translucent. Add the garlic and continue to sauté until the onion is lightly browned. Stir in the ginger. Combine the miso with the water or stock in a small bowl and stir until the miso is dissolved. Slowly pour into the saucepan. Simmer over very low heat for 3 to 4 minutes; do not boil. Add the sesame seeds and the cayenne if you wish. Serve at once.

• *Miso Salad Dressings:* Tangy, unusual dressings made with miso are suitable for crisp salads of Oriental vegetables (such as briefly steamed bean sprouts, bok choy, daikon radish, or snow peas). Miso salad dressings are also quite nice with cold rice or noodle salads or salads using sea vegetables. Use lighter misos with delicately flavored vegetables. Here's a basic recipe; add other seasonings, such as garlic or herbs, if you wish.

MISO SALAD DRESSING

Yield: About 1 cup

1 to 3 tablespoons miso, to taste
1/3 cup water

¼ cup safflower or peanut oil
3 tablespoons rice vinegar
1 tablespoon honey
1 tablespoon mirin (optional)
½ teaspoon dry mustard

Stir the miso and water together in a small bowl until smooth. Add the remaining ingredients and whisk together until smoothly blended.

• *Miso Dips*: The lighter, sweeter rice misos are great for making healthy, tasty dips. Tofu makes an excellent base or try yogurt for a tangy twist. The following dip is very good with crisp, raw vegetables:

DILLED MISO-TOFU DIP

Yield: About 1½ cups

½ pound soft tofu
2 to 3 tablespoons genmai, shiro, or
   mellow white miso, to taste
Juice of 1 small lemon
¼ teaspoon garlic powder
3 tablespoons chopped fresh dill
¼ teaspoon kelp powder (optional)
¼ cup soy milk or low-fat milk

Place all the ingredients in the container of a food processor or blender. Process until smooth.

MISO CONDIMENTS

Condiments with miso as their base are as common in Asian markets as ketchup is in American markets. Only two varieties have made any headway into the natural foods realm. One is *natto miso*, a thick, sticky traditional Japanese condiment that combines soybeans, barley koji, ginger, kombu, and barley malt. Its strong, savory-sweet taste makes it an unusual topping for grains, noodles, vegetables, tofu, tempeh, and potatoes. Natto may also be thinned with water to make a broth or sauce for these foods. Another miso condiment that has caught on to some degree with Western natural foods enthusiasts has the saucy name of *Finger Lickin' Miso*. Made with soybeans, koji, and minced pickled vegetables, this condiment may be used as a spread for crackers or bread, or as a topping for the same foods listed for natto miso, above.

SOY MILK

Expressed from soybeans that have been soaked and pureed, soy milk is a boon to those who are lactose-intolerant, since in cooking it produces a very good approximation of cow's milk. It compares favorably in nutritional value, too (see comparison chart, that follows). The flavor of pale, tan soy milk is unlike that of cow's milk, though. It has a somewhat nutty flavor that may occasionally taste slightly "beany." Homemade soy milk may taste too distinct to drink straight, as a beverage, but is improved when other flavorings, such as honey or natural sweeteners, are added. Some natural-food manufacturers produce soy milks with added natural flavorings that make them taste quite smooth and highly palatable.

Soy milk is available in bottles or cartons in the refrigerator section of natural-food stores. You can also buy individual servings in foil pouches. Refrigerated, soy milk will keep well for about a week to 10 days from the date it was made. Look for soy milk packaging that is dated. Also available in natural-food stores are flavored soy drinks in various flavors such as carob, banana, and strawberry. These are quite delicious, and though they are somewhat expensive, will not cost you much more than an additive-filled "milk shake" from a hamburger stands.

The chart on the next page shows how soy milk compares nutritionally with cow's milk.

Product (per 100 grams)	Protein (grams)	Fat (grams)	Calories	Calcium (milligrams)	Iron (milligrams)
Soy milk	3.4	1.5	33	21.0	0.8
Cow's milk (whole)	3.5	3.5	65	118.0	trace

	Niacin (milligrams)	Thiamine (milligrams)	Riboflavin (milligrams)	Vitamin A (IUs)
	0.2	0.08	0.03	40
	0.1	0.03	0.17	140

As an occasional purchase, soy milk is not prohibitively expensive, but if you'd like to make it a staple in your kitchen, you might want to save money by making it at home. You need no special equipment, as you do with tofu making, and the procedure is not complicated—just a bit messy and time-consuming. You will need a 3- or 4-quart pot, a colander, and several layers of cheesecloth. Here are the steps to make about 1 1/2 quarts. Start with this quantity on your first try, then when you are familiar with the procedure, you can easily double the recipe:

1. Rinse and sort 1 cup soybeans and place them in a container with 3 cups water. Cover and soak overnight, refrigerated.

2. Drain in a colander and rinse.

3. Place 1 cup of the soaked beans at a time with 1 cup of warm water in the container of a food processor or blender. Puree for 2 to 3 minutes.

4. Combine the pureed beans with 5 cups water in a 3- or 4-quart cooking pot. Bring to a boil over moderately high heat. When the foam begins to rise, quickly reduce the heat and simmer for 10 minutes.

5. Pour the mixture, a batch at a time, if necessary, into a colander lined with two layers of cheesecloth. When cool enough to handle, gather up the four corners of the cheesecloth and twist, wringing out as much soy milk as possible.

6. Place the wrapped soybean residue with the cheesecloth in a bowl of warm water for 5 minutes. Wring and squeeze again into the first batch of soy milk.

7. Pour the soy milk into a clean cooking pot. Bring to a boil, then reduce the heat and simmer gently for 5 to 7 minutes, stirring frequently. Let cool, then pour into jars and refrigerate.

The soybean pulp left over from making soy milk (and from the production of tofu, since making soy milk is the first step in that process) is called okara. This pulp retains a good deal of nutrients and, in Japan and China, is utilized as food. It may be used to add texture to soups, stews, casseroles, savory pancakes, and baked goods, or made into "beanburgers." Many interesting recipes for using okara are in The Book of Tofu by William Shurtleff and Akiko Aoyagi (see appendix C).

- Quick Soy Milk: If you don't want to go to the trouble of making soy milk from scratch, natural-food stores sell soy powder (see page 61), from which you can make an instant soy milk according to the package directions. The result is not quite as good as it would be if made from whole soybeans in that it tends to separate, but it produces a reasonable facsimile, good for use in soups, sauces, and baking.

Soy milk may be used in a variety of ways as a substitute for dairy milk. Try it in:

- Soups, especially chowders or cream soups
- Sauces, including cheese and béchamel
- Blended beverages and shakes, particularly those made with bananas, carob syrup, or strawberries
- Baked goods
- Egg dishes
- Hot and cold cereals

SOY MILK CRÊPES

Yield: About 1 dozen crepes

These tender crepes may be filled with sweet or savory fillings, as you like. As dinner crepes, try filling them with ricotta cheese or mashed tofu and topping with tomato sauce, or fill them with steamed vegetables and top with an herbed sauce, using soy milk as a substitute for dairy milk in a recipe for a white or béchamel sauce. As dessert crepes, fill them with crushed berries, fine preserves, or apple butter.

1 egg, beaten
1 1/2 cups soy milk
1/2 cup whole wheat pastry flour
1/4 cup barley or oat flour
1 tablespoon safflower oil
1/2 teaspoon salt

In a mixing bowl, combine the beaten egg with the soy milk. Sprinkle in the flours, then add the oil and salt. Whisk together until quite smooth. Heat a 6- or 7-inch nonstick skillet. When hot enough to make a drop of water sizzle, pour in 1/4 cup of the batter. Cook briefly on both sides until golden. Repeat with the remaining batter.

To assemble the crepes, spoon some filling down the middle of each, then fold one end over the other and serve at once, either with or without sauce.

——— SOY FLAKES ———

Not a commonly available product, soy flakes are made from soybeans that have been dry-roasted, split, and rolled in a roller mill, then dehydrated. Just a few nutrients are lost during this process, but soy flakes are very convenient, since they do not require presoaking and take only about 30 to 40 minutes to cook. Soy flakes retain the mild flavor of whole soybeans, minus a bit of that "beany" flavor, thanks to the roasting process.

Soy flakes are most often sold in bulk. They are made from full-fat soybeans, and so should be stored in a cool, dry place. They will keep for several months.

Basic Cooked Soy Flakes: Use 2 1/2 parts water to 1 part soy flakes. Bring the water to a boil, stir in the soy flakes, return to a boil, then lower the heat and simmer, stirring occasionally. Cook 35 to 40 minutes, or until the water is absorbed. The dry volume of soy flakes will double when cooked.

Soy flakes may be cooked together with grains that have approximately the same cooking time, such as brown rice or pearl barley; this boosts the protein usability of the grains enormously. When cooking soy flakes with rice or barley, use them in whatever ratio you wish— 1 part soy flakes to 2 or 3 parts grain is a good rule of thumb—with the same proportion of flakes to water given above.

- Cooked soy flakes give a "meaty" texture and add protein to stews, soups, and chilies. In these types of preparations, soy flakes may be added dry, rather than precooked, so long as they will be simmered for about 40 minutes and some extra water is added for them to absorb (a ratio of 2 parts water to 1 part soy flakes is sufficient if there is a liquidy base to begin with).
- Substitute cooked soy flakes for mashed whole soybeans in soyburgers (see page 52).
- Try combining soy flakes with hearty whole-grain noodles (buckwheat or udon noodles are good choices) and top with steamed or sautéed fresh vegetables. Season with natural soy sauce.
- Use soy flakes in tandem with grains such as bulgur as an excellent stuffing for squash, peppers, or tomatoes.

CURRIED SOY FLAKES WITH RICE AND PEAS

Yield: 4 to 6 servings

2/3 cup brown rice
3 cups water
2/3 cup soy flakes
2 tablespoons soy margarine
1 medium onion, chopped
2 cloves garlic, minced

1 tablespoon unbleached white flour
1 cup low-fat milk or soy milk
2 teaspoons good curry powder
1 teaspoon dried mint
3 tablespoons minced cilantro or fresh
   parsley
Salt to taste
Dash of nutmeg
Dash of cayenne pepper
2 cups freshly steamed or thawed frozen
   peas
1/2 cup yogurt

Bring the water to a boil. Stir in the rice and soy flakes and simmer, covered, for 35 to 40 minutes, or until the water is absorbed.

Heat the margarine in a large skillet. Add the onion and garlic and sauté until the onion is golden. Sprinkle in the flour and stir in until it disappears. Add the milk or soy milk slowly, stirring it in as you pour. Add the seasonings and simmer over low heat until the liquid has thickened. Add the rice and soy flakes mixture, then cover and simmer for 10 minutes over very low heat. Stir in the peas and cook for another 5 minutes. Remove from the heat and stir in the yogurt. Serve at once.

SOY FLOUR (see page 101)

——————— SOY GRANULES ———————

Soy granules are made from precooked, defatted, and dehydrated soybeans (not to be confused with soy grits, page 60, which are made from raw dry soybeans). Because of the way they are processed, soy granules are a very convenient product, ready to use in minutes. Their texture resembles that of finely cracked wheat, and their flavor is more reminiscent of nuts or grain than of soybeans.

You'll find soy granules in natural-food stores sold prepackaged in cardboard boxes. Stored in a cool, dry place, but not necessarily refrigerated, they will keep for several months.

To rehydrate soy granules, combine them in a bowl with tepid water in a ratio of 2 parts water to 1 part granules. Let stand for 5 minutes. The dry volume of the granules will double once rehydrated.

- Add a small amount of rehydrated granules to green salads, where they resemble grain or ground nuts.

- Toss a handful of soy granules into casseroles, soups, and stews for extra texture and protein. You need not soak them first.

- Rehydrated soy granules combined with sautéed onions, garlic, and green bell pepper have a perfect texture for use as a stuffing or, for that matter, simply as a side dish in place of grain.

- Add unsoaked soy granules directly to baked goods in place of nuts. In "wet" batters, such as for cakes and muffins, they will soften, but still provide nice texture; in "dry" batters, such as for cookies, they will retain a pleasant crispness.

- When cooking hot cereals, add 1 tablespoon of unsoaked granules and 1 extra tablespoon of water per serving and cook along with the cereal. This will improve the protein usability of the cereal, as well as add an interesting texture.

- Add 1/4 cup or so of unsoaked granules to pancake batter. Let the batter stand for 5 minutes before cooking.

——————— SOY GRITS ———————

Soy grits are made from whole, dry soybeans, which are sometimes lightly toasted, then cracked into several pieces. Soy grits are a convenient form in which to utilize relatively unprocessed soybeans. They retain the mild flavor and nutritional values of whole soybeans, but take far less time to cook (about 40 to 50 minutes, depending on the coarseness of the grind) and need no presoaking. Cooked soy grits have a texture resembling that of coarse cracked wheat.

Soy grits are most often sold in bulk and, like other full-fat soy products, should be stored in a well-sealed container in a cool, dry place. They will keep for several months. Occasionally, soy grits are available in packaged form. Follow the cooking instructions given on the package, rather than those given below, since prepackaged grits may be defatted or partially cooked, which affects their cooking time.

Basic Cooked Soy Grits: Use water in a ratio of 3 parts water to 1 part grits. Bring the water to a boil, stir in the grits, and return to a boil. Cover, with the lid slightly ajar to let steam escape, then lower the heat and simmer, stirring occasionally, until the water is absorbed, about

40 to 50 minutes. Adjust the heat as necessary to prevent the water from foaming. Cooked soy grits are rather firm and stay separate rather than becoming mushy. The dry volume of soy grits will yield a little more than double the volume when cooked.

The flavor of soy grits may be enhanced by toasting them before cooking. In a heavy skillet, heat a tablespoon of oil for each cup of grits. Add the grits and toast them over moderate heat, stirring for about 5 to 7 minutes, or until they become aromatic. Then proceed to cook as above.

- Cooked soy grits are excellent when combined with cooked grains (such as rice, barley, or quinoa) in as much as a fifty-fifty ratio. Topped with steamed vegetables and seasoned with natural soy sauce, this combination makes for a simple and very healthful main dish.

- Soy-grits-and-grain combinations can be used to create high-protein pilafs and stuffings.

- Like soy flakes, soy grits are a good texturizer for stews and chilies and can be used as a meat substitute or extender as well. Add a cup or so of cooked soy grits to your favorite spaghetti sauce as it simmers; they'll provide thick, "meaty" texture.

- Add a tablespoon or two to green salads, or grain salads such as tabouli, for a protein boost.

SAVORY SOY AND BREAD STUFFING

Yield: 6 or more servings as a side dish

2 tablespoons soy margarine
2 large onions, chopped
1 large stalk celery, minced
1 to 1 1/2 cups cooked soy grits
1 cup chopped mushrooms
3 medium slices whole-grain bread
3 tablespoons minced fresh parsley
1 1/2 teaspoons mixed dried herbs
1/2 teaspoon dry mustard
1/2 teaspoon paprika
1/4 teaspoon cumin
1 cup low-fat milk or soy milk
2 eggs, beaten
Salt and freshly ground pepper to taste

Preheat the oven to 375°F.

Heat the margarine in a large skillet until it foams. Add the onions and celery and sauté over moderate heat until the onions are lightly browned. Add the soy grits and sauté until they are lightly browned. Add the mushrooms and continue to sauté just until they are wilted. Remove from the heat.

Tear the bread into several smaller pieces and place in the container of a food processor or blender. Process until the bread is fine crumbs.

In a mixing bowl, combine the mixture from the skillet with the crumbs and all the remaining ingredients and mix well. Pour into an oiled 1 1/2-quart casserole dish and bake for 35 to 40 minutes, or until the top is brown and crusty.

SOY NUTS

Soy nuts are whole soybeans that have been partially cooked, split, and dry-roasted. At a whopping 47 percent protein, they make a very healthful snack. Available plain or lightly salted, soy nuts are quite tasty, with a mild, nutty flavor. Eat them as a snack, or incorporate them into dried fruit-and-nut mixes. Tossing a handful into green salads is another good way to use them.

SOY POWDER

Soy powder is ground from cooked, dehydrated soybeans. It is quite similar to soy flour (page 101), but has a finer texture and contains less hull material. Unlike soy flour, soy powder does not have to be cooked or baked to be fully digestible (though it can be used in many of the same ways) and is more readily soluble in liquid.

Soy powder is available in bulk or prepackaged. The boxed variety is usually full-fat and so retains most of the nutritional characteristics of whole cooked soybeans. If you buy it in bulk, ask your retailer whether it is defatted or full-fat. Full-fat powder is more susceptible to spoilage, and you will want to know if your bulk source has a good turnover. Refrigerate soy powder to keep it at optimal freshness.

Use soy powder to enhance the nutritional value of blender drinks. If a small amount is used (a tablespoon or so per serving), it will not impart a "beany" flavor. Use soy powder to add quality protein to baked goods. For every cup of flour used, substitute 2 to 3 tablespoons flour with soy powder. Since soy powder has a somewhat milder flavor than soy flour, it is fine for use in baked desserts. Sprinkle a tablespoon or so into hot or cold soups to add bulk and protein.

Soy powder may also be used to make a quick version of soy milk, without the hassle and mess of the whole-bean version. The result is fairly good, though not as tasty, and tends to separate as it stands. Here's the formula:

Combine 1 quart water with 1 cup soy powder. Let stand for 2 hours. Bring to a simmer and cook over low heat for 20 minutes. Let cool and strain through several layers of cheesecloth. Store in jars and use wherever you'd use dairy milk—in soups, beverages, sauces, cereals.

——————— TEMPEH ———————

A staple soyfood of Indonesia, tempeh (pronounced tem-PAY) is slowly gaining popularity in North America, much as tofu did before it. Whereas tofu is bland and soft, tempeh has a chewier texture and a flavor with a unique character all its own. A versatile food, it packs a nutritional wallop.

To make tempeh, cooked and hulled soybeans (or a combination of soybeans and grain) are spread out on trays and inoculated with a benefi-cial mold culture *(Rhizopus oligosporous)*. A fermentation process occurs as the mold multiplies on the cooked soybeans and binds them together to form firm cakes. The $3/4$-inch-thick cakes are sold in 8- to 12-ounce, plastic-wrapped portions. Look for them in the refrigerator sections of natural-food stores and co-ops. Spots of dark mold are sometimes visible on the cakes, usually at the corners; this mold is not harmful, but you can simply scrape away any dark spots if you wish. Packages of tempeh should be dated to indicate when they were packed. Use as soon as possible after this date; or pop the package immediately into the freezer, where it will keep for several months.

During the fermentation process, the indigestible sugars in the whole soybeans are broken down. Since these sugars, or oligosaccharides, cause intestinal gas in some people, tempeh is far easier to digest than whole cooked soybeans. Tempeh is prized not only for the quantity of its protein, which is 20 percent, but also for its quality. It is a complete protein, containing the full range of essential amino acids. In addition, tempeh is low in fat, high in fiber, and provides significant amounts of calcium, iron, phosphorus, vitamin A, and the B-complex vitamins, notably riboflavin and niacin. Here's how tempeh compares with hamburger meat:

Product (per 100 grams)	Protein (grams)	Cholestrol (milligrams)	Calories	Fat (grams)	Calcium (milligrams)
Soy tempeh	19.5	0	157	7.5	142
Hamburger (20% fat)	24.2	90	286	20.3	11

	Iron (milligrams)	Thiamine (milligrams)	Riboflavin (milligrams)	Niacin (milligrams)	
	5.0	0.28	0.65	2.52	
	3.2	0.09	0.21	5.4	

During its fermentation process, a good quantity of vitamin B_{12} is formed in tempeh (this vitamin is rare in plant foods, and those who eat no meat, eggs, or dairy products must be careful to obtain it). While tempeh is often touted as a rich source of this vitamin, the nutritionist Jane Brody, in her *Good Food Book* (1986), sounds a cautionary note, asserting that although tempeh does contain a great deal of B_{12}, it is present in a form the body cannot absorb.

How does tempeh taste? It has been described as tasting like chicken or mushrooms, but in fact, the flavor of tempeh defies comparison. It may be an acquired taste (though with creative preparation, not a difficult one to acquire). The flavor of tempeh varies somewhat according to the manufacturer, ranging from mildly nutty to distinctly fermented. Some people relish the more fermented flavor, whereas others prefer a milder tempeh. There's no way of telling what a particular brand tastes like until you buy it, so it's best to find a brand whose flavor you enjoy and stick with it.

Tempehs combining soy with other grains are just as common as the soy-only version. Soy and brown rice, soy and barley, soy and wheat, and even soy and quinoa are available, though their flavors and textures are not drastically different.

The definitive book on tempeh, *The Book of Tempeh*, by William Shurtleff and Akiko Aoyagi, is an invaluable source for nutritional and historical information, as well as traditional Indonesian and numerous Western-style recipes. There are also instructions for making homemade tempeh, a process that is somewhat easier than making tofu. Another good source for recipes is *Tofu, Tempeh and Other Soy Delights*, by Claire Cusumano (Rodale Press, 1984). Very few general vegetarian cookbooks include recipes for using tempeh, so these books will prove valuable if you'd like to make tempeh a more frequent part of your diet.

Tempeh is a convenient, practically ready-to-use food, and only a little imagination is required to appreciate its versatility.

- TEMPEH "CROUTONS": Slice through a cake of tempeh so that it is only half as thick, then cut into 1/2-inch dice. Heat just enough oil to coat the bottom of a large skillet, along with 2 tablespoons natural soy sauce. Add the tempeh dice and sauté over moderate heat, stirring frequently, until lightly browned on most sides. Sprinkle with spices if desired (ground coriander is a traditional flavoring; a touch of garlic powder, chili powder, or curry is also good). Add the croutons to stir-fried vegetables, noodle dishes, soups, stews, and green or grain salads. They make a particularly savory addition to buckwheat noodles, garnished with minced scallions.

- PAN-FRIED TEMPEH: Slice through a cake of tempeh so that it is only half as thick, then cut into rectangular pieces approximately 1 1/2 by 2 inches. Heat just enough oil to coat the bottom of a skillet, along with 2 tablespoons natural soy sauce. Shallow-fry the tempeh pieces over moderate heat until golden brown and crisp on both sides. Season with any combination of garlic powder, onion powder, and cumin or coriander if you wish. Eat plain, with a sauce, or smothered with mushrooms. This is also great in a sandwich with lettuce and tomato.

- TEMPEH CUTLETS: Cut tempeh as described above for pan-fried tempeh. Dip the pieces in beaten egg, then in seasoned dry bread crumbs, then shallow-fry in oil. Try these cutlets with tofu tartar sauce (see page 66) or with Ginger-Apple "Duck Sauce" (page 169).

- TEMPEH SLOPPY JOE OR TACO FILLING: Sauté 1 finely chopped onion in a small amount of oil in a skillet until it is golden. Add 8 ounces finely crumbled tempeh and about 1/4 cup finely chopped green bell pepper, and sauté until the tempeh is lightly browned. Add a cup or so of thick tomato sauce, 1 teaspoon each natural soy sauce and honey, and season to taste with chili powder, cumin, and garlic powder. Cook over low heat for 10 minutes. Serve on a whole wheat roll or in a taco shell with shredded lettuce.

- TEMPEH AS A GROUND-MEAT SUBSTITUTE: Tempeh works very well this way. To make "burgers," crumble an 8-ounce package finely and combine it in a mixing bowl with 2 beaten eggs, 1 small minced onion, 1 crushed garlic clove, natural soy sauce to taste, and seasonings (curry spices are nice, or a pinch of mixed dried herbs). Shallow-fry in oil or broil until both sides are golden brown. Try tempeh burgers in pita bread with sprouts, tomato, and Tahini Mayonnaise (page 86). Tempeh may also be pan-browned and used as a meat substitute in spaghetti sauce, chili, vegetable stews, or as a topping for pizza. Simply crumble tempeh, heat just enough oil to coat the bottom of a skillet, and sauté it, stirring frequently, until lightly browned.

- TEMPEH SANDWICH SPREAD: Mash tempeh, straight out of the package, to a fine texture and add mayonnaise, mustard, chopped celery, and scallions to make a quick and satisfying spread for sandwiches and crackers.

TEMPEH, CAULIFLOWER, AND CASHEW CURRY

Yield: 6 servings

2 medium potatoes
2 tablespoons soy margarine
1 large onion, chopped
2 cloves garlic, minced
2 heaping cups small cauliflower florets
One 14-ounce can imported plum
    tomatoes, with liquid
1 cup diced zucchini
1 teaspoon each: freshly grated ginger,
    cumin, ground coriander, and turmeric
1/2 teaspoon cinnamon
2 green chilies, chopped, or one 4-ounce
    can chopped mild chilies (optional)
1 tablespoon safflower oil
8 ounces tempeh, sliced through so that it
    is only half as thick, then into 1/2-inch
    dice
Salt to taste
1/2 cup cashew nuts

Cook or bake the potatoes in their skin. When cool, peel and dice, then set aside.

Melt the margarine in a large skillet. Add the onion and garlic and sauté until the onion is golden. Add the cauliflower and sauté another 5

minutes. Add the tomatoes, zucchini, spices, and optional chilies. Stir together, then cover and simmer over low heat for 15 minutes.

In the meantime, heat the safflower oil in a smaller skillet. Add the diced tempeh and sauté over moderate heat until golden on all sides. Add to the skillet along with salt to taste and simmer for another 10 to 15 minutes over low heat. Stir in the cashews and serve.

TEXTURIZED VEGETABLE PROTEIN (TVP)

TVP is a processed soy food made from high-protein defatted soy flour that is exposed to heat and pressure to form granules or small, fibrous chunks. It is commonly used as a meat extender in institutional cooking as a cost-cutting measure; up to 25 percent of the meat in ground beef may be replaced with TVP with no detectable change in flavor. It is also the main ingredient in meat-analog products, such as soy sausages, soy frankfurters, imitation bacon and bacon bits, and imitation meat patties. Though these are high-protein soy products, bear in mind that they are also highly salted and are sometimes made with a lot of added fat.

Natural-food stores carry the granular-style TVP more often than the chunk-style. You'll usually find it in packages printed with directions and serving ideas. TVP is a very concentrated source of protein, being approximately 70 to 90 percent protein. Though many of the original nutrients of soybeans are lost in the processing, packaged TVP is fortified with many nutrients, including the B-complex vitamins, notably niacin, thiamine, and vitamin B_{12}, plus a good deal of iron and calcium. A 1/2 cup serving provides a hefty 26 grams of protein.

To reconstitute granular TVP, combine 1 cup with 7/8 cup boiling water in a small bowl. Stir and let stand for 10 minutes. TVP takes on a chewy, meatlike consistency and, though it has little flavor of its own, absorbs other flavors easily. It may be used to add a meatlike quality to tacos, burritos, and other Mexican dishes, vegetable or bean stews and sloppy joes.

TOFU (BEAN CURD)

It is generally accepted that tofu was first used in China about two thousand years ago by a famous philosopher named Lord Liu An. Tofu reached Japan during the eighth century A.D., very likely carried over by the Buddhist monks, who traveled widely during that time. Today, tofu (its Japanese name), is a staple food both in China and in Japan. Tens of thousands of small shops in Japan make tofu fresh daily.

To make tofu, soybeans are partially cooked, then pureed. Soy milk is extracted from the puree, then poured into shaping containers and solidified with one of two natural coagulants—nigari or calcium sulphate. The process is somewhat analogous to making cheese from dairy milk.

In the Orient, many types of tofu are produced, ranging from silky, custardlike varieties to freeze-dried cakes and everything in between. In Western markets, however, our choices are more limited; apart from the occasional tofu exotica to be found in Oriental groceries, there is basically firm tofu and soft tofu. For the most part, they are not so different that they can't be used interchangeably. For best results, use firm tofu for dishes where you'd like the tofu to retain its shape, and use soft tofu in dishes where the tofu is to be mashed or pureed. Another form of tofu making occasional appearances in our part of the world is *silken tofu*, a very smooth, soft, custardlike variety that is excellent for making puddings and pie fillings.

Tofu, both firm and soft, is sold fresh in 1/2-pound cakes or 1-pound blocks that are immersed in water, or in 1-pound blocks packaged in plastic tubs and usually stamped with "best if used by" dates. If you buy fresh tofu from Oriental groceries or natural-food stores from a vat of water, make sure you know that there is a good turnover. The water should look clean and fairly clear, and the water and the tofu should have very little aroma. Slimy, thickened water and a peculiar odor are sure signs that the tofu is not fresh. At home, store it immersed in water in the refrigerator and change the water daily. Tofu bought from containers of water is best used within a week. Tofu packaged in tubs is best used by the date stamped on the package.

Tofu is an excellent source of protein. A 4-ounce serving provides an average of 13 grams of complete protein. The same portion contains about 130 calories and from 6 to 8 grams of fat. The exact proportion of protein, calories, fat, and nutrients depends on the density of the cake: Firm cakes contain less water, and hence slightly higher concentrations. Tofu is also a very good source of calcium and iron and provides modest amounts of the B-complex vitamins. Here's how tofu compares with Cheddar cheese:

Product (per 4-ounce portion)	Protein (grams)	Cholestrol (milligrams)	Calories	Sodium (milligrams)	Unsaturated Fat (grams)
Firm tofu	13.0	0	130	7.9	7.9
Cheddar cheese	28.0	376	450	790	37

	Saturated Fat (grams)	Calcium (milligrams)	Iron (milligrams)
	1.2	294	2.9
	22	850	1.1

Those who don't like tofu cite its blandness, but it is precisely that blandness that is tofu's greatest asset. The range of flavors, and even textures, that it can take on is almost endless. Nor does it require a great deal of advance preparation. For sheer variety, here are two optional techniques that may be used to alter the texture and consistency of tofu:

- *Pressed Tofu*: Pressing tofu is done to extract some of the water, giving it a firmer, chewier texture. It's best to use firm tofu for this. Slice a block or cake of tofu into 1/4- to 1/2-inch-thick slices. Arrange the slices on one or two layers of thick, absorbent dish towels, cover with another dish towel, then with a cutting board. Place some weight, such as a heavy skillet, on the board. Allow to sit for 20 to 45 minutes. Pressed tofu makes chewy, firm cutlets with a "chickeny" texture. Dice pressed tofu for use in soups or saucy dishes; it will retain its firm texture.

- *Frozen Tofu*: Freezing tofu transforms it into almost a different food. It turns tan, and the surface becomes quite porous. Once thawed, quite a bit of water may be pressed out, yielding an even more concentrated form of protein with a chewy, meatlike texture. Cut the tofu into approximately 4-ounce portions and place in a plastic container, or wrap in freezer wrap or foil. Freeze for at least 24 hours. Let thaw at room temperature or in the refrigerator. Cut into slices and squeeze each slice between your palms to extract most of the water. Thawed tofu slices can be made into cutlets by dipping in egg, then breading and frying. Or it may be crumbled and made into a mock chicken or tuna salad. Crumbled or diced, it also makes a good addition to macaroni-and-cheese casseroles or cold macaroni salads, in which it resembles flaked tuna.

It would be impossible to present within the limited space of this entry all the ways in which tofu may be used, but here are a number of basic ideas that will serve as an introduction to this marvelous food. For further information on cooking with tofu, see the listing of books in appendix C.

- SCRAMBLED TOFU: To serve 2, crumble 1/2-pound tofu coarsely with a fork. Heat enough oil or margarine to coat the bottom of a skillet. Sauté 1 medium onion until golden, then add 1 cup sliced mushrooms and 1/2 medium green bell pepper, minced. Cook until the mushrooms are wilted, then add the tofu and cook, stirring, until it begins to turn golden. Season with salt (or natural soy sauce) and pepper. Add a dash of turmeric for color if you wish.

- MARINATED TOFU: Cut tofu into 1/2-inch dice and marinate in Rice Vinegar Marinade (page 181), or your favorite marinade for several hours. Toss into stews, stir-fried vegetables, green salads, grain salads, or cold noodle dishes.

- PAN-FRIED TOFU: Cut tofu into 1/4-inch-thick slices, about 1 1/2 by 2 inches or so. Heat enough oil to coat the bottom of a heavy skillet. Add 1 to 1 1/2 tablespoons natural soy sauce per 1/2 pound tofu. Fry the slices over moderately high heat on both sides until browned and crisp. Serve as a simple supper entrée, topped with sautéed onions and green bell peppers. Pan-fried tofu is also delicious in sandwiches with lettuce, tomato, and mustard.

- TOFU MAYONNAISE: In a blender or food processor fitted with a steel blade, combine 1/2 pound soft tofu with 1/4 cup safflower oil, 1 tablespoon prepared mustard, 1/2 teaspoon salt, and 1 tablespoon lemon juice. Process until creamy and smooth. If the mayonnaise is too thick, whirl in 1 to 2 tablespoons water.

- TOFU TARTAR SAUCE: To the recipe for tofu mayonnaise (see above) add an additional teaspoon of prepared mustard and some pickle relish to taste.

- TOFU EGG SALAD: Finely crumble 1/2 pound soft or firm tofu. Add mayonnaise or tofu mayonnaise (see above) to taste, plus 1 to 2 teaspoons prepared mustard, 1 finely diced stalk celery, 1 to 2 tablespoons minced scallion or chives, and salt and pepper. This is delicious on whole wheat rolls.

- TOFU CUTLETS OR FILLETS: Cut 1/2 pound of tofu into 1/4-inch-thick slices, about 1 1/2 by 2 inches. Press as described on this page, or drain briefly on paper towels. Beat 1 egg with 1 tablespoon natural soy sauce. Dip each slice of tofu into the beaten egg, then into some fine dry bread crumbs or a mixture of wheat germ and cornmeal. Fry in oil until crisp and golden on both sides. Serve either topped with a sauce or in a sandwich. Either way, these are great with tofu tartar sauce (see above). These proportions yield 2 or 3 servings; double as needed.

- BROILED TOFU: Cut tofu into 1/4-inch slices, about 1 1/2 by 2 inches. Prepare Sweet and Savory Grilling Sauce (page 161) or use your favorite barbecue sauce. Spread a thin layer of the sauce in a shallow pan. Arrange the tofu slices on it and baste with additional sauce. Top with sautéed chopped onions, diced green or red bell peppers, sliced mushrooms, or a combination. Broil for 5 to 7 minutes, and serve immediately.

- TOFU RICOTTA: Finely crumbled soft tofu makes an excellent substitute for ricotta cheese in Italian-style recipes. Use in manicotti, lasagna, stuffed shells, and so on.

- TOFU DIPS: Pureed soft tofu makes an excellent base for dips for vegetables or chips instead of fattening sour cream. Combine with yogurt or buttermilk for a nice tang. Try this creamy tofu-avocado dip: In a food processor or blender fitted with a steel blade, combine 4 ounces tofu, 1 medium ripe avocado, 1/2 cup yogurt, 1 tablespoon lemon juice, and 1/2 teaspoon each cumin and dried oregano. Puree until smooth.

- TOFU SALAD DRESSINGS: As with dips, tofu makes a good base for creamy dressings. Combine with approximately equal amounts of buttermilk and oil (about 1/4 to 1/3 cup each), plus herbs and spices to taste in a food processor or blender and process until smooth.

- TOFU BURGERS: Finely mash 1/2 pound tofu and combine in a mixing bowl with 2 beaten eggs, a pinch of dried mixed herbs, 1 to 2 tablespoons natural soy sauce, and 1/4 cup finely ground nuts or dry bread crumbs. Shape into patties and fry on both sides in a small amount of oil until golden. This makes 8 to 10 "burgers."

- TOFU PIES: This easy-to-make fudge pie is wonderfully smooth and rich-tasting. In a small saucepan, melt 1 cup semisweet chocolate chips. In the container of a food processor or blender, combine 1 pound soft tofu with the melted chocolate, 1/4 cup low-fat milk or soy milk, 1/4 cup honey, and 1 tea-spoon vanilla extract. Process until velvety smooth. Pour into your favorite piecrust and bake at 350°F for 30 to 35 minutes, or until the filling is firm and the crust is golden. For another great-tasting tofu pie, try Carob-Rum-Raisin Pie (page 166).

- DICED TOFU FOR MANY PURPOSES: Simply cut into approximately 1/2- to 3/4-inch dice, tofu may be tossed into many types of dishes, including soups (they are especially nice in Oriental noodle or vegetable soups), stews, pastas, stir-fried vegetables, curries, rice, or other grain dishes—anywhere you'd like!

POTATOES WITH TOFU AND GREEN CHILI

Yield: 4 to 6 servings

4 or 5 medium potatoes, cooked or baked in their skins
2 tablespoons safflower oil
2 tablespoons natural soy sauce
1 pound tofu, diced
1 tablespoon olive oil
1 large onion, quartered and thinly sliced
1 to 2 cloves garlic, minced
One 4-ounce can green chilies, chopped
1/2 teaspoon each dried oregano and cumin
1 tablespoon unbleached white flour
2/3 cup low-fat milk or soy milk
1 1/2 cups grated Monterey Jack cheese

Preheat the oven to 375°F.

When the potatoes are cool enough to handle, peel and dice them. Transfer them to a large mixing bowl and set aside.

Heat the safflower oil and soy sauce in a large skillet. Add the diced tofu and cook over moderately high heat, stirring frequently, until the pieces are lightly golden on most sides. Transfer to the mixing bowl. In the same skillet, heat the olive oil. Add the onion and garlic and sauté until the onion is lightly browned. Stir in the chilies and seasonings. Sprinkle in the flour and stir until it disappears. Pour in the milk or soy milk and stir together. Simmer until the milk thickens. In the large mixing bowl, combine the skillet mixture with the potatoes and tofu. Pour into a lightly oiled large, shallow baking dish. Sprinkle with the grated cheese. Bake for 15 to 20 minutes, or until the cheese is bubbly.

Chapter 4

NUTS, SEEDS, AND NUT BUTTERS

Before the advent of agriculture, nuts and seeds were staple nourishment for nomadic tribes foraging for food. Far from diminishing their importance, the onset of civilized society elevated the use of nuts from basic sustenance to prized delicacies. Nuts are the hard-shelled fruits of nut trees (with the exception of peanuts, which are legumes), and the food group referred to as seeds comes from the fruits or flowers of plants.

Both nuts and seeds are a rich source of proteins, vitamins, and minerals. Their chief drawback is certainly their high fat content. Used in moderation, however, nuts and seeds can be an invaluable part of meatless diets and diets that are generally low in other fats. Excellent as high-energy snacks, this versatile food group can add savor and crunch to everything from soup to dessert.

NUTRITIONAL BENEFITS OF NUTS AND SEEDS

Nuts and seeds are a powerfully concentrated source of nutrients. Rivaling meat as a source of protein, they are actually better than beans in this respect because of the relative percentages of essential amino acids they contain. Even so, the protein in nuts and seeds is incomplete, that is, it lacks the exact proportions of all the essential amino acids to make it readily usable by the body. To make the protein complete, nuts may be eaten with other protein foods. Grain products are a particularly good complement, not only in terms of their protein, but also in that being low in fat and calories, they balance fat- and calorie-rich nuts and seeds nicely. Some of the typical uses for nuts and seeds (apart from their solo use as a snack) demonstrate this compatibility—for instance, peanut butter on bread, sesame noodles, pine nuts or walnuts with pasta, and grain pilafs topped with chopped nuts.

Nuts and seeds are good sources of the B vitamins niacin, thiamine, and riboflavin and are one of the best sources of vitamin E. They are high in fiber and are mineral-rich, providing generous quantities of iron, calcium, phosphorus, magnesium, and potassium. Though nuts and seeds are nutrient-dense, there is a price to pay for all this—as most of us know, they're quite high in fat and calories. Nuts and seeds are composed of from 50 to 70 percent fat, depending on the variety, and just 1 cupful averages about 800 calories. However, in most nuts and seeds the fat is composed mainly of polyunsaturates and monounsaturates, and these have been shown to help lower the blood cholesterol level. Harmful saturated fats, those that raise the blood cholesterol level, make up only a small percentage of the fat in most nuts and seeds (one notable exception is coconut, in which most of the fat is saturated). For a more detailed discussion of the properties of these components of fat, see page 137.

In moderation, and in combination with other foods, nuts and seeds are a marvelous addition to the diet, particularly a meatless one. But consuming cupsful of nuts daily is generally not considered a good idea. Avoid buying oil-roasted nuts; with all those natural oils, adding more oil to nuts seems awfully redundant—not to mention unhealthy.

BUYING NUTS AND SEEDS

The most important factor to consider when buying nuts and seeds in bulk is that their high fat content predisposes them to rancidity. Seek out a source that you know has a good turnover, so that you will be assured that the nuts and seeds you buy are as fresh as possible. Nuts and seeds found in the supermarket or in specialty food shops in jars, cans, and cellophane bags are protected from exposure to air, which helps retain freshness; however such packaging often adds cost to an already rather expensive food group. You will also have to read the labels to avoid buying those that are oil-roasted or that have additives.

When buying nuts and seeds in the shell, look for uniform-colored shells. Avoid buying those with shells that show cracks or holes. Nuts should feel weighty for their size and not rattle in the shell, which indicates that the nuts or seeds are plump and not shriveled. When buying shelled nuts and seeds, again look for uniformity, good color, and plumpness.

STORING NUTS AND SEEDS

Careful storage of nuts and seeds is crucial, since their high fat content causes rancidity to set in very soon after they are shelled. Nuts in the shell are less of a problem; they will keep for several months if stored in airtight containers in a cool, dry place. However, even nuts in the shell are best kept refrigerated during warm, humid summer months.

Shelled nuts and seeds stored in tightly lidded glass jars at room temperature and away from direct light will keep well from 1 to 2 months, depending on how fresh they were when first bought. It's a good idea to keep all shelled nuts and seeds in the refrigerator during the summer. Pine nuts are best kept refrigerated at all times—they contain oils that spoil particularly rapidly. Chestnuts, too, should be refrigerated unless used up immediately. Because they are about 50 percent water, they're almost more akin to vegetables than to nuts. Though available all year-round, most nuts are in season, and therefore at their freshest, in the fall and winter.

Shelled nuts and seeds freeze well. Packed in airtight plastic containers, they will keep for a year or more.

ROASTING NUTS AND SEEDS

The flavor of all nuts and seeds is enhanced by roasting. Pecans and walnuts are never sold roasted, and though roasting them before cooking or baking with them is not necessary, doing so before eating them as a snack is very nice. Pine nuts are often sold unroasted, but roasting them is highly recommended, since it improves the flavor immensely. Shelled peanuts, almonds, hazelnuts, and cashews are commonly roasted before they are sold, but when sold in bulk, they are often raw. These are definitely enhanced by roasting, whether to be used in cooking or baking or as a snack. Peanuts in particular must be roasted in order to destroy a substance they contain that interferes with the body's absorption of nutrients. Sunflower seeds, sesame seeds, and pumpkin seeds sold in bulk are also often unroasted. Their flavors, too, benefit by roasting.

Roasting Seeds: Shelled pumpkin, sesame, and sunflower seeds can be roasted on a dry, heavy skillet over moderate heat. Stir frequently until fragrant and lightly golden, 5 to 10 minutes.

Roasting Nuts: Shelled nuts may be spread on baking sheets and baked at 300°F for 10 to 15 minutes, depending on the size of the nut. Let your sense of smell be your guide—when the nuts are done, they will be quite fragrant; take care not to overbake.

MAKING NUT AND SEED BUTTERS

Making nut and seed butters at home is surprisingly easy and more economical than buying them ready-made. Natural nut and seed butters (other than peanut butter) can be rather expensive. The following will yield excellent results: cashews, peanuts, almonds, hazelnuts, and sunflower seeds. Expect the almonds and sunflower seeds to yield a slightly grainier butter than the others.

Simply place 1 cup of nuts at a time in the container of a food processor or blender (note: a food processor achieves better results). Process at high speed until the nuts begin to hold together as a mass. Add 1 tablespoon of oil and continue to process, scraping the sides of the container from time to time, until the desired consistency is achieved. Add a teaspoon of honey if you'd like a touch of sweetness. Repeat with another cup of nuts if you'd like a bigger batch, but working only with 1 cup at a time is easiest. Transfer the nut butter to a lidded container and keep refrigerated. Nut butter will keep for several months in the refrigerator. For easier spreading, remove from the refrigerator about 30 minutes before using.

GENERAL USES FOR NUTS AND SEEDS

- *Chopped nuts:* The easiest way to chop most nuts is to simply place ½ to 1 cup nuts in the container of a food processor or blender and pulse on and off until the pieces are about ¼ inch or so. Some soft nuts, such as walnuts or pecans, may be "chopped" by placing them between layers of wax paper and rolling with a rolling pin. For a finer texture, nuts may be ground in a meat grinder or food mill. Chopped nuts are most often used in cakes and breads, but consider using a small quantity to sprinkle over green vegetables such as green beans, spinach, or asparagus. Toss chopped nuts over pan-fried tofu or cold cereals, or incorporate them into grain pilafs or noodle dishes.

- *Trail mixes:* Made of several varieties of nuts and seeds in combination with chopped or whole dried fruits, trail mixes are one of the most appealing of nut snacks. Try mixing your own, using five or more different nuts, seeds, and dried fruits. There are no particular rules for proportions, but roughly equal volume of nuts and fruits works well. The prepackaged type found in natural-food stores, take-out shops, and supermarkets is really expensive for its weight. For variety, add carob chips and soy nuts to your mixes.

- *Ground nuts or nut meals:* To make a nut meal, place ½ to 1 cup whole shelled nuts or seeds in the container of a food processor or food mill, or ½ cup at a time in the container of a blender. The trick is to stop processing the minute they are finely ground, and not to overdo it, or you'll be well on your way to nut butter! Make only as much as you need, since grinding releases a lot of oils. A meal of very finely ground nuts will add a rich flavor and moist quality to cakes, breads, and pie-crusts. Simply replace 2 to 3 tablespoons of each cup of flour in the recipe with nut meal. Or, before baking, sprinkle the meal on top of cakes and breads as a garnish. Nut meal may also be combined with bread crumbs as a topping for casseroles.

——————— ALMONDS ———————

From biblical stories to European folk belief, almonds have carried through the ages a rich legacy of lore and symbolism; dreams of almonds were believed to have foretold good fortune, and the early blossoming of the almond tree made it a symbol of the arrival of spring. The high esteem in which almonds have long been held is certainly justified, both for their mildly sweet taste and their beneficial qualities.

Unroasted almonds in the shell are the most economical way to buy them. Their shell is easy to crack with a nutcracker. Shelled almonds are sold in bulk both roasted and raw. Raw almonds are sometimes less expensive and can be easily roasted at home (see page 73). Prepackaged almonds, available in supermarkets and specialty food shops, come in many forms: blanched (with the brown skins removed), slivered, sliced, salted, oil-roasted, and smoked.

Almonds are 54 percent fat. Most of the fat is monounsaturated, with some polyunsaturates; their saturated fat content is one of the lowest among nuts. They are 19 percent protein. One cup of almonds contains about 850 calories; 1 ounce, or about 22 nuts, contains 170 calories. They are rich in B vitamins and vitamin E. Minerals are in good supply, particularly iron, magnesium, and phosphorus. Of special interest is the relatively high calcium content in almonds. Though they can't be considered a high-calcium food when compared with most dairy products, they can be a good addition to the diet of those who must avoid dairy foods. Ten almonds contain more calcium than 2 tablespoons cream cheese.

Aside from eating them plain, as a snack, almonds may be used in a number of delectable ways:

- Toss a handful of chopped roasted almonds into stir-fried vegetable or noodle dishes and grain pilafs.

- Coarsely ground almonds add a pleasant crunch and protein boost to breakfast cereals and fruit salads. Allow 1 to 2 tablespoons per serving.

- Use chopped almonds as a garnish for steamed green vegetables such as green beans, Swiss chard, asparagus, or broccoli. Or garnish each serving of soups made from these ingredients with a sprinkling of chopped almonds.

- Almonds make a fine homemade nut butter, delicious eaten on a hearty bread with honey (see pages 70 and 72).

- Almonds are also a good choice for making nut meal (see page 71) to be incorporated into cookies and other baked goods.

- *Maple-Cinnamon Almond Snack:* Stir 1 cup almonds together with 3 tablespoons maple syrup and 1/2 teaspoon cinnamon. Bake in a shallow pan at 300°F for 10 to 12 minutes, stirring once or twice, until the glaze has dried. Let cool and break apart. This recipe may be easily doubled.

- Almond milk is a tasty substitute for dairy milk for use in delicately flavored soups and blended beverages. To make it, place 2 cups almonds in the container of a blender or food processor. Process until finely ground, then add 2 cups warm water and continue to process for 1 minute. Cover a bowl with four layers of cheesecloth. Pour the almond mixture over it. Gather up the corners of the cheesecloth and squeeze the liquid out. Save the remaining almond meal to use in cookies, muffins, quick breads, or casseroles.

BROCCOLI-ALMOND STIR-FRY

Yield: 4 to 6 servings

This quick and simple vegetable dish may be eaten on its own as a side dish or over grains or noodles.

2 large bunches broccoli (about 1 1/2 pounds)
1 tablespoon peanut oil
2 teaspoons sesame oil
1 clove garlic, minced
3 tablespoons dry sherry or dry white wine
3 tablespoons natural soy sauce, or to taste
1/2 teaspoon freshly grated ginger
1/2 cup coarsely chopped roasted almonds

Wash and trim the broccoli. Slice the stems thinly and break the rest into slightly larger than bite-size pieces. Heat the peanut and sesame oils in a wok. Add the garlic, sherry or wine, soy sauce, and ginger and stir to mix. Add the broccoli and stir until it is evenly coated with the sauce. Stir-fry over moderately high heat until it is bright green and tender-crisp. Stir in the almonds; stir-fry for another minute or so, then serve at once.

ALMOND BUTTER

An elegant-tasting nut butter that is becoming more and more common in natural-food and specialty shops, almond butter packs in all of the nutrition of whole almonds. A 2-tablespoon serving contains about 190 calories, 8 grams of protein, and 18 grams of fat.

Almond butter has a somewhat grainier texture than peanut butter; however, it concentrates the sweet, pleasant flavor of almonds and lends itself to many uses. Like other specialty nut butters, commercially prepared almond butter can be rather expensive. It can be made at home quickly and easily for a fraction of the cost (see page 70). Lightly roasted almonds result in the best flavor.

- Almond butter spread on good crackers and eaten with sliced pears or apples makes a satisfying light meal.

- Substitute almond butter in your favorite recipe for peanut butter cookies.

- Add 2 to 3 tablespoons almond butter, diluted in an equivalent amount of warm water, to stir-fried vegetables for added flavor and protein.

- Add 2 to 3 tablespoons almond butter, diluted as above, to soup bases. It's especially nice in pureed broccoli or squash soups.

- Spread almond butter and honey, apple butter, or peach butter on oatmeal bread (or any mild-flavored whole-grain bread) for a delicious sandwich. Or use sliced bananas instead of the honey or fruit butter.

ROASTED EGGPLANT AND ALMOND BUTTER SPREAD

Yield: About 2 cups

1 large eggplant (about 1 1/2 pounds)
1/4 cup almond butter
2 tablespoons safflower or peanut oil
1 clove garlic, crushed
Juice of 1/2 lemon
2 tablespoons finely minced parsley
1/2 teaspoon ground cumin
1/2 teaspoon ground coriander
Salt and freshly ground pepper to taste

Preheat the oven to 400°F.

Bake the eggplant whole, on a cookie sheet, for 30 to 40 minutes, or until it has collapsed. Allow it to cool.

When the eggplant is cool enough to handle, peel it and drain it of its excess liquid. Mash it well with a fork and place in a serving container. Add the remaining ingredients and stir together thoroughly. Serve with whole-grain crackers as an hors d'oeuvre.

———— BRAZIL NUTS ————

A large nut with rich, oily meat, the Brazil nut is the fruit of a mammoth tree native to the Amazon forests of South America. Occasionally known as cream nut, it is most widely grown in Brazil, Bolivia, and Peru.

Because their shell is extremely hard and difficult to crack, Brazil nuts are most often sold shelled. If you manage to find Brazil nuts in the shell and are willing to cope with cracking them, you'll find that they taste better and fresher. Because of their high fat content, they are particularly susceptible to rancidity, so buy shelled nuts only in small amounts. If you don't plan to use them right away, keep them refrigerated. It's best to buy them in season, which is fall and winter.

The fat content of Brazil nuts is 66 percent, one of the highest among all nuts. Brazil nuts are 16 percent saturated fat, a proportion also higher than that found in most other nuts. The remaining fat content is equally divided among monounsaturates and polyunsaturates. They are 14 percent protein. A cup of Brazil nuts contains about 920 calories; 1 ounce (6 large or 8 medium nuts) contains 185 calories. Brazil nuts are rich in the minerals phosphorus and potassium and also provide modest amounts of iron, calcium, and several B vitamins.

Brazil nuts are most commonly roasted and eaten whole or mixed with other nuts as a snack. Their rich, strong flavor is more compatible with savory preparations than with sweet dishes, and their hefty fat content warrants using them only in moderate amounts.

- Coarsely ground Brazil nuts make a tasty garnish for green vegetables, such as green beans or asparagus, and simple stir-fried noodle dishes.

- Finely ground into a meal, Brazil nuts combined with bread crumbs make a tasty topping for casseroles or a good stuffing for mushrooms or other small vegetables such as tomatoes and baby eggplant. Use 3 parts bread crumbs to 1 part Brazil nut meal. Season with salt and pepper and mixed dried herbs to taste.

BRAZIL NUT AND TOFU PATTIES

Yield: 15 to 18 small croquettes

3/4 cup whole Brazil nuts
1/2 pound tofu, cut into 4 or 5 pieces
1/2 cup toasted wheat germ
2 eggs, beaten
1 tablespoon safflower oil
1 shallot, minced
1/2 medium green bell pepper, minced
1/2 teaspoon each garlic powder and
    paprika
1/4 teaspoon each dried oregano and
    summer savory
1 tablespoon natural soy sauce
Soy margarine for frying

Place the Brazil nuts in the container of a food processor or blender. Process until they are coarsely ground. Add the tofu and wheat germ and continue to process until the mixture is smooth. Transfer to a mixing bowl and stir in the beaten eggs.

Heat the oil in a small skillet. Add the shallot and green pepper and sauté over moderate heat until they are lightly browned, about 5 minutes. Add them to the tofu-nut mixture along with the seasonings and mix well.

Shape into palm-sized croquettes and fry in margarine over moderate heat until they are golden brown on each side. Serve plain or in a pita sandwich with lettuce and dressing.

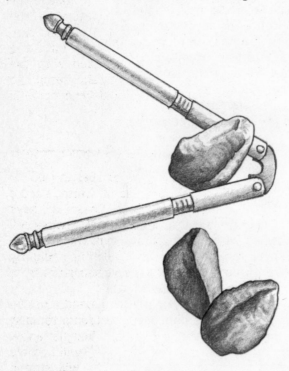

CASHEW NUTS

The cashew nut may be the closest rival to peanuts in terms of popularity in North America; they are held in high esteem in the Orient and India as well. The world's leading producer and exporter of cashews is India, which provides 90 percent of the world's supply. The large tropical evergreen on which they grow is believed to be native to South America.

Cashews grow on the bottom of an odd-looking, pear-shaped fruit, and before processing they are separated from it. The hard outer shell of the cashew consists of two layers, between which is a substance called cardol. This highly caustic substance can cause blisters and burns if it touches the skin. To release it, cashews are roasted at high temperatures. The nuts can then be removed from the shell; they are then heated again to remove an unwanted membrane layer. The necessity for these rigorous processing steps is the reason cashews are always sold shelled. The final step before exportation is sorting and grading cashews according to size.

Both raw and roasted cashews are available in bulk in natural-food stores. When labeled raw, that only means that the nuts haven't undergone an additional roasting process after the membrane has been removed. Roasting is easy to do at home (see page 70) and brings out their marvelous flavor. Broken cashew pieces are also available in bulk, offering a more economical alternative to buying them whole. These are fine for use in baking or cooking. Look for whole nuts or pieces that are fragrant and uniformly golden and plump.

Despite their creamy, rich quality, cashews are among the lowest in overall fat content of all the nuts, at 46 percent. The largest portion of the fat is monounsaturated, with small, roughly equal amounts of polyunsaturated and saturated fat. They are 15 percent protein. One cup of cashews contains about 780 calories; 1 ounce (18 medium or 14 large nuts) contains 185 calories. Cashews are rich in iron and zinc. They provide good amounts of other minerals as well, including phosphorus, potassium, and magnesium, as well as several B vitamins.

Look for recipes using cashews in Indian and Oriental cookbooks. Their delicious flavor adds a nice touch to stir-fried vegetables, seafood, or poultry dishes and to spicy curries (see the recipe for Tempeh, Cauliflower, and Cashew Curry, page 64). Here are some other ideas:

- Toss a handful of cashews into grain pilafs. They are compatible with long-grain brown rice and brown Basmati rice (see the recipe for Basmati and Wild Rice Pilaf, page 21).

- Add a sweet touch to salads of crisp Oriental vegetables. Combine a cup or so of steamed snow peas with an equal amount of raw, matchstick-cut white turnip or daikon radish. Add a 15- or 16-ounce can of drained baby corn and toss together. Dress with a miso salad dressing (see page 57) and toss again. Transfer to a serving bowl and garnish with chopped cashews. This makes 4 to 6 servings.

- Cashews are delicious tossed into winter fruit salads of apples, pears, and bananas. Dress in yogurt or buttermilk and add a touch of honey.

- Top each serving of cold or hot cereal with 2 tablespoons or so of chopped cashews.

- Use in cookies or shortbread. Because they tend to lose their crunch in baking, cashews are better in "dry" batters, such as those for cookies or shortbread, than in "wet" ones, such as for cakes and muffins.

CASHEW BUTTER

If you like cashews, you're bound to love cashew butter. Imagine the rich, slightly sweet flavor of cashews translated into a sensual, spreadable substance. The big mystery is why this product has not gained wider acceptance. The most obvious reason is surely the cost, since cashews often cost three to four times more than peanuts. Ready-made cashew butter is a somewhat costly treat, then, but the good news is that if you have a food processor or blender, you can easily make a very fine homemade version (see page 70).

Cashew butter is a concentrated source of all the nutrients in the nut. A 2-tablespoon serving contains approximately 190 calories, 16 grams of fat, and 6 grams of protein.

Use cashew butter wherever you'd use peanut butter. Your favorite peanut butter cookie recipe will be transformed into something a bit more special with cashew butter. For a twist on the classic peanut butter-and-jelly sandwich, try cashew butter on whole-grain bread with a natural fruit butter. Another satisfying sandwich is cashew butter with sliced banana on pumpernickel bread. For more ideas, see the suggestions listed under peanut butter (page 80).

CASHEW BUTTER SAUCE

Yield: About 2 cups

Cashew butter is the start of a heavenly sauce that is great over steamed green vegetables, noodles, grains, and even hard-boiled eggs.

1 tablespoon soy margarine
1 small onion, finely chopped
1/2 small green or red bell pepper, finely chopped
1 medium tomato, finely chopped
1 tablespoon unbleached white flour
1/2 cup cashew butter
1 cup water or vegetable stock
1/4 teaspoon chili powder
Salt and freshly ground pepper to taste
3 tablespoons finely chopped cashews (optional)

Melt the margarine in a heavy saucepan. Add the onion and sauté over moderate heat until it is translucent. Add the chopped bell pepper and sauté until the onion is golden. Add the tomatoes and cook, stirring occasionally, until they have softened, about 5 minutes. Sprinkle in the flour and stir until it disappears. Add the cashew butter and the water or stock and simmer for 5 to 7 minutes, stirring until the cashew butter is smoothly blended with the sauce. Stir in the chili powder and season to taste with salt and pepper. Add the optional chopped cashews and serve at once.

CHESTNUTS

Evoking nostalgic images of roasting on an open fire, chestnuts are one of winter's most delightful seasonal traditions. Chestnuts have long been regarded as a delicacy by diverse cultures, from the ancient Chinese to the southern Europeans of the present day. Their slightly sweet, soft, and mealy meat is a departure from the usual crunch of nuts.

Chestnuts are highly perishable and must be kept refrigerated. When kept at room temperature, they will start to go bad after just a few days; much longer than that, they will become moldy in the shell. Refrigeration will extend their life considerably; kept in ventilated plastic bags, they will remain fresh for 2 months. Choose firm, shiny-looking chestnuts during their fall and early winter season.

Because they are 50 percent water and 42 percent starch, chestnuts are not as dense in nutrients as other nuts. They are a mere 1.5 percent fat, and only 3 percent protein. A cup of chestnuts contains about 300 calories. They contain moderate amounts of vitamin A, several B vitamins, and the minerals iron, potassium, and phosphorus.

To prepare chestnuts for use, it's easiest to bake them. Cut an **x** into the domed part of the chestnut with a sharp knife. Arrange, cut side up, on baking sheets or in baking pans and cover with aluminum foil. Bake at 350°F for 40 to 50 minutes, depending on their size and how much of a roasted flavor you desire. Remove the foil and cool them until they can be handled. Shell while still warm, when they are easiest to peel, and eat as a snack or reserve for use in cooking.

- Sauté chopped roasted chestnuts in butter or margarine for 5 to 7 minutes and use as a side dish.

- Add a small amount of finely chopped roasted chestnuts to a basic recipe for béchamel sauce and serve over steamed green vegetables, such as asparagus or brussels sprouts.

- For an unusual salad, combine a cup or so of chopped roasted chestnuts with equal amounts of watercress and finely shredded red cabbage. Add tender lettuce (such as Boston or Bibb) as needed, depending on how many you are serving. Dress with good olive oil and red wine vinegar.

- Perhaps the most common use for chestnuts in cooking is as an element in stuffings. The stuffing that follows may be used as a side dish:

POTATO-CHESTNUT STUFFING

Yield: 6 to 8 servings as a side dish

18 medium chestnuts
4 medium potatoes, cooked in their
  skins, then cooled and peeled
³/₄ cup soy milk or low-fat milk
2 eggs, beaten
3 tablespoons soy margarine
1 cup chopped onion
2 large stalks celery
¹/₂ cup fine dry bread crumbs
3 tablespoons finely chopped parsley
¹/₄ teaspoon each: dried basil, dried
  thyme, and leaf sage
Salt and freshly ground pepper to taste

Bake the chestnuts as directed above. Allow to cool and peel off the shells. Chop each chestnut into quarters.

In a large mixing bowl, coarsely mash the potatoes and combine them with the milk and beaten eggs.

Preheat the oven to 350°F.

Melt the margarine in a skillet. Add the onion and celery and sauté over moderate heat until the onion is translucent. Add the chestnuts and continue to sauté until everything is lightly browned. Add to the potato mixture along with

all the remaining ingredients and mix well. Pour into a well-oiled 1 ¹/₂-quart casserole and bake 35 to 40 minutes, or until the sides and top begin to look crusty.

CHIA SEEDS

These minuscule shiny black seeds are native to the southwestern United States and Mexico, where they are gathered from a plant related to wild sage. Chia seeds are a fairly common offering in natural-food stores and through mail-order sources. Because they are so tiny and rather flavorless, they are used more as a supplement than as a food. Unlike other seeds, they can't be sprouted in the usual way, since they become gelatinous when soaked (a special clay sprouter is needed).

Chia seeds are 26 percent fat, which is low in comparison with other seeds, but they contain over 10 percent saturated fat. They are 16.5 percent protein and contain about 120 calories per ounce. Chia seeds are rich in calcium, phosphorus, and iron, as well as the B vitamin niacin. Comparing chia seeds with the more widely available sesame seeds, the nutritional profile provided by the USDA shows that sesame seeds are slightly higher in protein and contain higher amounts of minerals and a fuller range of B vitamins.

Grinding chia seeds before using them is often recommended to make them more digestible. They are commonly used to sprinkle over hot or cold cereals (a tablespoon or two per serving is sufficient) and can be mixed in small amounts into casseroles, bread doughs, or muffin batters.

COCONUT

The fruit of the coconut palm, the coconut is a staple food for a surprisingly large proportion of the world's population. This majestic tropical tree most commonly grows in the South Seas and the Pacific islands, including Hawaii and the Philippines, which boast thriving coconut industries. The sweet, distinct flavor and uniquely fibrous texture of coconut are relished by some and decidedly disliked by others.

Whole, fresh coconuts are available year-round in produce markets and supermarkets. A good one will feel heavy, and you will hear the liquid sloshing around inside when you shake it. To use whole coconut, pierce at least two of the "eyes" with an ice pick and allow the liquid (called *coconut water—coconut milk* is expressed from grated coconut meat) to run out into a bowl. Bake the coconut at 350°F for 25 to 30 minutes, or freeze it for an hour. Either of these methods will make the shell easier to crack and remove. Bring the coconut to room temperature, then place it on a firm surface and give it a sharp blow with a hammer. It should break easily. Then scoop out the meat with a short, sharp knife. Remove the dark skin from the outer meat with a vegetable peeler. Now the meat can be grated with a hand grater, or finely shredded in the container of a food processor or blender fitted with a metal blade. Freeze whatever coconut meat you are not going to use within a week and keep the rest refrigerated.

Natural-food stores offer grated, dried unsweetened coconut, packaged in cellophane bags or hermetically sealed cans. Supermarkets also carry commercial brands of dried coconut, but these are often loaded with sugar and contain additives that help retain moistness; they are not recommended. Dried, unsweetened coconut is a satisfactory substitute for freshly grated coconut in many recipes. After opening, grated coconut should be stored in a tightly lidded jar in the refrigerator and used within a month or so. If you don't plan to use it within that time, freeze it. It will keep almost indefinitely.

The fat content of coconut is high at 65 percent, and almost all of it is unhealthy, artery-clogging saturated fat. In other ways, coconut is fairly nourishing, providing particularly good amounts of the minerals potassium, phosphorus, and magnesium. Some B vitamins are present in modest amounts.

Coconut is often used for baking, especially as a topping for cakes and in cookies. If you'd like to try coconut and coconut milk in Indonesian-style cookery, consult *The Book of Tempeh*, by William Shurtleff and Akiko Aoyagi. A small amount of grated coconut is good in rice puddings and fruit salads. It is particularly compatible with pineapple.

PIÑA COLADA FREEZE

Yield: 4 servings

1 cup plain yogurt
One 8-ounce can crushed, unsweetened
pineapple with liquid
¹/₂ cup loosely packed grated,
unsweetened coconut
¹/₂ teaspoon vanilla extract
2 to 3 tablespoons honey, to taste

Combine the ingredients in a shallow pan. Freeze until nearly solid. Transfer, in chunks, to the container of a food processor. Process until smooth. Serve at once.

FLAXSEEDS

These tiny glossy-brown seeds are from the flax plant. The fibrous stems of the plant are used to produce the fiber of the same name, which goes into the making of rope and linen. Flaxseeds, also known as linseeds, are used to produce linseed oil.

Flaxseeds are occasionally available in natural-food stores as well as through mail-order sources, in whole as well as ground form. Both whole and ground seeds are best kept refrigerated. Though the seeds may be used whole, grinding them improves their digestibility.

Often sought more for health benefits than for culinary use (they have little flavor), flaxseeds are thought to be good for improving dry hair and for alleviating constipation. They have not been analyzed by the USDA, so information on specific nutrient composition is unavailable. However, they are thought to be high in unsaturated fats, protein, iron, phosphorus, and the B vitamin niacin.

Whole or ground flaxseeds can be sprinkled over yogurt, cottage cheese, salads, or cereals. Allow 1 to 2 tablespoons of flaxseeds per serving. Cook ground seeds along with hot cereals. Add a tablespoon or two to bread or muffin dough or combine with bread crumbs to make a topping for casseroles.

HAZELNUTS

These sweet-tasting, hard, roundish nuts are alternatively referred to as filberts, though technically, they are not exactly the same. Hazelnuts come from the wild, shrublike hazel tree, which grows primarily in the northwestern United States (Oregon and Washington States are leading producers) and in Mediterranean Europe. The filbert tree is a domesticated version of the wild hazel tree and is cultivated in groves.

Shelled hazelnuts are available in bulk in natural-food stores; they should look full and plump, and their skins should have a nice redbrown color. Hazelnuts in the shell are usually more economical than when they are bought shelled; their shiny brown shell is easy to crack, and since these nuts aren't generally used in large quantities, it isn't a daunting prospect to shell 1/2 cup or so as needed. The shells help keep the hazelnuts fresher longer, too. Hazelnuts in their shells keep at room temperature for several months; shelled hazelnuts should be refrigerated if they are to be kept for more than 2 months.

Hazelnuts are 66 percent fat, ranking high in fat content among nuts. The largest portion of the fat is monounsaturated. They are 11 percent protein. One cup of hazelnuts contains about 850 calories; one ounce (about 20 nuts) contains 180 calories. They provide relatively good amounts of several B vitamins and minerals, especially calcium, magnesium, and potassium.

Because hazelnuts taste so rich, they are particularly valued as a dessert nut. They're famed for their use in tortes and for their affinity with chocolate.

- Coarsely chopped hazelnuts may be used as a delicious topping for steamed broccoli, green beans, asparagus, and other green vegetables.

- Use hazelnuts as a substitute for chopped walnuts in cakes and muffins for a nice change of pace.

- Hazelnuts make delicious homemade nut butter (see page 70).

- Stuff hazelnuts into pitted dates and eat as a snack or serve with tea instead of cake.

- Finely ground hazelnuts are excellent for use as a garnish for cakes or as a stuffing for mushroom caps as an elegant hors d'oeuvre.

HAZELNUT-JAM COOKIES

Yield: About 3 dozen

1/2 cup (1 stick) soy margarine, softened
2/3 cup honey
1 egg, beaten
1 teaspoon vanilla extract
1 1/2 cups whole wheat pastry flour
1/2 cup toasted wheat germ
1 teaspoon baking powder
1/4 teaspoon each salt and cinnamon
1 cup finely ground hazelnuts
Blueberry or currant preserves

Preheat the oven to 350°F.

Cream together the margarine and the honey. Beat in the egg and vanilla.

In a mixing bowl, combine the remaining ingredients, except for the preserves. Work the wet ingredients into the dry to form a stiff batter. Drop by heaping teaspoonsfuls onto cookie sheets. Flatten slightly and make an indentation in the center of each cookie with your thumb. Fill the indentations with preserves. Bake for 10 to 12 minutes, then cool on a rack.

MACADAMIA NUTS

The round macadamia nut is native to Australia. It comes to the North American specialty-food market via a fast-growing Hawaiian macadamia industry. Macadamia nuts are encased in a hard shell that is very difficult to crack; they also have a tendency to mildew in their shells and so are usually sold shelled, either roasted or raw, whole or in pieces. Their creamy texture and lovely flavor contribute to their reputation as a prized delicacy.

Macadamias are more frequently found in supermarkets and specialty-food shops than in natural-food stores, packed in jars or cans. If you will be using them in baking or cooking, consider buying the more economical jars of broken pieces. For optimal storage, refrigerate them after their cans or jars have been opened.

Quite high in fat at 73 percent, macadamia nuts are 11 percent saturated fat; the remaining fat content is mostly monounsaturated. They are lower in protein than most other nuts at 7.8 percent. One cup of nuts contains about 940 calories; 1 ounce (about 15 halves) contains 200 calories. Macadamias contain all the nutrients generally provided by nuts—minerals such as potassium, phosphorus, iron, and magnesium, plus several B vitamins—but in relatively modest amounts.

Because macadamia nuts are a premium item, they are primarily eaten on their own, as a snack, so that their exquisite flavor may be fully enjoyed. Occasionally, they are used in rich baked desserts, very much as hazelnuts are. Macadamia nuts also appear in recipes from Southeast Asian countries such as Malaysia and Singapore, where small amounts are added to vegetable and seafood dishes.

————PEANUTS————

Botanically, the peanut is actually a legume, not a nut, for it comes from a vinelike plant and not a tree. The pods containing the peanuts grow underground, hence their archaic name groundnuts. However, the appearance, flavor, and ways of using peanuts are more closely related to nuts than to legumes, so for all practical purposes they can be classified together. Not only is the peanut the most widely used nut in the United States (Americans *daily* consume 4 million pounds of peanut products, including peanut butter), but it is also well loved in the Orient, Africa, and Southeast Asia, particularly Indonesia.

Peanuts are believed to have originated in South America several thousand years ago. Carried back to Spain and Portugal by early seventeenth-century explorers, the peanut came to American shores, via the African slave trade, only in the nineteenth century. George Washington Carver, the noted American botanist, is widely credited with popularizing the use of peanuts in this country by devising and promoting hundreds of recipes.

There are several varieties of peanuts. The two most common are the familiar jumbo, or Virginia, peanut and the small, red-skinned Spanish peanut. Peanuts are generally the most economical nuts you can buy, especially when purchased in the shell by the pound. When buying shelled peanuts, your best bet is the dry-roasted, unsalted variety. The flavor of peanuts is much improved by roasting. In fact, peanuts should never be eaten raw. They contain a substance (easily destroyed by roasting or even cooking) believed to interfere with the body's ability to absorb nutrients.

Unshelled peanuts will stay fresh for several months if kept in a cool, dry place, but refrigerate them during warm weather. Shelled peanuts will keep under cool, dry conditions for 2 months; if stored longer than that, they should be refrigerated.

Peanuts are 49 percent fat. Most of the fat is monounsaturated, with some polyunsaturates and very little saturated fat. Peanuts lead other nuts in protein content, at 26 percent. One cup of peanuts contains 840 calories; 1 ounce (from 10 jumbo nuts) contains 105 calories. Peanuts provide generous amounts of many minerals, including magnesium, phosphorus, and iron; they are particularly rich in potassium. Of the several B vitamins they contain, they are particularly high in niacin.

Versatile peanuts have a wide variety of uses in cooking and baking. They make an especially good nut meal (see page 71).

- For every cup of flour in quick bread, muffin, and cookie recipes, substitute 2 to 3 tablespoons peanut meal. The flavor of peanut meal is particularly compatible in cornbread.

- Use chopped peanuts as a substitute for walnuts in brownies and carrot cakes.

- Add peanuts to stir-fried vegetables just before serving, but don't incorporate them into the dish if you anticipate leftovers, since the peanuts will become soft by the next day.

- Top cooked brown rice, seasoned with freshly grated ginger, scallions, and natural soy sauce, with a handful of peanuts halves.

- Sauté 1/2 pound diced tofu in a small amount of oil until most of the sides are golden. Dissolve 2 tablespoons miso in 1/3 cup warm water. Pour over the tofu and stir in 1 teaspoon freshly grated ginger. Cook over low heat for 10 minutes. Stir in 1/2 cup peanut halves and serve as a protein-packed main dish. Garnish each serving with some thinly sliced scallions. This makes about 4 servings.

- Combine equal parts peanuts and raisins for a delicious snack. Use peanuts in other dried fruit-and-nut mixes.

- Add peanuts to fresh green salads. Combine strong greens such as spinach and romaine lettuce with cooked corn kernels, sprouts of any kind, and diced tomatoes. Toss in a handful of peanuts and dress with a light vinaigrette or a buttermilk dressing. Here's another peanut salad to try:

CRISP ORIENTAL VEGETABLE SALAD WITH PEANUTS

Yield: 6 or more servings

½ pound mung bean sprouts
¼ pound snow peas, trimmed
2 cups loosely packed shredded red
  cabbage
2 bunches scallions, finely chopped
½ cup shelled roasted peanuts
Sesame-Soy Salad Dressing (page 142),
  as needed

Steam the bean sprouts and the snow peas together until they are tender-crisp. Rinse immediately under cool water until the steaming stops and drain well. Combine with the cabbage, scallions, and peanuts in a serving bowl and toss well. Pour on enough dressing to coat the vegetables and toss again. Let the salad stand for 30 minutes before serving.

PEANUT BUTTER

Americans are passionate about peanut butter—more than a million pounds of it are consumed every day! This ubiquitous favorite first appeared in the United States in the 1890s, and large-scale commercial production began in 1907. In other countries, such as Indonesia and certain African nations, peanut paste is used in many traditional dishes, so where it actually originated is a matter for debate.

Most commercial brands of peanut butter contain sugar and salt; highly saturated, hydrogenated oils are added as stabilizers. Left at room temperature, natural peanut butter forms a layer of oil on top as a result of the settling of the solids. This oil may either be stirred back in or poured off. Natural peanut butter tastes very intense and peanutty, and after you get accustomed to using it, you'll wonder why anyone thought that salt, sugar, and additional oils need to be added to this excellent food. Refrigerate after opening to prevent further separation. For easier spreading, remove the peanut butter from the refrigerator about an hour before using it. Though natural peanut butter is a staple in natural-food stores, some national manufacturers have begun to make it for distribution in supermarkets.

Nutritionally, peanut butter has all the good-

ness of peanuts in concentrated form. A 2-tablespoon serving of peanut butter provides 9 grams of protein, 190 calories, and 16 grams of fat.

Don't limit your use of peanut butter to sandwiches alone. Use peanut butter in breads, bar cookies, drop cookies, cakes, and fudge. Such recipes are common in natural-food and vegetarian cookbooks. Look for recipes for peanut soup in American cookbooks—it's a Southern classic with a peanut butter base, and it's outstanding!

- *In piecrust:* Most standard crusts call for 6 tablespoons butter. Substitute 3 tablespoons peanut butter, and for the other 3 tablespoons use soy margarine for a really different, rich, and tasty crust.

- Mix peanut butter with an equal amount of warm water and stir until smoothly dissolved. Use as a quick and simple sauce for steamed green vegetables, noodles, or rice.

- Add a tablespoon or two of peanut butter (dissolved as above) to your favorite grilling sauce for an interesting flavor twist. Use to barbecue or broil tofu, seafood, or tempeh.

COLD NOODLES WITH SPICY PEANUT SAUCE

Yield: 6 servings

This sauce is inspired by an Indonesian classic. Consider using the peanut sauce over green vegetables, over Japanese noodles simply garnished with scallions, or over pan-fried tofu.

Peanut sauce:

1 tablespoon safflower oil
1 clove garlic, minced
1 small onion, chopped
1-inch piece fresh ginger, minced
½ cup natural chunky peanut butter
2 tablespoons natural soy sauce
1 tablespoon lemon juice
¾ cup water
1 teaspoon chili powder
Cayenne pepper to taste

Noodle salad:

½ medium head cauliflower, chopped into small florets
1 medium carrot, sliced diagonally
1 cup steamed fresh or frozen peas
1 large sweet red or green bell pepper, cut into thin strips
2 bunches scallions, minced
½ pound long noodles, such as buckwheat, udon, or somen, cooked and drained

To make the peanut sauce: Heat the oil in a small skillet. Sauté the onion and garlic until the onion is golden. Combine the onion and garlic with the remaining ingredients in the container of a food processor or blender. Process until creamy and smooth.

To make the noodle salad: Steam the cauliflower and carrots together until they are tender-crisp. Refresh under cool water briefly. Combine with the remaining ingredients in a large serving bowl. Pour the peanut sauce over and toss well. Serve at room temperature.

PECANS

If there is such a thing as an all-American nut, then the pecan is surely it. Native to the American South, pecans grow on a tall tree that is a species of hickory. A trip through the contemporary South confirms that the rich-tasting pecan is quite a favorite, showing up on nearly every menu in the form of pie and, in New Orleans, as the ubiquitous praline candy.

Pecans bought in their smooth, shiny brown shell are easily cracked with a nutcracker. They are even more widely available shelled, whether in bulk, cans, or cellophane bags. There are different grades and sizes of pecan halves, and they are priced accordingly. Oil-rich pecans are susceptible to rancidity. If you are buying in bulk, choose a source that has a good turnover. No matter how you buy them, it's a good idea to refrigerate pecans if you don't plan to use them within a month or so. In the summer, it's safest to refrigerate them from the start.

Pecans are 70 percent fat, second only to macadamia nuts in fat content. Most of the fat is in the form of monounsaturates, with only a small portion of saturates. They are just over 9 percent protein. One cup of pecans contains about 850 calories; 1 ounce (about 20 halves) contains 195 calories. The nutritional strength of pecans lies in their content of potassium and the B vitamin thiamine. Their vitamin A content is appreciable in comparison to other nuts. Other minerals and vitamins common to all nuts are present in modest amounts.

Pecans are highly compatible with sweet dishes and baked goods. They are interchangeable with walnuts in most recipes (especially where chopped nuts are called for in baked goods, such as brownies) and are, of course, commonly used in pies and tarts.

- Combine 1 part finely ground pecans with 3 parts fine dry bread crumbs to make a tasty topping for casseroles.

- Add a few pecan halves to summer or winter fruit salads or to stewed fruits.

- Garnish mashed sweet potatoes with a small amount of chopped pecans.

PECAN CANDIED YAMS

Yield: 4 to 6 servings

4 medium sweet potatoes
2 tablespoons soy margarine
Juice of 2 oranges (about 3/4 to 1 cup)
1/3 cup maple syrup or rice syrup
1/4 teaspoon each: cinnamon, ground
    nutmeg, salt
2/3 cup coarsely chopped pecans

Cook or bake the sweet potatoes in their skins until they are tender but still firm. When cool enough to handle, peel, then cut into quarters and slice into 1/4-inch thick slices.

In a large skillet, heat the margarine until it melts. Add the orange juice, maple or rice syrup, and seasonings. Stir in the potatoes and cook, uncovered, for 25 to 30 minutes, over medium heat stirring frequently, or until the potatoes are glazed and lightly browned. Stir in the pecans and serve at once.

PINE NUTS

Diminutive pine nuts are the seeds found in the pinecones of certain species of pine trees. They have achieved the rank of a delicacy. The pinecones are heated to help open them, then the nuts are removed by hand. The type most commonly found in natural-food and specialty stores is the pignolia, from the tree *Pinus pinea*, and is imported from Italy, Spain, or France. A somewhat different variety, the piñon, from the piñon tree, is used in the cuisines of North and South American Indians and of Mexico. In North America, the pinon is rarely marketed commercially outside the Southwest, so the comments in this entry pertain to pignolias.

Pine nuts are expensive, but with their rich and intense flavor a small amount goes a long way. If the pine nuts you buy are unroasted, it is highly recommended than you roast them before eating. The tangy, somewhat "piney" flavor of the raw seeds will mellow considerably. Some of the oils present in pine nuts go rancid quickly, so they are best kept refrigerated in airtight containers at all times.

The fat content of pine nuts is 47.5 percent. There is a roughly equal amount of monounsaturates and polyunsaturates, with only a small proportion of saturated fats. They are 25 percent protein. One cup contains about 700 calories; 1 ounce contains 156 calories. Pine nuts are strong in the minerals iron, potassium, phosphorus, and zinc. They contain modest amounts of several B vitamins.

Pine nuts are a common item in Mediterranean cookery, particularly that of Italy and Greece. They are occasionally used as an element in a stuffing for poultry, and in Greek cuisine they are sometimes used to stuff grape leaves or in pastries. Though they are eaten as a snack in their native regions, here we mainly use them in cooking.

- Toasted pine nuts are especially welcome in pasta dishes, particularly those using mild sauces or simply dressed with olive oil. Here's one idea: Cook 1/2 pound corkscrew-shaped pasta and combine with 1 large bunch steamed chopped broccoli and 1/4 cup toasted pine nuts. Add extra-virgin olive oil, salt, pepper, and finely chopped fresh basil as desired and toss together. Makes 4 servings.

- A handful of roasted pine nuts enhances grain salads, pasta salads, and even potato salads.

- Make an unusual salad by combining a cup or so of seedless green grapes sliced in half, 1/4 cup roasted pine nuts, and a tender lettuce such as red leaf or Bibb as needed. Dress in a light vinaigrette.

- Use crushed roasted pine nuts as an elegant

garnish for steamed green vegetables such as brussels sprouts, asparagus, or fresh green peas.

- Roasted pine nuts, like walnuts, are often used in pesto sauce. In any standard pesto recipe, simply replace the walnuts with an equivalent amount of pine nuts.

SPINACH FETTUCINE WITH PINE NUTS

Yield: 4 servings

1/2 pound spinach fettucine
2 tablespoons olive oil
2 to 3 cloves garlic, minced
2 heaping cups cauliflower, cut into bite-
    size pieces and florets
1/3 cup pine nuts, roasted
3 tablespoons finely chopped mixed
    fresh herbs or 2 teaspoons mixed
    dried herbs
1/3 cup grated Parmesan cheese
1 tablespoon soy margarine
Salt and freshly ground pepper to taste

Cook the spinach fettucine until it is *al dente*. Drain immediately and rinse briefly under cool water.

While the pasta is cooking, heat the olive oil in a large skillet. Add the garlic and sauté over moderate heat, stirring, for 1 minute. Add the cauliflower and sauté, stirring, until it is tender-crisp. Add the pine nuts and continue to sauté, another 3 minutes or so, until the pine nuts smell toasty. Toss in the cooked pasta and add the herbs, Parmesan cheese, margarine, and salt and pepper. Sauté, stirring frequently, for 5 minutes. If the mixture seems a bit dry, add a tablespoon or two of water. Serve at once.

———— PISTACHIO NUTS ————

The pistachio nut is revered in India and the Middle East for its delicate green color and its exquisite flavor. Pistachios grow on the tree *Pistacia vera*, which is native to central and western Asia. The pistachios available in North America are grown in the Middle East and in California.

Pistachios are most commonly sold roasted and salted in their hard, light-tan shell. The appeal of the red-dyed shell, originally conceived by street vendors to make them more enticing, is gradually wearing off. It takes a bit of work to shell pistachios, so when a quantity of them

is needed in a recipe, it is preferable to buy them shelled and unsalted, although these are more difficult to come by. You'll find them in Indian and Middle Eastern food stores or specialty food shops. They may be raw in this state, but it doesn't take long to roast them at home (see page 70). Pistachios in the shell will keep for several months under cool, dry conditions; refrigerate them during the summer. Shelled pistachios should be refrigerated at all times.

Pistachios are 54 percent fat. The fat is mostly monounsaturated, with small proportions each of polyunsaturated and saturated fat. They are 19 percent protein. One cup of pistachios contains about 770 calories; 1 ounce contains 168 calories. Pistachios are high in potassium and contain modest amounts of iron, phosphorus, calcium, and the B vitamins thiamine and niacin.

In North America, pistachios are eaten mainly as a snack and in pistachio ice cream. In Indian cooking they are used in spiced pilafs and to garnish puddings and other desserts. In the Middle East pistachios are used in pastries, such as baklava. If you are able to find them in shelled, unsalted form, it will be easy for you to use these delicious nuts in a variety of ways.

- Top steamed vegetables such as cauliflower, zucchini, or spinach with chopped pistachios. Or sprinkle some over curried eggs or baked egg dishes for an interesting flavor accent.

- For a superb relish, broil 2 sweet red bell peppers until charred on all sides. Let them cool inside a paper bag. Peel them and discard the core and seeds, then cut into 1-inch squares. Combine with 1/4 cup chopped pistachios, 2 tablespoons good olive oil, and 1 teaspoon red wine vinegar. Serve in small portions as a condiment for simple pasta or grain dishes.

- Toss freshly baked spaghetti squash with sautéed onions and soy margarine as desired. Top with a handful of whole pistachios and a sprinkling of Parmesan cheese.

- Sprinkle chopped, unsalted pistachios on fruit salads and sherbets.

PISTACHIO-APPLE SALAD

Yield: 4 servings

3 medium tart apples, peeled, cored, and sliced
¹/₃ cup raisins or other dried fruit
¹/₃ cup unsalted pistachios, coarsely chopped
1 medium stalk celery, finely diced

Dressing:

¹/₂ cup yogurt
1 tablespoon safflower oil
2 teaspoons honey
¹/₂ teaspoon dried mint
¹/₄ teaspoon cinnamon
¹/₄ teaspoon curry powder

Dark green lettuce leaves as needed

Combine the first four ingredients in a serving bowl. Combine the ingredients for the dressing in a small bowl and stir together. Pour the dressing over the salad and toss well. Serve at once, placing each serving on a bed of dark green lettuce leaves.

PUMPKIN SEEDS

Pumpkin seeds are not used as much as they deserve to be. High in protein, they have a unique flavor that makes them especially pleasant to eat as a snack.

When buying pumpkin seeds, you can choose between raw or roasted, shelled or unshelled, salted or unsalted. Roasting brings out their flavor and crunch, and you can easily roast them at home (see page 70). If you'll be using them primarily as a snack, buy them in the shell. They're more economical that way, and the extra time it takes to shell them will help limit the number eaten in one sitting. Avoid salted pumpkin seeds, which are usually quite salty, causing their flavor to be masked rather than enhanced. Pumpkin seeds in the shell will keep well for several months stored in an airtight container in a cool, dry place. Store shelled pumpkin seeds in the refrigerator if you don't think they'll be used up within 2 months.

Pumpkin seeds are 46 percent fat. The proportion of polyunsaturated fat is slightly greater than that of monounsaturated, with only a small percentage of it saturated fat. They are an impressive 29 percent protein. One cup contains 774 calories; one ounce contains 148 calories. Pumpkin seeds are quite high in phosphorus and iron and contain modest amounts of several B vitamins.

Don't throw away the seeds from your fall pumpkins! Rinse them well of the pulp and fibers and spread them on baking sheets or pans to dry for a week or so, stirring them daily. When they are completely dry, bake them at 300°F for 15 to 20 minutes, or until fragrant.

Apart from their preferred use as a snack, pumpkin seeds may be used in many ways that nuts are commonly used. The ideas given below are for toasted shelled seeds:

- Use pumpkin seeds in dried fruit-and-nut mixes. They're particularly good when mixed with raisins, dried apricots, and soy nuts.

- Sprinkle a tablespoon or so over a serving of cold cereal.

- Coarsely chop about ¹/₄ cup pumpkin seeds and add to batters for an average quick breads and muffins recipe. Try them in corn muffins.

- A handful of pumpkin seeds tossed into grain pilafs, green salads, and pasta salads will add an unusual flavor twist.

- Use pumpkin seeds to garnish steamed vegetables, such as cauliflower, or the pumpkin's kindred vegetables—the squashes.

SQUASH SEEDS

The seeds from the large squashes, such as butternut, acorn, and spaghetti, are quite similar to pumpkin seeds in appearance, flavor, and nutritional profile. The difference is that they are smaller and have thinner hulls, which are not as easy to crack as those of pumpkin seeds, because they have a bit too much "give." Squash seeds are rarely marketed, but you can salvage quite a number from your fall and winter squashes if you have the patience. Prepare them as directed for pumpkin seeds (see above) and use them for snacking; they're a bit too small and tedious to hull for use in any great extent in cooking.

SESAME SEEDS

These tiny seeds, relished in the Middle East, China, Japan, India, and Africa (they are sometimes referred to as *benne seeds*, their African name) are worth much more than their weight, both in nutritional benefits and in culinary properties. The flavor of sesame seeds is mild and nutty. It greatly intensifies when they are expressed into oil or are ground into a paste (known as tahini) or into a butter.

When buying sesame seeds, look for the whole, unhulled variety, which have not been stripped of their nutritious, deep-tan hulls. These are usually sold raw and may be roasted at home to bring out their flavor (see page 70). Whole sesame seeds will keep well for many months in a tightly lidded jar in a cool, dry place. Refrigerate them during the summer.

Sesame seeds are 48 percent fat, with roughly equal parts polyunsaturates and monounsaturates and only a small proportion of saturated fat. Sesame seeds are about 18 percent protein. Two tablespoons contain 110 calories. Though sesame seeds are quite rich in calcium (2 tablespoons contain an amount equal to that in an ounce of Cheddar cheese), some nutritionists have expressed doubts as to whether the calcium, present in a form called *calcium oxilate*, can be readily absorbed by the body. Studies done on this so far have been inconclusive. Sesame seeds are valued for their high vitamin-E content. They are also rich in the minerals iron, zinc, potassium, and phosphorus and provide substantial amounts of the B vitamins niacin and folacin.

Sesame seeds are well known for their extensive use in Middle Eastern cookery, where they appear in the sesame candy halvah and tahini (sesame paste). Oriental dishes that have become popular in the West are sesame noodles and sesame chicken.

- Sesame seeds are an excellent garnish sprinkled on almost any type of casserole, stir-fried vegetables, Oriental noodles dishes such as vegetable lo mein, and green salads.

- Sesame seeds may be sprinkled over or incorporated into yeasted breads, quick breads, crackers, and muffins.

- Use whole or ground sesame seeds in granola or sprinkle a tablespoon or so over a serving of cold cereal.

- Toss a small quantity of sesame seeds into simple cooked grains such as brown rice or bulgur or into grain pilafs.

- Sesame seeds are also nice in certain forms of sweet baking. Here is a recipe for some cookies with a very special flavor and crunch:

SESAME DROPS

Yield: About 3 dozen

1/2 cup (1 stick) soy margarine, softened
2/3 cup light brown sugar
1 egg, beaten
1/2 cup low-fat milk or soy milk
1/2 teaspoon vanilla extract
2 cups whole wheat pastry flour
1/2 teaspoon salt
1/2 teaspoon baking powder
1/4 teaspoon cinnamon
1/2 cup unhulled sesame seeds

Preheat the oven to 375°F.

Cream together the margarine and brown sugar. Combine with the beaten egg, the milk or soy milk, and the vanilla and beat until smooth. In another mixing bowl, combine the flour, salt, baking powder, cinnamon, and sesame seeds. Work the wet mixture into the dry until thoroughly combined into a stiff batter. Drop by heaping teaspoonfuls onto a cookie sheet. Bake for 10 to 12 minutes, or until lightly golden. Cool on a rack.

SESAME BUTTER

Ground from whole (unhulled) roasted sesame seeds, sesame butter is an intensely flavored spread. The hulls present in sesame butter make it thicker, grainier, and darker than tahini, which is made from hulled seeds. Commonly available in natural-food stores, sesame butter is more difficult than other nut or seed butters to produce at home because of the tiny size of the seeds. A 2-tablespoon serving of sesame butter contains 180 calories, 6 grams of protein, 15 grams of fat, and all the nutrients provided by whole sesame seeds. Once opened, sesame butter is best kept refrigerated. For easier spreading, let it stand at room temperature for an hour before using.

Use sesame butter as an interesting change of pace from peanut butter. It is useful as a spread for bread, crackers, or rice cakes. Try it in combination with strong-flavored fruit butters, such as plum butter, or mix it to taste with miso for a bold, savory spread.

SESAME PASTE (TAHINI)

A favorite Middle Eastern food, tahini is a rich paste ground from raw, hulled sesame seeds. Tahini comes in jars or preweighed plastic tubs; stir it well before using to mix the oil with the solids. Keep tahini refrigerated. Because the hull is not present, the nutrients in tahini are not as concentrated as they are in whole sesame seeds or sesame butter. Two tablespoons of tahini contain 170 calories, 16 grams of fat, and 5 grams of protein.

Tahini is combined with eggplant to make the classic baba ghanouj, and with chick-peas to make hummus, both delicious dips to be scooped up with pita bread. Many Middle Eastern and vegetarian cookbooks provide recipes for these and other dishes utilizing tahini. Tahini is also often used to flavor cold sesame noodles, an Oriental favorite.

- Dilute a tablespoon or two of tahini with an equal amount of water, just enough to make it smooth and pourable. Add to stir-fried vegetables, plain cooked grains, or to simple steamed vegetables such as broccoli or green beans with a squeeze of lemon juice.

- Add a tablespoon or two of tahini to recipes for bean or grain croquettes for extra flavor and a nutritional boost. It's particularly nice in chick-pea or brown rice croquettes.

- *Tahini mayonnaise:* This simple, tangy sauce is excellent as a dip for raw vegetables or as a dressing for pita sandwiches. Combine 1/4 cup each tahini and safflower mayonnaise with 1/2 cup plain yogurt and the juice of 1/2 lemon in a small mixing bowl. Whisk to blend thoroughly.

- Add a rich flavor to a simple oil-and-vinegar salad dressing with tahini. To every cup of dressing, whisk in 1 to 2 tablespoons of tahini, as desired. Serve over green salads.

SPICY SESAME EGGPLANT

Yield: 4 to 6 servings as a side dish

1 large eggplant (1 1/2 to 2 pounds)
1 tablespoon sesame oil
2 to 3 cloves garlic, crushed or minced
1/3 cup water
1 teaspoon grated ginger
4 bunches scallions, chopped, white and
   green parts seperated
3 tablespoons tahini
2 tablespoons natural soy sauce, or to
   taste
1 teaspoon chili powder or chili oil
1 teaspoon dry mustard

Peel the eggplant and slice into 1/4-inch-thick slices. Cut the slices into pieces approximately 1/2 inch wide by 2 inches long.

Heat the oil in a large, heavy skillet. Add the eggplant, garlic, water, ginger, and the white parts of the scallions. Cover and simmer over low heat, stirring occasionally, until the eggplant is nearly tender. Add more water if necessary to keep the bottom of the skillet moist. Add all the remaining ingredients except for the green parts of the scallions and simmer until the eggplant is quite tender. Stir in the scallions and serve at once as a side dish alone or over hot cooked grains.

SOY NUTS (see page 61)

————SUNFLOWER SEEDS————

The seeds of the majestic sunflower are a concentrated source of nutrition and flavor. Native to the Americas, the sunflower was introduced to the Mediterranean region in the early sixteenth century and, shortly after, to the Middle East. Though widely used, sunflower seeds are not particularly characteristic of any cuisine, save for some of those of Native Americans.

Sunflower seeds are available in a variety of forms—shelled, unshelled, salted or unsalted, raw, dry-roasted or oil-roasted. The most economical way of buying them is unshelled, in bulk. If you'll be using them in cooking or baking, buy them preshelled for easier use. Avoid salted and oil-roasted sunflower seeds. Whether you buy them raw or roasted is a matter of preference. Their flavor is definitely enhanced by roasting, and you can easily do so at home (see page 61). Sunflower seeds in the shell will keep for several months in a cool, dry place; refrigerate them during the summer. Shelled sunflower seeds are best kept refrigerated at all times.

Sunflower seeds are 47 percent fat, and the fat is highly polyunsaturated (the use of sunflower oil as a general-purpose cooking oil has grown tremendously over recent years). They are 22 percent protein. One cup of seeds contains about 810 calories; 1 ounce contains about 160 calories. Sunflower seeds are rich in vitamin E, niacin, and the minerals potassium, phosphorus, iron, and zinc.

- Combine sunflower seeds with other nuts and dried fruits of your choice for a healthful snack.

- Use sunflower seeds as an ingredient in homemade granolas, or toss a tablespoon or so of toasted seeds into a serving of your favorite cold cereal.

- Sunflower seeds are delicious tossed with green salads or added to cole slaw or potato salad for a nice crunch.

- Toasted sunflower seeds make a nice addition to grain pilafs and are a tasty topping for vegetable or noodle casseroles.

- For a simple side dish or entrée, cook 1/2 pound Oriental noodles such as udon or somen. Toss with 1/3 cup toasted sunflower seeds, 1 tablespoon sesame oil, and 2 minced scallions. Season to taste with natural soy sauce. This will serve 4.

- Incorporate whole or ground sunflower seeds into bread dough or muffin and quick-bread batters. Here's a tasty example:

ZUNI SUNFLOWER BREAD

Yield: 1 loaf

1 1/2 **cups whole wheat flour**
1/4 **cup cornmeal**
1/3 **cup ground toasted sunflower seeds**
2 **teaspoons baking powder**
1/2 **teaspoon baking soda**
1 **teaspoon salt**
2 **eggs, beaten**
1 **cup buttermilk**
2 **tablespoons molasses**
3 **tablespoons safflower oil**
1/4 **cup toasted sunflower seeds**

Preheat the oven to 350°F.

Combine the first six ingredients in a bowl. In another bowl, combine the beaten eggs with the buttermilk, molasses, and oil and beat until smooth. Combine the wet ingredients with the dry and stir vigorously until smooth. Stir in the sunflower seeds. Pour the batter into an oiled 9-by-five-by-3-inch loaf pan. Bake for 40 to 45 minutes, or until golden brown and a knife inserted tests clean.

SUNFLOWER BUTTER

An intensely flavored spread, sunflower butter is available in jars in natural-food stores and is easy to make at home with roasted sunflower seeds. Keep sunflower butter in the refrigerator. Providing all the nutrients in sunflower seeds, a 2-tablespoon serving of sunflower butter contains 180 calories, 6 grams of protein, and 15 grams of fat. Sunflower butter doesn't have the slight sweetness characteristic of nut butters and tastes more savory, almost like a pâté. Spread it on pumpernickel bread, rice cakes, or crackers. Add a tablespoon or two to recipes for grain, bean, or lentil croquettes.

——— WALNUTS ———

The familiar English walnut, so called to distinguish it from the rarely marketed black walnut, is believed to be Persian in origin. English walnuts established themselves in Europe soon after the beginning of the Christian era, then traveled to North America via the Spanish missionaries of the eighteenth century. The walnut tree found a perfect climatic niche in California, whose walnut industry supplies much of the product marketed in the United States. American, Chinese, and Italian cooks are among those who prize walnuts in their cuisines. The flavor of English walnuts is sweet with a slightly bitter undertone, making them compatible with both sweet and savory preparations. Black walnuts are not widely marketed, but are occasionally found in specialty-food stores. Their hard shells and sticky hulls make them more impractical to process and to use than English walnuts. The comments in this entry pertain only to the latter.

Walnuts are widely available both shelled and unshelled in supermarkets as well as natural-food stores. Despite the sturdiness of the shell, it is easy to crack. Walnuts come in three basic sizes—large, medium, and "baby"—and the difference in sizes does not affect their flavor or quality. Since walnuts are high in fat, shelled nuts should be refrigerated if they will not be used up within 2 months. Keep them refrigerated in any case during the summer. Walnuts in the shell will last for several months unrefrigerated if kept cool and dry. Walnuts are not customarily sold roasted, but you can do this at home (see page 70). It's not necessary to roast them before using in baking or cooking, but roasted walnuts are nice as a snack.

Walnuts rank high in fat content among nuts, at 64 percent. The fat is highly monounsaturated, with some polyunsaturates and very little saturated fat. One cup of walnuts contains 780 calories; 1 ounce contains 182 calories. They are 14 percent protein. Walnuts provide modest amounts of calcium, iron, phosphorus, potassium, and the B vitamin thiamine.

- Ground walnuts are a common addition to pesto sauce, which is delicious with pasta, potatoes, or even on top of pizza.

- Combine finely chopped walnuts with an equal volume of fresh bread crumbs to make a tasty topping for vegetable pies and casseroles.

- Toss a handful of coarsely chopped walnuts over steamed green vegetables such as green beans, broccoli, or asparagus; or toss them into Oriental-style stir-fried vegetables, curried vegetables, and grain pilafs.

- Make a Waldorf-style salad to serve 4 by combining 2 medium stalks celery, diced; 2 peeled and diced apples; 1/4 cup coarsely chopped walnuts; and 1/4 cup raisins. Mix 3/4 cup plain yogurt with 2 tablespoons honey and toss well with the salad.

- Add some chopped walnuts to cold grain salads. Here's one idea: Combine 2 1/2 cups cooked long-grain brown rice with 1/2 cup chopped walnuts, 1/2 pound asparagus (steamed and cut into 1-inch pieces), and 2 bunches scallions, sliced. Toss together and dress in a mild vinaigrette. Makes 4 to 6 servings.

- Walnuts are a favorite baking nut. Quick breads, fruit breads, muffins, brownies, and cakes are all familiar locales for walnuts.

WALNUT-CARROT CROQUETTES

Yield: About 1 dozen

These rich-tasting croquettes are excellent in pita sandwiches with shredded lettuce and a yogurt-based dressing.

1 tablespoon safflower oil
1 medium onion, chopped
3/4 cup walnut halves
1 1/2 cups finely grated carrot
1/4 cup wheat germ
2 eggs, beaten
2 tablespoons natural soy sauce
1/2 teaspoon each: paprika, cumin, dry mustard

¹/₄ teaspoon each dried basil and
   oregano
Dash of garlic powder
Freshly ground pepper to taste
Oil for frying

Heat the oil in a small skillet. Add the onion and sauté over moderate heat until it is golden. Combine the onion with the walnuts in the container of a food processor or blender and process until the walnuts are very finely ground and the mixture resembles a paste. Combine in a mixing bowl with the remaining ingredients and stir together until thoroughly mixed. Heat just enough oil to coat the bottom of a heavy skillet. Shape the walnut-carrot mixture into palm-size croquettes and fry on both sides until golden brown. Drain on paper towels.

Chapter 5

FLOURS AND MEALS

The growing awareness of the importance of complex carbohydrates in the diet has brought with it an enormous resurgence in the marketing of whole grains and whole-grain-flour products. With this increased acceptance of heartier, nuttier-tasting baked goods comes an interest in not only whole wheat flour but many other whole-grain flours and meals as well. These include barley, oat, rye, and rice flour, among others, as well as rich-tasting stone-ground cornmeals. Flours and meals such as these can be versatile staples in the kitchen, even if you don't have the time to make your own yeasted bread. Quick baked goods, such as muffins, pancakes, batter breads and crackers, can be equally rewarding.

NUTRITIONAL BENEFITS OF WHOLE-GRAIN FLOURS

The difference between refined and whole-grain flours is significant. Grains that are refined before milling lose their germ and bran, and with those goes up to 50 percent of the B vitamins and minerals as well as all of the vitamin-E content. Whole grains are excellent sources of minerals, including iron, potassium, phosphorus, and calcium. In cases where the bran is completely removed, almost all of the fiber content is lost. Grains that are commonly refined before milling, such as wheat and cornmeal, are enriched before being marketed, but only four nutrients are restored—the B vitamins niacin, thiamine, and riboflavin, plus iron.

In an age when new dietary guidelines call for less emphasis on protein and fat and more on complex carbohydrates, whole-grain-flour products are excellent choices for maintaining a healthy diet. Hearty breads, muffins, pancakes, and the like can be the cornerstones of any meal, providing high-quality protein and very little fat or calories (an average slice of whole wheat bread provides only 70 calories). The protein in most grain flours is incomplete, that is, the essential amino acids are not present in the precise proportions that make them readily usable by the body. The protein may be easily complemented with other protein foods, such as legumes, dairy products, and nut butters. Some common complementary pairings are peanut butter or cheese on bread, buttermilk in pancakes, and rolls or muffins with hearty bean soups.

BUYING WHOLE-GRAIN FLOURS AND MEALS

Most natural-food stores and co-ops carry an array of basic whole flours and meals. Less common flours, such as oat, barley, and amaranth, can be purchased through mail-order sources if you can't find them in your retail store. Flour mills are good sources, since their supply is likely to have a rapid turnover and be fresh (see appendix B). This is the most important criterion, whether you buy your flour from mills, in packages, or in bulk, because many whole-grain flours don't have a terribly long shelf life.

Many of the flours and meals offered in natural-food stores are labeled stone-ground. This is the traditional method of grinding grains; it utilizes a stone mill, which grinds the grains at a lower speed, generating less heat and thereby retaining more nutrients.

FLOUR STORAGE

Because milling grains releases their natural oils, flours and meals don't keep as long as whole grains. Rancidity sets in soon after the fats are exposed to air, and the flour begins to turn stale. Vitamin E acts as a natural preservative in some whole grains, but its strength diminishes after 3 months. If you are going to store whole-grain flours for more than 2 months, refrigerate them; during warm months, it is best to refrigerate them at all times. Otherwise, keep in a cool, dry place in tightly lidded jars or containers. A good practice is not to buy more flour than you think you can use up within 2 to 3 months. Buy no more than 1-pound bags of unusual flours that may be used only in small quantities or infrequently. It's especially important to keep flours dry, since they absorb moisture easily, which can contribute to their going stale quickly.

———— AMARANTH FLOUR ————

Amaranth flour is milled from the exceptionally nutritious seed referred to as grain amaranth. Having once been a revered crop of the ancient Aztecs, amaranth has been rediscovered and is now being watched with much interest as a "superfood" of the future. (For the story of amaranth's history and full nutritional benefits, see page 7.) Amaranth is 16 percent protein, a very high percentage in a grain, and in addition, the protein quality is superior to more common grains. It is quite high in fiber and rich in calcium and iron.

Amaranth is still a specialty crop, and the whole grain and flour are more readily available through mail-order sources than through retail outlets. Ask your retailer to order some or use the services of Walnut Acres. A free recipe sheet is included with your order of flour. Nu-World Amaranth is another good source. In addition to flour, they sell other amaranth products as well as an inexpensive book on baking with amaranth (see appendix B). Since amaranth flour is higher in fat than most flours, it should be refrigerated at all times.

Amaranth flour provides an easier and, to some tastes, a more palatable way of incorporating this highly beneficial food into the diet than the grain itself. The cooked grain tends to be rather sticky and heavy, thus limiting its versatility. The flour, distinctly though pleasantly flavored, adds a nutty character and rich aroma to whatever baked goods it is used in.

In yeasted breads, substitute up to 25 percent of the wheat flour with amaranth flour; in quick breads, muffins, griddle cakes, and pastries, substitute up to half the wheat flour with amaranth flour. In wheat-free recipes, amaranth works well with mild flours such as barley or oat. A mixture of equal parts amaranth flour and cornmeal makes a very tasty substitute for bread crumbs for dredging foods to be fried.

AMARANTH WALNUT-CHIP BARS

Yield: Approximately 2 dozen

1 cup semisweet chocolate chips or carob chips
1 cup walnuts
1 1/2 cups whole wheat pastry flour
1 cup amaranth flour
1 1/2 teaspoons baking powder
1 teaspoon salt
1/2 teaspoon cinnamon
2 eggs, beaten
1/3 cup soy margarine (about 2/3 stick), melted
2/3 cup light honey
1 teaspoon vanilla extract
3/4 cup low-fat milk or soy milk

Preheat the oven to 350°F.

Place the chips in the container of a food processor. Pulse on and off a few times, until they are roughly chopped. Add the walnuts and pulse on and off a few times, until the mixture resembles coarse crumbs.

In a mixing bowl, combine the next five ingredients. In a smaller bowl, combine the remaining ingredients and mix thoroughly. Add the wet ingredients to the dry and stir until thoroughly combined. Spread half the batter into an oiled, 8-by-13-inch baking pan or jelly roll pan. Sprinkle evenly with the walnut-chip mixture. Top with the remaining batter, spreading it carefully with a cake spatula. Bake for 25 to 30 minutes, or until the top is golden brown and springy. Cool, then cut into approximately 1-by-2-inch bars.

BARLEY FLOUR

Once a staple bread flour in northern Europe, mild-tasting barley flour can be incorporate into many types of baked goods. Milled from hulled and partially pearled barley, this flour has a delicately nutty aroma and contributes to a tender moist, cakelike crumb when combined with other flours. The nutrients in barley flour depend on how much of the outer bran layers have been removed, or pearled. Whole barley is rich in the B vitamins and the minerals potassium, phosphorus, and iron. Pearling the barley removes up to half the nutrients and most of the fiber.

Look for barley flour in bulk in natural-food stores or order it through mail-order sources (see appendix B). Barley flour is rather perishable and is best kept refrigerated.

Barley flour is very low in gluten, so best results are achieved when used with wheat flour when rising is needed, such as in quick breads and cakes. Barley flour may be used on its own to make tender pancakes; simply replace wheat flour with an equivalent amount of barley four in standard recipes. Or, use it in equal proportions with wheat flour in buttermilk pancake recipes or in piecrusts. Up to 30 percent of wheat flour may be replaced with barley flour in yeasted breads, and up to 50 percent in quick breads, muffins, and even cakes. It's also a good thickener for soups and sauces in place of wheat flour.

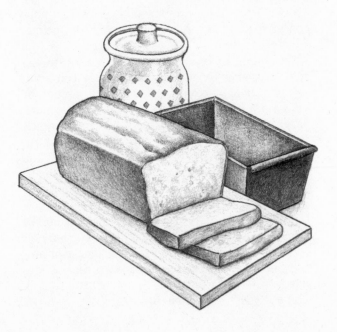

Many traditional Scandinavian breads utilize barley flour. Look for recipes in *Great Whole Grain Breads* by Beatrice Ojakangas (E. P. Dutton, 1984). In India, barley flour is combined with wheat flour to make some common breads. Explore Indian cookbooks for recipes.

BARLEY GRIDDLE SCONES

Yield: 8 servings

Make these easy scones while a pot of vegetable or bean soup is simmering and serve them warm with the soup.

¾ cup barley flour
½ cup whole wheat flour
1½ teaspoons baking powder
½ teaspoon baking soda
½ teaspoon salt
2 tablespoons poppy seeds
¼ cup (½ stick) soy margarine
⅓ cup low-fat milk or soy milk, or as needed

In a mixing bowl, combine the first five ingredients. Cut the margarine into bits and work into the flour with a pastry blender or the tines of a fork until the mixture resembles coarse crumbs. Add enough milk to hold the dough together. The dough should be light-textured, but not sticky. Turn the dough out onto a well-floured board and knead briefly. Form into a ball, then roll out into a round, about 10 inches in diameter. Cut into eight even pie-wedge shapes and arrange them on a heated griddle. Cook each wedge on both sides over moderate heat for about 8 to 10 minutes on each side, or until golden brown. Serve warm.

BUCKWHEAT FLOUR

Buckwheat flour is milled from buckwheat groats, the seeds of a plant that is not a grain at all but a relative of dock and rhubarb. Strong-flavored buckwheat flour is most familiar to North Americans from its use in buckwheat pancakes, a fixture on American tables in the nineteenth century and still quite popular in the southern states today. Buckwheat flour is also the basis of the famous Russian pancakes known as blini, which are traditionally embellished with sour cream and caviar. In Eastern and Northern Europe, buckwheat is used to make hearty sourdough breads, and in the Orient, to make the well-loved soba noodles.

Both dark and light buckwheat flours are available. The dark version is less refined and contains more of the hull. Dark buckwheat flour retains more of the valuable nutrients found in whole buckwheat, including a wide range of B vitamins and minerals such as calcium, phosphorus, and iron.

This powdery, grayish flour is commonly available in natural-food stores. Otherwise, you might contact Birkett Mills in Penn Yan, Pennsylvania; they specialize in buckwheat products (see appendix B.) Buckwheat flour keeps well for 2 to 3 months. For longer storage, refrigerate.

Buckwheat flour is heavy and low in gluten, so for successful use in yeast-risen breads, it's best to combine it with a high-gluten wheat flour, such as a spring wheat bread flour, or a high-gluten unbleached white flour. Substitute up to 30 percent of the wheat flour in yeasted breads with buckwheat flour. For use in pancakes, buckwheat may be used straight, or combine it with equal parts wheat flour of any kind. Up to 50 percent of wheat flour in recipes for muffins and quick breads may be substituted with buckwheat flour, but the more you use, the heavier the results will be. Buckwheat flour is good when combined with other distinctive flavors, such as molasses in breads and buttermilk in pancakes. It is also compatible in bread recipes that contain potato flour or mashed potatoes.

BUCKWHEAT FOCACCIA BREAD

Yield: 1 round loaf

The addition of buckwheat flour to this traditional Italian bread round gives it a robust flavor. Because only one brief rising is needed, this is not as time-consuming to make as most other yeasted breads. You might make it while waiting for a long-simmering soup; it makes an excellent accompaniment.

1 package active dry yeast
1 cup warm water
1/3 cup olive oil
1 teaspoon honey
1 teaspoon salt
3/4 cup buckwheat flour
3/4 cup whole wheat flour
1 cup unbleached white flour
1 clove garlic, minced, or garlic powder
  to taste
Coarse salt
Dried oregano or rosemary

Dissolve the yeast in the water for 5 to 10 minutes. Stir in half the olive oil, the honey, and the salt. In a mixing bowl, combine the flours and stir together. Work in the wet mixture until well blended. Turn out onto a well-floured board and knead for 5 minutes, adding additional wheat flour if necessary, just enough so that the dough loses its stickiness. Spread the dough out into a 12-inch circle. Smooth the top, then cover lightly with a thin tea towel and let rise for 40 to 50 minutes in a warm place.

When the dough had risen to about double its original bulk, poke shallow holes into the top at somewhat even intervals. Pour the remaining olive oil evenly over the surface, then sprinkle with the garlic, salt, and dried herbs. Bake in a preheated 400°F oven for 20 to 25 minutes, or until the round sounds hollow when tapped and it lightly golden. Tear at random or cut into wedges to serve.

—————CHICK-PEA FLOUR—————

This is not a flour in the usual sense, since it is finely milled from chick-peas and not from grain. Chick-pea flour is most prevalently used in Indian cuisine. Look for it in Indian specialty stores and through mail-order outlets. It is occasionally sold in bulk in natural-food stores. Store chick-pea flour in a tightly lidded jar in a cool, dry place. If you plan to keep it for more than 2 months, keep it refrigerated for optimal freshness.

The flavor of chick-pea flour is very reminiscent of these tasty legumes, without tasting raw or "beany." Replace up to 25 percent of wheat flour with chick-pea flour to make savory quick breads (it is especially nice in quick herb breads) and use the same replacement ratio in muffins, flat breads, and crackers. Use chick-pea flour for adding flavor and body to soup stock or add a small amount to fine bread crumbs to use for dredging foods to be fried.

Chick-pea flour is commonly used in Indian cuisine to make savory pancakes. These may be spread with spiced mung beans or lentils or any number of curried fillings. Here's a recipe I devised that is not particularly traditional, but it was a success nonetheless:

CHICK-PEA PANCAKES WITH CURRIED SWEET POTATOES

Yield: 4 servings

Pancakes:

1 cup chick-pea flour
1 cup water
1 teaspoon salt
1 teaspoon freshly grated ginger
Dash of cayenne pepper
2 teaspoons safflower oil

Filling:

2 tablespoons soy margarine
1 medium onion, chopped
**2 heaping cups diced cooked sweet
  potatoes**
2 teaspoons good curry powder
**1/2 teaspoon each: ground coriander, dry
  mustard, salt**
Dash of cayenne pepper
1/2 to 3/4 cup water
1/4 cup currants
1/4 cup slivered almonds

In a mixing bowl, combine the ingredients for the pancakes and beat together vigorously with a wire whisk until smoothly blended. Heat a 6- or 7-inch nonstick skillet. Pour 1/4 cup batter in at a time, tipping the skillet to coat it evenly. Cook on both sides until set. Repeat until eight pancakes have been made. Keep the pancakes covered until the filling is ready.

In a medium-sized skillet, melt the margarine. Add the onion and sauté until golden. Add the sweet potatoes, seasonings, and enough water to keep the bottom of the skillet moist. Simmer, covered, over low heat for 10 minutes, Add the currants and almonds and simmer for another 5 minutes.

To assemble, divide the filling among the eight pancakes, spooning some down the middle of each in the same way you'd fill a crepe. Fold one side over the other and arrange on plates, seam side down, allowing two per serving. Serve at once.

———— CORNMEAL ————

Corn has long been one of the most revered native crops of the Americas, and cornmeal was one of the important staples whose usage was passed on to the colonists by the Native Amer-icans to sustain them through arduous times. Cornmeal is milled from a variety of whole corn that has a high percentage of soft starch, allowing easy grinding.

There are several types of cornmeal available, some better than others. The best choice, whether buying it packaged or in bulk, is stone-ground, undegerminated whole cornmeal. In this case the corn has not been stripped of its nutritious germ. Undegerminated cornmeal spoils more quickly than the degerminated (and rather dry and flavorless) variety found in cardboard boxes in supermarkets. Spoilage need not be a concern, though, if you store the cornmeal in a cool, dry place and use it up within 2 to 3 months. During warm months, refrigeration is recommended. Whole cornmeal, at its freshest, will taste moister and sweeter in breads and other baked goods than the supermarket variety. The latter is refined to increase its shelf life but yields drier, more crumbly, and less flavorful results.

Cornmeal labeled *water-ground* is ground by millstones powered with water. This implies a smaller-scale production of meal and possibly a slightly better product, but it's more expensive. Another type of cornmeal is labeled *bolted*, meaning that it had been sifted, removing some hull material, which results in the loss of some nutrients and fiber. It's therefore not as desirable as stone-ground or water-ground meals.

In addition to these distinctions, there are also differences in the color of cornmeals. *Yellow cornmeal* is the most common, followed by *white cornmeal*, which is used more frequently in the southern United States. The flavor of white cornmeal is more delicate and slightly sweeter. Yellow cornmeal is slightly higher in protein and vitamin A, but the choice between the two is ultimately a matter of personal preference.

A relative newcomer to the speciality-food and natural-food markets is *blue cornmeal*. This is a product of the American Southwest, ground from blue corn. The color of the cornmeal is actually more of a slate blue-gray. It's flavor is nuttier than that of yellow or white cornmeal, and it yields moist results. Perhaps not as visually appealing in breads and muffins as it is in tortillas (blue corn tortillas are quite common in the Southwest), it is nevertheless very good in baked goods.

Whole cornmeal is high in calcium, vitamin A, and the valuable amino acid lysine, an amino acid usually in short supply in grains. It also provides modest amounts of phosphorus and B vitamins.

Cornmeal must be used in conjunction with wheat flour in yeasted breads, since it contains no gluten. Replacing up to 25 percent of the flour with cornmeal adds wonderful texture. In baking powder-risen pan breads, a quantity of wheat flour is also usually needed to improve the texture of the bread and make it less crumbly. More or less equal proportions of cornmeal and wheat flour is a good rule of thumb. Try replacing 25 percent of the flour in cookies with cornmeal for an unusual flavor twist.

Cornmeal is the basis of many classic American recipes, including the familiar pan cornbreads, as well as hoecakes, johnnycakes, hasty and Indian puddings, and much more. Explore American regional cookbooks for these (as well as many other) cornmeal recipes. If you want to use cornmeal more often, additional sources for recipes are natural-food and vegetarian cookbooks, which seem to favor its use, as well as books on whole-grain breads (see appendix C).

Here are a few other ideas:

Basic Cooked Cornmeal Bring 1 quart water to a boil in a large, heavy saucepan or double boiler. Add 1/2 teaspoon salt. Begin stirring the water with a whisk while sprinkling in the cornmeal in a thin, steady stream. Once all the cornmeal is in, turn the heat to very low and cook for 20 to 25 minutes, or until the water is absorbed and the mixture is thick and smooth. Here we call it cornmeal mush: in Italy, cooked cornmeal is called polenta.

- Cooked cornmeal may be buttered and eaten as a hot cereal.

- Spread cooked cornmeal on a lightly oiled dinner plate or in one or more pie pans in a thickness of about 1/2 inch. Refrigerate overnight. Cut into small squares and fry on a bit of soy margarine in a hot skillet until golden brown and crisp on each side. Serve hot, plain, or with maple syrup or fruit butter.

- Cook 1 cup cornmeal as directed in "Basic Cooked Cornmeal," above. When done, pour it into an oiled, round 1 1/2-quart casserole dish and bake at 375°F for 15 minutes. Remove from the oven and top with sautéed fresh mushrooms, tomatoes, zucchini, herbs, and grated mozzarella cheese. Return to the oven and bake for 15 to 20 minutes at 375°F. Allow to cool for 10 minutes, then cut into wedges to serve. Serves 4 to 6.

- Cooked cornmeal is the basis of a southern American classic known as spoonbread, which is more of a soufflé than a bread. Cook the cornmeal as directed above in "Basic Cooked Cornmeal," but use only half the quantity of water given in the directions and cook for 15 to 20 minutes. Stir 2 tablespoons soy margarine into the cornmeal, then whisk in 1 cup low-fat milk and 3 egg yolks. Beat 3 egg whites until they form stiff peaks and fold into the cornmeal mixture. Pour into an oiled 1 1/2-quart casserole dish or soufflé pan. Bake at 375°F for 30 to 35 minutes, or until puffed and lightly browned.

- *Cornmeal Dumplings*: Combine 1/2 cup cornmeal with 1/2 cup whole wheat flour. Add 1 teaspoon baking powder, 1 teaspoon salt, 1 tablespoon oil, and 1/2 cup water. Work together and shape into 1-inch balls. Drop into boiling water and cook at a steady simmer for 15 minutes.

- *Cornmeal Pizza Dough*: Substitute 1/2 cup of the wheat flour with cornmeal in your favorite pizza dough recipe (or see 100 Percent Whole Wheat Pizza Dough, page 104). Give the pizza a Mexican flavor by using Cheddar instead of mozzarella cheese and adding corn kernels, green chilies, and bell pepper strips to the topping.

- Finally, who can resist fresh, rich-tasting corn muffins or breads? Using buttermilk or yogurt instead of plain milk does a lot for the flavor of cornbreads. Make sure to use 1/2 teaspoon of baking soda for every cup of buttermilk or yogurt used.

CHEDDAR CORN MUFFINS

Yield: 1 dozen

3/4 cup whole wheat flour
3/4 cup cornmeal
1/4 cup unbleached white flour
1 teaspoon baking powder
1/2 teaspoon salt
1/2 teaspoon baking soda
2 eggs, beaten
2 tablespoons honey
1/4 cup soy margarine, melted
1 cup buttermilk or yogurt
1 cup grated Cheddar cheese
1/2 cup cooked corn kernels (optional)

Preheat the oven to 375°F.

Combine the first six ingredients in a mixing bowl.

In a smaller bowl, combine the remaining ingredients and mix thoroughly. Add the wet ingredients to the dry and stir vigorously to combine. Divide among oiled muffin cups. Bake for 12 to 15 minutes, or until a toothpick inserted into the center of one tests clean.

CORN FLOUR

Corn flour can be milled from either whole or hulled degerminated corn kernels. It's consistency is finer than that of cornmeal. It's not as commonly available as cornmeal, but may be used in most of the same ways, particularly where a finer texture is desired, such as in pancakes, cookies, and light-textured breads. Corn flour is used to make corn pastas.

MASA HARINA

Used primarily in making corn tortillas and tamales, masa harina is made from corn kernels that have been soaked in lime (calcium hydroxide) or other alkaline substance to remove the hulls. The hulled kernels are then dried and finely milled. Masa harina has a somewhat more distinct aroma and finer texture than cornmeal.

Masa harina is sold in 5- or 10-pound bags in supermarkets and Mexican speciality groceries. If stored in a cool, dry place, masa harina will keep well for several months. However, unless you plan to make tortillas or tamales on a reg-

ular basis (both rather involved productions), masa harina has limited use, and even a small bag may be hard to finish.

MILLET FLOUR

Ground from the highly nutritious millet seed, millet flour is a slightly coarse meal that resembles cornmeal. Millet flour is a staple in Africa, particularly Ethiopia, where it is used to make the national bread. In India, it is sometimes used to make the flat bread roti. Though infrequently used in Western cuisines, millet flour is occasionally available in natural-food stores and through mail-order sources (see appendix B). Millet is a nutritious, easily digested grain that provides high-quality protein. It contains a wide range of B vitamins and generous amounts of calcium and potassium. Millet is particularly rich in iron.

If millet flour is used on its own, without combining it with other flours, the results are dry, crumbly, and slightly bitter. Substituted for about 20 percent of the flour in yeast breads, batter breads, griddle cakes, or muffins, millet flour adds an interesting texture without being overpowering. It adds neither softness nor moistness to the crumb.

POTATO-MILLET DUMPLINGS

Yield: 12 to 14 dumplings

These flavorful dumplings can be used in soups, or as a side dish, sautéed in a bit of soy margarine and sprinkled with grated Parmesan cheese.

1 cup cold mashed potato
1 egg, beaten
1/2 cup millet flour
1/4 cup unbleached white flour
1 tablespoon minced fresh parsley
1 bunch scallions, green part only, minced
1/2 teaspoon salt

Combine the mashed potato with the beaten egg. Work in the flours, then stir in the parsley, scallions and salt. Shape into balls about 1 inch in diameter.

Bring 2 quarts of water to a rolling boil in a large soup kettle or Dutch oven. Drop the dumplings in gently. Reduce the heat until the water maintains a gentle simmer. Cook for 15 minutes and drain.

OAT FLOUR

Soft, delicate-flavored oat flour, finely milled from rolled oats, is a welcome addition to all forms of baking. Since oats are never refined before processing, the nutritious bran and germ remain intact. Thus, oat flour retains most of the nutrients present in whole oats, which are considerable. Oats contain seven B vitamins plus significant amounts of iron, calcium, and phosphorus. Oats are high in protein at 14 percent. The bran in oats has been shown to have properties that lower the blood cholesterol level.

Oat flour is occasionally available in natural-food stores, but if you can't find it, explore mail-order sources (see appendix B). Though oats contain more fat than most grains, they also contain a natural antioxidant, a substance that retards spoilage. Keep oat flour in a cool, dry place in a tightly lidded jar for up to 2 months. If you plan on keeping it more than 2 months, keep it refrigerated.

Commonly used in traditional Scottish cookery, oat flour added to baked goods contributes to a moist, tender crumb. Oat flour makes very tender, flavorful crêpes when substituted for wheat flour in whole or in part in crêpe recipes; the same is true for pancakes, where it can be substituted in whole or in any part for wheat flour. Three parts oat flour combined with 1 part cornmeal makes a wonderful mix in buttermilk pancakes. For wheat-free baked goods, oat flour may be substituted for 100 percent of wheat flour in baking-powder-risen recipes; it is particularly good in cookies, but in other recipes the results will be soft and crumbly. In yeasted breads, substitute oat flour for 20 percent of the wheat flour, and in quick breads and muffins, for up to 50 percent. Oat flour is especially good in fruit breads and cheese breads.

CHEDDAR-OAT BANNOCKS

Yield: 1 bannock bread

Bannocks are traditional Scottish flatbreads, similar to scones. These easy bannocks are wonderful served with hearty bean soups.

1 cup oat flour
½ cup rolled oats
½ cup whole wheat flour
1 teaspoon salt
1 teaspoon baking powder
¼ cup (½ stick) soy margarine, softened

1 cup firmly packed grated Cheddar cheese
¼ cup milk, or as needed
Poppy seeds for topping

Preheat the oven to 350°F.

Combine the first five ingredients in a mixing bowl. Blend the margarine into the mixture with the tines of a fork until the mixture resembles a coarse meal. Stir in the Cheddar cheese, then add milk as needed to form a soft dough. Turn out onto a floured board and knead briefly with floured hands. Form into a ball, then flatten. Roll into a round about ½ inch thick. Place on a lightly oiled baking sheet and sprinkle with poppy seeds. Score about halfway through with a knife to make six or eight wedges. Bake for 10 to 12 minutes, or until the top is nicely golden.

POTATO FLOUR

Not actually flour in the usual sense, potato flour is ground from cooked, dehydrated, potatoes. This versatile product is primarily sold in bulk in natural-food stores and co-ops. Potato flour may be stored in tightly lidded jars for several months in a cool, dry place. Potato flour is low in fat and contains moderate amounts of vitamin C, B vitamins, and minerals, such as iron and potassium.

Replace 25 percent of wheat flour with potato flour in recipes for yeasted breads. Replace up to 30 percent of the wheat flour with potato flour in quick breads, muffins, biscuits, and griddle cakes to add a subtle potato flavor. Sprinkle potato flour in soups to give body and flavor to the stock. Start with a tablespoon and add more if necessary. This is a tastier, less gummy thickener for soup stock than is wheat flour. Use it to thicken sauces as well. Here are two additional ways to make use of potato flour:

- *"Instant Mashed Potatoes":* This formula is quite handy to use in baking instead of fresh mashed potatoes if you're short on time. Whisk enough water or low-fat milk together with the potato flour to achieve the texture of mashed potatoes. About ⅓ cup potato flour and ⅔ cup liquid will make 1 cup "mashed potatoes." This adds a superb flavor and moist texture to breads, muffins, and biscuits.

- Use potato flour to make quick savory griddle cakes. Combine 1/2 cup potato flour, 1/4 cup wheat germ, 1 1/2 cups water, 1/4 cup yogurt, and salt and pepper. Work the mixture together, shape into palm-size croquettes, and fry in oil or soy margarine on both sides until golden and crisp. Makes about 18 small cakes.

POTATO-HERB BISCUITS

Yield: 1 dozen

1 1/2 cups whole wheat flour
2/3 cup potato flour
1 1/2 teaspoons baking powder
1/2 teaspoon baking soda
1 teaspoon salt
1/3 cup (2/3 stick) soy margarine
1 cup buttermilk
3 tablespoons finely minced fresh herbs

Preheat the oven to 425°F.

Combine the first five ingredients in a mixing bowl. Cut the soy margarine into bits and rub it into the flour mixture until the mixture resembles a coarse meal. Work in the buttermilk and herbs to form a soft dough. Divide into twelve parts; roll into balls and set on a baking sheet. Flatten the balls slightly. Bake for 10 to 12 minutes.

QUINOA FLOUR

A relative newcomer to the natural foods market, quinoa (pronounced KEENwa) flour is milled from the tiny, highly nutritious grain of the same name that was once a staple crop of ancient South American Indians. (For a more complete description of quinoa, see page 17.) Along with grain amaranth, quinoa is being promoted as a food of the future due to its unusually strong nutritional profile. Quinoa and amaranth are the only two grains that provide nearly complete protein. At 16 percent protein, they exceed most other grains in protein quantity as well. Like whole-grain quinoa, quinoa flour is nutrient-rich, providing generous amounts of the B-vitamin complex and vitamin E, and the minerals calcium, phosphorus, and iron.

Quinoa is still being grown as a specialty crop and is not a staple offering in every natural-food store. If your retailer doesn't carry it, you may order quinoa flour directly from the Quinoa Corporation (see appendix B). Quinoa flour is best kept refrigerated.

A flour higher in fat than most others, quinoa contributes to a tender, moist crumb and adds a rich, nutty taste to baked goods. Substitute up to 50 percent quinoa flour for wheat flour in baking-powder-risen recipes, such as quick breads, muffins, cookies, cakes, pancakes, and biscuits. For a real boost in nutrients and flavor, replace up to 25 percent of the wheat flour in yeasted-bread recipes with quinoa flour.

When ordering quinoa flour from the Quinoa Corporation, request their free recipe pamphlet. Recipes include crepes, breads, pizza crust, and even a béchamel sauce. The recipe for this flavorful wheat-free cracker is courtesy of the Quinoa Corporation:

QUINOA CRACKERS

Yield: 2 dozen 3-inch crackers

1 cup quinoa flour
1 cup rye flour
1 cup rolled oats
1/2 teaspoon salt
1/2 cup lightly refined corn or sesame oil
1/2 cup water, approximately
2 tablespoons hulled whole sesame seeds
Flour for dusting

Glaze:

2 teaspoons natural soy sauce
2 teaspoons oil

Preheat the oven to 425° F.

In a mixing bowl, combine the flours, oats, sesame seeds, and salt. With your fingertips or with the tines of a fork, rub in the oil. Gradually add water to form a workable but soft dough. Knead lightly for 2 to 3 minutes. Cover the dough and allow to rest for 10 minutes. On a well-floured pastry cloth or board, roll out the dough to 1/8 inch thickness (this is easier done if the dough is divided into two or three batches). Cut crackers into 3-inch circles and place on an oiled or seasoned cookie sheet.

In a small bowl, combine the soy sauce and oil. With a pastry brush, glaze the crackers. Bake for 7 to 10 minutes, or until the crackers are lightly browned. Remove and cool on a rack.

RICE FLOUR

Once a staple in the traditional baking of the southern United States (especially South Carolina), rice flour is widely available in natural-food stores. White rice and brown rice flours are marketed, and predictably brown rice flour is more flavorful and nutritious than refined white rice flour. White rice flour, like the polished grain, is low in fiber and protein and contains only the four nutrients with which it is enriched—iron and three B vitamins. Brown rice flour contains a wider range of B vitamins and minerals as well as vitamin E.

Natural-food stores are more likely to sell brown rice flour than the refined variety, and it comes in packages or in bulk. Store in a cool, dry place for 2 to 3 months. If you plan on keeping it longer than that, keep it refrigerated.

If used on its own or in great part in baking-powder-risen recipes, rice flour often yields disappointing results, with a dry, crumbly texture. It is more successful when combined in smaller ratios with other flours. Replace up to 30 percent of wheat flour with rice flour in baking-powder-risen recipes, such as quick breads, muffins, and griddle cakes. Replace up to 20 percent of wheat flour with rice flour in yeasted bread recipes. Rice flour adds softness, but not moistness, to the crumb. Frankly, it does not add a great deal of character or flavor to baked goods, though it is more successful in cracker recipes. If you like the idea of adding the goodness of brown rice to baked goods, consider adding well-cooked whole brown rice or cooked rice flakes (page 21) for tasty, moist, and chewy results.

Rice flour is a staple in West Africa, where it is used both in cooking and in baking. This unusual pancake was inspired by a West African recipe.

RICE FLOUR–PLANTAIN PANCAKES

Yield: 18–20 small pancakes

2 brown-ripe, medium-size plantains
1 cup rice flour
1 teaspoon baking powder
1/2 teaspoon salt
2 shallots, minced
1 or 2 green chilies, minced
1 egg, beaten
1 cup low-fat milk or soy milk, or as
  needed

Oil for frying
Plain yogurt for topping

Preheat the oven to 375°F.

Trim the tips off the plantains and cut a lengthwise slit down the middle of each. Set in a shallow baking pan covered with foil and bake for 35 to 40 minutes, or until tender. Remove and allow to cool. Peel and mash.

In a mixing bowl, combine the mashed plantain with the rice flour and the remaining ingredients, using enough water or milk to make a medium-thick batter. Drop in heaping tablespoonfuls onto a hot, oiled skillet and fry over moderate heat on both sides until golden brown and crisp. Serve warm and pass around yogurt for topping.

RYE FLOUR

Few breads are more irresistable than fresh, hearty dark rye bread—once considered a "peasant food." A classic bread grain in Scandinavia, Germany, and the Soviet Union, rye bread is also relished by North Americans for its pleasantly sour flavor and chewy texture.

Dark rye flour, the least refined form of rye flour, is even more nutritious than whole wheat flour. High in good-quality protein, minerals (especially potassium), and the B vitamins, dark rye flour (sometimes labeled stone-ground) is what you should look for in natural-food stores, where it is usually sold in bulk. It looks coarser than light and medium rye flours because it contains all the bran and germ of the whole rye berry. Light and even medium rye flours have been refined of much of the nutritious bran and germ and have a fine texture and pale-gray color. These are often sold in 5-pound bags in supermarkets. Store dark rye flour in a cool, dry place in a tightly lidded jar for up to 2 months. If you plan on keeping it longer than that, refrigerate it. Light and medium rye flours are less susceptible to spoilage and can be kept at room temperature somewhat longer.

It is rather impractical to make 100 percent rye bread, since the gluten content is low, and careful and expert handling are needed. In addition, the dough made from rye flour is very sticky and needs long rising periods. However, combined with wheat flour, it's not difficult to get great results. Equal proportions of rye and wheat flours can be used in yeasted breads. 30 to 50 percent of the wheat flour may be replaced with rye flour in quick bread, muffins, and flat breads. The results in baking-powder-risen baked goods are dense and somewhat crumbly. Replace up to 50 percent of the wheat flour with rye flour in buttermilk pancakes for a delicious breakfast treat.

Some great additions to rye breads are sprouted rye berries (see appendix A), caraway seeds, raisins or currants, and cornmeal. And what bread is more synonymous with sourdough than rye? Almost any book on baking with whole grains will have a good selection of rye bread recipes. A fine source is *Great Whole Grain Breads*, by Beatrice Ojakangas (E. P. Dutton, 1984), which features a lengthy section on tempting rye breads.

ONION-RYE DINNER ROLLS

Yield: 1 dozen rolls

1 envelope active dry yeast
2 cups warm water
3 tablespoons barley malt syrup or
 blackstrap molasses
¼ cup safflower oil
1 teaspoon salt
2½ cups rye flour
1 cup unbleached white flour
1½ cups whole wheat flour
½ cup cornmeal

1 tablespoon safflower oil
1 large onion, finely chopped

Combine the yeast with the lukewarm water in a small bowl and allow to stand for 10 minutes. Stir in the barley malt syrup or molasses and salt.

In a large mixing bowl, combine the flours and the cornmeal. Pour in the liquid and work together to form a dough. Turn out onto a floured board and add enough additional flour (either whole wheat or rye) until the dough loses some of its stickiness. Knead for 8 to 10 minutes, or until smooth and elastic. Form into a round and place in a floured bowl. Cover and let rise in a warm place until doubled in bulk, about 1½ hours. Punch down and divide into twelve more or less equal parts. Shape each into smooth rounds, flatten slightly, and arrange on two lightly oiled or seasoned cookie sheets. Allow to rise again, about 1 hour.

Heat the oil in a small skillet. Sauté the onion over moderate heat until lightly browned. Distribute evenly over the rolls. Bake in a pre-heated 350°F oven for 30 to 35 minutes, or until the rolls feel hollow when tapped. Cool on a rack.

SOY FLOUR

Two types of soy flour are commonly available in natural food stores, one called *full-fat soy flour* and the other *defatted soy flour*. Full-fat soy flour (occasionally labeled natural soy flour, since it is not processed as much as its counterpart) is made from whole, raw soybeans which have been dehulled, cracked, and finely ground. Sometimes the soybeans are heat-treated before being milled in order to deactivate an enzyme that inhibits digestion of soy protein. This process also helps tone down the raw, "beany" flavor. When buying soy flour in bulk, there is usually no way to know whether the soybeans were heated, but any cooking or baking you do with soy flour will deactivate this enzyme. To help coax the flavor of the flour from "beany" to nutty, toast the amount you will be using in a dry skillet over moderate heat for 5 to 7 minutes, stirring occasionally.

Full-fat soy flour, like whole soybeans, is 20 percent fat and 35 percent protein and retains most of the original nutrients, notably the B-complex vitamins, vitamin E, and the minerals phosphorus, calcium, and iron.

Defatted soy flour is made from the soybean pulp left over after expressing oil from the bean to make soybean oil. The oil is separated from the bean by the hexane solvent method, a chemical process; there is no evidence that this process is harmful. Because so much of the oil is removed, the protein in defatted soy flour becomes much more concentrated, the end result being anywhere from 40 to 60 percent protein and between 1 and 6 percent fat, depending on how much oil has been removed. The vitamin-E content goes out with the oil, but the other nutrients, as described for the full-fat version, remain intact.

Chances are that defatted soy flour will have been exposed to heat during processing, which destroys the unwanted protein-inhibiting enzyme. Toasting the flour or cooking or baking with it also ensures that this enzyme will no longer be present.

If the soy flour sold in bulk in your natural-food store is not specifically labeled, ask your retailer what you are getting. Full-fat flour is particularly susceptible to rancidity, so you need to know that your source has a good turnover. Both full-fat and defatted soy flours should be refrigerated once you get them home. The defatted flour might contain up to 6 percent fat, which is still higher than the fat content of whole wheat flour.

One additional difference between full-fat and defatted soy flours is the flavor. The defatted version tastes less "beany," but it may also have a slightly bitter aftertaste. The two may be used interchangeably in recipes, so from this point on, to avoid repetition, I'll simply refer to both as soy flour.

Soy flour contributes to a tender, moist, and nicely browned crumb to baked goods, but it has an assertive flavor, so is best used in moderation. Customarily, soy flour is mixed with other flours in baked goods. Soy flour can replace up to 15 percent (about 2 to 2 1/2 tablespoons per cup) of wheat flour in yeast baking and can be used to replace higher proportions (about 1/4 cup per cup) of flour in quick breads, muffins, biscuits, and griddle cakes. Even when used in small amounts, soy flour increases the usability of the proteins in grain flours significantly.

SOY-TOMATO QUICK BREAD

Yield: 1 loaf

This easy and unusual bread is a good companion to hearty soups.

2 1/4 cups whole wheat flour
1/2 cup soy flour
1 1/2 cups baking powder
1 teaspoon baking soda
1 teaspoon salt
2 eggs, beaten
1/4 cup safflower oil

2 tablespoons honey
2 tablespoons finely minced fresh parsley
One 14-ounce can imported plum tomatoes, with liquid
Poppy seeds for topping

Preheat the oven to 350°F.

Combine the first five ingredients in a mixing bowl. In another bowl, combine the beaten eggs with the oil, honey, and parsley. Crush the tomatoes with your hands to break them apart into small pieces. Add them to the liquid ingredients. Combine the wet and dry ingredients and stir until well blended. Pour into an oiled 9-by-5-by-3-inch loaf pan. Sprinkle poppy seeds over the top. Bake for 45 to 50 minutes, or until a knife tests clean when inserted in the middle and the top is nicely browned.

━━━━━━━TRITICALE FLOUR━━━━━━━

The world's first man-made grain, triticale (pronounced tri-ti-CAY-lee) is a specially developed hybrid of wheat and rye (for further information, see page 24). The flour resulting in milling of the whole grain has some of the characteristics of both its parent grains. At 16 percent protein, triticale is higher in protein than both rye or wheat and has greater percentages of the essential amino acids. Triticale, though not fully analyzed for nutrients by the USDA, is believed to be rich in B vitamins and minerals. Its flavor combines the nuttiness of whole wheat with a bit of the characteristic, pleasantly sour flavor of rye. Breads made with triticale flour are chewy, like rye bread.

Triticale flour is occasionally available in bulk or in packages in natural-food stores. If you can't find it, explore mail-order grain mills (see appendix B). Triticale flour may be stored in a cool, dry place for up to 2 months. If you plan on keeping it longer than that, store it in the refrigerator.

Triticale flour has a delicate gluten, so handling and kneading should be kept to a minimum. The gluten level is too low to be used entirely on its own in yeasted breads, so it is recommended that it be used in more or less equal parts with whole wheat bread flour or with a small portion of unbleached white flour or gluten flour. With whole wheat, a very dense, chewy texture is achieved, while with unbleached white, a fine, high-risen loaf will result. Only one rising is needed for triticale doughs. In baking-powder-risen recipes, such as quick breads, muffins, and griddle cakes, triticale flour may be used in equal proportions with whole wheat flour for good, hearty results.

TRITICALE HERB BREAD

Yield: 2 loaves

1 cup warm (110–115°F) low-fat milk or
    soy milk
1 cup warm (110–115°F) water
2 packages active dry yeast
3 tablespoons honey
3 tablespoons safflower oil
1 teaspoon salt
1 egg, beaten
2 cups triticale flour
1 1/2 cups whole wheat flour
1 1/2 cups unbleached white flour
2 teaspoons each: dried chives, dried dill,
    sesame seeds

In a mixing bowl, combine the first five ingredients. Let stand for 5 to 10 minutes, or until the yeast is dissolved. Stir in the salt and beaten egg. In a large bowl, combine the remaining ingredients and stir together. Make a well in the center and pour in the wet mixture. Work together just until well blended, using a wooden spoon at first and then well-floured hands. Transfer the dough to a well-floured board. Knead gently for 5 to 7 minutes, adding a bit more flour if necessary for the dough to lose its stickiness.

Divide the dough into two equal parts. Shape into loaves and place into two lightly oiled loaf pans. Let rise in a warm place until doubled in bulk, about 1 to 1 1/2 hours.

Heat the oven to 350°F. Bake the loaves for 45 to 50 minutes, or until they feel hollow when tapped and are nicely browned. When cool enough to handle, remove from the pans and cool on a rack.

——————WHEAT FLOUR——————

Concluding this chapter on the array of natural flours and meals is wheat flour, the cornerstone of bread making. What sets wheat flour apart from the others is its gluten content. Gluten, a protein that gives bread the ability to rise, is far more prevalent in wheat than in any other grain. It is the component of dough that becomes stretchy and elastic when kneaded. Some types of wheat flour have more gluten than others and produce different results in baking. These will be differentiated below.

Refined wheat flour was already the norm by the nineteenth century, when Sylvester Graham, the renowned American clergyman and reformer, raised vociferous objections against it. He claimed that the refinement of flour was "to put asunder what God joined together" and proceeded to promote a rather coarse, whole wheat flour, which came to be known as graham flour. From that time on, a small but vocal minority of wholefood advocates have sought to bring whole wheat flour back into general use.

Whole wheat flour is ground from the wheat berry, which is comprised of three basic components: the *bran*, which is the six or so outer layers of the grain; the *germ*, which is a very small area inside the base of the grain; and the *endosperm*, which comprises about 82 percent of the grain. The endosperm contains 70 percent of the protein and most of the starch. It is the bran and germ that contain most of the nutrients of the grain, and when these are removed, so goes most of the goodness of the wheat. The bran and germ contain 75 percent of the eleven B vitamins, plus the greater part of the minerals. The germ contains important amounts of vitamin E, and the fiber is concentrated in the bran. When the bran and germ are refined from the grain, 80 percent of the nutrients and most of the fiber leave with them.

What Americans have been consuming, for the most part, is refined, enriched, and bleached white flour. When flour is enriched, only four of the nutrients removed in processing are added back. The fiber is all but gone in refined flour and, once removed, cannot be put back.

Natural-food stores, food mills, and an increasing number of supermarkets are all sources for the various types of whole wheat flours outlined below. Unbleached flour and gluten flour, though refined, are also included, since their superb rising abilities often make them very useful as a component in whole-grain bread making.

Optimal storage time for whole wheat flour is 2 months, in a cool, dry place. During this time, the vitamin E acts as a natural preservative, but after this it diminishes. Some of the B vitamins, too, may begin to break down with lengthy storage. Refrigerate whole wheat flours if you plan to keep them for longer than 2 months, and at all times during warm weather.

WHOLE WHEAT BREAD FLOUR

This is usually termed simply *whole wheat flour* when bought packaged or in bulk, but sometimes the word *bread* is inserted to distinguish it from whole wheat pastry flour. For the most part, this is milled from winter wheats, which are good for bread making and for general baking purposes, or from spring wheats, which make for even better results in leavened breads. Winter wheats are grown in milder climates and are higher in starch. Spring wheats are higher in protein. Each comes in "soft" and "hard" varieties, the latter being higher in gluten and thus preferable for use in yeast-risen breads.

Whole wheat flours come in varying grinds, but are not always labeled accordingly, except in the case of "stone-ground" flour. This labeling implies a coarse grind. Stone-ground flour is generally considered the best choice. This method of grinding exposes the grain to less heat than does milling with steel blades, thus protecting the nutrients, notably the B vitamins and vitamin E.

Whole wheat bread flour can be the basis for an astonishing array of breads and other baked goods. Dense, chewy whole wheat breads can be varied in a number of ways, with added sprouts or wheat berries for extra texture, honey for a sweet touch, eggs for tenderness, buttermilk for a pleasant tartness, or molasses for an earthy flavor. Whole wheat flour combines well with almost any other flour to create a range of textures and densities. Though bread making requires a commitment of time and effort, there are few culinary experiences more rewarding than taking fresh bread out of the oven. (See appendix C for books on baking with whole-grain flours.)

---

100 PERCENT WHOLE WHEAT PIZZA DOUGH

---

1 package active dry yeast
1 cup warm water
3 tablespoons safflower oil
2 ½ cups whole wheat bread flour
1 teaspoon salt

Dissolve the yeast in the warm water for 5 to 10 minutes. Stir in the oil. Combine the flour in a mixing bowl with the salt. Slowly pour in the liquid, stirring it in. Work together to form a smooth dough. Cover and let rest for 10 minutes.

Turn the dough out onto a well-floured board. Knead for 8 to 10 minutes until smooth and elastic. Place in a floured bowl, cover, and let rise in a warm place until doubled in bulk, about 1 to 1 ½ hours. Punch down and roll out to fit a cookie sheet. Top with desired toppings. Bake in a preheated oven at 400°F for 15 minutes, or until the crust is golden.

Topping ideas:

Traditional: Well-seasoned marinara sauce; sautéed mushrooms, broccoli or eggplant, bell pepper, and onions; mozzarella cheese.

Light: Fresh plum tomatoes as a base, topped with sautéed zucchini rounds, marinated artichoke hearts, Parmesan cheese.

Mexican: Enchilada sauce, sautéed chopped onions and bell peppers, chopped green chilies, Cheddar cheese.

WHOLE WHEAT PASTRY FLOUR

Whole wheat pastry flour may be milled from either spring or winter wheats, but the distinguishing characteristic is that they are softer wheats with lower gluten content than those used to make whole wheat bread flour. Whole wheat pastry flour has a finer texture than bread flour, but retains the germ and bran. It is excellent for use in cakes, pastries, muffins, piecrusts, quick breads, and pancakes, resulting in light-textured baked goods. Whole wheat pastry flour and whole wheat bread flour should not be used interchangeably in recipes.

CLASSIC CARROT BREAD

Yield: 1 loaf

2 eggs, beaten
1/3 cup safflower oil
2/3 cup light brown sugar
1 teaspoon vanilla extract
1 cup finely grated carrot
3 tablespoons apple or orange juice
1 1/2 cups whole wheat pastry flour
1 1/2 teaspoons baking powder
1/2 teaspoon salt
1 teaspoon cinnamon
1/4 teaspoon each ground cloves and allspice
1/3 cup chopped walnuts
1/3 cup raisins or currants

Preheat the oven to 350°F.

In a mixing bowl, beat the eggs together with the oil. Stir in the sugar until dissolved. Add the vanilla, carrot, and apple or orange juice.

Combine the next five ingredients in another bowl. Add the wet ingredients to the dry; beat together until thoroughly mixed. Stir in the chopped nuts and raisins or currants. Pour into an oiled loaf pan and bake for 45 to 50 minutes, or until a knife inserted into the center tests clean.

GLUTEN FLOUR

Gluten flour is a refined wheat flour that contains additional dried ground gluten. Though not a whole-grain flour, it is useful for combining in small quantities with low-gluten flours, such as rye, in order to achieve well-risen loaves. Using 1 part gluten flour with 4 or 5 parts whole wheat flour improves the texture of the loaves. One part gluten flour, 2 parts whole wheat flour, and 2 parts rye, triticale, or buckwheat flour will also yield good results.

GRAHAM FLOUR

Graham flour is not made the same way by every manufacturer, so this labeling can result in confusion. The label *graham flour*, a term that has lingered since the nineteenth century, is used to describe whole wheat flours with only the coarsest bran sifted out, or whole wheat flours with very coarse grinds, or stone-ground flours in which the germ and starchy endosperm of the grain are finely milled and the bran is left coarse. If you buy anything labeled graham flour, read the package information to clarify what you are buying.

UNBLEACHED WHITE FLOUR

This widely available, all-purpose flour is a refined, enriched flour that has not been bleached by chlorine dioxide, as are bleached flours. It is most useful when combined with heavy flours, such as whole wheat, buckwheat, or triticale, when finer textures or lighter risings are desired.

Chapter 6

PASTA AND NOODLES

Pasta and noodle cuisine immediately brings to mind two distinct locales: Italy and the Orient. Records of noodle making in China date back thousands of years, and Italians have been savoring pasta for many hundreds of years. Popular legend has it that it was the explorer Marco Polo who first brought noodles to Italy in the thirteenth century after discovering them during a voyage to China. By the Middle Ages, pasta was known in England under the name macaroni. In eighteenth-century England, it was considered such a delicacy that anything desirable or fashionable was called "macaroni"—like the feather in Yankee Doodle's cap.

If you do your shopping for pasta strictly at the supermarket, you're literally missing out on a world of variety. Pasta and noodles offered in natural-food stores, ethnic groceries, and specialty-food shops come in all manner of flours, flavors, shapes, and sizes. The wheat-intolerant pasta lover will also be pleased to know that these markets are good sources for several types of wheat-free pastas. Having recently shed a false image as being fattening, pastas and noodles are satisfying and nutritious, quick and easy to cook, and lend themselves to a myriad of enticing preparations.

NUTRITIONAL BENEFITS OF PASTAS

The nutritional values of the different varieties of pastas and noodles depend on the particular flours used to make them. In general, most pastas are good sources of protein (although the protein is incomplete and must be eaten with other protein foods, such as legumes, dairy products, nuts, or soy foods, to be readily usable by the body) and excellent sources of carbohydrates (that is, starches, complex sugars, and fiber). Whole-grain pastas contain far more fiber than do refined ones, as well as a wider range of vitamins and minerals. Pasta has recently been popularized by competitive runners as a high-energy food that supplies quick fuel for the body. A new tradition among such athletes is to eat spaghetti or some other form of pasta before a race. Even ordinary refined durum wheat pastas cannot be dismissed. Though not high in fiber, they are a source of good-quality protein, and because the flour used is usually enriched, they supply generous amounts of iron and the B vitamins niacin, thiamine and riboflavin.

Pastas and noodles are easy to digest and are low in fat and calories. An average serving (2 ounces) of standard durum wheat pasta, for example, contains only 1 gram of fat and 210 calories and provides 8 grams of protein. Many of the pastas listed here have not been specifically analyzed for nutrients by the USDA, but further information on their benefits may be found under the entries for the particular grains or flours from which they are made.

COOKING PASTAS AND NOODLES

Cooking pasta and noodles is a simple undertaking, but here are a few basic guidelines:

- Use 1/2 pound dry pasta to make 4 average servings.

- It is not necessary to measure the amount of water precisely. There should be enough to give the pasta plenty of room to simmer, and the more water used, the less gummy the cooked texture will be. A standard rule of thumb, however is to use about 5 quarts of water per pound of pasta or noodles.

- Bring the water to a rolling boil in a deep, heavy saucepan or Dutch oven. Stir in the pasta or noodles, stirring again several times during the first minute or so to prevent clumping. Some people like to add a tablespoon or so of cooking oil to the water, but with careful stirring, this really isn't necessary. Lower the heat and cook at a steady simmer until *al dente*, as the Italians say—that is, until it is done, but still has a good resistance to the tooth. Drain at once. It's best to have a sauce or other ingredients to be used in the recipe ready by the time the pasta or noodles are done, so that you can combine them right away.

- Don't rinse the pasta after cooking unless it is to be used immediately in a cold salad.

- To salt or not to salt the cooking water is a matter of preference and is a hotly debated issue among pasta lovers. Most Japanese noodles are already lightly salted, so I would not recommend adding more salt to their water. If you do want to add a bit of salt to other types of pasta, add it to the water once it has boiled.

These are the general steps. Whenever the cooking instructions vary for any of the pastas or noodles listed below, this is indicated in the individual entry.

PASTA STORAGE

Storage of pasta is not a great problem, since it is a food that is likely to get used up quickly. Like all grain products, storage in tightly sealed containers or jars in a cool, dry place ensures that pastas will keep well for several months. Whole-grain pastas will stay fresher if kept under refrigeration during hot summer months.

——— BROWN RICE PASTA ———

This wheat-free pasta is usually available as elbows or other small shapes. Made only from brown rice flour and a vegetable gum, it is appropriate for use by those who have an intolerance to wheat. However, it's difficult to be enthusiastic about it as a general-purpose alternative pasta due to its rather gummy texture.

Brown rice pasta cooks very much the way a similarly shaped wheat pasta would. Follow the guidelines on page 107. Brown rice elbows take about 8 minutes to cook. They can go from underdone to overdone rather quickly, with little leeway in between, so test frequently. The texture of this pasta is not firm and chewy like wheat pasta, but rather gives the sensation of chewing mashed rice. For a general-purpose, wheat-free alternative, shaped corn pasta has a flavor and texture much more akin to wheat pasta than does rice pasta.

BUCKWHEAT NOODLES (SOBA)

One of the most relished of the traditional foods of Japan, buckwheat noodles, or soba, are so immensely popular that their very name is steeped in folklore and ritual. Expressions indicating affection or expressing superlatives use soba as an analogy. Soba shops are a common sight in Japanese cities—usually small, snack-bar-type restaurants serving buckwheat noodle specialties.

Buckwheat noodles are commonly available in natural-food stores, as several domestic companies are involved in their importation and distribution. These noodles are always thin and spaghetti-shaped, but their buckwheat flour content varies, from as much as 80 percent buckwheat flour to as little as 20 percent. The packages usually state the proportion. If you buy them in bulk, ask your retailer what you are getting. The remaining proportion in the noodle consists of wheat flour. Predictably, the more buckwheat flour in the noodle, the more distinct the flavor will be. These lightly salted noodles are quite flavorful and not as difficult to acquire a taste for as are their whole-grain parent, buckwheat groats.

To cook buckwheat noodles, use the guidelines given on page 107. They take approximately 5 to 7 minutes to cook. Since their flavor is not at all delicate, these dark-brown noodles stand up particularly well to robust-flavored sauces and accompaniments.

- Serve buckwheat noodles as a side dish simply seasoned with sesame oil, minced scallions, and natural soy sauce. For interest, add a small amount of sea vegetables, such as shredded nori or reconstituted arame. To make this a main dish, simply add diced tofu or tempeh "croutons" (see page 63).

- Add cooked buckwheat noodles, cut into 2-inch lengths, to miso soups. They are particularly good in a broth along with winter root vegetables, flavored with freshly grated ginger.

- Add cooked buckwheat noodles to pureed green vegetable soups composed of flavorful vegetables, such as cream of broccoli, asparagus, or green beans.

- In a wide skillet, sauté 2 minced cloves garlic, 1 sliced yellow summer squash, and 1 sliced zucchini in 3 tablespoons good olive oil. When the squashes begin to brown lightly, add 1/2 pound chopped spinach and cook, covered, just until the spinach wilts. Combine with 1/2 pound cooked buckwheat noodles in a serving bowl. Toss in 1/4 cup grated Parmesan cheese, grind in some black pepper, and serve at once. Makes 4 to 6 servings.

- Toss buckwheat noodles with any kind of tomato-based or sweet-and-sour sauce.

- Use buckwheat noodles to make marinated cold salads. Combine 1/2 pound cooked buckwheat noodles with 1 cup each peeled and seeded cucumber, lightly steamed mung bean or soybean sprouts, and snow peas. Toss together with 1/2 cup of your favorite vinaigrette dressing and 2 teaspoons natural soy sauce. Refrigerate for several hours, stirring occasionally. This makes 4 to 6 servings.

SWEET-AND-SOUR BUCKWHEAT NOODLES WITH ASPARAGUS

Yield: 4 to 6 servings

1 tablespoon safflower or peanut oil
1 tablespoon sesame oil
1 medium onion, chopped
2 cloves garlic, minced
1 1/2 pounds asparagus, trimmed and cut into 1-inch lengths
One 14-ounce can imported plum tomatoes, with liquid, chopped
1/4 cup dry white wine
3 tablespoons rice vinegar
3 tablespoons honey
3 tablespoons natural soy sauce
1 tablespoon fermented black beans, chopped
1 1/2 tablespoons cornstarch
1/2 pound buckwheat noodles, broken in half
Freshly ground black pepper

Heat the oils in a large skillet or wok. Add the onion and garlic and sauté until the onion is translucent. Add the asparagus and stir-fry over moderately high heat until it is tender-crisp, about 5 to 7 minutes. Add the tomatoes, wine, vinegar, honey, soy sauce, and optional black beans. Dissolve the cornstarch in a small amount of water and stir into the mixture. Lower the heat and simmer while cooking the buckwheat noodles. When the buckwheat noodles are done, drain and rinse briefly under cool running water. Stir them into the skillet or wok and season to taste with freshly ground black pepper. Simmer for another minute, then serve at once.

CELLOPHANE NOODLES (BEAN THREAD NOODLES)

A noodle with many names (in addition to the above, you may find them marketed as *mung bean noodles*, *saifun*, *fun-see*, or *harusame*), fine, transparent cellophane noodles are strands of mung bean starch. Silky and almost gelatinous in texture, they are used in Japan and China but are even more common in other Southeast Asian cuisines—you'll likely encounter them in dishes offered in Thai, Indonesian, and Vietnamese restaurants.

Cellophane noodles are very tough when dried, so it's not recommended (indeed, it's almost impossible) that you break them by hand. Available in natural-food stores and Oriental groceries, they often come in manageable, 2-ounce bundles, which expand greatly when cooked. There are two ways of cooking them. One is to presoak the noodles in warm water for 20 to 30 minutes. Then, cut them into 3- to 4-inch lengths, immerse in a pot of boiling water, simmer for 2 to 3 minutes, and drain. The second way is to simply immerse the bundle of noodles in cold water in a saucepan, bring to a boil, then remove from the heat, cover, and let sit for 3 to 5 minutes, or until *al dente*. When the noodles are done, drain and rinse briefly under cool water. Place them on a board and cut them into 3- to 4-inch lengths.

It is the silky texture and the transparency of the noodles that make them an exotic change of pace, since their flavor is quite bland. They are most successful in dishes with flavorful sauces, or in well-seasoned, brothy soups. Add the cooked noodles to your recipes at the end of their cooking time; if they are allowed to simmer further for any length of time, they become overcooked very quickly. Cellophane noodles are good combined with exotic, earthy mushrooms, such as shiitakes or cepes, and with stir-fried vegetables whose crunch provides a good textural contrast, such as snow peas or bok choy.

VIETNAMESE-STYLE CELLOPHANE NOODLES

Yield: 4 to 6 servings

2 tablespoons peanut oil
1 large onion, quartered and thinly sliced
2 cloves garlic, minced
2 heaping cups thinly shredded cabbage
2 heaping cups diced fresh tomatoes
1/2 pound mung bean sprouts
1/2 pound tofu, diced
2 to 3 tablespoons rice vinegar, to taste
Red pepper flakes to taste
2 ounces cellophane noodles
Salt to taste
Chopped peanuts for garnish

Heat the oil in a large, heavy skillet or wok. Add the onion and fry over moderate heat until it is translucent. Turn up the heat, add the garlic and cabbage and stir-fry until the cabbage is tender-crisp and lightly browned, about 5 to 7 minutes. Add the tomatoes and sprouts and continue to fry, stirring frequently, until the tomatoes are soft and the sprouts tender-crisp, about 5 to 7 minutes. Stir in the vinegar, tofu and red pepper flakes. Remove from the heat.

Cook the cellophane noodles in one of the two ways described above. Toss them into the vegetable mixture. Add salt to taste, toss well, and serve at once, garnished with chopped peanuts.

CORN PASTA

Pasta made of natural blends of corn flours is a relatively recent innovation. It is of particular value to those who suffer from an intolerance to wheat but would still like to enjoy traditional pasta dishes. Its use need not be limited to those who can't eat wheat pastas, however, since it can be a pleasant alternative for general purposes. Corn pasta has a mild flavor that is faintly reminiscent of cornmeal.

Available in packages or in bulk, corn pasta comes in a variety of shapes, including spaghetti, shells, and ribbons. In addition to natural-food stores, many supermarkets offer this product in their natural-food sections.

Cook corn pasta according to the guidelines on page 107. The exact cooking time depends on the shape and thickness of the noodle and will range from approximately 7 to 12 minutes. Follow the package instructions or test often. Corn pasta is a bit stickier than wheat pasta, so use plenty of cooking water and stir carefully and often when it is first immersed, to prevent clumping. Corn spaghetti has a rather brittle texture that doesn't hold up too well in cooking. The small shapes, such as shells and elbows, have firmer textures when cooked and seem to have a smoother texture, too.

Use corn pasta as a substitute for wheat pasta in any non-Oriental noodle dish requiring small, shaped noodles. These noodles work well with tomato sauces, in macaroni-and-cheese casseroles, tossed with steamed vegetables, and in cold pasta salads.

CORN PASTA WITH PESTO AND FRESH CORN

Yield: 4 to 6 servings

Abounding with fresh corn, basil, and tomatoes, this aromatic dish is perfect for a quick summer supper.

1/2 pound corn pasta, preferably shells or elbows

Pesto:

1 1/2 cups fresh basil leaves
1/2 cup fresh parsley leaves
1/2 cup pine nuts or walnuts
1 or 2 cloves garlic
1/3 cup freshly grated Parmesan cheese
1/3 cup extra-virgin olive oil
1/2 teaspoon salt
Freshly ground black pepper to taste

2 medium ears fresh, cooked sweet corn

2 large, ripe tomatoes
1 tablespoon lemon juice

Cook the pasta until *al dente*. In the meantime, prepare the pesto sauce by placing all the ingredients into the container of a food processor and processing to a coarse puree. When the pasta is done, drain it and transfer to a serving bowl. Toss gently with the pesto.

Scrape the corn kernels off the cob with a sharp knife. Add them, along with the tomatoes and lemon juice to the pasta mixture. Toss gently but thoroughly and serve at once.

EGG NOODLES

Egg noodles are usually made of the same refined, enriched durum wheat flour that is used to make standard pastas, with a minimum of 5 1/2 percent egg solids added. They are most commonly shaped as ribbons of varying widths. In supermarkets, these noodles are commonly marketed under names that evoke Jewish or Pennsylvania Dutch traditions, since they are common to both cuisines.

Egg noodles are also quite commonplace in Chinese, Thai, Indonesian, and other Southeast Asian cuisines. They are shaped either as ribbons or long, fine strands. Either way, they come in small, tight bundles. Their flavor is similar to, though perhaps a bit stronger than, that of domestic egg noodles. Look for dried Oriental egg noodles in Oriental groceries and through Oriental mail-order food sources.

Non-Oriental egg noodles are cooked much the same as any pasta (follow the guidelines on page 107, and read package instructions for the precise cooking time). Their cooked texture is somewhat more tender than that of standard pastas.

To cook Oriental egg noodles, soak them in hot water for 10 minutes to separate the bundled strands, then drain. Bring approximately 2 1/2 quarts water to a boil for every 1/2 pound noodles. Cook fine strands for 2 to 4 minutes, ribbons for 4 to 6 minutes. Test frequently for doneness.

Neither Oriental nor domestic egg noodles should be used as a substitute for standard pastas in Italian recipes. Their flavor and texture are most compatible with subtle sauces and seasonings. They're also a bit too tender for use in cold noodle salads, but they are delicious tossed with stir-fried vegetables or delicate bits of seafood. Egg noodles are great in brothy soups, added once the soup is done or else cooked right in the broth. Here are a few additional ideas for using domestic egg noodles, followed by a recipe for the Oriental variety:

- A famous Jewish "comfort food," noodle kugel is a pudding that can be eaten as a dessert or as a light lunch. In a mixing bowl, combine 1/2 pound cooked egg noodles with 2 beaten eggs; 1 cup small-curd cottage cheese; 1 medium apple, peeled and grated; 1/4 cup honey; 1/2 cup raisins; and 1 teaspoon cinnamon. Toss gently and pour into a buttered large, shallow casserole dish. Bake at 325°F for 40 to 45 minutes, or until the top is deep golden and crusty. Serve warm (not hot) or at room temperature. Makes 6 or more servings.

- Sauté a large, thinly sliced onion and 2 to 3 cups thinly shredded cabbage in safflower oil until both are golden brown. In a serving bowl, toss the cabbage mixture with 1/2 pound cooked egg noodles. Sprinkle in 2 tablespoons wheat germ and 1 tablespoon poppy seeds and toss again. Serve as a side dish. Makes 4 servings.

- Here's an idea from the Pennsylvania Dutch tradition that makes an easy summer supper dish: Melt 2 tablespoons soy margarine in a wide skillet. Add 2 chopped onions and sauté until they are golden. Stir in 3 cups diced very ripe tomatoes, 1/4 cup water, 2 cups cooked fresh corn kernels, and 1/4 cup chopped parsley. Cook over moderate heat for 2 to 3 minutes. In a serving bowl, combine the skillet mixture with 1/2 pound hot cooked egg noodles. Season to taste with salt and pepper and toss gently. Serve at once. Makes 4 servings.

FRIED EGG NOODLES

Yield: 4 to 6 servings

This recipe was inspired by those that are traditional to Malaysia and Singapore. Use Oriental egg noodles if you can find them, cooking as directed above. If not, substitute standard egg noodles.

6 to 8 dried shiitake mushrooms
1/2 pound ribbon egg noodles, cooked and drained
3 tablespoons peanut oil
3 large stalks celery, sliced diagonally
2 to 3 cloves garlic, minced

One 10-ounce package frozen French-cut green beans, thawed
One 8-ounce can bamboo shoots, drained
2 to 3 tablespoons natural soy sauce, to taste
1 tablespoon dry sherry (optional)
1 teaspoon freshly grated ginger
1 tablespoon soy margarine or oil
2 eggs, beaten
Minced scallions for garnish

Soak the mushrooms for 15 minutes in hot water. Drain and reserve the liquid for another use; trim and discard the tough stems and slice the caps into strips. Begin cooking the egg noodles as directed above or according to package instructions. When done, drain and set aside.

While the noodles are cooking, heat the oil in a large skillet or wok. Add the celery and garlic and stir-fry over moderately high heat until the celery is tender-crisp. Add the noodles, mushrooms, green beans, bamboo shoots, soy sauce, optional sherry, and ginger and stir-fry for 10 minutes. Lower the heat and continue to fry, stirring occasionally until the noodles begin to brown lightly.

Heat the margarine or oil in a small skillet. When hot enough to make a drop of water sizzle, pour in the beaten eggs. Fry until set on top, then flip and fry briefly on the other side. Remove from the skillet and cut into small strips.

Remove the noodle mixture from the heat. Serve at once, garnishing each serving with strips of egg and some minced scallion.

JINENJO NOODLES

Imported from Japan, these noodles combine wheat flour with flour derived from the jinenjo root, a nutritious wild mountain yam. These mild, smooth-textured, and lightly salted noodles are spaghetti-shaped and quick-cooking. Cook them according to the guidelines on page 107. They take from 5 to 7 minutes to cook.

Use jinenjo noodles in any Oriental recipe calling for long noodles. Because of their delicate flavor, jinenjo noodles are particularly good added to light broths or combined with delicately flavored stir-fried vegetables such as summer squashes. Jinenjo noodles are tasty enough to be served as a simple side dish, simply seasoned with natural soy sauce and scallions, and topped with a sprinkling of sesame seeds.

RAMEN NOODLES

Long, wavy ramen noodles have become familiar through their use in soup mixes. The supermarket variety of these soup mixes use refined noodles and are packaged with dried meat stocks and artificial additives. The mixes found in natural-food stores make tasty, healthy, and quick soups. They come in several varieties, incorporating sea vegetables, dried mushrooms, miso, or herbs. The ramen noodles themselves also vary, coming in whole wheat or whole wheat mixed with rice flour or buckwheat flour. You may further embellish these soups by adding to them fresh, sliced mushrooms, chopped scallions, or drizzling in a well-beaten egg for an egg drop soup. Children seem to love these ramen noodle soups.

Occasionally, though not as often, whole-grain ramen noodles may be purchased without soup mixes in natural-food stores. They usually come in small packages of about 2 to 3 ounces, and for their weight, they are rather expensive. Their flavor varies according to the precise proportions of flours used to make them, but they are always flavorful enough to stand up to bold seasoning. Cook them according to the guidelines given on page 107. They take approximately 5 to 7 minutes to cook.

The appealing shape and texture of ramen noodles make them a nice addition to simple broths, such as miso broths, with the same embellishments suggested above, or for use as a simple side dish, flavored with soy sauce, scallions, or chopped, reconstituted sea vegetables. A package of ramen noodles cooked and added to a dish of colorful stir-fried vegetables and tofu adds an appetizing visual touch.

RICE-STICK NOODLES (RICE VERMICELLI, BIFUN)

Imported from the Orient in cellophane-wrapped 8-ounce or 1-pound bundles, rice-stick noodles are used extensively in many Southeast Asian cuisines. These long, fine noodles are not a whole-grain product, since the noodles are made from white rice and thus lack fiber and many of the nutrients present in whole-grain pastas. Nevertheless, rice-stick noodles are an interesting and offbeat product to use on occasion in ethnic recipes. Rice-sticks are a common offering both in natural-food stores and in Oriental groceries. They have the same bland flavor as white rice and a rather tender texture when cooked. Those who are wheat-intolerant may use rice-sticks as a substitute for wheat noodles in Oriental noodle recipes.

There are two ways of cooking rice-stick noodles. One is to soak the bundles in cold water for 15 to 20 minutes, then separate the noodles and cut them into manageable lengths. Immerse in plenty of boiling water and cook for 2 to 3 minutes. The second way is to simply immerse the bundles in boiling water and simmer for 3 to 5 minutes, or just until they are *al dente*. Drain, then place on a board and cut them into the desired length. Either way, these cook very quickly and should be tested frequently to avoid overcooking.

- Rice-stick noodles can be used as an offbeat alternative to rice as a bed of grain for stir-fried vegetables or seafood dishes.

- Cook 4 to 6 ounces of rice-stick noodles as directed above. Drain and rinse under cold water until cool. Combine with 2 cups mixed matchstick-cut vegetables such as carrots, bok choy, and green or red bell pepper, plus a can of drained Oriental mushrooms, such as enoki or straw mushrooms. Dress in Sesame-Soy Salad Dressing (page 142) and serve cold as a salad. This makes 4 to 6 servings.

- Rice-stick noodles make a nice addition to brothy soups. Add noodles soaked and cut as described above to the soup just before it is done. Simmer until the noodles are tender but firm.

- Rice-sticks may also be fried in hot oil and used as a crisp garnish. Heat about 1/4-inch of oil in a heavy skillet. When very hot, add a good handful of broken raw noodles and stir constantly until they puff and become opaque. These are delicious as a topping for stir-fried vegetables.

RICE-STICKS WITH CABBAGE AND EXOTIC MUSHROOMS

Yield: 4 to 6 servings

1/2 ounce dried cloud-ear mushrooms or
1 ounce dried shiitake mushrooms
One 8-ounce bundle rice-sticks
2 tablespoons peanut oil
1 teaspoon sesame oil
1 medium onion, halved and sliced

2 cloves garlic, minced
2 cups firmly packed thinly sliced white
   or savoy cabbage
2 tablespoons natural soy sauce
One 15-ounce can oyster (shimeji) or
   straw mushrooms
Liquid from canned mushrooms and
   soaking water from dried mushrooms
   to make 1 1/2 cups
1 1/2 tablespoons cornstarch

If using cloud-ears, soak them in boiling water in a covered, ovenproof dish for about 45 minutes. Cut them into thin strips about 2 inches long; reserve the liquid. If using shiitakes, soak them in hot water for 15 minutes. Remove and discard the tough stems and slice the caps; reserve the liquid.

Prepare the rice-sticks in either of the two ways directed above. When they are done, drain and cover them.

In a large, heavy skillet or wok, heat the oils. Add the onion and stir-fry until it is translucent. Add the garlic and cabbage and stir-fry until the cabbage is tender-crisp. Add the soy sauce and mushrooms and stir-fry for another minute or so.

Use a bit of the mushroom liquid to dissolve the cornstarch. Pour the liquid into the skillet or wok, and stir in the cornstarch. Add the cooked rice-sticks and toss the mixture together thoroughly but gently. Serve at once.

——— SOMEN ———

These spaghetti-shaped noodles are another Japanese import and are traditionally eaten cold during the summer months. The version imported for the Western natural-food market is a lightly salted, 100 percent whole wheat product, with a very smooth texture in comparison to domestic whole wheat spaghetti. They are usually available in cellophane-wrapped, 8-ounce packages.

Cook somen according to the guidelines on page 107 or follow package directions. They take from 6 to 8 minutes to cook to an *al dente* texture. Test frequently toward the end of their cooking time, then drain when they are done.

To depart from tradition, you may substitute somen anywhere you'd use a medium-thickness spaghetti—even with Italian tomato-based sauces. The results are excellent, because so-men are more flavorful and a bit more wholesome than ordinary semolina spaghetti, yet are not as heavy and grainy as domestic whole wheat spaghetti. Raw somen are also very good added to light broths, simmered until done, then served simply garnished with scallions. If you wish to stay true to tradition, use them in cold noodle salads, such as this one:

COLD SOMEN
WITH DAIKON AND CARROTS

Yield: 4 to 6 servings

4 dried shiitake mushrooms
1 medium daikon radish, cut into
   matchsticks (if unavailable, substitute
   a crisp white turnip)
2 large carrots, cut into matchsticks
One 8-ounce package somen

Dressing:

2 tablespoons natural soy sauce
1 to 2 tablespoons rice vinegar, to taste
1 tablespoon peanut oil
1 tablespoon sesame seeds
1 teaspoon honey

2 bunches scallions, chopped, for garnish

Soak the shiitakes in hot water for 15 minutes. Pat them dry, remove and discard the tough stems, and slice the caps; reserve the liquid for another use.

Have the vegetables cut as directed above before cooking the noodles. Cook the somen until they are *al dente*, about 7 to 8 minutes. Drain the rinse under cold water until cool. Combine the dressing ingredients in a small bowl and stir together until blended.

Combine all the ingredients in a serving dish. Toss thoroughly and garnish with the scallions. Chill until needed or serve at once.

——— SOY PASTA ———

Pastas made with soy flour (for specific information on soy flour, see page 101) usually also contain whole wheat flour. Wheat flour is the primary ingredient, and the highly nutritious soy flour most often comprises from 10 to 20 percent of the noodle, depending on the manufacturer. Even a small amount of soy flour teamed with wheat flour substantially increases protein quality and usability.

Wheat-and-soy pastas have firm textures that are less grainy than 100 percent whole wheat pastas. The flavor is predominantly that of whole wheat. Cook according to the guidelines on page 107. They take approximately 7 to 12 minutes to cook, depending on the size and shape of the noodle. Follow package instructions or test frequently.

Use soy pasta anywhere you'd use whole wheat pasta—in dishes with robustly seasoned tomato sauces, in casseroles, soups, and cold, marinated noodle salads.

UDON NOODLES

Udon are a long, rather thick, light-colored noodle traditional to Japan and are usually sold in cellophane-wrapped 8-ounce packages. Though udon noodles available in Oriental groceries are made from refined wheat flour, natural-food stores offer lightly salted udon noodles made from whole wheat flour. Their shape and size are similar to linguine, and their smooth, pleasant texture make them quite versatile, welcome in almost any Oriental or Western recipe that calls for long noodles.

Cook udon noodles according to the guidelines on page 107. Udon noodles take from 5 to 7 minutes to cook to an *al dente* texture.

- For a tasty side dish, season udon noodles with soy sauce and garnish with scallions or sesame seeds. To make a quick and healthy main dish, add some diced tofu.

- Try substituting udon in for spaghetti or linguine in your favorite Italian recipe, with a herbed tomato sauce or pesto.

- Combine 1/2 pound cold cooked udon with the recipe for spicy peanut sauce on page 81. Cold udon noodles are also excellent with sesame sauce.

- Udon noodles are excellent combined with stir-fried vegetables.

- Cut cooked udon into 2-inch lengths and add to miso broth.

UDON WITH SPINACH-MISO PESTO

Yield: 4 to 6 servings

Miso adds a rich, hearty flavor to this pesto, making a bold substitute for Parmesan cheese.

Pesto sauce:

3/4 pound spinach, washed and stemmed
1/2 cup firmly packed fresh basil
1/4 cup walnuts
1/4 cup olive oil
2 tablespoons miso, more or less to taste
2 tablespoons chopped fresh parsley

8 ounces udon noodles
1 tablespoon olive oil
2 cloves garlic, crushed or minced
1 Italian frying pepper, seeded and minced
One 14-ounce can imported plum tomatoes, with liquid, chopped
1/4 cup black olives, sliced
Freshly ground black pepper to taste

Steam the spinach just until it is wilted. Squeeze out as much moisture as possible, then place it in the container of a food processor or blender along with the rest of the pesto ingredients. Process until the mixture is a rough paste.

Cook the udon noodles. When they are *al dente*, drain them immediately, and transfer them to a covered, ovenproof serving dish.

Meanwhile, heat the olive oil in a large skillet. Add the garlic and frying pepper and sauté over low heat until the garlic is golden. Add the tomatoes, olives, and black pepper and simmer over low heat for 5 minutes. Stir in the pesto sauce and simmer for another 5 minutes. Pour over the cooked, drained noodles and toss together well. Serve at once.

VEGETABLE PASTAS

Vegetable pastas are made primarily from the same refined durum wheat flour used in standard pastas (or, in the natural foods realm, from whole durum wheat flour) with the addition of about 10 percent vegetable flour (made from dried and powdered vegetables). The most familiar of these is *spinach pasta*; it has the most distinct flavor. Another is *tomato pasta*, which is reminiscent of tomatoes only because of its light-pinkish-red color, not its flavor. *Jerusalem artichoke pasta*, too, is made with only about 10 percent Jerusalem artichoke flour, so its pleasant and mild taste is little different from that of ordinary pasta. And finally, in multicolored mixes of vegetable pastas, you may occasionally see one that is a deep maroon—this is *beet pasta*. Multicolored vegetable pasta mixes are becoming quite common in both natural-food stores and supermarkets.

Vegetable pastas are more useful for adding a bit of elegance and variety to pasta recipes than for taste. The exception to this is spinach pasta (for a specific recipe using spinach pasta, see Spinach Fettucine with Pine Nuts, page 83). These pastas cook just like their nonvegetable counterparts (see page 107 or follow package directions) and can be readily substituted in Italian-style pasta dishes. Vegetable pastas are particularly nice for making colorful cold pasta salads.

MULTICOLORED PASTA SALAD FOR A CROWD

Yield: 10 to 12 servings

1 pound mixed-variety vegetable pasta
2 large bunches broccoli, cut into bite-size pieces
2 large carrots, thinly sliced diagonally
1/2 cup sliced radishes
1/2 cup sliced black olives
1 medium green or red bell pepper, cut into thin, 1-inch-long strips
One 6-ounce jar marinated artichoke hearts, chopped, with liquid
2 to 3 bunches scallions, minced
1/4 cup chopped fresh parsley
1/4 cup extra-virgin olive oil
1/4 cup safflower oil
1/4 cup red wine vinegar
1 teaspoon dried oregano

1/2 cup grated Parmesan cheese
Salt and freshly ground pepper to taste

Cook the pasta in a large kettle of rapidly simmering water until *al dente*. When done, drain and rinse under cool water.

While the pasta is cooking, steam the broccoli and carrots together until the broccoli is bright green. Rinse under cool water and allow to drain.

Combine the pasta, steamed vegetables, and all the remaining ingredients in a large serving bowl. Toss well and allow to sit for about an hour at room temperature before serving.

WHOLE WHEAT PASTAS

Whole wheat pastas, made from whole durum wheat, come in many shapes and sizes, from spaghetti to shells to twists, among others. Some shapes seem to have a smoother, less gritty texture than others; for instance, fettucine seems to have a smoother texture than whole wheat spaghetti. Experiment with different shapes to find your particular preference. A staple in natural-food stores, 100 percent whole wheat pastas have the hearty, nutty taste of whole wheat flour. They contain far more fiber and a wider range of nutrients than do standard refined durum pastas. The more assertive flavor and intensely chewy texture of whole wheat pasta may seem odd at first in familiar recipes, so if you'd like, try mixing them with standard pasta, cooked separately, until you get accustomed to them.

Available packaged or in bulk in natural-food stores, whole wheat pastas take a bit longer to cook than their refined equivalents. (See the guidelines on page 107.) Cooking times vary widely according to the shape; test frequently, or, if you feel you need more guidance, packaged whole wheat pastas give instructions with approximate cooking times.

Whole wheat pastas can be used in many types of recipes as a heartier, whole-grain alternative to standard refined pasta, with the exception of Oriental dishes, for which traditional noodles are better suited. They are particularly good with highly seasoned tomato sauces, cheese sauces, in casseroles, in hearty vegetable or bean soups, or combined with beans to make marinated cold salads.

WHOLE WHEAT PASTA WITH SWEET RED PEPPER SAUCE

Yield: 4 to 6 servings

4 large sweet red bell peppers
1/2 pound whole wheat pasta, preferably
   small shapes such as shells or twists
3 tablespoons extra-virgin olive oil
2 cloves garlic, minced
2 medium ripe, juicy tomatoes
2 tablespoons unbleached white flour or
   1 tablespoon arrowroot
1 cup low-fat milk or soy milk
2 to 3 tablespoons fresh chopped basil
1/2 teaspoon dried oregano
1 tablespoon red wine vinegar
Salt and freshly ground pepper to taste
Grated Parmesan cheese for topping
   (optional)

Place the red peppers under a broiler and broil on all sides until the skin is charred. Let them cool in a paper bag. Meanwhile, cook the pasta until *al dente*. When done, drain and place in a covered serving dish.

When the peppers are cool enough to handle, slip the skins off, core them, and cut them into approximately 1-inch by 1/2-inch pieces. Set aside.

In a heavy saucepan, heat the olive oil. Add the garlic and sauté over moderate heat for 1 minute. Add the tomatoes and cook until they have softened a bit, about 5 minutes. Sprinkle in the flour or arrowroot and continue to stir until it disappears. Reduce the heat and slowly stir in the milk or soy milk. Add the red peppers, basil, and oregano and cook, stirring, until the sauce thickens, about 5 to 8 minutes. Remove from the heat and stir in the vinegar. Pour over the pasta and toss together well. Season to taste with salt and pepper.

WHOLE WHEAT PASTA VARIATIONS

Some variations on whole wheat pasta that have already been covered are vegetable pastas (page 116) and soy pasta (page 114). A fairly recent addition to the selection of whole-grain pastas is whole wheat and quinoa pasta. Quinoa flour, milled from the supernutritious grain (see page 17), adds a subtle, pleasant flavor and contributes to a nice texture, somewhat smoother than 100 percent whole wheat pastas. If you can't find quinoa pasta, you may order it directly from the Quinoa Corporation (see appendix B). Another recent innovation is an 80 percent whole wheat pasta with 10 percent rice flour and 10 percent sesame flour—very nice and nutty. These specialty pastas may be cooked and used in precisely the same way as 100 percent whole wheat pastas.

Chapter 7

DAIRY PRODUCTS

Dairy products make up a very small part of the inventory of natural-food stores. Those that are offered, however, often have special nutritional features, such as inoculation with beneficial bacterial cultures to improve digestibility. Yogurt, kefir, and acidophilus milk are examples of such products. This chapter will focus on these and other less familiar milk products, rather than on the more common dairy foods, such as cheeses and butter.

Dairy products are highly nutritious foods. Though much of the world's adult population is unable to digest lactose (milk sugar) easily, in the Western world, at least, milk and its products—cheeses, cream, and butter, to name a few—are among the most popular and satisfying of foods. People who would like to enjoy dairy products as a regular part of their diet would be wise to choose those that are lowest in fat and most easily digestible. These include cultured dairy products, low-fat milk, low-fat cottage cheese, and ricotta cheese. Hard cheeses are hard to resist, but since they are high in saturated fat and cholestrol, moderation is important.

NUTRITIONAL BENEFITS OF DAIRY PRODUCTS

Dairy foods are rich in high-quality, complete protein and a wide range of vitamins, including vitamins A and D and the B-complex vitamins. Vitamin B_{12} is in good supply; rarely found in vegetable sources, many vegetarians rely on dairy products for this vitamin. Dairy products are by far the best food source of calcium, the mineral that promotes the strength and health of bones, teeth, and muscles. The recommended daily allowance for calcium is 800 milligrams, though experts feel that women should take in 1,200 milligrams. One cup of milk, buttermilk, kefir, or yogurt provides about 300 to 350 milligrams of calcium. Generous amounts of iron, phosphorus, potassium, and magnesium are provided as well.

DIGESTIVE PROBLEMS ASSOCIATED WITH MILK

As mentioned above, many people have difficulty digesting the milk sugar *lactose*. In fact, it is believed that this is true of the majority of the world's adult population, especially those of Asian, African, and Native American descent. To be lactose-intolerant means that you lack the ability to produce the enzyme *lactase*, which must be present in the intestine in order to break down the lactose into two digestible sugars, glucose and galactose. If milk is not properly broken down in the small intestine, the results may be nausea, cramps, and diarrhea. Lactose intolerance is not always an all-or-nothing situation. Some people who are intolerant might be able to digest cultured milk products, such as yogurt and kefir, whereas others might be totally incapable of assimilating any milk product whatsoever.

Another problem associated with dairy products is milk allergy. A small percentage of children and adults are allergic to the milk proteins lactalbumin and lactaglobulin. Many children outgrow this allergy at a very early age. The unpleasant side effects of this allergy include respiratory or digestive problems.

If you experience milk intolerance, you may want to have your physician refer you to a nutritionist; if you are actually allergic to milk, an allergist would be more appropriate.

BUYING AND STORING DAIRY PRODUCTS

Buying fresh dairy products from natural-food stores is little different from buying them in supermarkets. They should be sold from a refrigerated section, and their packages should be dated. Specific storage recommendations will be given under the individual entries that follow.

——— ACIDOPHILUS MILK ———

This milk product was a staple offering in dairy cases of natural-food stores in the 1970s, but now it seems to be offered only occasionally. Acidophilus milk is fresh, low-fat milk into which the bacteria *Lactobacillus acidophilus* has been introduced. Sometimes called sweet acidophilus, this differs from other cultured milk products in that it has a mild rather than tart flavor. Inconclusive studies done in the 1970s lead to the theory that the beneficial bacteria in acidophilus milk line the intestinal tract, aiding in digestion in general, as well as specifically aiding in the digestion of lactose in those who are sensitive or intolerant. Most studies neither strongly recommend nor warn against this product for the lactose intolerant, but rather are cautiously noncommittal. It seems that the evidence is not all in; consequently, the general interest in acidophilus milk is waning. It is generally agreed, however, that this milk should not be heated, since heat kills the beneficial bacterial and thus nullifies any potential benefit.

The nutrients in acidophilus milk are identical to those in low-fat milk. One cup contains 145 calories, 5 grams of fat, and significant amounts of vitamin A, D, and the B vitamins. It provides 350 milligrams of calcium and good quantities of phosphorus and potassium.

——— BUTTERMILK ———

Buttermilk is a product more likely found in the supermarket than in the natural-food store, but it is so closely related to those "health food" staples yogurt and kefir that I though it merited discussion. Many people misunderstand buttermilk, thinking it a rich, fattening food due to its name and rich consistency. At one time buttermilk was, quite literally, the residue from butter making. Today, buttermilk is simply a cultured milk product, as are yogurt and kefir. And because the lactose (milk sugar) in buttermilk is converted into lactic acid during the fermentation process, it may be more easily digested by those who are lactose sensitive.

What surprises people most often is that despite its thick, creamy appearance, buttermilk is the nutritional and caloric equivalent of skim milk, from which it is made. One cup contains about 88 calories, virtually no fat, and 9 grams of protein. It provides almost 300 milligrams of calcium, plus significant amounts of the minerals iron, potassium, and phosphorus. Like all milk products, buttermilk contains a wide range of vitamins, including vitamins A, the B complex, and D.

Buttermilk will keep longer in the refrigerator than regular milk—2 weeks is a maximum, once it has been opened. Buttermilk whose freshness is waning is better used in baking than in soups or beverages.

- A bit of buttermilk on a baked potato instead of butter and sour cream will save a lot of calories and fat.

- Buttermilk also makes a creamy base for low-calorie salad dressings. You can combine it with other ingredients such as herbs, mustard, or tomato juice or just pour it directly onto a green salad.

- Buttermilk is great to use in baking. A traditional ingredient in biscuits, muffins, breads, and pancakes, buttermilk contributes to tenderness and to a nice browning of crusts. Try substituting it in quick and yeasted breads when a recipe calls for milk. Baking soda must be used in conjunction with buttermilk to balance the acidity. The rule of thumb is 1/2 teaspoon soda for every cup of buttermilk.

- If you enjoy the tang of buttermilk, blend it with strawberries or other fruits for refreshing summer drinks. Add a touch of honey if you wish.

- Buttermilk makes a tangy base for refreshing, cold summer soups. Its flavor is especially compatible in soups containing potatoes, such as in the recipe that follows:

CHILLED POTATO-BUTTERMILK SOUP

Yield: 6 to 8 servings

5 or 6 medium potatoes
1 small onion, cut in half
1 clove garlic, crushed or minced
1 tablespoon soy margarine
2 bay leaves
Water or light vegetable stock to cover
1 cup steamed fresh peas
1 cup finely chopped fresh spinach
2 to 3 tablespoons chopped fresh dill, to
   taste
1 tablespoon chopped fresh parsley
2 1/2 to 3 cups buttermilk, or as needed
Salt and freshly ground pepper to taste

Scrub the potatoes well and cut into 1/2-inch dice. Place in a large soup kettle or Dutch oven with the halved onion, the garlic, margarine, bay leaves, and water or stock. Bring to a boil, then cover and simmer over low heat until the potatoes are tender, about 20 minutes. Remove and discard the onion. With a slotted spoon, remove 1 1/2 cups of the potato dice. Mash them coarsely, then stir back into the soup.

Stir in the peas, spinach, and herbs and simmer for 5 minutes. Allow the soup to cool to lukewarm. Add the buttermilk, more or less as needed to achieve a desired consistency. Season to taste with salt and pepper, then cover and chill.

CHEESE, RENNETLESS

Natural-food stores often carry common varieties of hard cheeses that are labeled rennetless. What this means is that the cheese has not been coagulated by rennet (sometimes called *rennin*), an enzyme extracted from the stomach lining of slaughtered calves that is used in most hard cheeses. Rennetless cheeses are coagulated with plant substances, such as lady's bedstraw, or with laboratory-produced "vegetable rennet," made from synthesized mold cultures. Kosher cheeses, too, are coagulated with plant substances. Rennetless cheeses are sought by those who keep kosher as well as by vegetarians who object to eating any product that entails the killing of animals.

GOAT'S MILK

Goat's milk is used extensively in regions where a rough or mountainous terrain is not hospitable to cows. It is closer in composition to mother's milk than is cow's milk and is sometimes recommended for infants and small children who cannot digest cow's milk. Don't use it for this purpose, however, without consulting a physician. Goat's milk is probably better known in our culture for its role in making sharp-flavored goat cheese, considered a gourmet item.

In natural-food stores, goat's milk is more likely to be sold condensed in cans than in fresh form. Fresh goat's milk spoils more quickly than cow's milk. The cans carry directions concerning how to reconstitute and use it.

Goat's milk is a bit lower in protein and higher in fat than whole cow's milk. It is also higher in sugar, which gives it a rather sweet flavor. Goat's milk contains no iron, but does provide more or less equivalent amounts of the other vitamins and minerals provided by cow's milk.

KEFIR

Kefir (pronounced ke-FEER) is beginning to make a rather noticeable appearance on the North American market, fueled by an intensive advertising campaign. Rising from obscurity as did its cousin, yogurt, kefir has likewise been a traditional favorite in the Middle East and in Eastern Europe. A fermented milk product, it differs from yogurt primarily in the type of culture used to ferment it. Kefir is cultured with what is called kefir grains, seedlike pellets comprised of yeast, bacteria, and milk protein. The final product is very similar to yogurt. According to an October 1986 report in the *New York Times,* a spokesperson for a major manufacturer of kefir conceded that their similarities far outweigh their differences.

Kefir is available in a custardlike, spoonable version, either plain, sweetened, or with fruit. It also comes in the same variations in a liquid version that is used as a beverage. Although claims are made that kefir is smoother and less tart than yogurt, it still has an unmistakable tang. Buy kefir well before the date stamped on the container. If unopened, kefir keeps in the refrigerator for 2 to 3 weeks after it is purchased. Once opened, it is best used up within a week. Sweetened kefir lasts longer than plain kefir, since the sugar acts as a preservative. Use plain kefir whose freshness is waning in baking as a substitute for buttermilk. If the kefir develops a sharp, fermented odor, it is spoiled and should be thrown away.

Like yogurt and other fermented dairy products, kefir may be more easily digested by those who are sensitive to lactose (milk sugar). One cup of whole-milk kefir contains 168 calories, 8.6 grams of fat, and 9.5 grams of protein. Full analysis on its vitamin and mineral content is incomplete, but it is believed to be nearly identical to yogurt in those respects.

Plain liquid kefir can be used as a substitute for buttermilk in baking, making blended drinks, and as a base for light salad dressings (see the list of ideas for buttermilk on page 120). Plain kefir in the custardlike version may be used exactly as recommended for yogurt (see the list of ideas on page 123).

——— POWDERED MILKS ———
(INSTANT NONFAT DRY MILK AND
NONINSTANT MILK POWDER)

The more familiar form of powdered milk is *instant nonfat dry milk*, which is available in supermarkets. This is made from the surplus skim milk from the manufacture of butter and cream. Instant nonfat dry milk is best used only in its reconstituted form rather than added straight to baked goods or hot liquids. To reconstitute, combine 4 parts cold water with 1 part dry milk. Use wherever you might use low-fat milk in cooking or baking. For a creamier flavor and texture, such as for use in "cream" soups or in sauces, use only 3 parts water with 1 part milk. Though fine for use in cooking or baking, the taste of reconstituted dry milk might seem a bit odd if used straight, as a beverage.

Noninstant milk powder is also a nonfat product and is a common offering in natural-food

stores. Literally a dry milk, made by a process called spray-drying, noninstant milk powder is preferable to the instant kind because it is dried at lower temperatures, thus retaining more of the nutrients. Unlike instant milk powder, noninstant milk powder may be used as a dry ingredient in baking, where it adds a protein and vitamin boost to cookies, muffins, cakes, and breads. Replace 2 tablespoons in each cup of flour used in recipes with noninstant milk powder.

To reconstitute, combine 4 parts cold water with 1 part milk powder. Let stand for several minutes, then stir or agitate to blend. Use less water if a richer milk is desired. Reconstituted milk powder can be used in any form of cooking or baking where you would use low-fat milk. It also works well for home yogurt making, where instant nonfat dry milk does not.

Stored in a cool, dry place in containers that are completely moistureproof, both forms of powdered milk will keep for up to 6 months. If kept refrigerated, they will keep for up to 2 years. Once reconstituted, they will keep for about a week, refrigerated.

The nutrients in both types of reconstituted powdered milk are roughly equivalent to those in skim milk. Spray-dried noninstant milk powder may have slightly greater amounts of nutrients because of the way in which it is processed. As a basis for general comparison, 1 cup of skim milk contains 88 calories, virtually no fat, and nearly 9 grams of protein. Also present are all the nutrients present in dairy products: vitamins A, D, and the B complex, and the minerals calcium, iron, phosphorus, and potassium, among others.

——————— RAW MILK ———————

Raw milk has not caught on in the natural-food market in any substantial way, but since it is a product that is controversial, a brief discussion is warranted. Raw milk is whole milk that is unpasteurized and unhomogenized. Proponents say that this milk contains vitamins that are lost in the pasteurization process, but they warn the consumer to buy this product only from "reputable dairies." Obviously, this is not an easy task, since consumers usually buy from a third party. Opponents state that the small loss of nutrients does not warrant risking the potentially serious dangers of raw milk—notably, microorganisms that can cause infection or disease.

YOGURT

Yogurt is a product that has made a dramatic resurgence from ancient origins, transcending the natural foods movement to become a multimillion-dollar industry. Now a staple in every supermarket dairy case, yogurt has been used for centuries in the Near and Middle East. Made from milk fermented with special bacterial cultures (either *Lactobacillus bulgaricus* or *Streptococcus thermophilus*), good-quality yogurts contain these live, beneficial cultures when purchased. They may thus be more easily digested by some people who are lactose sensitive, since the lactose is turned into lactic acid during fermentation.

There is now a proliferation of yogurt brands available almost everywhere. When buying flavored yogurts, avoid those containing gums, gelatins, and of course artificial flavorings and colorings. Even the most "natural" brands may be high in sugar or high-fructose corn syrup, and if those are a concern for you, stick with plain yogurt and embellish it yourself with fruit butters, unsweetened crushed pineapple, bananas, or chopped dried fruit. Just a touch of honey may be added if you'd like additional sweetness.

Buy yogurt well before the date stamped on the container. Yogurts keep from 2 to 3 weeks if unopened and refrigerated. Sweetened yogurts last longest, since the sugar acts as a preservative. Once opened, yogurt is best if used within a week. Yogurt whose freshness is waning can be used in baking in place of buttermilk. Yogurt with a sharp, fermented odor is spoiled and should not be used.

A cup of plain, low-fat yogurt contains approximately 120 calories and 4 grams of fat, whereas a whole-milk yogurt contains 152 calories and 8 grams of fat. Both contain approximately 8 grams of protein, 300 milligrams of calcium, and a range of other minerals, including iron, phosphorus, and potassium. Vitamins present include vitamins A, the B complex, C, and D.

There are numerous ways to use and enjoy plain yogurt. Start with these suggestions:

- Substitute yogurt for sour cream for topping baked potatoes or Mexican specialties such as enchiladas. If you'd like a little added richness, combine sour cream half-and-half with yogurt and mix thoroughly to blend.

- Use yogurt as a base for chilled summer soups. If necessary, thin with low-fat milk for the correct consistency. Make sure that the soup is no more than lukewarm when adding the yogurt, so that the yogurt doesn't separate. Potatoes, spinach or other greens, and cucumbers are especially compatible with yogurt bases.

- Add yogurt to hot grain dishes, such as fruit-and-nut rice pilafs. Stir in a small amount after the skillet has been removed from the heat. Yogurt adds a light tang and moistness to grain pilafs.

- Use yogurt as a basis for refreshing blended drinks. Bananas temper the tang nicely, as does honey. Try other fruits, such as peaches or berries. Sweeten if necessary with honey and thin as needed with low-fat milk or fruit juice.

- Combine yogurt with oils, herbs, spices, mustards, or pureed tomatoes to make great salad dressings. Here's a tangy dressing reminiscent of blue cheese: Combine 3/4 cup yogurt with 2 tablespoons safflower oil, 1 teaspoon prepared mustard, and 1/3 cup crumbled feta cheese. Mix thoroughly. This is very nice with endives and strong greens.

- Use yogurt instead of mayonnaise or sour cream to dress potato salads and cole slaws. Similarly, yogurt makes a great sandwich spread when combined with a bit of mustard or tahini.

- Use yogurt in baking as a substitute for milk or buttermilk. Like buttermilk, it contributes to a tender crumb and to nicely browned crusts. You'll need to use 1/2 teaspoon baking soda for every cup of yogurt used.

- Here's a simple and very tasty idea based on a Southeast Asian recipe: Combine a cup of yogurt with about 5 medium boiled and coarsely mashed potatoes. Flavor with fried onions, green chilies, and freshly ground ginger. This makes 4 to 6 servings.

- Yogurt is used extensively in Indian cookery, and if you're a yogurt enthusiast, you're sure to find many enticing ideas in Indian cookbooks. Yogurt is often used as a basis for palate-cooling relishes called raitas. These usually combine cucumbers or bananas with an approximately equal amount of yogurt.

Chapter 8

SEA VEGETABLES

The term *sea vegetables*, though perfectly interchangeable with *seaweeds*, has come to be the popular, more appetizing name for edible varieties of marine algae. The family of sea vegetation comprises over twenty thousand species, encompassing plants that range in size from one-celled organisms to giant kelps, whose fronds measure hundreds of feet in width. Sea vegetation is found both in fresh and salt water, where the plants live in the upper levels of water so that sunlight may reach them. Like land plants, sea vegetation relies on the sun to photosynthesize the nutrients necessary for its growth and development. The more commonly used sea vegetables come from coastal regions of oceans—bays, inlets, and peninsulas. The oceans of the world offer far more edible sea vegetables than are described in the following pages. The focus here is on those that are readily available through the natural-food market, including with those that have become familiar as a result of the popularity in the West of Japanese food.

The seas have long been an important source of food, providing both animal life and sea vegetables. The use of sea vegetables dates back thousands of years and crosses many cultural boundaries. One of the earliest records of their use is from China and dates back over twenty-five hundred years; it describes seaweeds as delicacies fit for an emperor. The ancient Greeks and Romans used them when they were at sea or when other foods were scarce during times of famine. Today, sea vegetables are correctly associated with the cuisine of Japan, but they have been a part of the culinary traditions of many other coastal locales as well. These include the British Isles (particularly Wales and Scotland), the Scandinavian nations, the northeastern and northwestern United States, Hawaii, and northeastern Canada. Some sea vegetables have come under cultivation, while others are still culled from the wild. Methods for foraging, sun-drying, and utilization have been passed down and improved upon for many centuries.

NUTRITIONAL BENEFITS OF SEA VEGETABLES

All sea vegetables are rich sources of vitamins and minerals. Because they have the ability to absorb nutrients from the surrounding waters many times over, they are among the most nutritious foods known. Sea vegetables contain significant amounts of calcium, iron, phosphorus, and magnesium, plus many trace elements, such as iodine, zinc, copper, and fluoride. They also provide an abundance of vitamins, which vary in quantity from type to type. Most are good sources of vitamin A and the B-vitamin complex, including niacin, thiamine, riboflavin, folic acid, and vitamin B_6. Importantly, sea vegetables are one of the few vegetable sources of vitamin B_{12}, so they can be a valuable addition to the diet of vegans (those vegetarians who, in addition to avoiding meat, also shun eggs and dairy products). They also provide varying amounts of vitamins E, K, and C. The vitamin-C content is particularly outstanding in dulse, nori, and alaria. Complete, high-quality protein is present in most sea vegetables, but few contain enough to be of much significance in the small portions usually consumed, with the exception of nori and dulse. Sea vegetables are very low in fat; the calories contained in an average portion are so low as to be almost negligible.

Apart from specific nutritional properties, sea vegetables have historically been regarded as possessing powerful medicinal properties for a wide range of complaints. Claims that they help prevent disease and promote cardiovascular health and longevity are also common. Scientific studies, though inconclusive, have shown some evidence to back up these claims. Some studies have also indicated that the minerals and enzymes present in sea vegetables may assist in eliminating toxins and pollutant residues from the body.

One drawback to sea vegetables is that many are very high in sodium. Among the highest are the kelps, dulse, nori, and wakame. Those concerned with salt intake should use sea vegetables sparingly or avoid these particular varieties altogether.

A CAUTIONARY NOTE ON POLLUTION

Though few conclusive studies have been done, there is some controversy over whether sea vegetables are safe from pollution. The world's oceans are virtual sewers for the industrial world, and since sea vegetables grow in shallow waters near coastal regions, the question of their ability to withstand large amounts of organic runoff and dumped toxins in a worrisome one.

The authors of *The Book of Tofu* and other milestone books on traditional foods of the Orient, William Shurtleff and Akiko Aoyagi, send a form letter to those who inquire stating that after years of research, they have discontinued work on a proposed book on sea vegetables. The reason cited is their concern about pollution, particularly in sea vegetables from Japan.

Evelyn McConnaughey, a West Coast expert on sea vegetables, writes that the sea vegetable industry of Japan has experienced problems due to pollution, which caused some operations to be moved to cleaner waters. She cites fuel oil, sewage, and radioactive substances as hazards that may have affected some sea vegetable crops. Sewage and organic agricultural runoff are believed to have little effect on sea vegetables in small quantities, but in large quantities these do cause problems. Some years back, contamination of sea vegetable crops from nuclear waste was documented off the coast of Ireland. Though the pollution of ocean water has had its damaging effects on sea vegetables in certain areas, the awareness of it has made the industry as a whole much more vigilant. In Japan, one solution has been to cultivate certain sea vegetables, such as nori, in aquacultural seaweed "farms." McConnaughey as well as other experts point out that the waters surrounding sea vegetables are constantly being renewed and that the plants' surfaces are continually rinsed by moving waters. Further, most proponents concur that the domestic and Japanese sea vegetable industries operate under extremely strict standards, and that contaminated sea vegetables would not be marketed.

With so little hard evidence in the way of definitive studies on this subject, it is a tough question for the consumer to decide. Specific information on the comparative cleanliness of waters from which imported or domestic brands are harvested is largely unavailable. Several national distributors sent me general statements: Eden foods states in company literature that their sea vegetables are harvested from "environmentally clean waters." U.S. Mills, Inc. states that their Erewhon Japanese sea vegetables are harvested from areas that either pass a "no heavy metals" test, pass a government test, or are from waters where there are no heavy industries. Maine Coast Sea Vegetables said that they have their products tested regularly for heavy metals, and are all well below FDA toxicity threshholds. Further, they never harvest near major harbors, nor are there any large industries up near their harvesting areas. If you have access to sea vegetables local to your area, you could call your state's department of conservation to get information on the waters from which they came. Dr. Robert Buchsbaum, coastal ecologist for the Massachusetts Audubon Society, suggests determining where the sea vegetables were harvested by means of labels or contact with the marketing organization. One can make the assumption, for example, that sea vegetables harvested from undeveloped areas around the Maine coast are more likely to be from clean water than anything harvested from much of the mid-Atlantic shore. He also suggests varying the sea vegetables you use unless you are certain they came from clean sources. Dr. Rod Fujita of the Harbor Branch Oceanographic Institute in Florida confirms that water quality studies pertinent to the Japanese seaweed industry are scarce. He states that from his observations, severe industrial pollution has been the most severe threat to nori production in Tokyo Bay. He goes on to say that there has been progress in offshore farming technology to cultivate nori in safer waters. The bottom line is that it's best to avoid any sea life that comes from waters around highly industrialized areas.

BUYING AND STORING DRIED SEA VEGETABLES

In natural-food stores, dried sea vegetables are most commonly sold in sealed cellophane packages. Occasionally, they are sold loose, by the ounce, and often come from the same distributors that produce the packages. Dried sea vegetables are a very hardy item, and there is no need to worry about freshness when buying them.

Storing dried sea vegetables is a very simple matter. If kept in tightly lidded jars in a cool, dry place, they will keep for up to 2 years.

————AGAR———— (AGAR-AGAR or KANTEN)

Agar, from the Malay word meaning "jelly," is a seaweed product long appreciated by many Eastern cultures for its gelling properties. Available in several forms, the most widely marketed are bars, sold tightly wrapped in cellophane, and flakes, sold in small cellophane packages. Agar bars have been in use for longer than the flakes and are made from a combination of several different red seaweeds belonging to the botanical family Gelidium. The method used to produce the bars is a long, tedious one that has changed little throughout the centuries since its discovery. Agar flakes are made by a more modern method and yield a product that is somewhat more convenient to use than the bars, containing a more concentrated, stronger gelatin. In either case, the gelatin yielded is flavorless, odorless, and colorless, making agar a product with endless possibilities.

Agar has virtually no calories. At 75 percent carbohydrate, it is high in a form of fiber that passes through the body undigested, adding bulk to the diet and creating a beneficial laxative effect. Although it is not quite as rich in nutrients as other sea vegetables, it does contain iron, calcium, potassium, and iodine, as well as a number of vitamins, including B_6, B_{12}, C, D, and K.

One agar bar will gel up to 3 cups of liquid. Use slightly less liquid if a firmer gel is desired. Break the bar up into several pieces and combine it with liquid in a saucepan. Bring to a boil, then lower the heat and simmer for 15 minutes, stirring occasionally. One tablespoon of agar flakes will gel 1 cup of liquid. Bring the liquid to a boil in a saucepan. Sprinkle in the flakes, then lower the heat and simmer for 2 to 3 minutes, stirring occasionally. The liquid used may be water, fruit juice, vegetable juice, or bouillon, depending on the needs of the recipe. Once prepared in the method described above, other flavorings and solid ingredients may be added to make aspics and puddings. Pour whatever mixture you've made into a heatproof bowl and allow to chill thoroughly, refrigerated, for at least 2 hours. The consistency, once chilled, resembles that of a firm pudding, but is not quite stiff enough to be cut into squares or molded the way you could commercial gelatins.

Certain substances interfere with the gelling action of agar. It will not set in the presence of acetic acid (found in vinegar) or oxalic acid (found in chocolate and spinach). With other acidic substances, such as pineapple or tomato juice, the agar will set, but not as firmly as it might otherwise.

Agar bars or flakes are easy and fun to experiment with. Use the proportions of agar to liquid given above. Here are just a few ways to try it:

- Cook agar in 1 cup pineapple juice. Allow to cool to room temperature. Stir in 1 cup each plain yogurt and crushed pineapple. Flavor with 2 to 3 tablespoons honey and stir together. Pour into individual serving cups or into a glass bowl and chill for at least 2 hours. Serve as part of a light lunch or as dessert. This makes 4 servings.

- Cook agar in 1/2 cup apple cider, then add an equivalent amount of applesauce and a pinch each of cinnamon and nutmeg. Chill for at least 2 hours, then use as a spread for breads and muffins.

- Try gelling stewed fruit compotes. Cook agar in 1 cup fruit juice and combine with 2 cups or so stewed fruits. Chill for at least 2 hours.

- Agar makes great vegetable aspics. Try gelling your leftover gazpacho, or other brothy vegetable soups. Strain the liquid from the soup and cook it with the proper amount of agar. Stir in the solid ingredients, pour into a container, and chill for at least 2 hours.

AVOCADO ASPIC

Yield: 4 servings

1 1/4 cups water
4 teaspoons agar flakes
1/4 cup firmly packed grated carrot
1/4 cup firmly packed seeded chopped
    cucumber
1/2 medium green bell pepper, finely
    chopped
1 tablespoon minced chives or scallion
1 tablespoon minced fresh dill
2 medium soft, ripe avocados, mashed
Juice of 1/2 lemon
1/4 teaspoon salt or to taste
Dash each of freshly ground pepper and
    cumin

Combine the water and agar in a small saucepan. Bring to a boil, then simmer for 5 minutes. In a mixing bowl, combine the liquid with the remaining ingredients. Stir briskly to combine thoroughly. Pour into a glass bowl or into individual serving cups. Chill for at least 2 hours before serving. If you did not pour the mixture into individual molds, you may serve each portion on a bed of lettuce.

━━━ ALARIA ━━━

Closely related to Japanese wakame, alaria is its Atlantic counterpart, growing wild near rocky, windy peninsulas of the northeast coast of North America. Most of the alaria marketed domestically comes from the Maine coast, but it is also known on the other side of the Atlantic as a traditional sea vegetable of the British Isles. Alaria comes in the form of a wavy frond with winglike leaves emanating from a thin but firm midrib. Like wakame, alaria has a mild flavor, but it is more resilient and needs longer cooking time. Unlike wakame, however, alaria has a very pungent scent, one that not everyone will like.

Alaria is a rich source of vitamins C, A, and the B vitamins, including folacin, niacin, and B_{12}. A 1-ounce serving provides 100 percent of the Recommended Daily Allowance of vitamin B_{12}, a vitamin rarely occurring in vegetable sources. It also provides a range of minerals, including magnesium and phosphorus, as well as many trace elements.

The firm texture of alaria makes it most appropriate for use in recipes that require long simmering. To make it easier to chop, first reconstitute it by soaking it in warm water for 10 to 15 minutes. The volume of alaria doubles when soaked. Alternatively, you may simply snip it with kitchen shears and add it directly to soups. Either way, check carefully for bits of shell that may be hiding in the tangled fronds.

- Marinate a small amount of reconstituted alaria overnight in a vinaigrette. Chop and add to grain salads, cucumber salads, or hot or cold cooked Oriental noodles such as somen or soba.

- Simmer a small amount of chopped reconstituted alaria in tomato sauce, flavored with dried or fresh herbs, for at least 30 minutes. Serve over cooked pasta.

- Make alaria "chips" by snipping the dried fronds into small pieces with kitchen shears and frying in a hot skillet with a small amount of oil until crisp and lightly browned. Drain on paper towels and serve with soy sauce.

- Add 1/2 cup or so of dried alaria, snipped into small pieces with kitchen shears, to long-simmering soups. Try it in bean or pea soups, grain soups (such as barley soup), or vegetable soups (such as minestrone).

HEARTY TEMPEH–SPLIT PEA SOUP WITH ALARIA

Yield: 6 servings

This filling, unusual soup comes courtesy of West Coast sea vegetable expert Evelyn McConnaughey.

1/2 to 3/4 cup dried alaria, snipped into pieces
6 cups water
1 cup green or yellow split peas
4 ounces tempeh, finely diced
1 cup chopped onion
2 to 3 cloves garlic, minced
1 stalk celery, diced
1 cup coarsely chopped carrot
1 teaspoon each: cumin, coriander, and Spike (a seasoning mix available in natural-food stores)
1/2 teaspoon oregano
1 tablespoon natural soy sauce
Salt and freshly ground pepper to taste

Place the alaria and the water in a large soup pot or Dutch oven. Allow to sit for 10 to 15 minutes. Add the remaining ingredients and heat slowly. Simmer for 1 1/2 hours, or until the split peas are tender. Taste, and correct the seasonings.

———— ARAME ————

Harvested in abundance primarily from the Sea of Japan, arame undergoes an extensive transformation from its original to its packaged form. The extra-tough, yellowish brown, foot-long fronds are cooked after harvesting, then sun-dried. Turning almost black in color once dried, they are then machine-sliced into short, ultrathin strands, resulting in a convenient, practically ready-to-use product. Because of its appearance and texture, arame is most readily compared with hijiki; though arame's flavor is noticeably milder than hijiki's, there is still an element of the distinct sea flavor.

Like the other sea vegetables, arame is rich in a variety of minerals, including calcium, iron, phosphorus, potassium, and iodine. It also provides modest amounts of vitamin A and several B vitamins.

To reconstitute arame, soak it for 5 minutes in warm water before adding it to your recipe. Arame doubles in volume when reconstituted.

- Heat 1 tablespoon each peanut oil and sesame oil in a skillet and sauté 2 large carrots, thinly sliced or grated and 1 large onion, quartered and thinly sliced, until both are golden. Add 1/2 cup or more reconstituted arame and season with natural soy sauce and the juice of 1/2 lemon. This is a customary way of preparing both arame and hijiki in Japan. Makes 4 servings.

- Stir-fry 1/2 pound diced tofu in a small amount of peanut oil until golden. Add 1/2 cup or more reconstituted arame and 1 thinly sliced sweet green or red bell pepper and sauté until the pepper is tender-crisp. Stir in 2 to 3 tablespoons toasted sunflower seeds, and natural soy sauce and lemon juice or rice vinegar to taste. Serve hot as a main dish with cooked grains. Makes 4 servings.

- Add 1/4 cup reconstituted arame to each cup of your favorite recipe for spaghetti sauce and serve over hot pasta.

- Add a small amount of reconstituted arame to Oriental-style noodle or vegetable soups. It's especially good in hot and sour soups.

- Use reconstituted arame as a garnish to add color and character to Oriental-style noodle dishes, vegetable salads, or stir fries, particularly those utilizing green vegetables such as green beans, broccoli, bok choy, or cabbage.

WASABI-FLAVORED ARAME, POTATO, AND BROCCOLI SALAD

Yield: 6 to 8 servings

1 1/2 pounds tiny new potatoes or russet potatoes
1 medium bunch broccoli, cut into bite-size pieces and florets
1/2 to 3/4 cup arame
1 large carrot, cut into matchsticks
2 bunches scallions, minced
1/4 cup toasted sunflower or pumpkin seeds
Salt and freshly ground pepper to taste
1 cup Wasabi Mayonnaise (page 182)

Scrub the potatoes well and cook them in their skins until tender. When cool enough to handle, cut the new potatoes in half, if using russet potatoes, cut them into large chunks, leaving their skins on.

Rinse the arame and soak in enough warm

water to cover for 5 minutes; drain well. While the arame is soaking, steam the broccoli pieces just until bright green; refresh immediately under cool running water.

Combine all of the ingredients in a serving bowl and toss gently; stir in the Wasabi Mayonnaise and toss again.

——— DULSE ———

Although they once grew prolifically in the waters around Western Europe, the wide, red, hand-shaped fronds of dulse are now harvested primarily off the coast of North America. Dulse gathered for commercial purposes comes from the northeast coast, from Maine to Newfoundland. Its tangy, sharp-and-salty flavor once made it a common pub snack in its native regions.

Dulse is 22 percent protein, second only to nori among common sea vegetables, and one of the few sea vegetables with enough protein to be of significance. It is quite rich in iron, potassium, magnesium, and fluoride and supplies significant amounts of vitamins C, B_6, and B_{12}.

Dulse is versatile in that it may be used straight from the package, toasted, or reconstituted. Here are some suggestions for using it in its dried form. Check for bits of shell clinging to the fronds before using.

- Use dulse straight from the package as a snack, either plain or with a yogurt-based dip.

- Cut a small amount of dulse into bite-size pieces with kitchen shears and sauté in a bit of butter or margarine until crisp. Use as a garnish for noodles or mashed potatoes.

- Cut a handful of dulse into 1/2-inch pieces with kitchen shears and add to chowders about 10 minutes before they are done. Used in this way, dulse is a terrific substitute for seafood.

Dried dulse may also be toasted. On a moderately hot, dry skillet, toast small pieces of dulse until they become a dull, brownish green. Here are some suggestions for using them:

- Use these crinkly and crisp pieces of dulse in lettuce and tomato in sandwiches as a tasty substitute for bacon.

- Crumble toasted dulse and sprinkle as a seasoning over green salads, hot or cold noodle dishes, and quiches.

Dulse is also versatile when reconstituted and used as a vegetable. Although soaking makes it a bit milder and less salty, you may want to start by using it sparingly at first until you are accustomed to its distinct flavor. Soak dried dulse in lukewarm water for 5 minutes. Its volume increases two to three times when reconstituted. Then it may be used in a variety of ways:

- In recipes calling for cooked spinach, chard, collard greens, or other strong, leafy vegetables, substitute about one-quarter the amount called for with reconstituted dulse.

- Dulse is compatible with the flavors of corn and potatoes. Add 1/4 cup or more chopped reconstituted dulse to succotash, creamed corn, sautéed potatoes, or potato salad to add a distinctive twist.

- Instead of soaking dulse in water, try reconstituting it in a vinaigrette, then chop and add to a salad of crisp greens or to a marinated salad of crisp, blanched vegetables such as cauliflower or green beans.

SPINACH-DULSE PIE

Yield: 6 servings

3/4 pound fresh spinach
1/4 to 1/2 cup dried dulse, or to taste
2 tablespoons soy margarine
1 large onion, chopped
1 clove garlic, minced
3 eggs, beaten
1 cup firmly packed grated Cheddar cheese
Juice of 1/2 lemon
1 teaspoon paprika
Freshly ground black pepper to taste
1/4 cup toasted wheat germ

Preheat the oven to 350°F.

Wash the spinach well. Stem it in a large, covered skillet or pot until it is wilted. Chop it finely, squeeze out the moisture, and set aside. Soak the dulse in warm water for 5 minutes, then drain well, chop, and set aside.

In a small skillet, heat the margarine until it foams. Add the onion and sauté over moderate heat until it is translucent. Add the garlic and continue to sauté until the onion is lightly browned.

In a mixing bowl, combine the beaten eggs with the spinach, dulse, and onion-garlic mixture. Add the grated cheese, lemon juice, seasonings, and half the wheat germ. Stir together thoroughly and pour into an oiled 9-inch deep-dish pie or quiche pan. Sprinkle the remaining wheat germ over the top and bake for 40 to 45 minutes, or until the pie is set and the top is nicely golden. Allow to cool for several minutes, then cut into wedges to serve.

———— HIJIKI ————

Of all the commonly used sea vegetables, hijiki has the strongest ocean flavor and is arguably the most difficult to acquire a taste for. Imported from Japan, hijiki is harvested from shallow coastal areas from Kyushu in the south to Hokkaido in the north. It spreads over rocks like a brown carpet. After the plants are harvested, they are sun-dried, cooked, then dried again. Hijiki is packaged as small, curly, dark frond pieces. Those who don't like strong "fishy" flavors may not like hijiki, but those who enjoy strong sea flavors may relish its assertive taste.

Hijiki is exceptionally high in calcium. Just 1 tablespoon provides more calcium than does a cup of milk. It also provides generous amounts of iron, phosphorus, and iodine, as well as several B vitamins, vitamin A, and vitamin E. *Hijiki* means "bearer of wealth and beauty," and in Japan, it is thought to promote healthy hair and skin coloring.

To reconstitute hijiki, soak it in warm water for 10 to 15 minutes. The volume of hijiki expands four times when reconstituted.

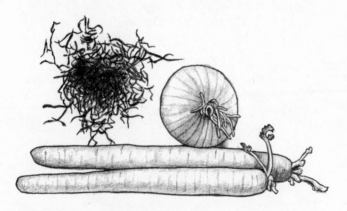

- Heat 2 tablespoons peanut oil in a skillet. Add 1 large chopped onion, 1 large thinly sliced carrot, 1 cup reconstituted hijiki, more or less to taste, and 1 cup grated daikon radish. Sauté until all the vegetables are golden. Season with natural soy sauce and lemon juice or rice vinegar. This recipe is based on a traditional Japanese preparation for hijiki. Makes 4 servings.

- Vary the recipe given above by adding 1/2 pound diced tofu and serve over brown rice for a high-protein main dish.

- Combine a small amount of reconstituted hijiki with shredded cabbage and a creamy buttermilk dressing for an unusual coleslaw.

- Use a small amount of reconstituted hijiki to garnish hot grain or noodle dishes or add a small quantity to tomato-based pasta sauces for an unusual twist.

SWEET VINEGAR-GINGER AND HIJIKI RICE

Yield: 4 servings

This unusual recipe is adapted from *Cooking with Sea Vegetables*, by Sharon Rhoads (Autumn Press, 1978).

Sweet Vinegar-Ginger Marinade:

1 teaspoon rice vinegar
1/2 teaspoon sake or mirin (optional)
1/2 teaspoon honey
1 tablespoon finely chopped fresh ginger

1/4 cup dried hijiki
3 tablespoons safflower oil
**1 pound tofu, cut into approximately 1-
   by-2-inch slices about 1/4 inch thick**
1 tablespoon rice vinegar
2 tablespoons honey
**2 tablespoons natural soy sauce, or to
   taste**
3 tablespoons water
1 tablespoon sake of mirin (optional)
3 cups hot cooked rice

Combine the marinade ingredients in a small bowl. Set aside and let stand for at least 30 minutes. In another bowl, refresh the hijiki in water to cover for 10 minutes.

In a wok or large skillet, heat 2 tablespoons of the oil. Fry the tofu over moderately high heat until golden on both sides. Drain on paper towels. Heat the remaining oil. Add the vinegar, honey, soy sauce, water, and optional mirin or sake. Add the hijiki and cook over low heat for 8 to 10 minutes. Stir in the fried tofu and cooked rice and fry for another 5 minutes. Serve at once, garnishing each serving with the marinated ginger.

IRISH MOSS (CARRAGEENAN)

Irish moss, along with agar, is a sea vegetable valued for its gelling properties. Carrageenan is the name of the gelling extract in Irish moss. Named after the Irish coastal town Carraghean, it is widely used commercially as a thickener in ice cream, cottage cheese, and other prepared foods. It is also used as a stabilizer in the production of beer. Irish moss was introduced to the United States in the nineteenth century and quickly came under cultivation. Apart from its thickening qualities, Irish moss has historically been valued in its native habitats for numerous medicinal uses, from heart ailments to kidney disorders. Carrageenan is used even in present-day medicines for ulcers. Specific nutritional information on Irish moss is not available.

As a thickener, Irish moss is effective, but it's not nearly as practical for home use as agar. It must be used in twice the quantity as agar and is not as completely flavorless. Thus, where agar flakes or bars are ready-to-use, Irish moss must be presoaked and rinsed to rid it of any vestiges of sea flavors that may not be desirable in some gelled dishes, such as desserts. Then it must be tied up in cheesecloth and immersed in cooking liquid and continuously pressed with a spoon to express the gel. Homemade dishes (as opposed to commercial preparations) thickened with Irish moss tend not to retain their firmness if left unrefrigerated for some time. These drawbacks make a strong case for choosing agar as a vegetable gelling agent. Not only is it much easier to use, but it is more commonly available as well.

KELP AND KOMBU

Belonging to the family of brown seaweeds called kelp are actually nearly nine hundred different species. The varieties most commonly marketed through the natural-food market are Japanese kombu and Atlantic kelp, related varieties that have similar flavors and culinary usages. Packaged in wide, flat frond pieces, they are both deep olive-green and are sometimes covered with a whitish powder, which is nothing more than the natural salts and sugars that come to the surface as they dry.

Atlantic kelp has until recently been marketed under the name Atlantic kombu, and it looks and tastes like the thinner varieties of Japanese kombu. It is harvested from the waters of the quiet bays of the northeast coast. Japanese kombu comes from the waters off the coast of Hokkaido, the northernmost island of Japan. Both have a fairly mild flavor in relation to other sea vegetables; they taste somewhat salty and have a hint of ocean flavor.

Kombu and kelp are nutritionally similar. Both are rich sources of minerals such as calcium, iron, magnesium, potassium, and iodine, as well as the trace minerals copper and zinc. Kombu and kelp provide a good supply of vitamins A, C, and D, and several of the B vitamins, including riboflavin, niacin, and pantothenic acid.

Reconstitute kombu and kelp by cutting 4- to 5-inch lengths with kitchen shears and soaking in warm water for 5 to 10 minutes. Then, to use as a vegetable, cut into strips or small squares and add to stir-fried vegetables, bean stews, soups, hot cooked grains, or simple Oriental noodles flavored with miso or soy sauce. Many uses for kombu and kelp do not require presoaking, however. Here are a few:

- *KOMBU DASHI*: Kombu is especially well known as an important element in making this basic Japanese broth. Combine 4 to 5 cups water with a 5-inch piece of kombu and 5 to 6 dried shiitake mushrooms. Bring to a boil, then remove from the heat and let stand for 30 minutes. Strain and reserve the kombu and mushrooms for other uses. Flavor the stock with natural soy sauce and use its stock for cooking vegetables or simply as a light broth, adding cooked noodles such as jinenjo, somen, or udon, diced tofu, and minced scallions.

- Both kombu and kelp may be used as a tenderizer for cooking beans, peas, and lentils. They contain a substance (glutamic acid) that softens the beans, helping them to cook more quickly and making them more digestible. Simply add a 4-inch piece of kelp or kombu per every pound of dried beans used and cook until the beans are tender.

- *KOMBU OR KELP "CHIPS"*: Cut dried kombu or kelp into 1- to 2-inch squares with kitchen shears. Bake at 350° F for 15 to 20 minutes, or until lightly browned and crisp. Serve as a snack with Soy Dipping Sauce (page 180) or tofu tartar sauce (page 66).

SIMMERED KOMBU OR KELP WITH MUSHROOMS

Yield: 4 to 6 servings

Kombu and kelp have a special affinity with mushrooms. Try this simple and aromatic dish.

12- to 18-inch length of kombu or kelp,
    as desired
8 dried shiitake mushrooms
1 cup warm water
1 teaspoon sesame oil
1 clove garlic, crushed
One 15-ounce can straw or oyster
    mushrooms, with liquid
1 cup fresh white mushrooms, sliced
1-inch piece ginger, minced
2 tablespoons sherry or dry wine
1 tablespoon natural soy sauce
2 tablespoons cornstarch
Dash of cayenne pepper

With kitchen shears, cut the kombu or kelp into two or three pieces. Soak them in enough water to cover for 5 minutes. Drain and cut them into 1-inch squares.

Soak the shiitakes in the warm water for 15 minutes. When done, reserve the liquid, squeeze the shiitake caps, and remove the tough stems. Slice the caps. In a large skillet, heat the sesame oil. Add the straw or oyster mushrooms with their liquid, the white mushrooms, ginger, sherry or wine, and soy sauce. Bring to a simmer, then add the kombu and the shiitakes and their liquid. Simmer over low heat for 10 minutes.

Dissolve the cornstarch in just enough cold water to make it smooth and pourable. Pour into the skillet and stir in. Add a dash of cayenne and simmer for another 5 to 10 minutes over very low heat. Serve in bowls or over hot cooked rice.

KELP POWDER

Kelp powder, dried and ground from kelp, is more likely to be found in the spice section of your natural-food store than it is alongside other sea vegetables. Used as a seasoning, it imparts a slightly salty, tangy flavor and may be used as a general-purpose seasoning or a table condiment instead of salt. Kelp powder is especially good for seasoning soups and tempura batter. Add 1 to 2 teaspoons to a cup of dry bread crumbs and use for dredging foods before frying. Dip slices of tofu into beaten egg and use this mixture for breading, then fry the tofu until golden on both sides; the flavor of the kelp creates an effect of fish filet.

LAVER (WILD NORI)

Closely related to the cultivated nori that is pressed into thin sheets, laver is its uncultivated cousin. It grows wild on ocean granite beds and is harvested during low tides. Laver is a traditional sea vegetable of the northeastern United States and Canadian provinces as well as the northern Pacific coast, but it is best known for its use in traditional Scottish and Welsh cooking, where it is called *sloke* and is famous as the basis of the fried cakes known as laverbread. Much of the laver marketed in North America comes from the Maine coast and is packaged in masses of dark, tangled fronds. Laver is a strong-flavored sea vegetable with a salty-sweet, distinctive ocean taste.

Laver, like nori, is just about tops in nutrition among sea vegetables. High in protein at 28 percent, laver is an excellent source of trace minerals, such as manganese, fluoride, copper, and zinc, as well as the more common iron, calcium, and phosphorus. Laver is one of the richest sea-vegetable sources of vitamins A, B complex, C, and E.

To use dry laver as a condiment, detangle some of the fronds and spread them on a baking sheet. Bake in a 350°F oven for 5 to 8 minutes or toast in a heavy skillet for several minutes until dry and crisp. Crumble and sprinkle over noodles, grains, steamed vegetables, soups, or sauces.

To reconstitute, soak laver in warm water for 5 to 10 minutes. The volume increases two to three times.

- Stir-fry 2 large onions and 2 cloves minced garlic in a small amount of sesame or peanut oil until translucent, then add 1 to 1 1/2 cups reconstituted laver and continue to stir-fry until the onions are lightly browned. Season with natural soy sauce and lots of freshly grated ginger. Toss in a handful of roasted peanut halves and serve over brown rice or noodles. This makes about 4 servings.

- Combine 1/4 cup chopped reconstituted laver with 3 or 4 beaten eggs and 2 bunches scallions, minced. Pour into a lightly oiled hot skillet and cook on both sides until golden to make an unusual flat omelet. Cut into 4 wedges to make 2 to 4 servings.

- Substitute reconstituted laver for all or part of the spinach called for in a recipe for spinach quiche. This offbeat quiche is for those who enjoy bold sea flavors.

- Combine steamed vegetables of your choice with a small amount of reconstituted laver. Dress with Seasame-Soy Salad Dressing (page 142) as needed and serve as a warm salad.

NORI

Nori is the most popular sea vegetable in Japan, made for over three hundred years from the red algae cultivated in that country's bays and inlets. In its uncultivated form, nori is closely related to laver (see page 133). Nori is harvested in the colder months, sun-dried on bamboo mats, then pressed into sheets. Its unique, salty-sweet flavor seems to be one of the more appealing among sea vegetables to Western palates.

Available in Oriental groceries as well as in natural-food stores, nori comes in deep-purplish or olive-brown sheets, wrapped in cellophane packages. It is also available in the form of *sushi nori*, already toasted, and *kizami nori*, toasted and shredded for ready use as a condiment.

Of all the varieties of commercially distributed sea vegetables, it is hard to match nori in nutritional value. It's the richest in high-quality protein, at 35 percent, and is as rich in vitamin A as are carrots. High in vitamin C, the B vitamins, calcium, magnesium, potassium, and phosphorus, nori also contains enzymes that are believed to aid digestion.

Unlike most other sea vegetables, nori is never reconstituted but is rather used toasted. To prepare nori that's not pretoasted, use a pair of tongs to hold one sheet at a time about 7 to 8 inches away from a medium flame on your stove, just until it turns a bright olive-green.

In Japanese cuisine, nori is use to wrap seasoned rice for sushi or rice balls. Look for recipes in Japanese cookbooks. Here are more ways to use it:

- Cut sheets of toasted nori into 2-inch-wide strips with kitchen shears. Use the strips to wrap oblong pieces of tofu or cucumber (cut into pieces 1/2 inch by 1/2 inch by 2 inches). Secure with toothpicks and serve with Soy Dipping Sauce (page 180) as an hors d'oeuvre or as part of a meal.

- Cut and tear toasted nori into bite-sized pieces and eat just as is with a dipping sauce.

- Cut toasted nori into fine strips (1/2 inch by 2 inches or so) or simply crumble or tear it and use as a garnish for Oriental noodles, simple miso broths, and rice dishes. Add one or two sheets of crumbled nori to stir-fried brown rice and season with natural soy sauce, rice vinegar, a touch of honey, and minced scallions and serve as a side dish. With the addition of some diced tofu, this would become an excellent main dish.

SHORT-GRAIN RICE WITH NORI AND CRISP VEGETABLES

Yield: 4 to 6 servings

Use short-grain, but not glutinous, rice to create this unusual warm salad.

Dressing:

2 tablespoons natural soy sauce
1 tablespoon rice vinegar
2 teaspoons peanut oil
1 teaspoon mirin (optional)
1 tablespoon water
1 teaspoon honey

2 1/2 cups warm cooked short-grain brown rice (about 1 cup dry)
1 cup finely shredded red cabbage
1/2 large cucumber, seeded and cut into matchsticks
1 large turnip or medium daikon radish, cut into matchsticks
2 bunches scallions, minced
2 sheets nori, toasted and cut into thin, 2-inch-long strips

Combine the dressing ingredients in a small bowl. Set aside. Combine the remaining ingredients in a serving bowl. Pour the dressing ingredients over them and toss well. Serve at once.

WAKAME

After nori and kombu, wakame is the third most widely used sea vegetable of Japan. Most of this dark-green long-leafed sea vegetable is harvested from the Hokkaido area of the Sea of Japan. Wakame is closest in appearance and use to kombu and is quite mild-flavored, making it a good choice for those who are shy of a strong sea flavor.

Wakame is quite rich in calcium and also provides good amounts of phosphorus and iron. It also contains an array of trace minerals. such as iodine and selenium, and moderate amounts of several B vitamins and vitamin C.

Dried wakame comes in long strands about 2 inches or so wide. To reconstitute, cut or tear off as much as needed and soak in warm water for 10 minutes. Wakame expands two to three times its dry volume.

- One of the most common uses for wakame is as an ingredient in simple miso broths. Use about 1/4 cup chopped reconstituted wakame per cup of water and simmer for 15 to 20 minutes. Add miso to taste, diluted in enough water to make it pourable before adding to the broth. Embellish with noodles if you'd like, such as soba or somen. Chopped wakame is equally welcome in more elaborate Oriental-style soups, such as hot-and-sour vegetable soups. It is also commonly used as an element in cold salads, particularly those containing cucumbers (see recipe that follows).

- Add a small amount of chopped reconstituted wakame and scallions to scrambled eggs.

- Combine 1/4 cup or so finely chopped reconstituted wakame, 3/4 cup yogurt, 1/4 cup safflower mayonnaise, 1 teaspoon prepared mustard, and the juice of 1/2 lemon. This makes a tangy, offbeat dip for vegetables, batter-fried tofu, crackers, or chips or an unusual dressing for seafood.

- Add 1/2 to 1 cup chopped reconstituted wakame to your favorite split pea soup about 30 minutes before the soup is done.

- Combine 1/4 to 1/2 cup chopped reconstituted wakame with a large grated daikon radish. Season with natural soy sauce, sesame oil, and rice vinegar and use as a condiment.

- Add some reconstituted wakame, cut into strips, to highly marinated salads. Try it with steamed cauliflower and sweet red pepper strips in a vinaigrette.

SWEET-AND-SOUR CUCUMBER AND WAKAME SALAD

Yield: 4 to 6 servings

1 large cucumber, cut into paper-thin slices
10- to 12-inch length of wakame
1 cup matchstick-cut daikon radish or white turnip
2 tablespoons minced scallion
2 tablespoons rice vinegar
1 tablespoon honey
1 tablespoon safflower or peanut oil
1 teaspoon sesame oil
2 teaspoons sesame seeds
Freshly ground pepper to taste

Salt the thinly sliced cucumber lightly and leave in a colander for 15 to 20 minutes. Spread on several layers of paper towel, cover with more paper towel and squeeze to extract moisture.

In the meantime, reconstitute the wakame by soaking for 10 minutes in lukewarm water. Drain well and chop finely. Combine the wakame in a serving bowl with the cucumber, daikon or turnip, and scallion.

Combine the vinegar, honey, and oils in a small bowl and mix well. Add to the cucumber mixture along with the sesame seeds and pepper and toss well to combine. Cover and let stand for 1 hour or so before serving, stirring a few times while it is marinating.

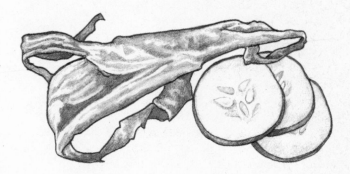

Chapter 9

OILS AND FATS

There has been much emphasis in recent years on the importance of reducing fat intake in a healthy diet. Eating excessive fat has been associated with heart disease and obesity, among other ailments. Nevertheless, fat is vital to the body in small amounts and, along with protein and carbohydrates, is one of the three "large nutrients." One of the best ways of providing the body with the small amount of fat it requires is with good-quality, polyunsaturated or monounsaturated oils from vegetable sources. Among these are oils expressed from nuts, seeds, soybeans, olives, and corn. Both natural-food stores and supermarkets offer quite a variety of these oils.

NUTRITIONAL BENEFITS OF OILS AND FATS

Fats are essential to the body in limited amounts. They are most important in helping to absorb the fat-soluble vitamins A, D, E, and K. Polyunsaturated oils are also thought to promote the body's utilization of B vitamins. Fat is a concentrated source of energy for the body—it can be stored, then used quickly when needed. Fats and oils are beneficial for the skin, hair, cells, and capillaries. When fats are eaten, the body breaks them down into fatty acids. All but two essential fatty acids can be manufactured by the body—*linoleic acid* and *linolenic acid*. Linoleic acid is an important component of most food oils, and when it is ingested, it helps the body synthesize linolenic acid. It is also associated with cardiovascular health, since it is believed to help lower blood cholesterol levels.

Many oils, particularly nut and seed oils, are good sources of vitamin E, which is not only a valuable nutrient essential for the function of the muscles and the endocrine system but is also a natural antioxidant that helps preserve freshness in oil. Up to one-third of the vitamin E in oils is lost during the refining process. Food oils also contain very small amounts of B vitamins and trace amounts of many minerals.

Experts concur that fats and oils are healthful but that they should be taken in great moderation. Current wisdom generally dictates that 1 tablespoon of fat per day from all sources is sufficient, though the average American's intake is an alarmingly high 6 to 8 tablespoons per day. All oils contain about 120 calories and 14 grams of fat per tablespoon.

POLYUNSATURATED, MONOUNSATURATED, AND SATURATED FATS

The dietary significance of the various types of fat is in the way that they affect the blood cholesterol level. Cholesterol is a fatty, waxlike substance essential to the blood in small quantities. The liver manufactures all the cholesterol the body needs. The trouble is that many foods contain cholesterol and can add superfluous levels to the blood. A high-fat, high-cholesterol diet can lead to clogged arteries, in turn leading to cardiovascular disease.

The chemical compositions of fatty acids determine whether fats are saturated, polyunsaturated, or monounsaturated.

Saturated fats are solid or semisolid at room temperature. Some examples of these are butter, shortening, lard, coconut oil, palm oil, and cocoa butter (found in chocolate). Fatty meats and hard cheeses are also high in saturated fats. Saturated fats have been shown to raise blood cholesterol levels.

Polyunsaturated fats are liquid at room temperature and have been shown to lower the overall level of blood cholesterol. These beneficial fats are found in safflower oil, sunflower oil, sesame oil, and other nuts and seeds and their oils, as well as in fish oils.

Monounsaturated fats are also liquid at room temperature and thicken slightly under refrigeration. Like polyunsaturates, they have been shown to lower the total level of blood cholesterol. Monounsaturated fats have the added bonus of helping the blood maintain a high level of high-density lipoproteins (HDLs). These are blood particles that assist the body in ridding itself of excess cholesterol and unneeded fatty acids. Olive oil, cashews, peanuts and their oil, and avocados are all rich in monounsaturated fats.

BUYING OILS

Some vegetable oil labels make a point of advertising that they have "no cholesterol," but the fact is that no vegetable oils contain cholesterol. The absence of cholesterol differentiates vegetable oils not from each other but from animal-derived fats, which do in fact contain cholesterol.

General-purpose oils offered in supermarkets, such as safflower, sunflower, corn oil, or "vegetable oil" (a generic label for oil blends or for soybean oil), are heavily refined to produce a light color, mild flavor, and lack of aroma. If they were placed in unlabeled bottles, it would be nearly impossible to tell one from the other. These oils are processed with a series of chemical bleachings and filterings. Most large-scale manufacturers of oil use the *solvent method* to express oil. The seeds, nuts, or beans are soaked in hexane or other chemical solvent. The oil is then heated to evaporate the solvent. In smaller-scale oil production, or for foods that yield their oil easily, the *expeller method* is used. In this process, the nuts or seeds are placed in a cylinder and are then exposed to heat and pressure to extract the oils. Other steps involved in the refining process include bleaching, degumming, and deodorizing. Many oils sold in natural-food stores also undergo these processes unless they are specifically labeled *unrefined*. Although these refining processes render common oils rather characterless, there is no evidence that they are actually harmful.

A source of confusion arises with the term *cold-pressed*. Many oils sold in natural-food stores are labeled as such, but this can be misleading, since it implies that no heat was used to express the oil. In fact, when an oil is labeled cold-pressed, it often simply means that it was processed by the expeller method rather than the chemical-solvent method, but the oils are still exposed to heat levels from 120° to 150°F. The term *cold-pressed* is not standardized by law, so it does not mean the same thing to every manufacturer. Cold-pressed oils, though somewhat more "natural" in one sense, are often still refined (that is, bleached and deodorized) to the point where they have very little color, flavor, and aroma. Technically, the only truly cold-pressed oils are virgin olive oils.

If expeller-pressed oil is simply filtered and bottled without further refinement, then it is termed unrefined on the label, and this is your best bet for getting an oil that has undergone minimal processing. Unrefined oils retain much more of the flavor of their source. They are, in addition, darker and more aromatic than their refined counterparts, and proponents say that they retain more of the original nutrients of their source. Many times you will see some sediment at the bottom of the bottle. This is harmless and is only further proof that the product is unrefined. Before you spend a lot of extra money on a cold-pressed oil, make sure that you see the word *unrefined* on the label, otherwise your taste buds will be disappointed.

STORING OILS AND FATS

Most oils keep well for several months in a cool, dark place. Unrefined or minimally refined oils will keep well for 4 to 6 months, provided they are kept cool. Refrigerate them during the summer, otherwise they will be susceptible to rancidity. Monounsaturated oils will thicken slightly under refrigeration. Let them come to room temperature before using. Refined oils will keep for up to a year in cool, dry, dark conditions.

ALMOND OIL (see NUT OILS)

APRICOT KERNEL OIL (see FRUIT OILS)

AVOCADO OIL (see FRUIT OILS)

COCONUT OIL

Expressed from the rich meat of ground and dried coconuts, this oil is used extensively in Southeastern Asian cuisines, where coconut in all forms is a staple food. Parts of India, Malaysia, and especially Indonesia are among those countries that use coconut products extensively.

Coconut oil is marketed in natural-food markets domestically and is considered an excellent frying oil. However, coconut oil is one of the least healthful of oils, and its usefulness is thus questionable. It is extremely high in saturated fat (nearly 90 percent).

Coconut oil is used by North American manufacturers in candy, cereals, and cosmetics. It has been said that women in Southeast Asia prize this oil for its benefits when applied directly to the hair and scalp. So, should you find yourself with some coconut oil that you'd like to use up, consider using it externally rather than internally!

CORN OIL

Extracted from the corn germ, corn oil has for many years been a popular general-purpose oil. Depending on the extent to which it has been refined, corn oil will range from pale yellow to deep amber. Corn oil has a polyunsaturate content of 60 percent. Its high vitamin-E content and rich linoleic-acid content make it a good choice as a general-purpose oil. It is easily digested and is a common component in margarines.

Corn oil has a high smoke point, so it is excellent for use in deep-frying or for popping corn (using unrefined corn oil to pop corn imparts a buttery flavor). Use it also for sautéeing, for making breads, particularly corn breads, and in piecrusts.

Look for cold-pressed, unrefined corn oil in natural-food stores. This deep amber oil has a rich flavor and a rather heady aroma.

FRUIT OILS

Fruit oils, available through natural- and specialty-food markets, include avocado oil and apricot kernel oil. Both of these oils are high in monounsaturated fats, very low in saturates, and high in vitamin E. They're expensive, and even their manufacturers offer little information on how—or why—they should be used, save that they are appropriate for cosmetic (presumably for the skin and hair) as well as culinary purposes. Avocado oil is recommended for use in salads, and apricot kernel oil is recommended for general use in cooking.

HAZELNUT OIL (see NUT OILS)

LINSEED OILS

Linseed oil is expressed from flaxseeds. It is an oil primarily distributed through natural-food stores and mail-order outlets and is valued for its high vitamin-E content. A mild, light all-purpose oil, linseed oil is high in polyunsaturated fat and linoleic acid. However, as a general-purpose oil, it is expensive. Safflower oil, similar in vitamin-E content and even higher in polyunsaturates, is considerably less expensive.

MARGARINE

Margarines offered in natural-food stores differ little from those in the supermarket in their overall nutritional profiles. Where they part ways is that natural-food margarines are free of the preservatives, artificial flavors and colors, and other additives loaded into their supermarket counterparts.

Margarine is made by a process of hydrogenation, that is, the introduction of hydrogen gas into liquid oils. The oils solidify, and in the process become more saturated. The chief advantages of vegetable margarines over butter is that they contain less saturated fat overall and contain no cholesterol, compared with the 35 grams in butter. The actual amount of total fat and calories is similar. One tablespoon of margarine or butter contains 100 calories and 12 grams of fat.

Some margarines are less saturated than others. It's usually the case that the softer the margarine is, the less saturated fat it contains. According to Jane Brody in *Jane Brody's Nutrition Book* (W. W. Norton, 1981), the best margarine for you is one that, according to its label, has a polyunsaturated-to-saturated-fat ratio of 2 to 1 or better. Further, the first ingredient of the margarine should be liquid vegetable oil, followed by partially hydrogenated vegetable oil. Most common to natural-food stores is soy margarine. Its polyunsaturated-to-saturated fat ratio is 3 to 2.

It almost goes without saying that margarine should be kept refrigerated. It may also be frozen until needed.

MAYONNAISE

Mayonnaise, by definition (and by law), must contain 65 percent oil. Mayonnaise-type dressings labeled otherwise do not need to adhere to this rule. Most natural-food stores carry mayonnaise that is made from oils high in polyunsaturates, such as safflower oil. Whatever oil is used, mayonnaise is still highly caloric (1 tablespoon contains 100 calories) and is best used sparingly. A nice way to bring the flavor and smoothness of mayonnaise to salads is to mix it in equal parts with low-fat yogurt, whose light texture and tang nicely balance the oily texture of mayonnaise.

NUT OILS

Available through the natural- and specialty-food markets, nut oils are more expensive than most other oils and are generally sold in smaller quantities. Fortunately, they are so flavorful that a little goes a long way. Almond, walnut, and hazelnut oils have become among the most coveted in recent years. Almond and hazelnut oils are rich in monounsaturated fats; walnut oil is high in polyunsaturates. All are rich in vitamin E.

Some nut oils are cold-pressed, but then they are refined to the point that they are as light in color and bland in flavor as general-purpose oils. Avoid these; they are too bland to justify the price. The darker the oil, the richer the flavor and the more distinct the aroma will be. Good-quality nut oils, often imported, have a rich, nutty flavor and pleasant aroma.

Nut oils are quite a treat in green or grain salads, on pasta, or used on fresh vegetables instead of butter. Served in these ways, their flavors may be appreciated more so than in frying or baking, where they can get lost. Combine the oils with a small quantity of the nuts from which they are derived to heighten their flavor even further. Use nut oils for grilling seafood and in homemade mayonnaise.

OLIVE OIL

The olive, ancient symbol of peace and prosperity, has given the culinary world one of its most valuable oils. The olive yields its oil easily; the first and second pressings require no heat or chemicals, so a good olive oil is therefore very pure. The best olive oils come from Italy, Greece, France, and Spain, and their respective flavor, consistency, and color all vary. Though the virgin oils from these locales are all good, the brand you choose is ultimately a matter of personal preference. There are three basic types of olive oil:

- *Extra-virgin olive oil* is the top grade, and is the first pressing of oil extracted from the choicest hand-selected olives. This oil has a rich yellow-green color and the strong, fruity scent and flavor of olives. No heat is used to express this oil. It is the only truly "cold-pressed" oil.

- Virgin olive oil, sometimes called *fine olive oil*, is pressed from olives that are not necessarily of the top, hand-selected grade, or it may be from the second pressing of those olives. High pressure and heat may be used.

- *Commercial grade*, or "pure," olive oil is extracted from pulp and pits left after the second pressing of olives, or else it is pressed from lesser-quality olives. Heat and high pressure are used, and sometimes a small amount of better-grade olive oil is mixed in for better flavor. The term *pure* refers only to the fact that no other types of oils are mixed in.

Olive oil is low in the essential fatty acid linoleic acid, but is high in oleic acid, which is effective in the absorption of fat-soluble vitamins A, D, E, and K and makes the oil highly digestible. It is composed primarily of monounsaturated fat, and several studies have shown that olive oil helps to lower the blood cholesterol.

Good olive oil adds wonderful flavor to Italian, Greek, Mexican, and Spanish recipes. It is delicious in many types of salads as well, especially when combined with wine vinegar. Use olive oil to make pesto sauce and mayonnaise. Add it to pasta sauces or use directly on pasta. Olive oil adds a lot of flavor to fresh vegetables when used for sautéeing. If you are a bit shy of the strong flavor of extra-virgin oil, you might dilute its strength by combining it with safflower oil, whose mild flavor and high linoleic-acid content complement it well. Olive oil has a fairly low smoke point, meaning that it does not tolerate high temperatures as well as do some other oils. It is therefore unsuitable for high-temperature frying.

PEANUT OIL

This oil has long been a favorite, both among commercial users and consumers. Depending on the manufacturer and how heavily the oil has been refined, its flavor and aroma range from completely mild to pleasantly nutty. Peanut oil is a common frying oil in many Oriental and Southeast Asian cuisines.

Peanut oil, like olive oil, is rich in monounsaturated fats, which have the effect of lowering the blood cholesterol level. It is considered a fairly healthy oil and is high in oleic acid, making it highly digestible.

If you wish to use a peanut oil with a peanutty character, look for an unrefined peanut oil. Some of these good peanut oils are imported from China or France. Warm brown in color, they are more expensive than the refined variety. Use peanut oil in place of sesame oil in sauces, marinades, and stir-fries. It is also excellent in cookies, muffins, and nut breads. Peanut oil has a high smoke point, making it suitable for frying at high temperatures.

SAFFLOWER OIL

In recent years, this oil has begun to catch up with corn, peanut, and soybean oils as a very fine, all-purpose oil. Safflower oil is generally available in both natural-food stores and supermarkets. They differ very little from one another and are often made by the same manufacturer. Extruded from safflower seeds, this oil has an outstanding polyunsaturated fat content of 90 percent and is also very high in linoleic acid, both which aid in lowering the blood cholesterol level. Safflower is also among the oils highest in vitamin E.

Safflower oil has a high smoke point, making it suitable for frying at high temperatures. It may be used for just about any culinary purpose where a mild oil is needed. As a salad oil, it is acceptable, if somewhat bland, but it is excellent for cooking, baking, and sautéeing.

SAFFLOWER MAYONNAISE

Yield: About 1 cup

This makes for a mayonnaise that is rich in polyunsaturates. However, if you'd like to experiment, use this formula to make more exotic mayonnaise, using olive oil or unrefined nut oils.

1 small egg
1 1/2 tablespoons lemon juice
1/2 teaspoon prepared mustard
1/4 teaspoon salt
1 cup safflower oil

Combine the first four ingredients in the container of a food processor. Process for several seconds or until smooth and light. With the food processor running, add the oil in a thin stream through the feed tube. Once it's all in, continue to process for only a few more seconds. Transfer to a jar and keep refrigerated.

SESAME OIL

The nutritious sesame seed yields its rich oil easily and can be processed without being exposed to an excessive amount of heat or solvents. Two types of sesame oil are available. *Light sesame oil*, found primarily in natural-food stores, is pressed from raw seeds and has a very mild flavor and aroma, suitable for sautéeing and for salads. Don't expect it to add any particular character to foods. *Dark sesame oil*, which is available both in natural-food stores and in Oriental groceries, is pressed from roasted sesame seeds. It has a deep amber-brown color and a distinct, almost smoked flavor, which is essential in many Oriental dishes. It is minimally refined, unlike light sesame oil.

When sesame oil is called for in recipes, it is almost undoubtedly the dark sesame oil that is required. Sesame oil is approximately equal parts polyunsaturated and monounsaturated fat and is very high in vitamin E. It has a long shelf life.

The flavor of dark sesame oil goes a long way. As little as 1 teaspoon to 1 tablespoon is enough to give character to a dish, even when used in combination with another, milder oil (such as safflower or peanut) in stir-frying. Sesame oil also makes for a tasty ingredient, in greater concentration, in marinades, dipping sauces, and dressings, as well as to flavor noodles. It has a high smoke point, making it suitable for frying at high temperatures. You'll find this oil used in many of the recipes in this book.

SESAME-SOY SALAD DRESSING

Yield: About 3/4 cup

This is a very tasty, offbeat dressing for crisp salads, especially those containing cabbage, sprouts, snow peas, and other characteristically Oriental vegetables.

3 tablespoons sesame oil
1/4 cup safflower or peanut oil
2 to 3 tablespoons natural soy sauce
3 tablespoons rice vinegar
1 teaspoon honey
2 teaspoons sesame seeds
1/2 teaspoon chili powder

Combine all the ingredients in a small bowl or cruet. Shake or stir well before each use.

SOYBEAN OIL

Often used to make margarines and mayonnaise, soybean oil is also a common element in oils labeled simply vegetable oil. In fact, 80 percent of commercial margarines, cooking oils, and mayonnaise are made with soybean oil. With 60 percent polyunsaturated fat, soy oil has a fairly good standing among oils. It is a rich source of vitamin E, linoleic acid, and lecithin, providing that the lecithin has not been removed in the processing. Soybean oil must be heavily refined in order to give it a palatable flavor. Unrefined oil has a strong "beany" flavor and odor.

Refined soybean oil is a good, general-purpose oil that can be used in baking, sautéeing, salad dressings, and in homemade mayonnaise. It is

142

not recommended that unrefined soy oil be used for frying, since it can become malodorous at very high temperatures. Unrefined soy oil has a flavor too strong for most palates.

SUNFLOWER OIL

Another very popular all-purpose oil, sunflower, like safflower, is a relatively recent fixture on both supermarket and natural-food-store shelves, but its use is growing. It ranks second to safflower oil in polyunsaturated fat content, at 65 to 70 percent, and is rich in linoleic acid. Like the seeds from which it is derived, sunflower oil is rich in vitamin E. It is available primarily as a refined, very mild, and light oil.

Sunflower oil is suitable for just about any-thing as an all-purpose oil; for example, in baking, sautéeing, salad dressings, and homemade mayonnaise. It has a fairly high smoke point, so it's fine for frying at high temperatures.

WHEAT GERM OIL

Wheat germ oil is a specialty oil occasionally found in natural-food stores. It is particularly high in vitamin E (its concentration is twice that of most other common oils) and is rich in linoleic acid and polyunsaturated fat. Try wheat germ oil, with its somewhat stronger, nuttier flavor, in salads, on pasta, to sauté vegetables, and in baking. It is expensive, so use it where its flavor will be most appreciated. Once opened, wheat germ oil must be refrigerated or it will go rancid quickly.

Chapter 10

DRIED FRUITS

Concentrated sources of natural sweetness, highly nutritious dried fruits have a long history as relished foods and as condiments. The drying of fruits is documented in wall paintings done in Egypt during the time of the pharaohs. King David of biblical times accepted raisins instead of taxes, and in classical Greece, dried fruits were extolled as preventative medicines. Natural-food stores and imported-food shops often provide an impressive variety of dried fruits that goes beyond the usual raisins and prunes (not to disparage the quality of these two excellent dried fruits) offered in supermarkets.

NUTRITIONAL BENEFITS OF DRIED FRUITS

All dried fruits are excellent sources of dietary fiber and are high in carbohydrates in the form of natural sugars. These natural sugars make dried fruits valuable additions to many foods such as cereals and baked goods to help cut down on the need for refined sugars. Dried fruits are rich in minerals, such as iron, calcium, magnesium, phosphorus, and potassium. They contain varying amounts of vitamins A and C and trace amounts of some of the B vitamins, such as niacin, thiamine, and riboflavin. Dried fruits are low in fat. A 1/4 cup serving of most dried fruits averages about 120 to 170 calories.

BUYING DRIED FRUITS

Much of the fruit prepared for commercial marketing is dried in the sun, and some is heat-dried. Some dried fruits are sulfured, a process in which the fruit is passed through sulfur dioxide, a poisonous gas, before it is dried. This is done to certain dried fruits so that they retain their color. Some fruits that commonly undergo this process are apricots, golden raisins, and peaches. Exposure to air, or oxidation, causes dried fruits to turn brown, but this discoloration has no significance whatever, except that the fruit is less visually appealing. On the plus side, it should be noted that sulfur processing is thought to help fruits retain their vitamin C content. Though the thought of using a poisonous gas on fruits may seem obnoxious, sulfur has in fact long been used as a preservative and is on the list of preservatives defined as GRAS (Generally Recognized as Safe) by the Food and Drug Administration (FDA). Even though this processing is considered harmless, it is also rather unnecessary except for cosmetic purposes. Consumers who would in any case like to avoid sulfured fruits will often have a variety of fruits to choose from in natural-food stores and through mail-order outlets.

Aside from sulfuring, commercially processed dried fruits may undergo other treatments, such as hydration and the addition of certain preservatives, so that they look glossier and retain their moistness. Potassium sorbate, or sorbic acid, is one such preservative used for this purpose. It is often used on prunes and figs to keep them moist and retard the growth of mold. This preservative is broken down by the body and used as food energy. It is also on the GRAS list. Other possible processes that dried fruits may undergo are being dipped in sugar (sometimes erroneously labeled honey-dipped) or coated with mineral oils to improve flavor or appearance.

Though the boxes in which dried fruits are packaged will sometimes indicate the extent to which they have been processed, it is not often clear which, if any, of these processes have been used on the dried fruits you buy, especially when buying in bulk. Often, natural-food stores and mail-order sources selling dried fruit will have information on the extent of the processing they've undergone. If you're not sure, ask your retailer. If you'd like to buy dried fruits that are as untreated as possible and also have the option of choosing organically grown dried fruits, Walnut Acres is a good source to explore (see appendix B).

STORING DRIED FRUIT

Store dried fruits in tightly lidded jars away from heat and light and they will keep for several months to a year. However, the sooner they are eaten, the moister and more nutritious they will be. Long storage causes deterioration of vitamin C. If dried fruits are stored in too warm a place, they may ferment and become unpalatable.

GENERAL USES FOR DRIED FRUITS

The sweetness and chewiness of most dried fruits make many of them interchangeable for general use. Try them in the following ways:

- *As a snack*: It almost goes without saying that most dried fruits are excellent as a naturally sweet snack for children and adults alike!

- *In baked goods*: Raisins, dates, and currants are commonly used in muffins and batter breads, but for a change of pace try using chopped apricots, peaches, pears, or prunes.

- *In trail mixes*: Combine whole or chopped dried fruits with nuts and seeds to make high-energy snacks. Mix together two or three different types of dried fruits with two or three different types of nuts and seeds in whatever proportions you'd like. Store in a jar.

- *In cereals*: Raisins are commonly used to sweeten hot or cold cereals. In addition try using diced dried peaches, prunes, apricots, apples—actually, any dried fruit is great for this purpose. They not only add natural sweetness but contribute to an interesting texture.

- *Stewed fruits*: To plump dried fruits, cover them with hot or cold water or fruit juice and let stand overnight. Try combining several types to make an interesting winter fruit compote. Top with wheat germ and eat for breakfast or mix with yogurt.

- *Fancy fruit salads*: Add any type of dried fruit to fresh fruit salads for variety and texture.

- *Fruit-and-nut grain pilafs*: Almost any type of dried fruit is good in grain pilafs, with perhaps the exception of dates, which are too soft and may disintegrate. Combine cooked grain (fluffy grains are best, such as brown rice, quinoa, couscous, pot barley) with dried fruits, chopped nuts, and whole or ground spices.

- *Sweet side dishes*: Combine dried fruits with sautéed sweet vegetables, such as carrots, winter squashes, or sweet potatoes. Especially good for this purpose are chopped pitted prunes, Calimyrna or mission figs, and raisins.

APPLES

Chewy and sweet, dried apples make a good snack for children (or for adults, for that matter). They contain modest amounts of vitamin C and traces of B vitamins. Minerals in good supply include calcium, iron, magnesium, and potassium. Dried apples are high in fiber, especially in the beneficial fiber pectin.

Dried apples may be used in many of the ways listed on page 146. Chop them and add to cold cereals and to grain pilafs (try them in a wild-rice pilaf), Combine them with nuts and other dried fruits in trail mixes. Soaked with other dried fruits, they make an excellent compote that is good served warm on its own or with yogurt.

APPLE-YOGURT COMPOTE

Yield: 4 servings

1 cup dried apples
¹/₃ cup raisins or pitted prunes
²/₃ cup apple juice
¹/₂ teaspoon cinnamon
¹/₄ teaspoon ground cloves (optional)
1 cup applesauce
¹/₂ cup plain yogurt
2 tablespoons honey
¹/₄ cup crushed almonds

Combine the dried apples and raisins or prunes with the apple juice and spices in a small saucepan. Soak overnight or simmer over low heat until the apple juice is absorbed. Allow the mixture to cool to room temperature, then combine in a mixing bowl with the applesauce, yogurt, and honey and stir to combine. Distribute among four serving bowls and top each serving with some crushed almonds.

APRICOTS

Apricot trees were originally cultivated in China, and the stones of their fruit were eventually carried over by traders to the Middle East and Europe. The Spanish settlers of early California brought the fruit with them, and it was there that the method of producing the moist and chewy dried apricot was developed.

Apricots are among the highest in food value of all dried fruits. Exceptionally high in fiber, apricots contain significant amounts of iron, calcium, and other minerals, as well as vitamin C. It is their vitamin A content that is the most outstanding, ¹/₄ cup serving providing nearly all of the adult Recommended Daily Allowance.

Most useful as a snack food, dried apricots are also nice chopped and added to winter fruit salads and trail mixes. Consider adding them, finely diced, to breakfast cereals and baked goods as a change of pace from raisins. Add finely diced apricots and a touch of honey to plain yogurt and eat as a light lunch. Their sweet and slightly tangy flavor gives grain pilafs an exotic twist.

APRICOT BLONDIES

Yield: 9 to 12 servings

¹/₄ cup (¹/₂ stick) soy margarine, softened
¹/₂ cup honey
2 eggs, well beaten
¹/₃ cup low-fat milk or soy milk
1 teaspoon vanilla extract
1 ¹/₂ cups whole wheat pastry flour, or 1 cup whole wheat pastry flour plus ¹/₂ cup oat or barley flour
1 ¹/₂ teaspoons baking powder
¹/₂ teaspoon salt
¹/₂ teaspoon cinnamon
¹/₄ teaspoon each ground cloves and allspice
³/₄ cup finely diced apricots
¹/₂ cup chopped pecans or walnuts

Preheat the oven to 350°F.
In a mixing bowl, cream the margarine with

the honey. Add the eggs and milk and beat together until smooth.

In another mixing bowl, sift together the flour, baking powder, salt, and spices. Add the wet mixture to the dry and beat together until smoothly blended. Stir in the apricots and nuts. Pour the mixture into an oiled 9-by-9-inch baking pan. Bake for 25 to 30 minutes, or until the top is golden and a knife inserted into the center tests clean. Cool in the pan, then cut into nine or twelve squares to serve.

BANANA CHIPS

Banana chips are a bit different from other dried fruits in that, unlike their counterparts, which are chewy and very sweet, banana chips are crunchy, almost like potato chips, and are far less sweet than fresh bananas. They retain a mild banana flavor and aroma. Like the fresh fruit, they are rich in potassium and also supply significant amounts of magnesium and vitamin A, as well as small amounts of vitamin C and the B vitamins. Occasionally, banana chips are sold sweetened with sugar, but there seems to be little merit in eating sweetened dried bananas; you're better off eating a fresh banana.

Banana chips are not as versatile as other dried fruits and are not appropriate for most of the general uses listed on page 146. They are

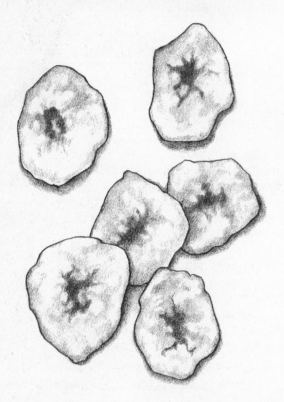

most useful as part of fruit-and-nut trail mixes or incorporated into homemade granolas, where they add a nice crunch and scent.

CURRANTS

The fruit of a shrub that grows both wild and under cultivation, currants are a type of berry. Fresh black currants are used to make excellent jams or are dried to become the tiniest of all dried fruits. Currants can be described as looking and tasting like miniature raisins, despite the fact that raisins are dried from a different type of fruit. Currants are particularly rich in fiber, iron, and vitamin C.

Since they are similar in texture and flavor to raisins, though perhaps slightly less sweet, currants may be substituted for them in many recipes. Currants make wonderful additions to baked goods such as cookies, muffins, and quick breads. They are particularly good in hot or cold cereals, pancakes, and scones, but they may get a bit lost in grain pilafs and trail mixes.

DATES

Prized for their extramoist, supersweet qualities since ancient times, the fruit of the date palm was introduced to California by the Spanish missionaries in the eighteenth century. Dates sold domestically come from California or else are imported from the Middle East or North Africa.

Dates are most often sold in preweighed plastic containers or bags, since their stickiness makes them hard to handle. Several types are available. The most common is *Deglet Noor*, which are the smaller, more familiar, smooth-skinned type. *Zahidi* are medium-size, less sweet, light-colored dates. *Medjool* dates are large, with a soft, wrinkled skin and an exceptionally sugary flavor. These dates may be used fairly interchangeably.

Dates supply moderate amounts of vitamins A, B complex, and C. They are a good source of minerals such as iron, potassium, magnesium, phosphorus, and calcium. Dates contain a high percentage of natural sugars and are fairly high in fiber.

Date-nut seems to be as much of a culinary expression as *salt and pepper*. Indeed, date-nut breads are ubiquitous, and recipes may be found in both natural-food and general cookbooks. Pitted dates have a well in the center that provides a perfect place for stuffing peanuts or almonds, to be eaten as a snack. Their flavor has an affinity with both bananas and apples, so you might try adding some, chopped, to your favorite banana bread or apple dessert recipes.

The texture of dried dates is a bit too soft for use in hot or cold cereals or grain pilafs, but it does make them one of the only dried fruits that can be used in blended beverages, and they also make wonderful chutneys. Try the following quick chutney:

MINTED DATE-APPLE CHUTNEY

Yield: About 2 cups

This chutney keeps for several weeks under refrigeration.

2 tablespoons soy margarine
1 large onion, chopped
2 medium apples, peeled and diced
1 heaping cup chopped dates
1/2 cup apple juice
1/4 cup chopped fresh mint
1 teaspoon freshly grated ginger
1/4 cup (scant) cider vinegar
1 teaspoon chili powder

Melt the margarine in a heavy saucepan. Add the onion and sauté until it is golden. Add the remaining ingredients and simmer, covered, over low heat for 35 to 40 minutes, or until the liquid is absorbed. If necessary, simmer, uncovered, for another 5 minutes or so to thicken the liquid. Allow to cool and store in jars, refrigerated. Serve at room temperature with Indian-style dishes or with simple grain dishes as a relish. Or spread on crackers or rice cakes.

FIGS

CALIMYRNA OR SMYRNA FIGS

These firm, chewy brown figs have a long history as a favored food in ancient Egypt and classical Rome. The Smyrna fig was brought to California by the Spanish missionaries in the eighteenth century. It found warm, dry growing conditions similar to those in its native Mediterranean regions. The fig grown in California has appropriately been given the name Calimyrna.

Imported Smyrna figs found in natural- and imported-food stores are often flattened and strung through the centers to form a round,

then wrapped in cellophane. The Calimyrna are often sold in bulk or in colorful packages in supermarkets in their unflattened form.

Figs are a concentrated source of minerals such as calcium, iron, potassium, and phosphorus. They are also an excellent source of dietary fiber and contain small amounts of vitamin A and the B vitamins.

Calimyrna or Smyrna figs are often eaten on their own as a snack but may also be incorporated into recipes in many interesting ways. Remove their tough stem before using them in recipes. Chopped figs may be used in rice or bulgur pilafs and are good sautéed with sweet vegetables such as squash or carrots. Stew them with other fresh or dried fruits in fruit juice, spices, and wine. Use them chopped as a change of pace from raisins in spice cakes, puddings, fruit crisps, and other baked goods. See the list on page 146 for more ideas.

FIG RUGLACH

Dough:

1 1/2 cups whole wheat pastry flour
3 tablespoons light brown sugar
1/2 teaspoon baking powder
1/4 teaspoon baking soda
1/4 teaspoon salt
1/2 cup (1 stick) soy margarine
1 egg, unbeaten
1 tablespoon apple juice

Filling:

1/2 pound figs, stemmed and finely chopped

½ cup apple juice
¼ cup (scant) honey or rice syrup
1 teaspoon cinnamon
1 teaspoon vanilla extract
⅓ cup finely chopped walnuts

In a mixing bowl, combine the first five ingredients. Cut the margarine into bits and cut it into the flour mixture until the mixture resembles a coarse meal. Work in the unbeaten egg and the apple juice, with a fork first and then with your hands, to form a smooth, soft dough. Place the dough in a bowl, then cover and refrigerate while making the filling.

Combine all the ingredients for the filling, except for the walnuts, in a saucepan and bring to a simmer. Simmer over low heat, covered, for 10 minutes. Stir in the walnuts.

Preheat the oven to 375°F.

Divide the dough into two parts. Roll each part into an approximately 11-by-12-inch rectangle, trimming the sides to make a neat rectangle. Spread the filling evenly over each rectangle, leaving a ½-inch border all around. Roll the rectangles up and crimp the sides. Place on an oiled cookie sheet, seam side down.

Bake for 20 minutes, or until the dough is golden. Allow to cool, then cut across in 1-inch sections.

MISSION FIGS

Mission figs, like Calimyrna figs, were brought to California in the eighteenth century by the Spanish missionaries. Still cultivated primarily in California, this plump black fig is moister and slightly sweeter than the Smyrna or Calimyrna type.

Although mission figs are sold in bulk in natural-food and specialty stores, they are beginning to appear in supermarkets, packaged in boxes.

Mission figs are rich in minerals, supplying calcium, iron, magnesium, and potassium. They contain small amounts of the B vitamins and vitamin C.

These sweet figs make an appealing snack simply eaten on their own; however, they lend themselves to any number of preparations, particularly as an interesting substitute for raisins in cooking, baking, or as an addition to cold or hot cereals. Just make sure to trim their tough stems before using them. Like Smyrna and Calimyrna figs, they work nicely in pilafs or sautéed with sweet vegetables such as squash, sweet potatoes, or carrots. For more ideas, see the list on page 146.

CARROTS WITH MISSION FIGS

Yield: 6 servings

This makes a nice side dish when served with curried vegetable or grain dishes.

2½ tablespoons soy margarine
1 medium onion, quartered and sliced
¾ pound carrots (about 5 medium),
   thinly sliced
⅔ cup mission figs, trimmed and sliced
1 teaspoon honey
½ teaspoon freshly grated ginger
¼ teaspoon salt
Dash of cinnamon

In a heavy skillet, heat the margarine until it foams. Add the onion and sauté over moderate heat until the rings separate. Add the carrots and sauté for 5 minutes. Add the remaining ingredients and sauté for another 7 to 10 minutes, stirring frequently, until the carrots are tender-crisp and lightly golden. Serve at once.

PAPAYA

This avocado-shaped fruit grows among the huge leaves of a tropical tree. Most of the papaya sold in the United States comes from Hawaii. In dried form, papaya is often sold in long strips that are very sweet, with a texture that almost resembles a gumdrop candy. Look for papaya that is not sugar-dipped. Papaya is high in vitamin C, potassium, and fiber and is very low in calories. Dried papaya is rather expensive, and its usefulness in cooking is limited. It is most useful eaten on its own, as an excellent snack. Its natural sweetness makes it especially appealing to children.

PEACHES

A favorite American fruit, the peach is perhaps most characteristic of Southern cookery. In dried form, however, peaches are one of the less common dried fruits, although they concentrate the sweetness and nutrition of fresh peaches in a very pleasant way. Dried peaches tend to be very expensive. Dried peaches are quite rich in vitamins A and C as well as iron. They provide modest amounts of the B vitamins, phosphorus, potassium, and magnesium.

Dried peaches can be used in most of the ways suggested on page 146. They are very good stewed, then eaten with yogurt as a light meal. They work well in fruit-and-nut mixes and as a change of pace in baking, in grain pilafs, and added to hot or cold cereals.

PEARS

Large, brown, and leathery, dried pears tend to look uninviting, but they are actually an interesting dried fruit to experiment with, perhaps because they are rather offbeat. High in fiber and potassium, dried pears also provide modest amounts of vitamins C and A and minerals such as calcium, phosphorus, and iron.

Dried pears come in halves that may be eaten straight as a chewy snack. Trim the core before using them in cooking or baking. Plumping them by soaking overnight or simmering briefly in water or fruit juice makes them a bit more palatable. They are good chopped and added to yogurt with a bit of chopped nuts and honey. Cut dried pears into strips and use them as an unusual element in fruit salads. They're especially nice if combined with tart fruits such as grapefruit, pineapple, and kiwi. They work well in fruit compote, combining fresh and dried fruits, but are not as successful in grain pilafs or in baking. For more ideas, see page 146.

PEAR BUTTER

Yield: About 1 cup

This quick and easy fruit spread is excellent on bread with cream cheese or nut butters.

1 heaping cup dried pears
1 cup apple juice
1 tablespoon dry red wine
½ teaspoon cinnamon
½ teaspoon allspice
Dash of nutmeg

Core the dried pears and chop them very fine, either by hand or in a food processor or blender. Place them in a saucepan along with the remaining ingredients and cook over low heat for 40 minutes, or until the mixture has the consistency of thick preserves. Allow to cool, then store in a tightly lidded jar in the refrigerator.

PINEAPPLE

This well-loved tropical fruit becomes almost a candy when it is dried. Dried pineapple is often sold in rings or chunks and is rather expensive. It's surprising that many natural-food stores sell sugared (sometimes called honey-dipped) pineapple, since it's so naturally sweet. Look for dried pineapple labeled unsweetened or natural. Dried pineapple, like the fresh fruit, is exceptionally high in vitamins A and C and in potassium.

Unsweetened pineapple rings make a good snack for children. Chopped dried pineapple adds an exotic touch to trail mixes, hot or cold cereals, rice puddings, and grain pilafs. It also adds an interesting touch to squash breads and sweet muffins.

PRUNES

Despite their geriatric connotations, prunes are a tasty and highly nutritious dried fruit that don't deserve their stodgy reputation. Prunes are dried plums, and most of those sold domestically come from California.

Prunes are often available in bulk, in addition to their more commonplace boxed form in supermarkets. In most cases, prunes are treated in various ways to make them more moist and plump (see page 145 for specifics). Though these processes are not generally considered harmful, those wishing to buy untreated prunes can ask their natural-food retailer about the extent to which the prunes sold in bulk have been treated, or else explore mail-order sources. Completely untreated prunes will need more soaking and coaxing to be equally palatable. Pitted prunes, are, of course, the most convenient to use.

Prunes are perhaps most valued for the fact that they are one of the foods richest in dietary fiber. A 1/4 cup serving contains 9 grams of fiber, about one-third of the fiber needed daily for a diet to be considered high in fiber. Exceptionally high in potassium, prunes also provide good quantities of iron, phosphorus, and magnesium. They are high in vitamin A and provide modest amounts of the B vitamins.

To soften prunes, either cover them with hot water or fruit juice and let stand overnight or combine them with an equal amount of water and boil for 3 to 4 minutes. Serve stewed prunes with citrus fruit sections, yogurt or applesauce.

Chopped prunes are a very good substitute for raisins in breads, muffins, and cookies. Use them for topping hot or cold cereals or incorporate them into grain dishes. Stuff pitted prunes with peanuts or cashews and serve as a snack. Slice prunes and add them to fresh fruit salads. Prunes are appropriate for all the uses listed on page 146.

WINTER FRUIT CRISP

Yield: 6 servings

2 medium apples, peeled, cored, and thinly sliced
3 medium pears, cored and thinly sliced
1 cup chopped pitted prunes
1/4 cup chopped walnuts or pecans (optional)
1/3 cup barley malt syrup or carob syrup
1/4 cup apple juice
1/2 teaspoon cinnamon
1/4 teaspoon each ground nutmeg and allspice

Topping:

3/4 cup rolled oats
1/2 cup toasted wheat germ
1/4 cup whole wheat flour
1/4 cup (1/2 stick) soy margarine, melted
2 tablespoons light brown sugar

Preheat the oven to 350°F.
Combine the ingredients for the filling in a large mixing bowl and stir together well.

In another bowl, combine the ingredients for the topping. Spread half the crumbs mixture in the bottom of a lightly oiled 9-by-9-inch baking pan. Pour in the fruit mixture, pat it in, then top with the remaining crumbs mixture. Bake

for 40 to 45 minutes, or until the fruit is tender and the crumbs are golden.

RAISINS

Mineral-rich raisins are the most abundantly used dried fruit in North America and are a favorite for snacking and cereals. Raisins are dried from grapes, and different types of grapes yield different types of raisins. A large percentage of the raisins sold are *Thompson* raisins. *Sultana* is the European name for Thompson raisins. *Monukka* raisins are larger raisins and are occasionally offered in specialty-food shops. *Zante currants* are not really currants, but are miniature raisins dried from a small grape. *Golden* raisins are Thompson raisins that have been sulfured to retain their light color. The differences in the flavors of the various raisins are not appreciable.

Nutritionally, raisins compare quite favorably with other dried fruits. Along with generous quantities of minerals such as iron, potassium, calcium, and magnesium, raisins are quite high in fiber. They also provide vitamin A and modest amounts of the B vitamins.

Raisins are such a ubiquitous kitchen staple that it hardly seems necessary to enumerate their uses. The use of raisins in baking breads, muffins, and cookies and in hot or cold cereals cuts down tremendously on the need for sugar. They are highly compatible with apples and pears and add an extra sweetness to most fruit salads. Raisins are always welcome in trail mixes and grain pilafs and can add an offbeat twist to curried vegetables, pastas, and spinach dishes.

MULTICOLORED AVOCADO-RAISIN SALAD

Yield: 4 to 6 servings

1 sweet red bell pepper, cut into long, thin strips
1 cup finely shredded red cabbage
1 medium bunch broccoli, cut into bite-size pieces and steamed tender-crisp
1 medium avocado, quartered and thinly sliced
1/2 cup raisins
1/4 cup toasted sunflower seeds

Dressing:

1/2 cup plain yogurt
Juice of 1/2 lemon
3 tablespoons safflower oil
1/2 teaspoon each dried dill and dry mustard

Combine the salad ingredients in a serving bowl. Combine the dressing ingredients in a small mixing bowl. Stir well and pour into the salad. Toss well and serve at once.

Chapter 11

SWEETENERS

Let's face it—most Americans have an enormous sweet tooth. While the detrimental effects of sugar are still being debated, most experts agree that in general, we consume far too much of it. Sugar is a catchall term, for there are actually many forms of sugar: sucrose, fructose, maltose, and dextrose, among others. Sugars are carbohydrates that occur naturally in fruits, vegetables, grains, and other foods. At the center of controversy are simple sugars, especially sucrose, or table sugar. Most people would be loath to give up eating sugar altogether, no matter how bad the news. The natural foods marketplace offers a good number of alternatives to simple sugar—some better than others, to be sure, but most at least somewhat better and less shocking to the system than table sugar. A few even contain measurable nutrients. The biggest drawback to some of these products is their cost, always a stumbling block in such supply-and-demand situations. But read on, since many of these products, used, of course, in moderation, are definitely worth exploring.

NUTRITIONAL BENEFITS OF SWEETENERS

Sweeteners are not consumed for their nutritional benefits, so instead, their effects on the system will be briefly defined here. As mentioned above, sugars are carbohydrates, chemical compounds that the body uses for quick fuel supply. The specific chemical composition of various sugars determines whether they are monosaccharides, disaccharides, or polysaccharides. *Monosaccharides* are the simple sugars such as sucrose, composed of one glucose molecule that enter the bloodstream rapidly. This is thought to "shock" the blood sugar level and upset metabolism. While eating foods that are simple sugars may result in an immediate boost in energy, the aftermath may be an equally quick drop in energy, renewed sugar craving, and hunger. Some sweetners that are mostly simple sugars include granulated sugar, corn syrup, honey, maple syrup, molasses, and some fruit sugars. *Polysaccharides*, on the other hand, are complex sugars composed of many glucose molecules. These are found in starchy foods, such as grains, potatoes and other vegetables, legumes, and some fruits. These sugars are absorbed into the blood much more slowly, providing a steady source of energy and a feeling of satiation.

Some natural sweeteners made from grain, such as rice syrup and barley malt syrup, are *disaccharides*, sugars composed of two glucose molecules. They are less shocking to the system than monosaccharides, because they don't have an immediate, dramatic effect on the blood sugar level.

The effects of simple sugars on the body are constantly being studied and debated. Findings are inconclusive, but most experts agree that sugar does not have the same effect on everybody. It is generally accepted, however, that excessive intake of simple sugars can contribute to obesity and tooth decay.

BUYING AND STORING SWEETENERS

Since most sweeteners available in natural-food stores come in jars or packages, where they remain for the duration of their shelf life, no special guidelines are needed for buying them. Sugar is a natural preservative, so products that are pure sugar, whether simple or complex, are in little danger of spoilage. As a general rule, sweeteners should be kept in a cool, dark dry place, where they will keep for up to a year. Any exceptions and special recommendations will be given under the individual entries that follow.

AMAZAKE

This traditional Japanese sweetener is a relatively recent import to the North American natural foods market. To make amazake, brown rice is cooked, then inoculated with rice koji, the same enzymatic culture used to ferment rice miso. The koji breaks the starches down into complex sugars. The end product is highly digestible, with a very concentrated sweetness. The complex sugars are released slowly into the bloodstream and so do not upset the blood sugar level, and the enzymes present aid in general digestion.

Depending on the manufacturer and the specific formula used to make it, amazake may be syrupy and flowing, or rather thick, like a pudding. The thicker it is, the more concentrated the sweetness. The flavor is quite pleasant and may have a slight bite due to the fermentation process. The only drawback of amazake is that it is rather expensive, so one may feel inhibited about using it freely. Store amazake in the refrigerator. The fact that amazake is not overly viscous and sticky makes it pleasant to use.

- Thick amazake is an excellent sweetener for puddings, such as rice or banana puddings.

- Thick amazake can be used in baking as a substitute for honey. It is not as sweet, so use slightly more.

- Either thick or liquid amazake can be used to sweeten hot or cold cereals and blended beverages such as fruit shakes or milk shakes.

- Stir amazake into yogurt to sweeten it, or use it as a topping for fresh or stewed fruits.

AMAZAKE-APPLE UPSIDE-DOWN CAKE

Yield: 6 servings

4 large apples, peeled, cored, and thinly sliced
1/2 cup thick amazake
1/2 teaspoon cinnamon
Dash of nutmeg

1 cup whole wheat pastry flour
1 teaspoon baking powder
1/4 teaspoon toasted wheat germ
1/4 teaspoon each salt and cinnamon
1 egg, beaten
1/4 cup honey
1/4 cup (1/2 stick) soy margarine, melted
1/4 cup low-fat milk
1 teaspoon vanilla extract
1/3 cup currants

Preheat the oven to 350°F.

Combine the first four ingredients in a mixing bowl and toss well, until the apples are evenly coated with the amazake and cinnamon. Pat into a buttered 9-by-9-inch baking dish.

In another mixing bowl, combine the beaten egg with the remaining ingredients. Combine the wet and dry ingredients and stir vigorously to combine. Spoon the batter evenly over the apples. Bake for 35 to 40 minutes, or until the top is golden brown and the apples are soft. Let cool somehat, then cut into nine squares to serve. Serve warm.

BARLEY MALT SYRUP

This robust-flavored natural sweetener has become a fixture on the shelves of natural-food stores in recent years. It is made by malting barley grains, an elaborate procedure that starts by sprouting the barley and ends by heating the sprouts slowly in brewing vats to make a syrup (this syrup, called *wort*, is the brewer's malt used to make beer). The syrup is then drawn off and evaporated, resulting in a highly concentrated sweetener.

Barley malt syrup has an assertive flavor, though not as overpowering as that of blackstrap molasses. It is almost as thick as molasses and is just as dark and sticky. Barley malt is less sweet than both molasses and honey. Store in a cool, dry place to prevent fermentation, and to be safe during warmer months, refrigerate it. If the barley malt hardens, place it in a pot of hot water until it regains its fluidity.

Barley malt syrup is 65 percent maltose, a sugar that enters the bloodstream more slowly than simple sugars and so is less shocking to the system. The malting process also increases the levels of B vitamins in the product, and it contains trace amounts of some minerals. Barley malt syrup is usually somewhat more expensive than honey, but due to its stronger flavor, there is a tendency to use it sparingly. It's a useful sweetener that may be used in a number of interesting ways:

- Substitute barley malt syrup for honey in muffins and quick breads that need a richness rather than a sweetness to their flavoring. Try it in squash or pumpkin breads and in bran muffins.

- Barley malt is excellent for use in yeasted breads, such as pumpernickel or hearty rye breads. Use about 3 tablespoons in a recipe that will yield 2 loaves. Its use not only contributes to the flavor but encourages the leavening process.

- Use barley malt syrup as a glazing agent for sweet potatoes. Combine 1/3 cup syrup with hot water in a small bowl and stir until it is dissolved. Combine the mixture with 2 large cooked peeled and sliced sweet potatoes in a large skillet with 2 tablespoons soy margarine and cook over low heat, covered, until the potatoes are evenly browned and glazed.

- Use barley malt syrup to sweeten hot cereals.

- Barley malt syrup makes terrific "malteds." For 2 servings, combine 1 banana, 1 cup milk or soy milk, 6 ice cubes, 3 tablespoons carob, and 1/4 cup barley malt syrup in the container of a blender or food processor. Process until frothy.

- Substitute barley malt syrup for blackstrap molasses in recipes if you find the flavor of molasses too strong. For instance, the molasses in the traditional Pennsylvania Dutch molasses pie that follows is replaced with barley malt syrup.

BARLEY-MALT SHOOFLY PIE

Crumbs mixture:

3/4 cup whole wheat pastry flour
1/4 cup toasted wheat germ
1/3 cup firmly packed light brown sugar
  or date sugar (see entry below)
1 teaspoon cinnamon
1/4 teaspoon each ground ginger and
  ground cloves
1/4 cup (1/2 stick) soy margarine,
  softened and cut into bits

2/3 cup barley malt syrup
1/2 cup boiling water
1/2 teaspoon baking soda
One 9-inch piecrust

Preheat the oven to 375°F.

In a mixing bowl, combine the ingredients for the crumbs mixture, working the margarine in with a pastry blender or with the tines of a fork until the mixture resembles a coarse meal.

In another bowl, dissolve the barley malt syrup in the boiling water. Sprinkle in the baking soda and stir until it dissolves. Add about two-thirds of the crumbs mixture and stir until moistened, but it need not be smooth. Pour into the piecrust and top with the remaining crumbs. Bake for 30 to 35 minutes, or until the crust and crumbs are golden and the filling is set. Serve warm or at room temperature.

DATE SUGAR

Not actually a sugar in the conventional sense, date sugar is ground from dehydrated dates. This interesting sweetener is quite expensive, so it's hard to feel free to use it liberally. Dates are nutritious dried fruits, high in fiber and rich in a wide range of vitamins and minerals, such as vitamin A, iron, and potassium.

Date sugar is most often sold in bulk or by weight in natural-food stores. It will keep well for several months if stored in a cool, dry place. If it hardens, place it in the container of a food processor or blender fitted with a metal blade and process until the granules separate.

Date sugar is very sweet and can be used interchangeably with sugar in baking. It does not work for sweetening coffee or tea, since the tiny pieces don't dissolve. It is very effective as a sugar substitute, used measure for measure in cakes, muffins, and batter breads. Date sugar is also an excellent substitute for brown sugar in making crumb toppings for fruit desserts such as apple crisp. Use it to sweeten cold or hot cereals, too.

DATE-SUGAR BLACK CAKE

This dark, moist cake tastes richer than it actually is.

1/4 cup (1/2 stick) soy margarine,
  softened
3/4 cup date sugar
1/4 cup light brown sugar
2 eggs, beaten
1/4 cup blackstrap or sorghum molasses
1 tablespoon grain coffee beverage,
  dissolved in 1/2 cup boiling water
1/3 cup low-fat milk
1 teaspoon vanilla extract
1 1/2 cups whole wheat pastry flour
1/3 cup unsweetened cocoa powder or 1/2
  cup carob powder
1 1/2 teaspoons baking powder
1/4 teaspoon each cinnamon, ground
  cloves, allspice
1/3 cup finely chopped walnuts

Preheat the oven to 350°F.

In a mixing bowl, cream together the margarine, date sugar, and light brown sugar. Add the beaten eggs and molasses and beat together until smooth. Add the dissolved grain coffee, milk, and vanilla

In another mixing bowl, combine the remaining ingredients, except for the walnuts. Add the wet mixture to the dry and stir vigorously to combine. Stir in the walnuts, then pour into a lightly oiled 10-inch tube pan or a 9-by-9-inch cake pan. Bake for 35 to 40 minutes, or until a

knife inserted into the center tests clean. Let cool in the pan, then cut into squares or slices to serve.

FRUCTOSE

Fructose is fruit sugar and is sold in natural-food stores as a white powder packaged in cellophane bags. Since it is extremely concentrated and much sweeter than sucrose (table sugar), much less is required for similar effect. This is a relatively new product, and information is just beginning to come to light, much of it positive. What is known so far is that fructose requires no insulin to be digested, so it does not disturb the blood sugar level as much as sucrose. It is broken down somewhat more slowly, without sending an immediate jolt to the bloodstream. It has been shown that some diabetics may use fructose with little ill effect, but this should not be done without medical advice.

On the minus side, fructose may cause tooth decay at an even faster rate than sucrose and in large amounts may cause gastrointestinal upsets and allergic reactions. Like sucrose, fructose has virtually no nutrients.

HONEY

Honey is the product of the blossom nectar that is gathered, converted, and stored by bees in their geometric honeycombs. Long revered both for its flavor and for cosmetic and medicinal purposes, the use of honey has been traced back to the ancient Egyptian, Roman, and Greek civilizations.

If it seems that clover honey is all there is, then one has only to go to farm markets, specialty-food stores, and of course, natural-food stores to discover a vast array of honeys. These range from the light and mild alfalfa, through the various stronger flavors of wildflower honeys, to the dark, almost opaque buckwheat honey. The flavors and viscosities of honeys are determined by the type of plant from which the nectar was gathered, the season, the specific weather conditions, and even the condition of the soil in which the plants lived.

When buying honey, it's important to remember that there are no standard federal labeling laws governing its sale. What is labeled pure honey, however, must be entirely honey and not a honey blend, although it is permissible that up to 8 percent sucrose may be added. Because of the lack of standardization of labeling, any term other than *pure*, such as *raw*, *organic*, *uncooked*, or *unfiltered*, may not always mean the same thing to every manufacturer, so these terms are rendered somewhat meaningless.

Most honeys are heated lightly before being put into jars to prevent crystallization for several months. Many mass-produced honeys are also filtered to produce clarity. These processes do not necessarily mean that the product is better.

Honey is primarily glucose, a simple sugar that is absorbed rapidly into the bloodstream, immediately raising the blood sugar level. The remaining component of honey is fructose. There is little agreement about whether or not honey is much better for you than sugar. The majority of experts concede that the effects of honey on the system are too similar to those of sugar to make much of a difference. Nutritional charts comparing honey with brown sugar actually show that brown sugar contains more nutrients, which is no doubt due to the molasses that the sugar is coated with. Here are a few additional points to consider:

- Honey contains several B vitamins, some vitamin C, and trace amounts of many minerals, including calcium, iron, copper, and potassium. However, these nutrients are not present in significant enough quantities to be of great importance.

- It is generally agreed that the darker the honey, the more nutrients are present, especially minerals. The darkest honey is buckwheat, and next are some robust wildflower varieties.

- Tablespoon for tablespoon, honey is more caloric than sugar (64 versus 54 calories), but honey is sweeter than sugar, so chances are you'd need to use less to achieve a particular level of sweetness.

- Experts who aren't sold on honey say that it is worse for the teeth than sugar, thereby promoting tooth decay.

- As is the case with sugars and most other sweeteners, moderation is the most sensible course. Think of honey as a delicious condiment to be enjoyed on occasion, rather than as a staple to be used in quantity every day.

Store honey in a cool, dark dry place, where it will keep for several months to a year. If the honey crystallizes, place it in a pot of hot water until it becomes fluid again.

As mentioned above, natural-food stores, specialty-food stores, and well-stocked farm markets are good sources for a variety of honeys. When experimenting with new honeys, a good rule of thumb to follow is that the lighter in color a honey is, the milder its flavor will be. Following are descriptions of some varieties:

Alfalfa honey and *orange blossom honey* are very similar to clover honey in flavor and color and may be used interchangeably in all forms of cooking, baking, and in tea.

Wildflower honey, which may vary in flavor and color depending on the specific wildflowers that were used by the bees, is a somewhat darker and stronger-tasting honey than those mentioned above, as is *tupelo honey*, which originates from the flowers of trees native to the Everglades. Both should be used with discretion at first, but if you like the fuller flavor, by all means use them as you would lighter honeys.

Buckwheat honey is perhaps the most unusual of these special honeys, quite dark, thick, and robust. It is reminiscent of barley malt syrup and may be used as a substitute for either barley malt syrup or molasses. Modify the amount, though, since the honey is sweeter. Buckwheat honey is most appropriate for use in baked goods made with hearty flours such as rye, or hearty grains such as bran, but may not be the best choice for sweetening tea or other beverages.

Apart from its familiar use as a spread for breads, in baking, cooking, and in beverages, here are some additional ways of using honey:

- Combine an equal amount of honey, natural soy sauce, and safflower or peanut oil. Heat the mixture in a skillet, then sauté slices of tofu, tempeh, or seitan on both sides until glazed and golden brown. Serve topped with browned onions. Use the same proportions as a glazing agent for grilling.

- Just a small amount of honey goes a long way to temper the tartness of yogurt. Add a small amount of honey and a dash of cinnamon to make a simple and refreshing dressing for fruit salad.

- Combine tomato sauce, honey, and apple cider vinegar in more or less equal amounts to make a quick sweet-and-sour sauce.

- Add a teaspoon or two of honey to vinaigrette dressings to mellow their bite. This type of dressing adds zest to coleslaw and corn relish and is very good for marinating mushrooms.

- Use honey in small amounts to heighten the flavor of cooked carrots, sweet potatoes, and winter squashes.

- Blend a bit of honey into nut butters or cream cheese and use as a spread for bread, rice cakes or crackers.

MAPLE SYRUP

Maple syrup, a well-loved, traditional sweetener in the United States and Canada, is the product of the brief yearly sap-producing season of sugar maple trees. The clear sap is tapped through holes drilled into the trees. About forty gallons of the sap, or "sugar water," must be boiled down in huge, outdoor vats in order to make 1 gallon of syrup. The hand labor and sheer quantity of sap needed make it easy to understand why genuine maple syrup is expensive.

Real maple syrup marked "fancy" is the best, followed by syrups that are graded accordingly A, B, and C. Maple syrup is prized for its exquisite flavor rather than its nutritive qualities, of which it has little. It is 60 to 65 percent sucrose (see page 155); most of the remaining portion is water, with only small traces of minerals.

Inexpensive supermarket brands of syrup might contain as little as 3 percent real maple syrup—the rest is sugar and water. Genuine maple syrup, if not particularly beneficial, is at least enough of a taste treat to warrant its use on special occasions. There is little reason to use the imitation, despite the lower cost.

Store maple syrup in a cool, dry dark place. It will keep for up to a year under these conditions. If the syrup crystallizes, place the bottle in a pot of hot water until it becomes fluid again.

Maple syrup is most commonly eaten, of course, on pancakes, waffles and French toast and also adds a delectable flavor to puddings. Use it in baked goods as a substitute for honey.

MAPLE-APPLE BREAD PUDDING

Yield: 4 to 6 servings

4 average-size slices soft whole-grain bread, cut into 1/2-inch cubes
1 cup low-fat milk or soy milk
2 eggs, beaten until light
1 cup firmly packed grated peeled apple
1/2 cup raisins
1/2 cup maple syrup
1 teaspoon vanilla extract

2 1/2 tablespoons soy margarine, melted
1/2 teaspoon cinnamon

Preheat the oven to 350°F.

Place the cubed bread in a mixing bowl and pour the milk over it. Allow to soak for 5 minutes. Add the remaining ingredients and mix thoroughly. Pour into an oiled 9-by-9-inch baking dish. Bake for 35 to 40 minutes, or until the top is golden brown and crusty. Allow to cool somewhat, then cut into nine squares to serve. Serve warm.

─────── MOLASSES ───────

Molasses has long been a staple sweetener in the southern United States, where it has always been inexpensive and abundant. Molasses comes in several grades. The one to look for is blackstrap, the highest quality molasses. This is the residue recovered from the final stages of the refining process of sugar, in which the cane or beet sugar crystals are separated from the syrup. In the process of refining cane or beet sugar, the nutrients end up in the syrupy residue, which is molasses.

Blackstrap molasses is considered the most nutritious of common sweeteners, with a good mineral content, particularly iron, as well as a range of B vitamins. It is the best known source of vitamin B_6 after yeast. Vitamin B_6 helps the body to assimilate iron. On the minus side, molasses is 65 percent sucrose (see page 155) and is associated with tooth decay and cavities.

Molasses has an assertive, bittersweet flavor. It is not as sweet as honey, but if the quantity used were increased to provide equal sweetness, most would find it downright overpowering. If you do like the taste of molasses, however, you can use it in moderate amounts to lend an interesting flavor element without knocking out all other flavors.

Traditional American recipes, especially those from the South, are the best sources for molasses recipes. Indian pudding and other cornmeal puddings are traditionally sweetened with molasses, as are some sweet-potato dishes and breads. A molasses-based pie called shoofly pie comes from the Pennsylvania-Dutch tradition. Molasses is often used to give color and hearty flavor to pumpernickel breads. Molasses lends itself quite well, in fact, to many hearty whole-grain breads, particularly those that feature rye flour or cornmeal.

SWEET AND SAVORY GRILLING SAUCE

Yield: About 2 cups

This strong-flavored sauce is excellent for broiling or simmering tofu, tempeh, or seitan.

1 tablespoon safflower oil
1 small ônion, finely chopped
1 clove garlic, minced
1 1/2 cups thick tomato sauce
1/4 cup molasses
3 tablespoons natural soy sauce, or to taste
1/2 teaspoon freshly grated ginger
1 teaspoon chili powder
1/2 teaspoon each dry mustard and paprika

In a heavy saucepan, heat the oil. Add the onion and garlic and sauté over moderate heat until they are golden. Add the remaining ingredients and stir to mix. Simmer over low heat, uncovered, for 15 minutes.

─────── RICE SYRUP ───────

Rice syrup is a traditional sweetener of the Orient. To make it, cooked rice is combined with malted barley. As it stands, the rice starch is converted into maltose, resulting in a thick, naturally sweet syrup. The sugar in rice syrup is primarily maltose, a more complex sugar that enters the bloodstream slower than do simple sugars such as sucrose. Rice syrup does not contain as high a concentration of nutrients as does barley malt syrup, but it contains enough trace amounts of minerals and B vitamins to give it an edge over honey.

One drawback to rice syrup is that it's very thick and sticky, making it tricky to measure or pour. It's easier to spread with a knife, like a jam, than to spoon or pour. Some brands have a better flavor than others, so if you like this mild sweetener, you might like to try a few types and stick with the brand you like most. Brown rice syrup has a fuller flavor than white rice syrup. Rice syrup is not as sweet as honey, but the two are fairly interchangeable in recipes if your palate can adjust to the milder flavor.

Rice syrup keeps well stored in a cool, dark place and does not crystallize or harden. Try rice syrup to sweeten coffee, hot tea, or blended beverages. Use it instead of jam to spread on muffins, griddle cakes, and breads.

SORGHUM MOLASSES

Sometimes called *sorghum syrup*, this form of molasses was quite common in North America from about the midnineteenth to the mid-twentieth centuries, then all but faded away before it began to make a reappearance through the natural foods market. Sorghum, sometimes called *Chinese sugarcane*, is a plant related to millet that has much in common with sugarcane. The process of producing this syrup is similar to that which makes common molasses. The stalks of the plant are crushed, and the sweet syrup is released. It is then cooked and clarified into a thick, almost black syrup. The sorghum syrup available in natural-food stores is either domestically produced or imported from Barbados.

Like blackstrap molasses, sorghum molasses is rich in minerals, such as potassium, iron, and calcium, and contains a good range of B vitamins. It is 65 to 70 percent sucrose (see page 155).

The characteristics of sorghum molasses are similar to those of blackstrap molasses in every way, except that its flavor is milder (though still very bold), without as much "bite." It can therefore be used a bit more freely without fear of overpowering other flavors. Use exactly as you would molasses (see page 161 for suggestions).

SORGHUM-SQUASH BREAD

Yield: 1 loaf

1 1/2 cups whole wheat flour
1/4 cup soy flour
2 teaspoons baking powder
1 teaspoon cinnamon
1/2 teaspoon ground ginger
1/4 teaspoon ground cloves or allspice
1/4 cup soy margarine, softened
1/4 cup light brown sugar
2 eggs, beaten
1 cup well-pureed cooked butternut
   squash
1/3 cup sorghum molasses
Juice of 1/2 lemon
1/2 cup chopped walnuts
1/2 cup finely chopped pitted prunes or
   mission figs

Preheat the oven to 350°F.

In a mixing bowl, combine the first six ingredients. In another mixing bowl, cream the margarine with the brown sugar. Beat in the eggs until smooth, then add the squash, molasses, and lemon juice. Beat until smooth. Combine the wet and dry ingredients together and stir vigorously until well blended. Stir in the chopped nuts and dried fruits. Pour into an oiled 9-by-5-by-3-inch loaf pan. Bake for 45 to 50 minutes, or until a knife inserted into the center tests clean.

SUGARS

As the intake of refined sugars by Americans surpasses even the sky-high levels set during the last century, its effects on the human system continue to be analyzed and argued. Still, the results are not definitive, and the findings remain controversial. The average American's sugar intake is considered high by any standard. These simple sugars are taken in not only as table sugar but in the form of processed foods, cereals, beverages, and so on.

One may or may not subscribe to the view that alarming physical problems are clearly associated with sugar intake. However, most nutrition experts agree that caution and moderation are a good course to take as far as sugar consumption is concerned. Furthermore, it is widely believed that sugar affects each person's system differently.

Defined below are the most commonly available types of sugar:

Table sugar, or refined white sugar is certainly not an item found in the realm of natural foods, but it is defined here in order to provide a basis for comparison. White, granulated sugar is the end product of chemical and mechanical processes that separate the sugarcane into crystals and syrup (which is known as molasses). The crystals are then further refined into granulated sugar. Table sugar is sucrose, the most simple form of sugar. It enters the bloodstream without having to be broken down, thereby raising the blood sugar level rapidly. It contains no nutrients whatsoever.

Brown sugar is simply the refined white sugar crystals to which some molasses has been added. It seems to be a bit more concentrated than plain white sugar, so that, in baking, less may be used for similar effect. The USDA's data show that brown sugar has a modest mineral content, and this is due to the added molasses.

Turbinado sugar is the form of sugar that appears most often in natural-food stores and restaurants. Sometimes labeled "sugar in the raw," it is not really raw sugar, the sale of which is illegal in North America. Turbinado has a pale-brown color and is somewhat less refined than white sugar, but is no more nutritious and, like table sugar, is pure sucrose, the simplest sugar. Most experts agree that the biggest difference between turbinado and white sugar is price, with turbinado sugar costing three to four times more. Analogous to the sea salt versus table salt question, the most logical answer seems to be to cut down on sugar altogether rather than to fret over minor differences.

Chapter 12

CONDIMENTS, FLAVORINGS, AND OTHER SEASONINGS

Natural condiments go hand in hand with whole foods, many of which benefit greatly from just the right touch from a sauce, a seasoning, or a tangy vinegar. The use of condiments both plain and fancy is an ancient art form, but many of the ones listed in this chapter are relatively new to the Western palate. The use of these products has grown in popularity with the various ethnic cuisines that have captured our national fancy and our desire to reproduce these ethnic specialties at home. Many of the condiments listed below, all fixtures of the natural foods market, are, in fact, imports from Japan and other parts of the Orient. An appreciation for the use of condiments and seasonings goes a long way toward making the "wholefood cuisine" a sensually satisfying, as well as a healthy, experience.

———— ARROWROOT ————

Derived from the powdered root of the tropical arrowroot plant, this silky white thickening agent has become a standard in the pages of natural-food cookbooks. Why it has come to be favored over cornstarch in that context is unclear, since the two are completely interchangeable in terms of culinary properties. Both are excellent thickeners, and neither has any nutritional advantage over the other. Arrowroot is usually sold by the ounce in natural-food stores. It will keep indefinitely if stored in a tightly lidded jar in a cool, dry place.

Arrowroot thickens liquid quickly, without the gummy texture and raw flavor that flour sometimes imparts. One tablespoon of arrowroot will thicken 1 cup of liquid. For every cup of liquid used, bring three-quarters of it to a simmer in a heavy saucepan or double boiler. Dissolve the arrowroot in the reserved 1/4 cup liquid. Slowly pour it into the saucepan. Cook over very low heat, stirring frequently, until the liquid thickens, for 8 to 10 minutes. It's important to stir as often as possible to prevent the arrowroot from sinking to the bottom of the

saucepan. Increase the amount of arrowroot to 2 tablespoons per cup if you'd like a firmer texture, such as for a pie filling or a firm pudding.

Use arrowroot as a substitute in any recipe calling for cornstarch or flour as a thickener. Aside from puddings and pie fillings, use arrowroot to thicken soups and sauces. Always dissolve the arrowroot in enough liquid to make it smooth and pourable.

TROPICAL ARROWROOT PUDDING

Yield: 4 to 6 servings

2 cups low-fat milk
1/4 cup arrowroot
1 cup peeled and diced mango or papaya
1 cup crushed pineapple
2 tablespoons unsweetened shredded coconut
Honey to taste
Dash of ground ginger
2 kiwi fruits, peeled and sliced

Heat 1 1/2 cups of the milk in a heavy saucepan or the top of a double boiler. Dissolve the arrowroot in the remaining milk. When the milk comes to a simmer, turn the heat to low, and slowly pour in the remaining milk and dissolved arrowroot. Stir constantly until the mixture thickens. Turn the heat down as low as possible and cook for 8 to 10 minutes, stirring frequently. Remove from the heat.

In the container of a food processor or blender, puree the mango or papaya with half the pineapple. Stir the mixture into the thickened milk along with the remaining pineapple, coconut, honey, and ginger. Distribute among serving dishes and chill for at least 3 hours. Before serving, garnish with the kiwi slices.

CAROB

This naturally sweet powder is ground from the pods of the evergreen carob tree. In the past, carob was known as locust bean or Saint-John's-Bread. Saint John the Baptist is said to have survived in the wilderness by eating carob pods and wild honey. Carob is most commonly used as a substitute for cocoa due to the similarity of color, texture, and cooking properties. Does it really taste like chocolate? Opinions vary, but it's hard to deny that it is at least similar.

Commonly sold in vacuum-packed cans in natural-food stores, carob may less frequently be sold in bulk. Store carob in a tightly lidded container in a cool, dry place. It will last for at least a year if kept free of moisture. Carob is often an ingredient in so-called health candy bars—however, be aware that those are often loaded with refined sweeteners and fats that emulsify the carob.

Comparisons to chocolate notwithstanding, carob has enough going for it to be appreciated for its own merits. Unlike chocolate, carob has a negligible amount of fat (1/4 cup contains 0 grams), far fewer calories, no caffeine, and no oxalic acid (a naturally occurring substance found in chocolate and other foods that inhibits the body's absorption of calcium). Carob contains moderate amounts of calcium and phosphorus, as well as smaller amounts of iron and some B vitamins. Studies have shown that the pectin (a form of fiber that is a natural gelling substance) in carob is effective in soothing stomach upsets.

The flavor of carob is a bit milder than that of cocoa powder, so use a bit more for similar effect. Here are a few suggestions for its use:

- *Carob Brownies*: In an average brownie recipe for a 9-by-9-inch pan of brownies that calls for 1/4 to 1/3 cup cocoa powder, substitute 1/2 cup carob powder.

- *Carob Shake*: For 2 servings, combine in the container of a food processor or blender 1 cup low-fat milk, 2 tablespoons carob powder, 3 or 4 ice cubes, and barley malt syrup (this really makes it a "malted") or honey to taste. Process until frothy for a delicious and refreshing drink.

- *Carob Fudge Sauce*: Combine carob in a small bowl with enough warm water to achieve a smooth, slightly thick consistency. Sweeten to taste with barley malt syrup or honey and serve over ice cream or fruit. Try it over pears.

- Sprinkle a tablespoon or so of carob over a serving of cold breakfast cereal.

- To add a rich flavor to breads, substitute 2 to 3 tablespoons of each cup of flour with carob powder. This is especially nice in hearty dark rye breads.

CAROB-RUM-RAISIN PIE

Yield: 1 pie, 6 to 8 servings

This dark pie tastes so rich, you won't believe you're eating something healthy.

1 recipe Rolled-Oat Piecrust (page 16)

Filling:

1/2 pound well-drained soft or silken tofu
1 medium banana
1/3 cup carob powder
3 tablespoons honey or maple syrup
1 tablespoon soy margarine
2 tablespoons rum
1/2 teaspoon vanilla extract
1/4 teaspoon each cinnamon and nutmeg
1/3 cup lightly floured raisins
1/4 cup finely ground almonds for topping

Prepare the piecrust as directed in the recipe. Allow to cool before preparing the filling.

Place all the filling ingredients except for the raisins in the container of a food processor or blender. Process until smoothly pureed. Add the raisins and pulse on and off until they are chopped. Pour the filling into the cooled piecrust and sprinkle the ground almonds over the top. Chill for 1 to 2 hours before serving.

CHILI OIL

Also labeled *hot pepper oil* or *hot chili oil*, this is sesame oil in which hot red chili peppers have been marinated. Use this as a condiment rather than as a cooking oil. Add a few dashes to spicy Oriental eggplant recipes, cold sesame noodles, and hot-and-sour soups. Don't limit its use to Oriental recipes—try adding a few dashes to enchilada sauce and to barbecue sauce for grilled foods.

CHILI PEPPERS

Chili peppers, (or *chiles*, as in the Mexican spelling) are an indispensible part of many ethnic cuisines that have become intrinsic to the healthy cook's home repertoire. Though they are not commonly sold in natural-food stores, especially not in their fresh form, they are fairly standard in Oriental and other ethnic groceries. Though volumes can be written on chili peppers, this brief entry is for the purpose of definition.

Chili peppers are members of the *Capsicum* genus. With flavors ranging from mild and sweet to explosively hot, chilies are the most widely produced and utilized condiment in the world after salt and black pepper. There are hundreds of varieties, with inconsistent names and little standardization of labeling. Here are a few basic guidelines to help the confused chili lover:

- In general, the smaller the pepper, the hotter it is. Large peppers are generally milder, though there are certain exceptions to that rule. To name a few common varieties, jalapeño, serrano, and cherry peppers are incendiary; Anaheim and poblano peppers are mildly hot to hot; Italian frying peppers are quite mild. Get to know the varieties your local market carries.

- When using whole chilies, whether fresh, canned, or frozen, remove the seeds before using. They taste extremely hot.

- If you are going to be handling hot chilies to any great extent for a given recipe, for instance when peeling and chopping them after roasting, wear rubber gloves to prevent skin irritation.

- Frozen chilies, available in Spanish or Mexican groceries, are generally very good and are more economical than canned chilies.

- Canned green chilies (packaged in the Southwest and labeled according to their degree of hotness) are good, but those little 4-ounce cans are rather expensive, and the small portion may be frustrating for chili lovers.

- Use pickled chili peppers for garnish purposes only.

- Red chili peppers are generally hotter than green chilies.

All chilies are rich in vitamins A and C. They are widely credited with having an ability to fight bacteria, and many cultures use them for medicinal purposes. Chilies are extensively used in Mexican, Native American, Indian, Indonesian, African, and Chinese cuisines.

COFFEE SUBSTITUTES

As long as the controversy rages on about the possible ill effects of caffeine, there will be coffee substitutes. The purpose of this entry is not to argue the case against caffeine, since the findings vary from one study to another, but to briefly describe its alternatives.

Substitute coffee beverages are made from various combinations of roasted grains and roots. Two well-known brands are Postum, made from bran, wheat, and molasses, and Cafix, made from rye, barley, and chicory. Chicory,

167

a root, is also used in combination with ordinary coffee in some national brands, since it is supposed to have a somewhat mellowing effect on caffeine.

While these beverages are low in calories, and in the small quantities consumed are neither harmful nor particularly nutritious, they don't really taste like coffee. To avoid disappointment, it's best to enjoy them for themselves, for their flavors can be rather pleasant. Like all good things, moderation is the key, since these beverages, like coffee, can easily become vehicles for lots of milk and sugar.

Grain coffees make fine substitutes for instant coffee in baking where a "mocha" effect is desired (see Date-Sugar Black Cake, page 158).

——DAIKON RADISH, DRIED——

Grated dried daikon radish is found in both natural-food stores and Oriental groceries. To use, simply reconstitute the stringy shreds in warm water for 5 to 10 minutes, then drain. They may be added to soups, shredded-vegetable salads, and grain dishes. However the texture of dried daikon is quite chewy and dry, and since fresh daikon is at least as easily available, there is little reason to seek out the dried version.

——FERMENTED BLACK BEANS—— (SALTED BLACK BEANS, FERMENTED BLACK SOYBEANS)

These fermented and aged soybeans have a salty, intense flavor. They are found in Oriental food stores and specialty-food shops as well as natural-food stores, usually in small glass jars. In some cases, they come simply plain and salted, while occasionally, they may be found in the form of a ready-to-use condiment, with added ginger and various spices. Once opened, the jars are best kept refrigerated. These little beans add a special earthy flavor to sauces for use in Oriental-style recipes. The following sauce is wonderful over tender-crisp green beans, tofu, mushrooms, or bok choy.

BLACK BEAN SAUCE

Yield: About 1 cup

2 teaspoons sesame oil
2 cloves garlic, minced
3 tablespoons fermented black beans,

rinsed and chopped
1 to 2 teaspoons fresh ginger, minced
³/₄ cup water
1 tablespoon natural soy sauce
2 tablespoons dry sherry or mirin
2 teaspoons cornstarch
¹/₂ teaspoon dry mustard
¹/₄ teaspoon five-spice powder (optional)

Heat the oil in a heavy saucepan. Add the garlic and sauté over moderate heat for 1 minute, stirring. Add the black beans and ginger and sauté for another minute, stirring. Add the water, soy sauce, and sherry or mirin. Dissolve the cornstarch in just enough water to make it smooth and pourable. Stir it into the saucepan along with the mustard and optional five-spice powder. Simmer over low heat, covered, for 10 minutes.

——GINGER——

In recent years, this knobby root has made its way from being a specialty item in Oriental groceries to becoming a fixture in supermarkets and produce stands. Its fresh, biting, and slightly sweet flavor and aroma are essential to many Asian cuisines, and it is one of the most characteristic flavorings in Indian cookery. In its powdered-spice form it is useful for baking (see page 172), but afficionados agree that dried ginger should not be used when fresh is called for.

When buying fresh gingerroot, it should feel rock hard, and the tan skin should look smooth and taut. Any root that feels light or has wrinkled-looking skin should be avoided. It's best to buy a small amount at a time, say, a root section that fits onto your palm. Store the root in a plastic bag in the crisper of your refrigerator. If you don't anticipate using it up within a week or two at the most, wrap the root in a paper towel to absorb moisture before placing in a plastic bag.

One unpredictable factor in buying fresh ginger is whether it will be fibrous. A root that was harvested when more mature will have more stringy fibers, making it more difficult to use, especially when fine grating is called for. If you've got a stringy specimen, opt for mincing it with a sharp knife rather than grating it, to minimize the problem. Another alternative for ginger that is stringy or nearing the end of its freshness is to cut it into thin slices and use them in recipes where simmering is called for, as in soups, sauces, and curried vegetables; remove and discard the slices before serving. When ginger is not fibrous, adding it to a recipe grated is desirable, since its flavor will permeate readily. Use a very fine grater. Some gourmet cookwear shops may carry a special Japanese grater made especially for this purpose. Ginger is usually peeled before using, mostly as a matter of aesthetics.

Ginger has been esteemed since ancient times not only for is remarkable flavor but also for its medicinal qualities. It has long been used, in both Oriental and European cultures, for its ability to settle the stomach and relieve nausea caused by motion sickness and pregnancy. This belief was born out by scientific studies in the early 1980s, which proved ginger more effective than Dramamine. Ginger has also been used in many cultures as an aid to digestion and as an appetite restorative, since it seems to stimulate the production of saliva.

As previously mentioned, ginger is used extensively in many Asian cuisines, particularly Chinese, Japanese, and Indian. It is also favored in West African cookery, where one specialty is a bracing beverage called ginger beer. The warm, spicy flavor of ginger also enhances sauces and dressings in a very special way. Ginger is used in many recipes in this book.

GINGER-APPLE "DUCK SAUCE"

Yield: About 1 1/2 cups

This sweet and spicy sauce is especially good as a dip for crisp Chinese noodles and as a dressing for egg rolls.

1 tablespoon sesame oil
1 small onion, minced
1 small apple, peeled, cored, and finely
** diced**
1 1/2 to 2 teaspoons freshly grated
** ginger, more or less to taste**
2 tablespoons rice vinegar
2 tablespoons natural soy sauce
1 cup apple juice
1 tablespoon cornstarch or arrowroot

Heat the oil in a saucepan. Add the onion and sauté over moderate heat until it is lightly golden. Add the apple and sauté until it has softened, about 5 minutes. Stir in the ginger, rice vinegar, soy sauce, and about 3/4 cup of the apple juice. Use the remaining apple juice to dissolve the cornstarch or arrowroot. Slowly pour

it into the saucepan and stir well. Bring to a simmer and cook over low heat until the liquid has thickened, about 5 to 8 minutes. Allow to cool somewhat before serving; serve at room temperature.

HERBS AND SPICES, COMMON CULINARY

As the popularity of cooking healthy, ethnic specialties at home grows, our pantries will invariably expand to accommodate the seasonings that go into giving these various dishes their unique characters. The natural and ethnic food markets offer a multitude of herbs and spices. Inasmuch as volumes can be written on the healing aspect of herbs, the focus here is culinary. This section will give a brief overview of those seasonings most commonly utilized in the preparation of international wholefood recipes.

BUYING, STORAGE, AND USAGE TIPS

- When buying herbs and spices by weight, buy only what will fit into an average-size spice jar. In other words, don't stock up. Most go a very long way and are at their optimal flavor for up to a year, after which they begin losing their potency.

- Keep dried herbs and spices in a place in your kitchen that is away from heat and moisture.

- When substituting fresh herbs for dry, use about three times the amount of fresh herb as the dry.

- Introduce dried herbs and spices into your recipe as early in the cooking process as possible, so that they have a chance to develop flavor. Add fresh herbs toward the middle or even the end of the cooking if you'd like to retain their pronounced flavor.

ANISE or ANISEED is an aromatic spice that imparts a distinct flavor of licorice and is commonly used to make the liqueurs ouzo, anisette, and pernod. Anise is used in cookies and cakes, and a sprinkling of the seeds adds an unusual twist to fruit salads, particularly those utilizing citrus fruits. Try adding anise to fruit pies, relishes and chutneys, and dark breads. In Indian cuisine, anise is occasionally used in pilafs and braised dishes.

ALLSPICE is the hard berry of an evergreen tree native to the West Indies and Central America. Its name quite possibly reflects its flavor, which as a hint of the flavors of several spices, including cinnamon, nutmeg, and cloves. It is most commonly sold in ground form, though the whole berry is available in spice shops and is used in pickling and to flavor broths and marinades. The mildly spicy-sweet flavor of ground allspice enhances apple desserts, banana breads, spice cakes, cookies, chutneys, and recipes utilizing squash, pumpkin, or sweet potatoes.

BASIL is one of the most relished of herbs and one that has an important place in herbal lore and legend, spanning many ages and cultures. In the summer, the intoxicating scent of fresh sweet basil fills produce markets, and its brief season should be fully enjoyed. Though basil makes an excellent dried herb whose sweet-and-spicy flavor is welcome in many dishes, the result is very different when using it fresh. Fresh basil is the main component of pesto sauces and has a special affinity with tomato-based pasta sauces and fresh tomato salads (as in the classic tomato, mozzarella, and basil salad). Dried basil is good in soups, marinades and vinaigrettes, grain dishes, herb breads, and omelets. It may also be used to flavor tomato sauces when fresh basil is unavailable.

BAY LEAVES are the whole, dried leaves of the bay laurel tree and are most useful in long-simmering recipes, such as soups and stews, where their flavor has a chance to permeate. Its warm, somewhat "woodsy" character lends itself especially well to recipes that contain tomatoes, beans, corn, and potatoes.

CARAWAY SEEDS, the seeds of a biennial plant native to Europe, have a sharp, distinctive taste that puts them in that category of flavorings that are either loved or intensely disliked. They are best known for adding zest to rye and pumpernickel breads; try expanding their use to flavor recipes emphasizing potatoes or other root vegetables (such as parsnips or turnips), cheese, and cabbage.

CARDAMOM, derived from a plant native to India, is available in whole or ground form. Bought whole, the seed pods must be opened, revealing several small, dark seeds. These aromatic seeds have a flavor that is hard to describe, but is appropriate for both sweet and savory dishes. The whole seeds lend an aromatic quality to grain dishes, especially fruit-and-nut grain pilafs as well as curries containing potatoes or peas. In ground form, cardamom may be used in the same sort of baked goods in which you'd use allspice—squash, pumpkin, or sweet-potato pies, for example, or batter breads. It may also be used to season those same vegetables when they are served as side dishes.

CAYENNE PEPPER is perhaps the hottest of ground spices, ground and dried from a very hot variety of a pepper of the *Capsicum* genus. A small amount goes a long way and is used to give fiery flavor to Mexican, Indian, and some Southeast Asian cuisines and is also useful in spicing Creole and Cajun specialties. Cayenne pepper lends itself to cheese dishes, vegetable or bean stews, curries, chilies, spicy cold noodle dishes, and hot-and-sour dishes.

CHILI POWDER is a blend of spices with dried, ground red chili pepper as its base. The blends available in Spanish groceries, spice shops, and natural-food stores will be more robust and aromatic than those bought in supermarkets; you will also be able to choose from among milder and hotter varieties. The consistent ingredients, along with chili pepper, often include cumin, oregano, and garlic, but may also contain salt and other seasonings as well. Use chili powder to flavor bean stews and soups. It's a logical addition to tomato-based enchilada sauces, but try adding it to tomato-based pasta sauces as well to add a warm note. Chili powder is good in some Oriental-style sauces such as peanut or sesame sauce for noodles.

CHIVES are a member of the lily family, whose relatives include onions, scallions, and garlic. Fresh chives are rarely seen in produce markets, but are easily grown in the kitchen garden—in fact, they proliferate like mad. Dried chives are commonly available, on the other hand. The flavor of chives is very much akin to that of scallions, yet more delicate, which makes them delightful to use raw when available fresh. Fresh chives add flavor to baked potatoes (along with a spoonful of yogurt), cottage cheese salads, potato salads, and in fact, most any fresh vegetable salad. Use dried chives in dips, dressings, soups, and sauces, where they will have a chance to reconstitute.

CILANTRO is an herb that is never available in dried form, since its pungent flavor and aroma seem to dissipate almost entirely when dried. Sometimes referred to as Spanish or Chinese parsley, this is the same herb whose seeds are the spice coriander. Fresh cilantro is becoming more widely available in produce markets. Italian parsley is often recommended as a substitute for cilantro, although the effect is not the same at all. Cilantro has a very unique flavor and aroma that some savor and others dislike. It is used widely in Mexican, Indian, and to a lesser extent, Oriental cookery. Cilantro adds an unusual zest to pinto bean stews, Spanish-style tomato sauces for enchiladas, tacos and the like, curried vegetable stews, and corn dishes such as corn-stuffed peppers.

CINNAMON is derived from the dried inner bark of the cassia tree, a small evergreen. One of the earliest spices recorded, cinnamon is also one of the most familiar and commonly used. A sweet, aromatic spice, cinnamon is often a component of curry blends and is a fixture in many baked goods, including custards, puddings, cakes, cookies, and fruit pies. Squash, pumpkin, and sweet potatoes, whether in pies or as side dishes, always benefit from a sprinkling of cinnamon. Whole cinnamon sticks are nice to add to stewing fruits and simmering beverages, such as hot mulled cider.

CLOVES are a pleasant, sweet spice like cinnamon, but have a stronger flavor and a sharp aroma. Whole cloves are the buds of the evergreen clove tree. Stewed fruits benefit from a handful of whole cloves while they are simmering, and fragrant pilafs are made even more so by the addition of some whole cloves. You may leave the cloves in the dishes you are making, but you may not enjoy biting into one, since the flavor is somewhat bitter. Ground cloves are often used in conjunction with cinnamon in baked goods, fruit pies, and squash, sweet-potato, and pumpkin recipes. Cloves enhance the flavors of apples and bananas in desserts and are occasionally used in curries and chutneys.

CORIANDER is the aromatic seed of the herbal plant whose leaves are known as cilantro. This is a spice whose complex flavor falls somewhere between sweet and spicy. It's usually one of the three main components of curry mixes along with cumin and turmeric. In Indonesian cookery, coriander is a common seasoning for tempeh recipes. In general, it's an excellent flavoring for bean dishes of many sorts. Corn and cabbage recipes as well as vegetable relishes and hot-sweet chutneys are enhanced by the flavor of coriander.

CUMIN is the golden-brown seed of a small herbal plant native to the Mediterranean, Middle East, and North Africa. Cumin's spicy and pleasantly hot flavor makes it a favorite seasoning in several ethnic cuisines; its zesty quality reduces the need for salt. You will find cumin used extensively in curry blends and chili powder; in those spice mixes or on its own, it is an important seasoning in Indian and Mexican cuisines. Cumin is also frequently used in Middle Eastern and Spanish cookery. Use cumin in soups, tomato-based enchilada sauces, cheese dishes, bean dishes, and vegetable stews. Spinach, lentil, and tempeh recipes often benefit from the addition of cumin. A pinch of cumin in breads is an old European tradition, and this works particularly well in cornbread.

CURRY POWDER is a blend of spices used in Indian cuisine with some constant ingredients and some that vary. Indian specialty-food stores and spice shops are good places to get fresh, aromatic curry blends with a choice of varying degrees of hotness. The supermarket variety often tastes and smells rather flat. The most notable and constant elements of curry powders are cumin, coriander, and turmeric; the variables may be any of cayenne pepper, mustard, fenugreek, along with some sweet aromatics such as cinnamon, nutmeg, cloves, or cardamon. Almost any good Indian cookbook will give several variations of curry spice blends, which may be made at home by grinding whole spices or, even simpler, by combining good, fresh ground spices. Aside from its obvious use in simplified Indian curry recipes (authentic Indian dishes usually combine individual curry spices in the recipe rather than using prepared curry powder), use curry powder to add zest and color to simple grain pilafs, lentil soups and stews, potato dishes, and egg recipes such as quiches or frittatas.

DILL WEED and DILL SEED are both products of a tall, feathery annual plant that is a favorite kitchen-garden herb. The seeds, less commonly used than the leaves, are used in pickling and may also be used as a milder substitute for caraway seeds in breads or as a topping for potato, cabbage, or cheese casseroles. Fresh dill is available for a few months out of the year, but may be hard to come by during the colder months. Dried dill is a fairly good standby for fresh when necessary. Fresh or dried, dill has a special affinity with tomatoes and cucumbers. Few summer salads are more simple or more refreshing than sliced cucumbers with yogurt and chopped dill. Fresh or dried, dill is an excellent herb in hot and cold soups and is an offbeat addition to omelets. Use dill in spinach pies and herb breads as well.

FENNEL SEED is a small, elongated seed that, used whole or ground, imparts a subtle anise or licorice flavor. Fennel seeds are used in some traditional Italian bread recipes and stews. In Indian cookery, they add a pleasant flavor and aroma to grain pilafs and curries. A few fennel seeds tossed into fresh fruit salads add an offbeat twist. Try green beans or root vegetables such as parsnips with a hint of the whole or ground seeds.

FENUGREEK is a less common aromatic spice and is actually a legume, something like a mung bean. Its somewhat bitter flavor and strong aroma warrant subtle application. Fenugreek appears as an element in Indian curries and chutneys and is used as a pickling spice in the Far East.

FIVE-SPICE POWDER, a blend of spices used in Oriental cookery, is increasingly available in natural-food stores as well as in spice shops and Oriental groceries. The same five spices are not always used, but some of the most common components are anise, fennel, cloves, black pepper, cinnamon, and ginger. The overall effect is sweet and slightly spicy, with a licorice undertone, since either anise or fennel is always present. Five-spice powder, subtly used, is a nice addition to grilling sauces, black bean sauce, and miso sauces.

GARLIC is well known and almost universally loved by good cooks across many cultures. A member of the lily family and related to onions, shallots, and the like, garlic has long been esteemed equally for its medicinal properties and its culinary qualities. The uses of garlic are familiar and too numerous to list. It appears extensively in the cuisines of Italy, India, Mexico, the Orient, Southeast Asia, the Middle East, and many more. Fresh garlic is almost always preferable, but garlic powder is an acceptable substitute in breading mixes for frying foods or in blended dips, where the flavor of raw garlic may be too strong.

GINGER is the underground rhizomelike root of a tropical plant. There's much to say about fresh ginger, so it is under a separate entry (page 168). Ground ginger should generally not be considered a substitute for fresh ginger, but rather as a hot-sweet, fragrant spice more appropriate to baked goods. Gingerbread is one that comes to mind immediately, but it is almost as common a spice for pumpkin and squash pies. Ground ginger is also a pleasing enhancement for apple desserts, as well as for sweet-potato or winter-squash side dishes.

172

GINSENG is the name of a root whose shape often resembles the human figure. Though it is not a culinary herb in the strict sense, it is included here for definition. Ginseng's presumed medicinal powers have been widely publicized. Ginseng is frequently marketed as a universal tonic for well-being, a general panacea for numerous ailments, and for its supposed powers as an aphrodisiac. No conclusive proof is available for its claims, but the commercial value of ginseng continues to grow. It has been brought under cultivation both in Asia (particularly in Korea) and in North America. Ginseng is now being incorporated into soft drinks marketed by natural-food companies and is also available in the form of liquids and powders (to be used in beverages or as tea) as well as in capsule form to be taken as a supplement.

MACE, the filigreed, red encasement surrounding the nutmeg kernel, is dried and ground for use as a spice. The flavor is similar to that of nutmeg, but milder. Like nutmeg, a little mace goes a long way. Substitute mace for nutmeg wherever you wish (see nutmeg entry for suggestions).

MARJORAM is an herb so closely related to oregano that the two share the botanical name *origanum,* which is from the Latin meaning "joy of the mountain." Marjoram is slightly sweeter, yet somewhat sharper than oregano, so inasmuch as the two may be used interchangeably, marjoram should be used more sparingly. Use marjoram in conjunction with other dried herbs to flavor vegetable dishes, Italian-style tomato sauces, bean stews, pizza sauces, soups, grain dishes, and vinaigrette salad dressings.

MINT is the general term used for a variety of highly aromatic herbs, the most common of which, for culinary purposes, are peppermint and spearmint. The fresh scent and menthol flavor of the mints are delightful, and they are popular and prolific kitchen-garden herbs. In Indian cuisine, fresh mint is commonly used in chutneys and in the palate-cooling relishes know as raitas, to add a refreshing note. Fresh mint is also a standard ingredient in the popular Middle Eastern tabouli. In a pinch, use dried mint as a substitute for fresh in such recipes, but the effect will not be the same. There is no substitute for fresh mint in beverages or as a garnish for fresh strawberries or melons, fruit salads, and chocolate puddings.

MUSTARD is the tiny, round seed of an annual plant native to Asia and is the spice used to make the popular condiment of the same name. Available in whole or ground form, the flavor of mustard seeds is subtly hot and slightly biting. Use dry mustard in cheese and egg dishes, soups, sauces, salad dressings, grain dishes, potato dishes, chilies, and curries.

NUTMEG is the seed of the small pear-shaped fruit of the nutmeg tree. The hard, nutlike nutmeg seed is optimally used freshly grated, however, the spice is more commonly sold and used in its dried, ground form. A sweet spice, nutmeg is a familiar flavoring in eggnog, custards, pumpkin and sweet-potato pies, and spice cakes. It is often one of the spices used in curry mixes, and has a special affinity with winter squashes and spinach.

OREGANO, a close botanical relation to marjoram, has become familiar to the North American palate through its use in popular Italian dishes such as pizza and spaghetti sauces. Oregano is a splendid kitchen-garden herb. Used fresh, it is especially nice in green salads and tomato salads. In dried form, it is a widely available, inexpensive herb useful in traditional Mexican, Italian, Greek, and Spanish recipes. It's also a common addition to salad dressings and does much to enhance the flavor of soups, grains, bean dishes, and pasta sauces.

PAPRIKA is ground from a dried, sweet *Capsicum* pepper. Its slightly sweet, warm flavor adds savor to tomato-based sauces, cheese dishes, egg dishes, pastas, French-style salad dressing, and potato dishes. Its bright red color makes it an excellent garnish sprinkled on quiches, casseroles, vegetable pies, and pâtés.

PARSLEY is a commonly used fresh herb that just doesn't translate well into dried form. Fortunately, fresh parsley is easy to grow on the windowsill and is also available inexpensively year-round, so there is little reason to buy this nutritious herb in dried form. The fresh, mild herbal flavor of parsley is welcome in many culinary categories, including salads and salad dressings, soups, grain and bean dishes, casseroles, omelets, vegetable dishes, and herb breads. When buying parsley, choose the Italian, flat-leafed parsley for cooking, since it's more flavorful, and reserve the use of the curly-leafed parsley for garnishing.

PEPPERCORNS are the whole, dried berries of an evergreen vine. Pepper is the second most commonly used seasoning after salt, not surprisingly, so its uses are too numerous, and too obvious, to enumerate here. It is worth noting, however, that it's preferable to buy whole black or white peppercorns and grind them as needed than to buy preground pepper. The difference in aroma and flavor is appreciable.

POPPY SEEDS are the tiny, round seeds of the beautiful and notorious opium poppy flower. The seeds contain none of the drug, but are thought to have a slight calming effect. Poppy seeds come in colors ranging from white to gray to black, but the best ones are the darkest. Their nutty flavor makes them a special addition to spice cakes and seed cakes and an excellent topping for breads and rolls. In addition, poppy seeds are a nice seasoning for egg noodle dishes, cabbage dishes, egg pies, potato and cheese casseroles, and dishes utilizing root vegetables such as parsnips.

RED PEPPER FLAKES come from the fruit of a pungent, fiery member of the *Capsicum* genus. Combining the seeds with the dried flesh of the pepper, this extremely hot spice is used in some of the incendiary dishes of India, Southeast Asia, Mexico, and in Cajun recipes from Louisiana. Even 1/4 teaspoon added to an average recipe will yield quite a nippy result.

ROSEMARY is the slender leaves of a small evergreen shrub and has a well-known legacy in folklore as the herb of remembrance. You'll certainly remember rosemary if you don't use it sparingly, since its strong, piney flavor can be overwhelming. Rosemary is traditionally used to

season lamb, chicken, and stuffings. In the vegetarian realm, it may be used to flavor vegetable stews, herb breads, and tomato soups or sauces.

SAFFRON, by far the most expensive of all spices, is derived from the dried, brilliant-yellow stigma of the autumn crocus. It lends its color to any food it touches; its flavor, on the other hand, is delicate. Saffron is primarily used in rice dishes, such as fruit-and-nut pilafs or the Spanish classic arroz con pollo, and is also utilized in some French and Middle and Far Eastern cookery and sometimes, but less commonly, in Indian cuisine. A common substitute for saffron is turmeric.

SAGE is the leaves of a small evergreen plant. Its strong, complex taste is best known as a flavoring for stuffings and sausages. When preparing foods such a TVP, tempeh, or seitan, all of which can be used as meat substitutes, seasoning with sage can add to the meatlike sensation. Sage may also be used, rather sparingly, in salad dressings, grain dishes (try it in wild-rice pilaf) and soups, particularly pumpkin or squash soups. Dried leaf sage is preferable to ground sage.

SAVORY comes in summer and winter varieties that may be used interchangeably. Summer savory, an annual plant, is more widely available and has a milder, sweeter flavor than the perennial winter savory. Savory is a useful seasoning that imparts a subtle flavor that tastes like a cross between parsley and thyme. Use it wherever a mixture of dried herbs is called for (in salad dreessings, herb breads, soups, and sauces) or as a milder substitute for thyme, oregano, or marjoram. Savory is known tradionally as the bean herb, because its flavor is thought to have a special affinity with most beans. Try it in bean soups and stews.

TARRAGON is an expensive herb best known for its role in making an elegant vinegar. It has a sharp-sweet, aniselike flavor and scent. Tarragon adds a distinctive touch to fresh green vegetables and green salads. Try sprinkling some on fresh peas, green beans, asparagus, or Swiss chard. Tarragon makes ordinary mayonnaise special and adds an unusual touch to omelets and tomato dishes. Tarragon is also used in the preparation of fish and chicken.

THYME is a popular herb related to the mints. Even when used sparingly, it imparts a vivid flavor and aroma. Thyme is an important seasoning in classic French and Creole recipes and is good used whenever a mixture of dried herbs is called for. Soups, vinaigrettes, grain and bean dishes, corn dishes, and tomato sauces all benefit from the distinctive flavor of thyme.

TURMERIC is the product of a dried, ground, fleshy root and is prized for its brilliant yellow color, much as is saffron, although turmeric is not nearly so expensive. This spice has a unique, rather "woodsy" flavor and scent and is almost invariably one of the main components of curry mixes. Use it to brighten rice pilafs, egg and cheese dishes, corn dishes, pickles, and relishes.

KUDZU

Kudzu (also spelled kuzu) is a starch powder extracted from the roots of the wild kudzu vine. This plant grows abundantly in eastern Asia as well as in the southeastern United States. Used medicinally in the Orient, kudzu is sold in the West as a culinary thickener.

Kudzu may be used for the same thickening purposes as arrowroot or cornstarch but is by far the most expensive of the three, and possibly the most difficult to work with. It comes in chunks, making it tricky to measure. To make measuring easier you can crush the chunks with a rolling pin. Manufacturers recommend 1 to 2 teaspoons of kudzu chunks per cup of liquid to be thickened. Bring the liquid to a simmer in a saucepan or double boiler, then lower the heat. In the meantime, dissolve the kudzu in water to cover. Pour into the simmering liquid and cook over low heat for 10 to 15 minutes. After using kudzu several times, my results led me to believe that it is not as effective a thickener as arrowroot or cornstarch. A nutritional comparison of kudzu to other starches does not reveal any great advantages in that department either. As a thickening agent, kudzu just doesn't seem worth the extra money.

MIRIN

A traditional Japanese condiment, mirin is syrupy rice wine. With an alcohol content of 8 percent or less, it is fermented naturally from sweet rice. Mirin is used primarily as a seasoning and glazing agent and has a pleasing, sweet-and-pungent taste.

Mirin is sold in bottled form; stored in a cool, dry place it will keep nearly indefinitely. Wipe the rim after each use to prevent the lid from sticking. Beware of some so-called mirins that are sold in natural-food stores—full of artificial ingredients, these imitators are not made of sweet rice at all!

Add a tablespoon or two of mirin to enhance soy dipping sauces. Likewise, add a tablespoon or two to add zest to vegetable stir-fries, Oriental-style crisp salads, fried rice, or simple Oriental noodle dishes. In the same quantity, it also lends an interesting spark to marinades and grilling sauces.

MUSHROOMS

Mushrooms are in a league of their own, with volumes having been devoted to them. It would be impossible to enumerate the myriad varieties of mushrooms available today, so the entries here are limited to a handful that have become most known and relatively popular through natural and Oriental food markets in dried or canned form.

CLOUD-EAR MUSHROOMS (Wood-ear, Tree-ear, Black Tree Fungus)

If one were to go by appearance alone, it would be hard to think of a more exotic-looking mushroom than the cloud-ear. Paper-thin when dried, one side is almost black and the other side is tan, with fluted edges. The dried cloud-ear, a staple in Chinese cookery, is becoming increasingly available in the West. It has little flavor, so its appeal lies in its chewy, almost crunchy texture. The Chinese have traditionally associated the cloud-ear with longevity.

Dried cloud-ear mushrooms are available in natural-food stores and Oriental groceries. Store them in a tightly lidded jar in a cool, dry place and they will keep for at least a year.

When reconstituted, the cloud-ear increases almost alarmingly in volume. Just $1/4$ to $1/2$ ounce of dried cloud-ear is sufficient for an average recipe, unless you have an unusually strong passion for it. Sources differ widely as to how long it must be soaked, ranging from a mere soaking in hot water for 30 minutes to several hours' simmering. I have found that covering them with boiling water in an oven-proof dish and letting them stand, off the heat and covered, for 45 to 60 minutes (depending on whether they'll be further cooked in a recipe) is sufficient. Longer soaking does not seem to change the texture. To use, drain them, then

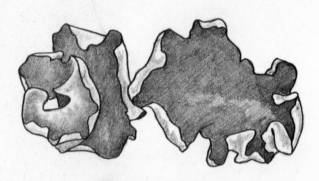

cut into thin strips. Reserve the liquid for use in soup stocks and sauces.

Exotic as cloud-ears are, they simply aren't flavorful enough to be the focus of a dish. Add them to stir-fried vegetable or seafood dishes, soups, and Oriental noodle dishes. Stir-fry them in a combination of soy sauce, sesame oil, and dry sherry and use them as garnish for pan-fried tofu or simple cooked brown rice. They're especially nice in dishes containing other types of mushrooms. For a specific recipe, see Rice-Sticks with Cabbage and Exotic Mushrooms, page 113.

ENOKI (Enokitake, Enokidake)

With their long, slender stems and tiny caps, enoki are among the most exotic mushrooms readily available today. The shape and delicate flavor of the enoki mushroom might fool the eye and palate into believing that it is some sort of noodle. Generally imported from Japan, the cultivation of this mushroom is just beginning in North America.

You'll find canned enoki mushrooms in natural-food stores and Oriental groceries. Occasionally, they may be sold fresh in Oriental groceries, but this is less common, since in that form they are highly perishable. Canned enoki are ready-to-eat, and are especially nice in a warm salad combined with steamed or stir-fried tender-crisp vegetables such as snow peas, bok choy, or sprouts and dressed in an Oriental-flavored dressing (such as

Sesame-Soy Salad Dressing, page 142). They may also be added to brothy soups or used as a garnish for steamed vegetables, notably fresh peas or green beans, simply seasoned with butter, pepper, and perhaps a dash of vinegar.

MARINATED ENOKI AND ASPARAGUS SALAD

Yield: 4 to 6 servings

1 pound asparagus, trimmed and cut into 2-inch lengths, steamed
One 7- or 8-ounce can enoki mushrooms, drained (reserve the liquid for another use)
³/₄ cup coarsely grated daikon radish or white turnip
2 medium carrots, diagonally sliced
2 bunches scallions, minced
1 tablespoon sesame seeds
¹/₂ cup Rice Vinegar Marinade (page 181)

Simply combine all the ingredients in a serving bowl and toss together to combine. Allow to marinate, refrigerated, for 1 to 2 hours before serving, stirring occasionally to distribute the marinade.

OYSTER MUSHROOMS (Shimeji)

These mild, silky-capped mushrooms are supposedly so named because they are thought to taste like and resemble oysters when prepared in certain ways. Oyster mushrooms grow prolifically in many parts of the world, but they are particularly well loved in both China and Japan.

Oyster mushrooms are available canned in Oriental groceries and natural-food stores. Their mild flavor and firm texture make them versatile enough to use absolutely anywhere you'd use ordinary mushrooms. They take to marinating beautifully, after which they may be sliced and used as a condiment or added to green salads or pasta salads. They may also be simply sliced and added to broth, where their delicate flavor can be appreciated. To serve as an appetizer, cut them in half and sauté in a small amount of soy margarine until golden brown. Add a squeeze of lemon and some minced scallion; they are also very good when breaded before sautéeing. Try substituting oyster mushrooms for ordinary mushrooms in omelets.

BROILED OYSTER MUSHROOMS

Yield: 4 servings

This makes a good appetizer or a tasty side dish.

1 tablespoon soy margarine
1 medium onion, quartered and thinly
  sliced
1 tablespoon natural soy sauce
1 teaspoon sesame oil
1 teaspoon honey
1 teaspoon mirin or dry sherry
¹/₄ teaspoon chili powder
Dash of garlic powder
One 15-ounce can oyster mushrooms,
  drained (reserve the liquid for use in
  soups or sauces)

In a small skillet, heat the margarine until it foams. Add the onion and sauté over moderate heat until it is lightly browned. In a small bowl, combine the onion with the remaining ingredients, except for the mushrooms, and stir well to combine. Stir in the mushrooms until they are evenly coated with the sauce. Arrange the mushrooms in a shallow, ovenproof dish and broil for 7 to 10 minutes, stirring once to turn the mushrooms over, or until the sauce has been nicely absorbed and the edges of the mushrooms have turned lightly brown.

SHIITAKE MUSHROOMS

The deep brown, intensely flavored shiitake mushroom is a favorite in several Southeast Asian cuisines. Sometimes known as black forest mushroom, chewy shiitakes are now being cultivated in the United States as well as imported from Japan.

Available in dried form in Oriental groceries and natural-food stores, shiitakes are usually

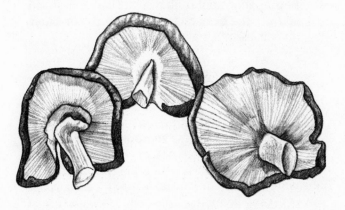

sold by the ounce. Store them in a tightly capped jar in a cool, dry place and they will keep for at least a year.

To use, soak the mushrooms in hot water to cover for about 15 minutes, or until they become pliable. Squeeze them lightly, then remove and discard the tough stems and slice the caps. Save the flavorful soaking liquid for use in stocks and sauces. Shiitakes and their liquid are among traditional ingredients used in making the Japanese soup stock dashi.

Shiitakes are quite versatile, and their uses should not be limited to the traditional. Use them in any recipe where standard mushrooms are called for, so long as they are not needed in great quantity (shiitakes tend to be expensive). Shiitakes transform an ordinary mushroom omelet into something special. Use them as you would ordinary mushrooms in grain pilafs, pasta or noodle dishes, and bean stews. Add them to give flavor and texture to simple seafood, sea vegetable, and vegetable stir-fry recipes.

STIR-FRIED BOK CHOY WITH SHIITAKE MUSHROOMS

Yield: 4 to 6 servings

1 cup loosely packed shiitake
  mushrooms, soaked in 1 cup hot
  water
1 tablespoon sesame oil
1 tablespoon peanut oil
1 medium onion, halved and sliced
6 medium stalks bok choy, sliced
  diagonally
1 heaping cup snow peas, trimmed and
  cut in half
2 tablespoons natural soy sauce
3 tablespoons dry sherry or mirin
¹/₂ teaspoon freshly grated ginger
Dash of cayenne pepper or hot chili oil
¹/₄ pound tofu, finely diced (optional)
1 tablespoon cornstarch

Soak the shiitakes in the hot water for 15 minutes. While they are soaking, heat the sesame and peanut oils in a large skillet or wok. Add the onion and stir-fry over moderately high heat until translucent. Add the bok choy, snow peas, soy sauce, sherry or mirin, and ginger. Stir-fry until the vegetables are tender-crisp. When the shiitakes are pliable, trim and discard the stems and slice the caps. Add them to the wok along with the cayenne or hot chili oil and optional tofu. Dissolve the cornstarch in a bit of the soaking liquid from the shiitakes. Add it, along with the remaining soaking liquid, to the vegetables and stir in. Allow to simmer until the sauce has thickened, about 3 to 5 minutes. Remove from the heat and serve at once over rice or noodles.

STRAW MUSHROOMS

Like shiitakes, straw mushrooms have become known to the Western palate through their use in Cantonese-style Chinese fare. They are small, mild-flavored mushrooms whose long cap and short stem are equally silky, almost slippery.

These mushrooms, imported in cans from the Orient, are ready to use; in fact, I would recommend adding them to your recipes only toward the end of the cooking time, because they are so delicate they are likely to fall apart if cooked for too long. The liquid in which they are canned may be used in soup stocks and sauces.

Straw mushrooms lend themselves to use primarily in Oriental vegetable or seafood dishes and in soups and sauces. They are widely used in Vietnamese cuisine, teamed with such vegetables as cauliflower, leeks, and tomatoes, with the occasional addition of cellophane noodles and tofu. This is an offbeat departure from the more familiar type of vegetable stir-fry. Here is a simple adaptation of this combination of ingredients:

CAULIFLOWER WITH STRAW MUSHROOMS AND LEEKS

Yield: 4 to 6 servings

1 large leek, white part only
2 tablespoons peanut oil
3 heaping cups cauliflower, broken into
   bite-size pieces and florets
2 cloves garlic, minced
2 large, ripe tomatoes (about 1 pound),
   chopped
One 15- or 16-ounce can straw
   mushrooms
1/2 pound tofu, diced
Salt and freshly ground pepper to taste
Dash of chili powder or cayenne pepper

Slice the leek into 1/4-inch slices. Separate the slices into rings and wash well to remove the grit.

Heat the oil in a large skillet or wok. Add the leeks and stir-fry over moderately high heat for

2 to 3 minutes. Add the cauliflower and garlic; stir-fry until the cauliflower is just tender-crisp. Add the tomatoes and reduce the heat to moderate. Simmer until the tomatoes have softened, about 5 minutes, then add the remaining ingredients and simmer for another 5 to 7 minutes. Remove from the heat and serve at once over hot rice.

━━━━━ SEA SALT ━━━━━

Many natural-food companies use sea salt in their prepared products and snack foods, giving the impression that it is somehow more pure and natural than ordinary table salt. Sea salt is also sold by weight in natural-food stores at significantly higher prices than is its supermarket counterpart.

Is sea salt really better? David Armstrong, in *The Insider's Guide to Health Food* (Bantam Books, 1983), offers the following thoughts, which are echoed by other nutrition experts as well:

- Sea salt is evaporated crystals from sea water, whereas table salt is mined from beneath the earth's surface, but both are essentially sodium chloride.

- Sea salt must be heavily refined to remove minerals.

- The seas serve as sewers for the industrial world.

- Whereas sea salt is said to be purer because it is sold without additives, those in table salt, dextrose and sodium bicarbonate, are present only in minute amounts and are in any case harmless; and the added iodine is a necessary nutrient.

- Rather than agonizing over which kind of salt to buy, the best tactic is simply to cut down on salt as much as possible.

━━━━━ SESAME SALT ━━━━━ (GOMASIO)

A simple condiment, sesame salt, or gomasio, is a traditional Japanese seasoning consisting of approximately 8 parts ground sesame seeds to 1 part sea salt. Its use as a table condiment has became popular in natural foods restaurants over recent years. Sesame salt has widespread uses as a general table condiment, rather than as a cooking seasoning, and may be helpful to those wishing to cut down on salt by adding an interesting flavor element. Use it as you would normally use salt on grain dishes, salads, green vegetables, and the like. Remember that sesame seeds contain fat that is released when they are ground, so store it in the refrigerator.

SOY SAUCE
(SHOYU, TAMARI)

Until the 1960s, the only type of soy sauce available in this country was the mass-produced, commercial variety. In the mid-1960s, George Ohsawa, father of the macrobiotic diet, introduced the natural, Japanese product to North America. This is what is commonly found in natural-food stores, inaccurately labeled tamari. What we buy as tamari (or in some instances labeled shoyu-tamari) is actually what is known in Japan as shoyu. Tamari in Japan is a by-product of miso and is a thicker, stronger tasting sauce. True tamari is rare in this country, so when you buy a product labeled tamari, chances are very good that you are really buying shoyu, or natural soy sauce.

Natural soy sauce is made from a combination of soybeans, roasted hard red wheat, sea salt, and water in more or less equal proportions. The mixture is ideally allowed to ferment in cedar vats for at least 18 months. When fully aged, the mixture is pressed to extract the liquid. Results vary according to specific recipes and regional preferences in Japan and China. The color of soy sauce ranges from light amber to black, and the flavor from pungent and salty to a more mellow salty-sweet. The quality and precise proportions of ingredients, the length of time aged, and the vats used in fermentation all contribute to differences in the flavor, color, and aroma of the sauce.

Mass-produced commercial soy sauces are made both in North America and in the Orient. The processes used to manufacture these are markedly different from the traditional ones used to create natural soy sauce, the most important of which are the following:

- Mass-produced soy sauces are made from chemically produced defatted soybean pulp. This process strips soybeans of much flavor and some nutrition.

- By using temperature controls, the fermentation process is artificially speeded up to be accomplished in no more than 3 to 4 months, which, some argue, does not allow as fine a flavor to develop.

- Chemicals and coloring agents are sometimes used to enhance the product. Because the shoyu is a product of naturally occurring biochemical processes, the compositions of the natural and mass-produced products are very different.

The Japanese-style natural soy sauce (shoyu) that is sold in natural-food stores has a more full-bodied flavor and tastes less salty than commercial soy sauce. Also available are a reduced-sodium natural soy sauce, which is allowed to ferment for 3 years to develop additional flavor (and again, by means of a much different process than mass-produced low-salt soy sauce), and a wheat-free natural soy sauce for those with wheat intolerance. Stored at room temperature, soy sauce will keep indefinitely.

Natural soy sauce has been shown to contain enzymes that aid in digestion and promote the production of beneficial bacterial cultures in the intestinal tract. The amino acids found in natural soy sauce complement those found in grains.

Soy sauce is a product familiar enough that its endless uses as a condiment for the table and in cooking need hardly be enumerated. You will find it used in many recipes throughout this book. Soy sauce is also superb in simple combinations with other condiments. Here are a few possibilities to try:

- Combine equal parts shoyu and rice vinegar (and water, if a milder flavor is desired) and use as a dipping sauce for steamed vegetables, diced tofu, seafood, and toasted sea vegetables.

- A traditional Japanese condiment called umejoya is made by combining equal parts mashed umeboshi pulp (see page 180) and soy sauce. Use as a relish with fish or sushi, or spread on pan-fried tofu, sea vegetables, and steamed vegetables.

- Combine lemon juice and soy sauce in approximately equal proportions. Use as a flavoring for steamed vegetables or sea vegetables, or as a baste for broiled fish or poultry.

- Combine 1/3 cup safflower mayonnaise with 1 tablespoon shoyu to make a tasty spread for sandwiches or a dressing for potato, tofu, or seafood salads.

SOY DIPPING SAUCE

Yield: About 1 cup

Use for dipping tofu, sushi, sea vegetables, and steamed vegetables.

1/2 cup water or light vegetable stock
1/4 cup natural soy sauce
1 tablespoon rice vinegar
1 tablespoon sesame seeds (optional)
1 teaspoon honey
1 teaspoon sesame oil
1/2 teaspoon dry mustard

Combine all the ingredients in a small bowl and mix well.

UMEBOSHI PLUMS

Umeboshi plums are part of the long list of Japanese food imports that have become staples on the shelves of natural-food stores. The ume is a sour plum that was once used for medicinal purposes. To make umeboshi (literally meaning "salted plum"), ume plums are pickled in cedar vats for 3 to 4 weeks to draw out their juices. They are then sun-dried and returned to their vats with crushed shiso (beefsteak plant) leaves, which give them their characteristic dark pink color. Good-quality umeboshi plums are then allowed to age for 1 year. The result is a powerfully sour and salty taste sensation concentrated into these little plums.

In natural- or specialty-food stores, umeboshi are sold in plastic tubs or, occasionally, glass jars. Take note of the ingredients on the label—cheaper brands use artificial flavorings and red dyes. Those plums look and smell like maraschino cherries and are no bargain. The only ingredients listed should be ume plums, shiso or beefsteak leaves, and sea salt.

Ume plums contain iron, calcium, and traces of other minerals, plus vitamin C and enzymes that are believed to aid digestion and settle stomach discomforts.

One of the most common ways of using these pungent plums is to insert a piece of one into a sushi roll or rice ball. The pulp of 1 plum blended with a cup or so of an oil and vinegar dressing goes a long way toward making a unique flavor statement and is very good on a salad of strong greens. Umeboshi pulp may also be spread thinly on corn on the cob. Or, you may do as many Japanese have always done—simply eat a whole umeboshi upon awakening. It is a most mouth-puckering way to wake up!

UMEBOSHI PASTE

This paste consists of pitted, pureed umeboshi plums, making it easy to blend with other ingredients such as soy sauce, mayonnaise, and oil and vinegar dressings. It may also be used as a sharp, salty condiment for spreading on crackers, rice cakes, or crisp vegetables.

UMEBOSHI VINEGAR

With the same sour and salty flavor of the plums, this liquid is derived from the pickling of ume plums. Use it as you would any other vinegar—in salad dressings, marinades, and pickles—but do so sparingly, since its powerful flavor goes a long way.

VINEGARS

Vinegar, from the French words *vin* ("wine") and *aigre* ("sour"), has been made since ancient times by fermenting various liquids. There are numerous types of vinegar, from the cheap, harsh white distilled vinegar to precious varieties, such as well-aged balsamic vinegar that can cost up to one hundred dollars a bottle. This section will give a brief overview of just a handful of vinegars—those most commonly found in natural-food stores or those that are common to ethnic cuisines popular in the wholefoods realm.

A fine vinegar doesn't have to be terribly expensive to be good and, used even in minute amounts, can do wonders to wake up the flavors of foods. Vinegars add a zest that helps reduce the need for salt. For connoisseurs of vinegars, or those who'd like to be, an excellent guide to them is contained in *Condiments* by Kathy Gunst (see appendix C).

APPLE CIDER VINEGAR

Made from apple cider, this all-time favorite is mellower than distilled vinegar, yet its tart-sweet flavor is sharp enough to make a statement in dressings, marinades, and pickling, as well as directly on salads. There are varying grades of apple cider vinegar. For superior quality, look for one labeled "aged on wood" or "made with whole apples."

BALSAMIC VINEGAR

An aged, sweet-wine vinegar, the mellow flavor of balsamic vinegar is welcome anywhere a mild vinegar flavor is desired—with salads of mild greens, in light vinaigrette marinades or dressings, or just dashed on freshly steamed vegetables. Dark brown in color, balsamic vinegar is made of grapes with a high sugar content. Its flavor is so mellow that you might even like to splash it on fruit salad. Though usually very expensive, balsamic vinegar will go a long way.

HERB VINEGARS

These gourmet-quality vinegars are flavored with fresh herbs, such as tarragon, basil, or mixed herbs. Exceptionally flavorful, they are superb used directly on fresh salads or to marinate salads. Try splashing a bit over freshly steamed vegetables to reduce the need for salt.

MALT VINEGAR

This vinegar is fermented from barley malt; it has a deep-amber color and a very distinct, sharp flavor that many will find too strong for salads. Malt vinegar is traditionally used in some of the British Isles and in some cold North American climates for sprinkling over fried potatoes and fried seafood (namely, that famous duo fish and chips). Try it in potato salads, pickles, chutneys, grilling sauces, and in recipes using strong-flavored sea vegetables such as hijiki.

RICE VINEGAR

Once you try rice vinegar, you may never want to use ordinary white vinegar again. Rice vinegar is subtle, fragrant, and just slightly sweet. Good-quality rice vinegar is extracted from the first pressing of fermented rice. Its most traditional use is as a seasoning for short-grain rice used in making sushi, but is it welcome almost anywhere a mild vinegar is needed.

In Oriental food stores, the rice vinegar sold is usually white. It may also be found in natural-food stores along with brown rice vinegar and sweet brown rice vinegar, the latter being the mellowest of the three. They're all excellent, with only slight differences in flavor. Which one you choose is a matter of personal preference. The brown rice vinegars come in small quantities and are expensive.

Rice vinegar is widely used as an ingredient in soy-based dipping sauces. It is also good in marinades and dressings, or in pickling. A splash of it added to a simple brown-rice-and-vegetables dish or noodle stir-fries will impart a subtle zest.

RICE VINEGAR MARINADE

Yield: About 1 1/4 cups

Use this to marinate steamed vegetables, tofu, tempeh, or seitan.

1/3 cup brown or white rice vinegar
1/4 cup peanut oil
2 tablespoons sesame oil
1/4 cup natural soy sauce
1 clove garlic, crushed
1/4 teaspoon chili powder
2 to 3 tablespoons honey, to taste

Combine all the ingredients in a small bowl and whisk together briskly to combine. Use as a marinade for tofu, tempeh, seitan, or seafood before grilling them or adding them to other recipes. This may also be used as a salad dressing.

UMEBOSHI VINEGAR (see page 180)

WINE VINEGAR

Processed from grapes, this vinegar comes in various shades, from white to rose to deep red. The darker the color, the stronger the flavor. Wine vinegar is most commonly used in dressings for green salads and is also good for marinated salads, coleslaws, and in dressings teamed with olive oil. The quality of wine vinegar varies with the price; you need not spend a fortune, but in this case, the cheapest is not the best.

———— WASABI ————

Wasabi is sometimes known as Japanese horseradish, an apt description, since its flavor is so reminiscent of the horseradish we know. The word *wasabi* is translated from the Japanese as "mountain hollyhock," and it is from the ground, dried root of this plant that the hot spice is derived. Its fresh, pungent taste has made it a traditional condiment to serve alongside of sushi and sashimi dishes.

You will most often find wasabi sold in powdered form, either in tins or small cellophane packets. Individually wrapped packets, which contain 1 to 2 tablespoons of the potent powder, will keep indefinitely stored in a cool, dry place. A small tin of the powder will keep for several months or longer once it has been opened. A little wasabi goes a long way, so buying it in small amounts may be wise.

Traditionally esteemed as an appetite stimulant, wasabi has also been said to aid digestion. In ancient Japan it was used for its powerful antiseptic qualities, and today, it is known to have a high vitamin-C content.

Reconstitute wasabi by blending it with enough water to form a firm paste, with a consistency similar to miso or nut butter. Let the paste stand for 10 minutes or so before using to allow its flavor to develop. If you've ever seen wasabi paste served in a Japanese restaurant, you'll note that only about a teaspoon is given with any serving. Apart from its use as a condiment with sushi and sashimi, wasabi is sometimes rolled into sushi as one of its elements. A dab of wasabi paste can be equally interesting served alongside seafood, sea vegetables, or root vegetables. A little of its pungent flavor can also add a delightful bite to dressings, as in this nontraditional recipe that follows.

WASABI MAYONNAISE

Yield: About 1 1/3 cups

Try this dressing on potato salads, seafood, or sea vegetables, or as a dip with raw vegetables or with fried tofu.

1 to 2 tablespoons wasabi powder
3/4 cup yogurt
1/2 cup safflower mayonnaise
Juice of 1/2 lemon
1/4 teaspoon garlic powder

Mix the wasabi powder with just enough water to form a paste. Allow the mixture to stand for 10 minutes.

Combine the wasabi paste with the remaining ingredients in a small bowl. Stir well to combine.

———— YEASTS ————

BAKER'S YEAST

Listed here just to differentiate it from the ones below, this is the yeast that is used as a leavening agent for breads. It should never be eaten straight, without being baked, because since this is a live yeast, it can continue to grow in the intestine and use up the B vitamins in the body.

BREWER'S YEAST

Brewer's yeast is a popular nutritional supplement that is an incredibly concentrated source of nutrients. It is particularly rich in B vitamins (check the label to make sure it contains B_{12}, an important vitamin for vegetarians) and contains all the essential amino acids, making it high in good-quality protein. Brewer's yeast contains generous amounts of several major minerals, including phosphorus, iron, and calcium. Trace elements, such as chromium and selenium, are also included. Brewer's yeast comes in tablet or powdered form. The powder is sometimes debittered in order to improve the flavor, which, many would agree, is pretty awful. Follow label recommendations for amount of daily intake. Powdered brewer's yeast is usually stirred into juice, blended into beverages, or sprinkled into cereals.

NUTRITIONAL YEAST

This yeast stands apart from the others listed here in that it is flavorful, so it can double as both a condiment and a supplement. Nutritional yeast is particularly rich in the B-vitamin complex; its yellowish color comes from the concentration of the B vitamin riboflavin it contains. It is also very high in protein and carbohydrates. The exact nutritional makeup of nutritional yeast varies according to the medium on which it was grown, so read the label when you buy it. If you are concerned about getting vitamin B_{12} in your diet (this is the vitamin rarely found in plant sources), check the label to make sure the brand you are buying supplies it. Nutritional yeast has a rather savory flavor that can taste nutty or cheeselike, depending on how it is used. A tablespoon or two may be added to sauces or soups, blended into dips or beverages, or incorporated into casseroles. Use it as a nondairy substitute for Parmesan cheese for sprinkling over pasta.

TORULA YEAST

Torula yeast is another form of yeast grown for use as a food supplement. It is 50 percent protein and contains all the essential amino acids, the full range of the B vitamins, and several major minerals, including calcium and potassium. Some of the methods used to produce torula yeast have become controversial. It may be grown on waste sulphite liquid from wood pulp or in broths of petrochemicals. Some consumer groups have questioned the safety of these methods. Though some torula yeasts are grown on more benign mediums, the method used is not usually listed on the package labels.

AMINO ACIDS: An amino acid is a building block of protein. There are some twenty amino acids required to make a complete protein. The body can manufacture all but eight; these are referred to as the *essential amino acids*. Foods that contain all eight essential amino acids in the correct proportions necessary to be readily utilized by the body are considered *complete proteins*.

CALORIE: A calorie is a unit of energy measured in terms of heat. As it pertains to food, food contains calories that, when burned, produce a specific amount of energy. If more calories are taken in than burned off, they are stored as fat, resulting in weight gain.

CARBOHYDRATES: Along with fat and protein, carbohydrates are chemical compounds known as the *large nutrients*. Carbohydrates are the body's ideal fuel source and have recently had their wrongful reputation for being "fattening" redressed. Starches, sugars, and fiber are all carbohydrates. Foods referred to as *complex carbohydrates* contain starch, the main form of carbohydrate energy, and fiber, the parts of plant foods that pass through the body undigested. Complex carbohydrates are important energy sources, since they are broken down and used slowly by the body.

CHOLESTEROL: This chemical compound is actually of great importance to several functions of the internal organs and is a part of every cell. The problem lies in the fact that the liver can manufacture all the cholesterol the body needs for its essential functions; when excessive cholesterol is ingested in the form of food, it causes buildup of plaque in the arteries, which is said to lead to heart disease. Foods high in cholesterol are eggs, fatty meats, butter, and some dairy products.

ENRICHED: When whole grains are refined of their nutritious bran and germ, they are then usually enriched with specific added nutrients as established by federal guidelines. The nutrients added back are iron and three of the B vitamins: thiamine, niacin, and riboflavin.

FAT: Fat is an organic compound of fatty acids and is one of the three "large nutrients," along with carbohydrates and protein. It provides a very concentrated source of stored energy for the body. An explanation of why some fat is essential can be found on page 137, along with a differentiation of the three types of dietary fat—saturated, polyunsaturated, and monounsaturated. The average American's fat intake has until recently been about 40 percent of total food intake. A 1977 Senate committee recommended that this be cut down to 30 percent, a figure most nutritionists feel is still much too high.

FIBER: This is actually a general term for a family of plant substances including pectin, cellulose, lignin, hemicellulose, gums, mucilage, and others. These are the parts of plants that pass through the body undigested, adding the bulk that is crucial for the regulation of the digestive system. Fiber is concentrated in the bran of grains, skins of certain fruits, filaments found in the flesh of vegetables, and so on.

According to nutritionist Jane Brody, a leading proponent of high-carbohydrate diets, fiber fills the stomach and small intestine, absorbing water and slowing down digestion enough to prolong the feeling of fullness. Further, she says that those living on high-fiber diets rarely suffer from constipation or hemorrhoids and are less likely to develop colonic cancer.

High-fiber foods include whole grains, legumes, nuts and seeds, fruits and vegetables. Twenty-five to thirty-five grams of fiber a day constitute what is considered a diet high in fiber.

LACTOSE: Lactose is milk sugar, the component of milk that makes it indigestible to many adults and some children. In order to digest lactose, the body must be able to produce an enzyme that converts the lactose to lactic acid. Several of the dairy products described in chapter 7 contain added bacterial cultures that convert most of the lactose to lactic acid, making them more digestible.

MACROBIOTICS: Ostensibly the name of a diet, the proponents of macrobiotics point out that it is above all a philosophy of a way of life. The two men most instrumental in teaching this system are George Ohsawa and Michio Kushi. Look for books by these authors for a fuller understanding of their tenets. It is impossible to define the macrobiotic diet fully in the space of a glossary entry, but its basic dietary precepts are as follows:

- The diet should comprise the following: 50 to 60 percent whole-grain foods; 20 to 30 percent vegetables that are grown as locally to their consumer as possible; 10 to 15 percent legumes; 5 to 10 percent sea vegetables; and no more than 5 percent fruit.

- Be aware of the yin-yang, or acid-alkaline, qualities of foods.

- Eat fresh foods that are seasonal and are as local to the area in which you live as possible. This is in keeping with the belief that each region places particular stresses on the body due to conditions of climate and terrain.

- Avoid meat, fish (except for occasional nonoily fish), sugar and other sweeteners (except for rice syrup and barley malt syrup), coffee, and alcohol.

Perhaps the most important aspect of the macrobiotic philosophy is to aspire toward balance, both in the body and in one's life.

MINERALS: These elemental substances are essential nutrients needed to regulate many bodily functions. Two types of minerals are utilized; these are the *major minerals* and the *trace minerals*. Both are vital, but the distinction lies in the amounts present in the body. Here is a description of some of the most important minerals:

CALCIUM is best known for its role in the formation and maintenance of bones and teeth. It also assists in blood clotting and the functions of the tissues. Some good sources are dairy products, nuts, soy foods, and dark-green leafy vegetables.

IRON is important in the functions of the blood, including its formation and the carrying of oxygen to the tissues. Some good sources are dried fruits, molasses, legumes, certain grains, especially whole wheat and its components, and sunflower seeds.

MAGNESIUM is needed for the functions of the cells, nerves, muscles, the heart and other organs, as well as in the overall metabolic functions. Some good sources are nuts, grains, legumes, dark-green vegetables, seafoods, and soy foods.

PHOSPHORUS plays an essential role in all cell functions and activates enzymes and B vitamins. Some good sources are dairy products, eggs, meats, nuts, and grains.

POTASSIUM is also important to cell functions, as well as those of the kidneys, muscles, and in maintaining the heartbeat. It is a mineral common to many foods; there is little danger of deficiency. Some good sources are dried fruits and fresh fruits, particularly bananas and oranges, molasses, seeds, potatoes, and wheat germ.

ZINC is needed for the production of new cells and is important for enzyme functions. Some good sources are whole grains, particularly wheat germ, fresh beans, nuts, and milk products.

ORGANIC FOODS: These are foods grown in soils fertilized with organic rather than synthetic fertilizers and are not sprayed with inorganic chemicals. Foods described as "whole" or "natural" are not necessarily organically grown. Organically grown foods are more expensive, but in certain cases, such as with grains or legumes bought in bulk, not so much more as to make them prohibitive. Natural-food stores and food co-ops often offer this choice to consumers concerned with the effects of pesticides, additives, and chemical fertilizers.

PROTEIN: Along with carbohydrates and fats, protein is one of the three "large nutrients," and often a misunderstood one. Protein is an essential factor in the building and maintenance of all bodily tissues and in the formation of enzymes and hormones. Protein is composed of some twenty amino acids, eight of which the body cannot manufacture, and these are taken in as food. Foods that have all eight essential amino acids in the precise proportions necessary to be readily usable by the body are considered "complete proteins." Vital as protein is, it has recently been accepted that more protein is not necessarily better. Many nutritionists recommend taking in what your body needs and no more, since excess protein cannot be stored. Eliminating excess protein puts great stress on several of the body's organs, and eating too much of it can make you fat. Protein is also not, as is commonly believed, the body's ideal source of energy—it comes in third after carbohydrates and fats. The Recommended Daily Allowance has been set at .8 grams per kilogram (2.2 pounds) of body weight. Thus, a 120-pound woman needs about 44 grams of protein a day; a 160-pound man, about 58 grams.

PROTEIN COMPLEMENTARITY: Certain protein foods contain all eight essential amino acids in the precise proportions necessary to be readily usable by the body and therefore are *complete proteins*. Other protein foods are high in some amino acids and in short supply in others and are referred to as incomplete proteins. In order to complete their protein, such foods can be eaten with other protein foods whose amino acid structure complements their own, thus forming complete protein. The most common form of protein complementarity is combining grain products with legumes. Other complementary combinations are grains or legumes combined with dairy products.

VEGETARIANISM: Many people who are vegetarians think of their diet as a way of life rather than merely as a way of eating. It's not necessary to be a strict vegetarian to be a practitioner of a natural foods diet; but generally, vegetarians almost by definition are more conscientious about the foods they eat. Here are the primary forms of vegetarianism that are practiced:

LACTO-VEGETARIAN: Dairy products such as milk and cheese are included in the diet, but not eggs.

LACTO-OVO (or vice versa) VEGETARIAN: The diet includes both dairy products and eggs.

VEGAN: No eggs or dairy products are used at all. This diet relies primarily on grains, legumes, and soy foods as protein sources.

VITAMINS: Vitamins are complex organic compounds, essential in minute quantities to assist the metabolic functions of the body. Here are some of the most common vitamins and what they do for you:

VITAMIN A is important to vision, for the maintenance of healthy skin and mucous membranes, and for resistance to infectious diseases. Some good sources are dark-green vegetables; deep-yellow vegetables, such as squashes, carrots, peas, dried apricots; and prunes.

VITAMIN B_1 (thiamine) prevents depression and assists in the functions of the nervous and digestive systems. Some good sources are legumes, whole grains, dark-green vegetables, seeds, and wheat germ.

VITAMIN B_2 (riboflavin) is important in cell functions, enzyme functions, and to assist normal growth. Some good sources are dairy products, eggs, whole grains, broccoli, almonds, and wheat germ.

VITAMIN B_6 (pyridoxine) regulates the nervous system and produces antibodies. It also promotes healthy skin. Some good sources are nuts, seeds, whole grains, bananas, tomatoes, and some sea vegetables.

VITAMIN B_{12} is essential for general growth and for the functions of the blood cells and nervous system. Some good sources are meats, eggs, fish, dairy products, tempeh, miso, and sea vegetables.

NIACIN, another B vitamin, is needed by the cells to utilize oxygen and also aids in metabolism. Some good sources are legumes, nuts, and whole grains.

VITAMIN C is vital in forming collagen, which binds the body cells, and is also needed for the health of the tissues. Vitamin C is also thought to be of benefit to wound healing and resistance to infection. Some good sources are citrus fruits, melons, dark-green vegetables, tomatoes, green peppers and other *Capsicum* peppers, currants, and apricots.

VITAMIN D is needed to absorb calcium and phosphorus, which are crucial to the formation and maintenance of bones and teeth. Some good sources are fish, fortified milk, and sunlight.

VITAMIN E is important in the functions of the heart, blood cells, endocrine system, and muscles. It is also believed to have properties that retard aging and promote general well-being. Some good sources are wheat germ, oats, nuts, sunflower seeds, sesame seeds, nut and seed oils, and safflower oil.

Appendix A

SPROUTING GRAINS, LEGUMES, AND SEEDS

Sprouting is an easy way to increase the usability of many types of grains, seeds, and beans. All are actually seeds, since they contain the germ, which carries the capacity to begin a new life, which in turn is the sprout. For the sake of brevity, then, I will henceforth refer to all these sproutable foods as seeds.

Watching the indoor garden grow is fascinating, and the resulting sprouts are tasty, inexpensive, and highly nutritious. Sprouting dramatically increases the content of present minerals and vitamins A, B complex, C, and E, sometimes tenfold. Occasionally, new nutrients appear that are not thought to be present in the original seed. Also increased are the quantity and quality of protein, with new amino acids forming as the seed sprouts. Sprouts are highly digestible and may be used in a number of interesting ways. Raw or briefly steamed, they are good in salads and sandwiches; they are perfect for use in stir-fries or along with other freshly steamed vegetables such as peas or green beans; and, if they are of the "short-tailed" variety, sprouts add great texture and a slightly sweet flavor to breads.

Natural-food stores and mail-order sources offer special equipment for sprouting, but this is entirely optional, since all that's really required is a Mason jar or two, some cheesecloth, and a rubber band. Here is the simple process, which is the same for all seeds. Refer to the chart on the next page for the varying times for soaking and sprouting and the amount of rinses required per day.

1. Place the seeds you are using in a quart jar and soak them in plenty of water for the time recommended in the chart on the next page. Keep the jar in a dark place, not too cool, such as a room-temperature pantry.

2. Drain and rinse the seeds. Now cover the opening of the jar with two or three layers of cheesecloth and secure this with a rubber band. Position the jar on its side, with the open end tilted slightly downward, and keep in the same dark place.

3. Rinse the sprouts through the cheesecloth several times a day, as specified for each type on the chart. Do this by filling the jar with water, swirling it around, then draining. Replace each time in the same position as before.

4. After the number of days designated on the chart, your sprouts are ready. Rinse them well and allow them to dry somewhat before placing them in a storage container in the refrigerator. Use them up as quickly as possible—5 or 6 days is optimal.

	Dry Amount	Soaking Time (hours)	Rinses per Day	Sprouting Time (days)	Length of Sprout (inches)	Approximate Yield (cups)
Adzuki beans	1/2 cup	12–18	3–4	4–5	1/2–1	2
Alfalfa seeds	3 tablespoons	4–8	2–3	3–5	1 1/2–2	4
Amaranth	1/4 cup	4–8	2–3	2–3	1/4	1 1/4
Barley	1 cup	4–8	2–3	3–4	1/4	2
Buckwheat (whole)	1/2 cup	4–8	2–3	3–5	1/4–1/2	1–1 1/2
Lentils	1/2 cup	8–12	3–4	3–4	1/2–1	3–4
Millet	1 cup	4–8	2–3	3–4	1/4	2
Mung beans	1/2 cup	8–12	3–4	4–5	1 1/2–2	2–3
Oats (whole)	1 cup	4–8	2–3	3–4	1/4–1/2	2
Peas, split	1 cup	8–12	2–3	3–4	1/4–1/2	2–2 1/2
Rice, brown	1/2 cup	4–8	2–3	3–4	1/4	1 1/2–2
Rye (whole)	1/2 cup	4–8	2–3	3–4	1/4	1 1/2–2
Soybeans*	1/2 cup	18–24	4–5	4–5	1 1/2–2	2–2 1/2
Triticale berries	1 cup	8	2–3	2–3	1/4	1 1/2–2
Wheat berries	1/2 cup	4–8	2–3	2–3	1/4	1 1/2–2

*Soybean sprouts must be steamed or cooked before eating in order to destroy an antinutrient present in them.

Appendix B

WHOLEFOODS BY MAIL

If you live in an area that is not served by a local natural foods retailer or are looking for particular products that your retailer doesn't carry, here are some additional sources that you may explore. Write to the individual companies for current price lists, product listings, or catalogs.

Anzen Japanese Foods and Imports
736 North East Union Avenue
Portland, Oregon 97232

Products include: grains, seeds, Oriental noodles, sea vegetables, sauces, condiments, mushrooms, Oriental teas.

Birkett Mills
P.O. Box 440
Penn Yan, New York 14527

Products include: buckwheat products (grits, groats, and pancake mixes) and stone-ground flours.

Butte Creek Mill
Box 561
Eagle Point, Oregon 97524

Products include: cereals, rolled grains, stone-ground flours and meals, whole grains, bran, grits, and pancake mixes.

Cape Ann Seaweeds
2 Stage Fort
Gloucester, Massachusetts 01930

This small company harvests or distributes Atlantic nori, alaria, dulse and kombu. They also do a small mail-order business. Write to them for current prices.

Deer Valley Farm
R.D. 1
Guilford, New York 13780

Products include: baked goods, dairy products, unsulfured dried fruits, grains, seeds, herbs, cereals, honeys, flours, nuts, oils, and natural cosmetics.

Ener-G Foods, Inc.
6901 Fox Avenue South
P.O. Box 24723
Seattle, Washington 98124-0723

Ener-G Foods specializes in allergy, dietetic, and low-sodium products, among them wheat-free and gluten-free mixes and baked goods.

Foods of India
Sinha Trading Co., Inc.
120 Lexington Avenue
New York, New York 10016

Products include: legumes, rice and rice products, flours, spices, spice mixes, nuts, oils, chutneys, and pickles.

Garden Spot Distributors
Route 1, Box 729A
New Holland, Pennsylvania 17557

Distributors of Shiloh Farms and other products, including baked-goods mixes, grains, cereals, dried fruits, flours, snacks, nuts, beans, seeds, herbal formulas, ointments, supplements, natural pet foods, and pet-care products.

Hodgson Mills Enterprises, Inc.
Industrial Park
Gainesville, Missouri 65655

Products include: whole-grain flours, cornmeals, bread and muffin mixes, and whole wheat pastas. Mail order is by case lots only.

New Hope Mills, Inc.
RR #2, Box 269A
Moravia, New York 13118

Products include: water-ground flours and cornmeal and pancake mixes.

Nu-World Amaranth, Inc.
P.O. Box 2202
Naperville, Illinois 60540

Products include: whole-grain amaranth; amaranth flour; amaranth and wheat-, rye-, or oat-flour blends; puffed amaranth; and a cookbook entitled *Baking with Amaranth*.

Old Mill of Guilford
1340 NC68 North
Oak Ridge, North Carolina 27310

Products include: water-ground and stone-ground flours and cornmeal, grits, muffin mixes, pancake mixes, and a special hushpuppy mix.

Quinoa Corporation
2300 Central Avenue
Suite G
Boulder, Colorado 80301

If your local retailer does not carry quinoa or quinoa flour, you may order directly from the Quinoa Corporation. They also offer a tasty quinoa pasta. Write for their current prices and ask them to include their useful recipe pamphlets as well.

The Sprout House
Box 700
Sheffield, Massachusetts 01257

Products include: sprouting seeds, sprouting indoor garden kits, nutritional guidebooks, juicers, and water purification systems.

Walnut Acres
Penns Creek, Pennsylvania 17862

An enticing full-color catalog features this established company's wide array of products, including grains, cereals, baking mixes, pancake mixes, seeds, beans, flours, nuts, herbs and spices, natural soups, unsulfured dried fruits, nut butters, juices, oils, and more. They also feature high-quality cookware for what they call "the natural kitchen."

Appendix C

TO LEARN MORE: BOOKS, ORGANIZATIONS, AND MANUFACTURERS

BOOKS

This selected list of books will lead you to more in-depth information covering areas of wholefoods that may be of particular interest to you. Many are still in print, while others may be found only in the library.

GENERAL BOOKS ON COOKING WITH WHOLEFOODS

Atlas, Nava. *Vegetariana*. New York: The Dial Press/Doubleday, 1984.

———. *American Harvest*. New York: Fawcett Columbine/Ballantine Books, 1987.

My first two books, the first is an eclectic, international collection of vegetarian recipes, whereas the second focuses on American regional recipes adapted to the wholefoods style. *American Harvest* contains lots of recipes that feature beans, corn, and cornmeal.

Brody, Jane. *Jane Brody's Good Food Book*. New York: W. W. Norton, 1985.

Jane Brody, The *New York Times*'s personal-health columnist, promotes the use of high-carbohydrate foods with a large volume of readable nutritional information as well as recipes.

Colbin, Annemarie. *The Book of Whole Meals*. New York: Ballantine Books, 1983.

Emphasizes seasonal menus.

Goldbeck, Nikki and David. *American Whole-foods Cuisine*. New York: New American Library, 1983.

An encyclopedic, *Joy of Cooking* style natural foods cookbook for the new age.

Jaffrey, Madhur. *World-of-the-East Vegetarian Cookery*. New York: Alfred A. Knopf, 1981.

An attractive book with a stunning array of dishes from the Near and Middle East, the Orient, Indian, and Southeast Asia. Many of the recipes emphasize grains, legumes, soy foods, and exotic seasonings.

Katzen, Mollie. *The Moosewood Cookbook*. Berkley, Calif.: The Ten Speed Press, 1977.

———. *The Enchanted Broccoli Forest*. Berkley, Calif.: Ten Speed Press, 1982.

Now-classic vegetarian cookbooks, these fun, lighthearted volumes offer a wide array of wholesome recipes.

Kushi, Aveline, and Esko, Wendy. *The Changing Seasons Macrobiotic Cookbook*. Wayne, N.J.: Avery Publishing Groups, 1985.

A good and very authentic book on macrobiotic cookery.

Lappé, Frances Moore. *Diet for a Small Planet*. New York: Ballantine Books, 1981.

A pioneer book in the realm of the meatless way of life. Includes important political, economic, and health points of view.

Robertson, Laurel, et al. *Laurel's Kitchen*. New York: Bantam Books, 1976.

A best-selling book featuring hundreds of straightforward recipes utilizing a wide range of natural foods, plus extensive nutritional information.

Rodale's Basic Natural Foods Cookbook. Emmaus, Pa.: Rodale Press Books, 1984.

A big book covering a wide array of foods. One of the few general natural foods cookbooks that contains chapters on sea vegetables and sprouts. Lots of grain and legume dishes are featured, and there is a good deal of supplemental information.

Sanhi, Julie. *Classic Indian Vegetarian and Grain Cooking*. New York: William Morrow, 1985.

For more advanced cooks, this is nonetheless a superb collection of exotic meatless recipes, many featuring grains and legumes.

Shulman, Martha Rose. *The Vegetarian Feast*. New York: Harper and Row, 1979.

———. *Fast Vegetarian Feasts*. New York: The Dial Press/Doubleday, 1982.

Shulman is a health-conscious cook who utilizes a wide variety of wholefoods in low-fat, appealing ways.

SOY FOODS (Including Tofu, Tempeh, and Miso)

Clarke, Christina. *Cook with Tofu*. New York: Avon Books, 1981.

A compact book filled with a wide variety of imaginative recipes utilizing tofu, from soups to desserts.

Cusumano, Claire. *Tofu, Tempeh, and Other Soy Delights*. Emmaus, Pa.: Rodale Press Books, 1984.

An informative book with good, Western-style recipes featuring tofu, tempeh, miso, and soy milk. Contains instructions on how to make tofu and tempeh at home.

Shurtleff, William, and Aoyagi, Akiko. *The Book of Tofu*. Berkley, Calif.: Ten Speed Press, 1983.

———. *The Book of Tempeh*. New York: Harper and Row, 1979.

———. *The Book of Miso*. Brookline, Mass.: Autumn Press, 1976 (large format); New York: Ballantine Books, 1976 (small format).

From these experts on soy foods come three definitive volumes containing hundreds of recipes, including traditional as well as Western-style uses for these foods, along with historic and nutritional information. Small-format paperbacks are slightly abridged versions of the large.

WHOLE GRAINS

Bumgarner, Marlene Anne. *The Book of Whole Grains*. New York: Saint Martin's Press, 1976.

Pitzer, Sara. *Whole Grains: Grow, Harvest and Cook Your Own*. Charlotte, Vt.: Garden Way Publishing, 1981.

Both of these books cover a good array of grains for use in cooking and baking. The recipes are more basic than imaginative, but are useful nonetheless.

London, Sheryl and Mel. *Creative Cooking with Grains and Pasta*. Emmaus, Pa.: Rodale Press Books, 1982.

The most thorough book I've seen on whole grains and whole-grain flours. Written in an informal, informative, and very inviting style, this is definitely worth looking for.

BAKING WITH WHOLE-GRAIN FLOURS

Ojakangas, Beatrice. *Great Whole Grain Breads*. New York: E. P. Dutton, 1984.

The recipes in this book cover a wide variety of whole-grain breads made from many different types of flour. You will find recipes that are very basic and those that are very sophisticated, but all are explained in a way that is never complicated.

Robertson, Laurel, et al. *Laurel's Kitchen Bread Book*. New York: Random House, 1984.

The authors of *Laurel's Kitchen* offer a large and definitive volume on wholesome home baking.

SEA VEGETABLES

Arasaki, Seibun and Teruko. *Vegetables from the Sea*. New York: Japan Publications/ Harper & Row, 1983.

This is a concise, yet comprehensive guide.

Madlener, Judith C. *The Sea Vegetable Book*. New York: Clarkson Potter, 1977.

A thoroughly researched volume, this is considered one of the most definitive on the subject of sea vegetables, containing technical information as well as recipes. The abundance of scientific names and data, however, may be a bit intimidating to the beginner.

McConnaughey, Evelyn. *Sea Vegetables: Harvesting Guide and Cookbook*. Happy Camp, Calif.: Naturegraph Publishers, Inc., 1985.

Ms. McConnaughey harvests sea vegetables on the Oregon coast and shares her expertise and recipes. If you can't find this book, write to the publishers at P.O. Box 1075, Happy Camp, California 96039.

Rhoads, Sharon A. *Cooking with Sea Vegetables*. Brookline, Mass.: Autumn Press, 1978.

A straightforward book, this is a good choice for those just getting acquainted with sea vegetables.

NUTS

Frank, Dorothy C. *Cooking with Nuts*. New York: Clarkson Potter, 1979.

This book offers interesting lore on almost all the different kinds of common edible nuts, along with a good number of recipes, not always in the wholefood style, but inspiring many good ideas nonetheless.

CONDIMENTS

Cost, Bruce. *Ginger East to West: A Cook's Tour*. Berkley, Calif.: Aris Books/Harris Publishing Co., 1984.

A fascinating, witty book on ginger, with recipes that often incorporate other interesting ingredients.

Gunst, Kathy. *Condiments: The Art of Buying, Making and Using Mustards, Oils, Vinegars, Chutneys, Relishes, Sauces, Savory Jellies, and More*. New York: G. P. Putnam's Sons, 1984.

The title says it all. Learning to make and use delicious condiments is a good idea for people who wish to keep flavor in their food while reducing their intake of salt and sugar.

NUTRITION, DIETS, AND CONSUMER INFORMATION

Armstrong, David. *The Insider's Guide to Health Food*. New York: Bantam Books, 1983.

An objective view of natural foods, supplements, and related products, separating the good from the not-so-good in no uncertain terms. Enjoyable reading.

Brody, Jane. *Jane Brody's Nutrition Book*. New York: W. W. Norton, 1981.

A complete, commonsense guide to good nutrition, written in highly readable language.

Carroll, David. *The Complete Book of Natural Foods*. New York: Summit Books, 1985.

A guide to sensible eating, divided into four sections: carbohydrates, fats, proteins, and natural diets.

Kushi, Michio. *The Book of Macrobiotics*. Tokyo: Japan Publications, 1977.

A discussion of the macrobiotic philosophy and way of life.

Rohe, Fred. *The Complete Book of Natural Foods*. Boulder, Colo.: Shambala Publications, 1983.

A big, informative book focusing on various aspects of natural foods and natural-food diets.

Taub, Harald Jay. *The Health Food Shopper's Guide*. New York: Dell Publishing, 1982.

The title is a bit misleading, since this book focuses more on vitamins, minerals, supplements, obscure herbs, and cosmetics, with only one section on food.

Tracy, Lisa. *The Gradual Vegetarian*. New York: M. Evans and Co., 1985.

A step-by-step approach to phasing meat out of your diet.

ORGANIZATIONS

Amaranth Research
Rodale Food Center
Food Research and Development
33 East Minor Street
Emmaus, Pennsylvania 18049

Research, development, and promotion of amaranth, the newly rediscovered high-potential grain, are the functions of this organization. Amaranth Research is the primary source for the dissemination of technical, agricultural, and nutritional information on grain amaranth. In addition, a new subscription newsletter has just begun distribution, called *Amaranth Today*. For information on this, simply write to Amaranth Today at the address listed above.

Natural Food Associates
P.O. Box 210
Atlanta, Texas 75111

A nonprofit membership organization, NFA promotes organic agriculture and is of particular interest to those involved in this type of work. In addition, this organization produces educational materials on natural foods and runs an educational center. NFA publishes a monthly magazine called *Natural Food and Farming*, and hosts a yearly convention.

The Soyfoods Center
P.O. Box 234
Lafayette, California 94549

Founded by the authors William Shurtleff and Akiko Aoyagi, this organization is a clearinghouse of information and materials on soy foods for consumers and professionals. Write to them for their brochure, which features books, pamphlets, and materials in other media that may be purchased from the center. The center also produces materials for people wishing to start soy foods businesses.

MANUFACTURERS AND DISTRIBUTORS OF NATURAL FOODS

Arrowhead Mills, Inc.
P.O. Box 2059
Hereford, Texas 79045

Arrowhead Mills is a major producer and distrib-

utor of grain products and flours. Consumers may write to them for free recipe folders for specific Arrowhead Mills products.

Eden Foods, Inc.
701 Tecumseh Road
Clinton, Michigan 49236

A major producer and distributor of a very wide range of natural foods, Eden Foods products include domestically made goods as well as imports from Europe and Japan. Among their offerings are organically grown cooked beans, whole-grain pastas, imported Japanese noodles, soy sauce, miso, bulk and packaged grains, beans and flours, sea vegetables, oils, condiments, sweeteners, snacks, and more. Eden produces literature pertaining to their products. Write to them with questions on specific Eden products.

Erewhon (U.S. Mills, Inc.)
5 Waltham Street
Wilmington, Massachusetts 01887

Formerly Erewhon, Inc., U.S. Mills, Inc., is the new corporate name of this well-known natural foods company. Their products are still distributed under the Erewhon brand name and include ready-to-eat hot cereals, granolas, nut and seed butters, soy sauce, noodles, miso, sea vegetables, various natural snack foods, and condiments. Many of their foods are certified kosher. U.S. Mills prints product description sheets. Write to them for further information on specific products.

Fearn Natural Foods
4520 James Place
Melrose Park, Illinois 60160

Fearn produces soy products, such as soy powder and soy granules. They also offer nonfat dry milk and numerous natural whole-grain cake, bread, and pancake mixes. They sell their products directly only by the caseload, so contact them only if you are interested in bulk buying, such as for a co-op or buying club. On the boxes of some of its products, Fearn offers free recipe booklets to consumers who send in a request with a self-addressed stamped envelope (SASE).

Grainaissance
800 Heinz Avenue
Berkley, California 94710

Grainaissance produces brown-rice mochi cakes.

196

Write to them for free pamphlets with recipes and ideas for using mochi; include SASE.

Great Eastern Sun
P.O. Box 237
Enka, North Carolina 28728

This company is an importer of high-quality natural foods from Japan, including soy products, snacks, and noodles. Two affiliates of Great Eastern Sun are the Macrobiotic Wholesale Company, which sells their products to natural-food stores, food co-ops, and buying clubs; and the American Miso Company, which manufactures traditional-style misos. Great Eastern Sun prints recipe cards for miso, noodles, and other products. They are available free of charge to consumers who write in with requests along with SASE.

Hain Pure Food Company
P.O. Box 54841 Terminal Annex
Los Angeles, California 90054

This company's products include nut butters, oils, mayonnaise, and snacks. They maintain an information hotline (toll-free, 1-800-HAIN-123; in New York State, 1-800-223-4242), which is staffed by a registered dietitian who will answer questions regarding nutrition. Consumers may also write in for Hain's nutritionally oriented pamphlets featuring tips and recipes.

Health Valley Foods
700 Union Street
Montebello, California 90640

This large company produces numerous packaged natural-food products, including cereals, snacks, canned goods, pet foods, soy products, condiments, and oils. Health Valley is very generous about sending product information, including nutritional analyses, to consumers who

write in requesting information.

Maine Coast Sea Vegetables
Shore Road
Franklin, Maine 04634

This company's sea vegetables—alaria, kelp, dulse, and Atlantic nori (laver) are available in natural-food outlets. Maine Coast also produces sea vegetable seasonings. Write to them for their useful informational pamphlets, which describe their products in some depth.

Quinoa Corporation (see page 192)

Tomsun Foods, Inc.
305 Wells Street
Greenfield, Massachusetts 01310

Tomsun is a large-scale maker of tofu and related products. One of their newer offerings is Jofu, a custardlike blend of silken tofu, fruits, and sweeteners in individual serving cups akin to those in which yogurt is packaged. It's an interesting alternative for those who eat no dairy at all or who don't like yogurt's tartness. Tomsun produces a delightful herbed tofu, as well as egg roll and wonton wrappers. Their products are often distributed to supermarkets. Write to Tomsun for information on where to buy these tofu products, or on ordering their free tofu cookbook. Send SASE for their free tofu recipe brochures.

U.S. Mills, Inc. (see Erewhon, page 196)

Upcountry Seitan
25 Church Street
Lenox, Massachusetts 01240

Upcountry, one of the few producers of seitan, prints a useful recipe pamphlet with ideas for using seitan. Send SASE with your request.

In addition to the books mentioned in this appendix and the material sent to me by the manufacturers and distributors of natural foods, these are some additional sources that were helpful in the preparation of this book.

Adams, Catherine F. *Encyclopedia of Food and Nutrition*. New York: Drake Publishers, Inc. 1977.

Staff of *Organic Gardening and Farming. Basic Book of Organically Grown Foods*. Emmaus, Pa.: Rodale Press Book Division, 1972.

Carroll, A. and De Persiis Vona, E. *Health Food Dictionary with Recipes*. New York: Weathervane Books, 1973.

Health and Human Services Publications, Public Health Service. Food and Drug Administration, Rockville, Md.

Margolis, Sidney. *Health Food: Facts and Fakes*. New York: Walker and Co., 1973.

Nugent, Nancy, and the editors of *Prevention Magazine. Food and Nutrition*. Emmaus, Pa.: Rodale Press Book Division, 1983.

Roehl, Evelyn. *Food Facts*. Seattle, Wash.: Food Learning Center, 1984.

United States Department of Agriculture. *Agricultural Handbook No. 8. Composition of Foods*, 1975.

Weiss, Theodore, J., Ph.D. *Food Oils and Their Uses*, 2d ed. Westport, Conn.: AVI Publishing Co., Inc., 1983.

Index